An Introduction to
European Law

Thought-provoking and accessible in approach, this book offers a
classic introduction to European law. Taking a clear structural
framework, it guides the student through the subject's core elements
from the creation of European law and its enforcement to the
workings of the internal market. A flowing writing style combines with
the use of illustrations and diagrams throughout the text to ensure the
student understands even the most complex of concepts. This succinct
and enlightening overview is required reading for all students of
European law.

Robert Schütze is Professor of European Law at Durham University.

An Introduction to

European Law

Robert Schütze

CAMBRIDGE
UNIVERSITY PRESS

CAMBRIDGE
UNIVERSITY PRESS

University Printing House, Cambridge CB2 8BS, United Kingdom

Published in the United States of America by Cambridge University Press, New York

Cambridge University Press is part of the University of Cambridge.

It furthers the University's mission by disseminating knowledge in the pursuit of education, learning and research at the highest international levels of excellence.

www.cambridge.org
Information on this title: www.cambridge.org/9781107025103

© Cambridge University Press 2012

First published 2012
3rd printing 2013

Printed in the United Kingdom by Clays, St Ives plc

A catalogue record for this publication is available from the British Library

Library of Congress Cataloguing in Publication data
Schütze, Robert.
Introduction to European law / Robert Schütze.
    p.   cm.
ISBN 978-1-107-02510-3
1. Law – European Union countries.   I. Title.
KJE947.S385   2012
349.24–dc23

2012010503

ISBN 978-1-107-02510-3 Hardback
ISBN 978-1-107-65444-0 Paperback

In Memory of Boris Rotenberg: Debater, Dreamer, Traveller

Summary Contents

Contents

Illustrations

Tables

Acknowledgements

Grateful acknowledgements are made to Hart Publishing, Kluwer Law International, Oxford University Press, and Sweet & Maxwell for their kind permission to incorporate sections from previously published material. Parts I and II of this book draw on my *European Constitutional Law* (Cambridge University Press, 2012). Thanks go to many a colleague and friend, especially Amandine Garde and Dieter Isolde Schütze. Sinéad Moloney of Cambridge University Press has again been very patient with me, and I thank her for this as well as for her professionalism. The book is dedicated to Boris Rotenberg (European University Institute, 2000), who died much too young.

Table of Cases

Contents

1. Court of Justice of the European Union

(a) European Court of Justice: Cases (numerical)

Case 8/55, *Fédération Charbonnière de Belgique* v. *High Authority of the European Coal and Steel Community*, [1954–56] ECR 245   191

Case 1/58, *Stork & Cie* v. *High Authority of the European Coal and Steel Community*, [1958] ECR 17   85–6

Case 20/59, *Italy* v. *High Authority*, [1960] ECR 325   180

Joined Cases 36, 37, 38 and 40/59, *Geitling Ruhrkohlen-Verkaufsgesellschaft mbH, Mausegatt Ruhrkohlen-Verkaufsgesellschaft mbH and I. Nold KG* v. *High Authority of the European Coal and Steel Community*, [1959] ECR 423   85, 86

Case 10/61, *Commission* v. *Italy*, [1962] ECR 1   138–9

Joinded Cases 2 and 3/62, *Commission* v. *Luxembourg and Belgium*, [1962] ECR 425   209

Case 16–17/62, *Confédération nationale des producteurs de fruits et légumes and others* v. *Council*, [1962] ECR 471   194

Case 25/62, *Plaumann* v. *Commission*, [1963] ECR 95   196–7, 199–200, 201–2

Case 26/62, *Van Gend en Loos* v. *Netherlands Inland Revenue Administration*, [1963] ECR (Special English Edition) 1   110–11, 112–15, 118, 122, 161–2

Joined Cases 28–30/62, *Da Costa et al.* v. *Netherlands Inland Revenue Administration*, [1963] ECR 31   154, 161–2, 163

Joined Cases 31 and 33/62, *Lütticke et al.* v. *Commission*, [1962] ECR 501   202

Case 75/63, *Hoekstra (née Unger)*, v. *Bestuur der Bedrijfsvereniging voor detailhandel en Amba* [1964] ECR 177   153, 236

Joined Cases 90–91/63, *Commission* v. *Luxemburg and Belgium*, [1963] ECR 625   182

Case 6/64, *Costa* v. *ENEL*, [1964] ECR 585   136–7, 153–4, 160, 163

(b) European Court of Justice: Opinions (numerical)

(c) General Court: Cases (numerical)

2. Other Jurisdictions

(a) American Supreme Court: Cases (chronological)

(b) European Court of Human Rights: Cases (chronological)

(c) German Constitutional Court: Cases (chronological)

Abbreviations

Bull. EC	Bulletin of the European Communities
CEE	Charges having equivalent effect
CFSP	Common Foreign and Security Policy
Coreper	Committee of the Permanent Representatives
CST	Civil Service Tribunal
DR	European Commission on Human Rights Decisions and Reports
EC	European Community (Treaty)
ECHR	European Convention on Human Rights
ECJ	European Court of Justice
ECR	European Court Reports
ECSC	European Coal and Steel Community
ECtHR	European Court of Human Rights
EEC	European Economic Community (Treaty)
EU (old)	European Union (Maastricht Treaty)
Euratom	European Atomic Energy Community
GATT	General Agreement on Tariffs and Trade
GC	General Court
MEEQR	Measures having an Equivalent Effect to Quantitative Restrictions
MEP	Member of the European Parliament
OJ	Official Journal of the European Union
QMV	Qualified Majority Voting
SEA	Single European Act
TEU	Treaty on European Union (post-Lisbon)
TFEU	Treaty on the Functioning of the European Union
UN	United Nations
US	United States
WTO	World Trade Organization

Introduction

The idea of European union is as old as the European idea of the sovereign State.[1] Yet the spectacular rise of the latter overshadowed the idea of European union for centuries. Within the twentieth century, two ruinous world wars and the social forces of globalization, however, discredited the idea of the sovereign State. The decline of the monadic State found expression in the spread of inter-state cooperation.[2] The various efforts at European cooperation after the Second World War indeed formed part of a general transition from an international law of coexistence to an international law of cooperation.[3]

The European Union was born in 1952 with the coming into being of the European Coal and Steel Community (ECSC).[4] Its original members were six European States: Belgium, France, Germany, Italy, Luxembourg, and the Netherlands. The Community had been created to *integrate* one industrial sector; and the very concept of *integration* indicated the wish of the contracting States "to break with the ordinary forms of international treaties and organizations".[5] The 1957 Treaty of Rome created two additional Communities: the European Atomic Energy Community and the European (Economic) Community. The "three Communities" were partly "merged" in 1967,[6] but continued to exist in relative independence. A major organizational leap was taken with the 1992 Maastricht Treaty. It integrated the three Communities into the European Union. But for a decade, this European Union was under constant constitutional construction. In an

---

[1] R. H. Foerster, *Die Idee Europa 1300–1946, Quellen zur Geschichte der politischen Einigung* (Deutscher Taschenbuchverlag, 1963).

[2] G. Schwarzenberger, *The Frontiers of International Law* (Stevens, 1962).

[3] W. G. Friedmann, *The Changing Structure of International Law* (Stevens, 1964).

[4] For a detailed discussion of the negotiations leading up to the signature of the ECSC Treaty, see: H. Mosler, "Der Vertrag über die Europäische Gemeinschaft für Kohle und Stahl", 14 (1951/2) *Zeitschrift für ausländisches öffentliches Recht und Völkerrecht*, 1.

[5] *Ibid.*, 24 (translation – RS).

[6] This was achieved through the 1965 "Merger Treaty" (see Treaty establishing a Single Council and a Single Commission of the European Communities).

attempt to prepare the Union for the twenty-first century, a European Convention was charged to draft a Constitutional Treaty in 2001. But this Treaty failed; and it took almost another decade to rescue the reform into the 2007 Reform (Lisbon) Treaty that came into force on 1 December 2009. The Lisbon Treaty has replaced the "old" European Union with the "new" European Union. It is this European Union that will be analysed in this "Introduction to European Law".

What is the structure of this book on European Union law? The book is divided into three parts, which correspond to the three themes of "creation", "enforcement", and "substance" of European law.

Part I analyses the Union as an institutional "creature", and considers the creation of European (secondary) law. It starts with an overview of the four major Union institutions: the European Parliament, the Council, the Commission, and the European Court in Chapter 1. Chapter 2 investigates how these institutions cooperate in the creation of European legislation. The Union cannot legislate in all areas of social life; and Chapters 3 and 4 look at two constitutional limits to Union legislation. Based on the principle of conferral, the Union must act within the scope of competences conferred upon it by the Member States. The scope of these competences – and their nature – will be discussed in Chapter 3. The final chapter within this part analyses the second constitutional limit to the exercise of Union

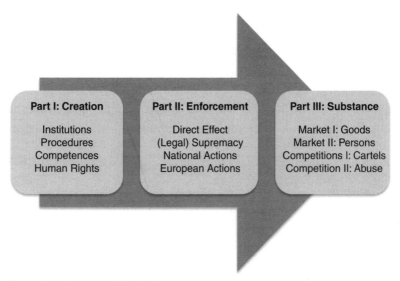

Part I: Creation	Part II: Enforcement	Part III: Substance
Institutions	Direct Effect	Market I: Goods
Procedures	(Legal) Supremacy	Market II: Persons
Competences	National Actions	Competitions I: Cartels
Human Rights	European Actions	Competition II: Abuse

Figure 0.1 Structure of the book

competences: European fundamental rights. These rights first emerged as general principles of Union law, but have now been codified in the Union's Charter of Fundamental Rights.

Part II concentrates on the "enforcement" of European law in the courts. We shall see that European law establishes rights and obligations that directly affect individuals. The direct effect of European law in the national legal orders will be discussed in Chapter 5. Where a European norm is directly effective, it will also be "supreme" over national law. The "supremacy" of European law is the subject of Chapter 6. But how will individuals enforce their "supreme" European rights? Chapters 7 and 8 look at the dual enforcement machinery within the Union legal order. Individuals will typically enforce their European rights in national courts. In order to assist these courts in the interpretation and application of European law, the Union envisages a preliminary reference procedure. The Union legal order has equally required national courts to provide effective remedies for the enforcement of European rights, and has even created a European remedy of state liability. The indirect enforcement of European law through the national courts is discussed in Chapter 7. It is complemented by the direct enforcement of European law in the European Courts, and Chapter 8 explores these direct actions.

Part III analyses the substantive heart of European law, that is: the law governing the internal market and European competition law. From the very beginning, *the* central economic task of the European Union was the creation of a "common market". The Rome Treaty had thereby not solely provided for a common market in goods. It equally required the abolition of obstacles to the free movement of persons, services, and capital. Europe's "internal market" was thus to comprise four fundamental freedoms. Two of these freedoms will be discussed in turn: Chapter 9 looks at the free movement of goods, while Chapter 10 examines the free movement of persons. The two subsequent chapters, Chapters 11 and 12, analyse the two pillars of European competition law: Articles 101 and 102 TFEU. The former deals with anti-competitive agreements, the latter prohibits the abuse of a dominant position by an undertaking. European competition law is thereby traditionally seen as a functional complement to the internal market. It would – primarily – protect the internal market from *private* power.

This book is (relatively) short for a book on European law. But brevity is the spice of language; and in order to keep this book as spicy as possible, many selective choices had to be made. Inevitably, some aspects will not be covered, others only marginally. Nevertheless, this "Introduction to European Law" will deal with all essential aspects of this complex area. And by concentrating on the "essence" of the subject, the book aims to help seeing the proverbial "wood" instead of the trees. For these European trees are ever growing and multiplying, and it is no wonder that many a student might get lost in the legal undergrowth! But if there is a second wish which this "Introduction to European Law" has, it is also to make the reader "thirsty" for more. Yet this thirst will have to be quenched by one of the larger generalist textbooks,[7] or one of the major textbooks dedicated to a specialized branch of European law.[8]

---

[7] The three traditional textbooks in English are: D. Chalmers et al., *European Union Law* (Cambridge University Press, 2010), P. Craig and G. de Búrca, *EU Law: Text, Cases, and Materials* (Oxford University Press, 2011), and A. Dashwood et al., *European Union Law* (Hart, 2011).

[8] European law is traditionally divided into three major branches: European *constitutional* law (see T. Hartley, *The Foundations of European Union Law* (Oxford University Press, 2010); and: R. Schütze, *European Constitutional Law* (Cambridge University Press, 2012)), European *internal market* law (see C. Barnard, *The Substantive Law of the EU* (Oxford University Press, 2010); and: G. Davies, *European Union Internal Market Law* (Routledge, 2006)), and European *competition* law (see J. Goyder and A. Albors-Llorens, *EC Competition Law* (Oxford University Press, 2009), and: A. Jones & B. Sufrin, *EU Competition Law* (Oxford University Press, 2011)). In addition to these three principal branches, the last two decades have seen the emergence of many smaller branches, such as European *external relations* law (see P. Eeckhout, *EU External Relations Law* (Oxford University Press, 2011), and: P. Koutrakos, *EU International Relations Law* (Hart, 2006)), and European *environmental* law (see J. H. Jans and H. Vedder, *European Environmental Law* (Europa Law Publishing, 2008), and: L. Krämer, *EC Environmental Law* (Sweet & Maxwell, 2006)).

Part I

European Law: Creation

This Part analyses the Union as an institutional "creature", and considers the creation of European (secondary) law. It starts in Chapter 1 with an overview of the four major Union institutions: the European Parliament, the Council, the Commission, and the European Court. Chapter 2 investigates how these institutions cooperate in the creation of European legislation. The Union cannot legislate in all areas of social life; and Chapters 3 and 4 look at two constitutional limits to Union legislation. Based on the principle of conferral, the Union must act within the scope of competences conferred upon it by the Member States. The scope of these competences – and their nature – will be discussed in Chapter 3. Chapter 4 analyses the second constitutional limit to the exercise of Union competences: European fundamental rights. These rights first emerged as general principles of Union law, but have now been codified in the Union's Charter of Fundamental Rights.

Chapter 1 Union institutions

Chapter 2 Union legislation

Chapter 3 Union competences

Chapter 4 Fundamental rights

Introduction

The creation of governmental institutions is *the* central task of all constitutions. Each political community needs institutions to govern its society; as each society needs common rules and a method for their making, execution, and arbitration. The European Treaties establish a number of European institutions to make, execute, and arbitrate European law. The Union's institutions and their core tasks are defined in Title III of the Treaty on European Union (TEU). The central provision here is Article 13 TEU:

The Union shall have an institutional framework which shall aim to promote its values, advance its objectives, serve its interests, those of its citizens and those of the Member States, and ensure the consistency, effectiveness and continuity of its policies and actions.

The Union's institutions shall be:

- the European Parliament,
- the European Council,
- the Council,
- the European Commission (hereinafter referred to as 'the Commission'),
- the Court of Justice of the European Union,
- the European Central Bank,
- the Court of Auditors.[1]

The provision lists seven governmental institutions of the European Union. They constitute the core "players" in the Union legal order.[2] What strikes the attentive eye first is the number of institutions: unlike a tripartite institutional structure, the Union offers more than twice that number. The two institutions that do not – at first sight – seem to directly correspond to "national" institutions are the (European) Council and the Commission. The name "Council" represents a reminder of the "international" origins of the European Union, but the institution can equally be found in the governmental structure of Federal States. It will be harder to find the name "Commission" among the public institutions of States, where the executive is typically referred to as the "government". By contrast, central banks and courts of auditors exist in many national legal orders.

Where do the Treaties define the Union institutions? The provisions on the Union institutions are split between the Treaty on European Union and the Treaty on the Functioning of the European Union in the following way:

---

[1] Article 13(1) TEU. Paragraph 2 adds: "Each institution shall act within the limits of the powers conferred on it in the Treaties, and in conformity with the procedures, conditions and objectives set out in them. The institutions shall practise mutual sincere cooperation."

[2] While the Treaties set up seven "institutions", they do acknowledge the existence of other "bodies". First, according to Article 13 (4) TEU, the Parliament, the Council and the Commission "shall be assisted by an Economic and Social Committee and a Committee of the Regions acting in an advisory capacity". The composition and powers of the "Economic and Social Committee" are set out in Articles 301–4 TFEU. The composition and powers of the "Committee of the Regions" are defined by Articles 305–7 TFEU. In addition to the Union's "Advisory Bodies", the Treaties also acknowledge the existence of a "European Investment Bank" (Articles 308–9 TFEU; as well as Protocol No. 5 on the Statute of the European Investment Bank).

Table 1 Treaty provisions on the Institutions

Provisions on the Institutions	
EU Treaty – Title III	FEU Treaty – Part VI – Title I – Chapter 1
Article 13 Institutional Framework	Section 1 European Parliament (Arts. 223–234)
Article 14 European Parliament	
Article 15 European Council	Section 2 European Council (Arts. 235–236)
Article 16 Council	Section 3 Council (Arts. 237–243)
Article 17 Commission	Section 4 Commission (Arts. 244–250)
Article 18 High Representative	Section 5 Court of Justice (Arts. 251–281)
Article 19 Court of Justice	Section 6 European Central Bank (Arts. 282–284)
	Section 7 Court of Auditors (Arts. 285–287)
Protocol (No.3): Statute of the Court of Justice Protocol (No.4): Statute of the ESCB and the ECB Protocol (No.6): Location of the Seats of the Institutions etc. (Internal) Rules of Procedure of the Institution	

The four sections of this chapter will concentrate on the classic four Union institutions: the Parliament, the Council, the Commission, and the Court.[3]

1. The European Parliament

Despite its formal place in the Treaties, the European Parliament has never been the Union's "first" institution. For a long time it followed, in rank, behind the Council and the Commission. Its original powers were indeed minimal. It was an "auxiliary" organ that was to assist the institutional duopoly of Council and Commission. This minimal role gradually increased from the 1970s onwards. Today the Parliament constitutes – with the Council – a chamber of the Union legislature. Directly elected by the European citizens,[4] Parliament constitutes not only the most

---

[3] For an analysis of the three other Union institutions, see R. Schütze, *European Constitutional Law* (Cambridge University Press, 2012), Chapters 3 and 4.

[4] Article 10(2) TEU: "Citizens are directly represented at Union level in the European Parliament."

democratic institution; in light of its elective "appointment", it is also the most supranational institution of the European Union.

This section will analyse two aspects of the European Parliament. First, we shall look at its formation through European elections. A second subsection provides an overview of Parliament's powers in the various governmental functions of the Union.

(a) Formation: electing Parliament

When the European Union was born, the European Treaties envisaged that its Parliament was to be composed of "representatives of the peoples of the States".[5] This characterization corresponded to its formation. For the European Parliament was not directly elected. It was to "consist of delegates who shall be designated by the respective Parliaments from among their members in accordance with the procedure laid down by each Member State".[6] European parliamentarians were thus – delegated – *national* parliamentarians. This formation method brought Parliament close to an (international) "assembly". The founding Treaties did nonetheless breach the classic international law logic already in two ways. First, they had abandoned the idea of sovereign equality of the Member States by recognizing different sizes for national parliamentary delegations.[7] Second, and more importantly, the Treaties already envisaged that Parliament would eventually be formed through "elections by direct universal suffrage in accordance with a uniform procedure in all Member States".[8]

When did the transformation of the European Parliament from an "assembly" of national parliamentarians into a directly elected Parliament take place? It took two decades before the Union's 1976 "Election Act" was adopted.[9] And ever since the first parliamentary elections in 1979, the European Parliament ceased to be composed of "representatives of the peoples of the States". It constituted henceforth the representative of a European people. The Lisbon Treaty has – belatedly – recognized this dramatic constitutional change. It now characterizes the European

---

[5] Article 137 EEC. See also Article 20 ECSC.   [6] Article 138 EEC. See also Article 21 ECSC.
[7] Originally, the EEC Treaty granted thirty-six delegates to Germany, France and Italy; fourteen delegates to Belgium and the Netherlands; and six delegates to Luxembourg.
[8] Article 138 (3) EEC. See also Article 21 (3) ECSC.
[9] "Act concerning the Election of the Members of the European Parliament by direct universal Suffrage." The Act was adopted in 1976 ([1976] OJ L278/5).

Parliament as being "composed of representatives of the Union's citizens".[10]

What is the size and composition of the European Parliament? How are elections conducted? The Treaties stipulate the following on the size and composition of the European Parliament:

The European Parliament shall be composed of representatives of the Union's citizens. They shall not exceed seven hundred and fifty in number, plus the President. Representation of citizens shall be degressively proportional, with a minimum threshold of six members per Member State. No Member State shall be allocated more than ninety-six seats.

The European Council shall adopt by unanimity, on the initiative of the European Parliament and with its consent, a decision establishing the composition of the European Parliament, respecting the principles referred to in the first subparagraph.[11]

The European Parliament has a maximum size of 751 members.[12] While relatively big in comparison with the (American) House of Representatives, it is still smaller than the (British) House of Lords.[13] The Treaties themselves no longer determine its composition.[14] It is the European Council that must decide on the national "quotas" for the Union's parliamentary representatives. The distribution of seats must however be "degressively proportional" within a range spanning from six to ninety-six seats. While the European Council has not yet taken a formal decision, it has given its political endorsement to a proposal by the European Parliament.[15] In its proposal, Parliament

---

[10] Article 14 (2) TEU.   [11] *Ibid.*

[12] The 2009 Parliamentary Elections were still held under the pre-Lisbon arrangement. Under that arrangement, there existed only 736 seats with Germany having 99 seats. To bring the number up to 751 and to reduce the German MEPs by three, Spain proposed a Treaty amendment to Protocol (No. 36) on Transitional Provisions. However, the final proposal suggested adding 18 MEPs for the 2009–14 parliamentary term *without* reducing the mandate of the three (already) elected German MEPs. Parliament would thus – temporarily – have 754 members! This proposal has received the consent of the Commission, the Parliament, and the European Council (see Decision of the European Council of 17 June 2010 on the examination by a conference of representatives of the governments of the Member States of the amendments to the Treaties proposed by the Spanish Government concerning the composition of the European Parliament and not to convene a Convention (2010/350/EU)).

[13] To compare: the (American) House of Representatives has 435 members. The (British) House of Commons has 648 members, while the (British) House of Lords currently has 829 members.

[14] This had been the case prior to the Lisbon Treaty.

[15] See Declaration (No. 5) on the political agreement by the European Council concerning the draft Decision on the composition of the European Parliament. For the draft decision, see European Parliament Resolution (11 October 2007) on the composition of the European Parliament ([2008] OJ C227/132).

Table 2 Distribution of seats in the European Parliament (Member States)

Member State (Seats)		
Belgium (22)	Ireland (12)	Austria (19)
Bulgaria (18)	Italy (72+1)[17]	Poland (51)
Czech Republic (22)	Cyprus (6)	Portugal (22)
Denmark (13)	Latvia (9)	Romania (33)
Germany (96)	Lithuania (12)	Slovenia (8)
Estonia (6)	Luxembourg (6)	Slovakia (13)
Greece (22)	Hungary (22)	Finland (13)
Spain (54)	Malta (6)	Sweden (20)
France (74)	Netherlands (26)	United Kingdom (73)

provided a definition of "degressively proportional",[16] and has suggested the concrete distribution of seats among Member States shown in Table 2.

The national "quotas" for European parliamentary seats constitute a compromise between the democratic principle and the federal principle. For while the democratic principle would demand that each citizen in the Union has equal voting power ("one person, one vote"), the federal principle insists on the political existence of States. The result of this compromise was the rejection of a *purely* proportional distribution in favour of a *degressively* proportional system. The degressive element within that system unfortunately means that a Luxembourg citizen has ten times more voting power than a British, French, or German citizen.

How are the *individual* members of Parliament elected? The Treaties solely provide us with the most general of rules: "The members of the European Parliament shall be elected for a term of five years by direct universal suffrage in a free and secret ballot."[18] More precise rules are set out in the (amended) 1976 Election Act. Article 1 of the Act commands that the elections must be conducted "on the basis of proportional representation".[19] This outlaws the

---

[16] *Ibid.*, para. 6: "[T]he principle of degressive proportionality means that the ratio between the population and the number of seats of each Member State must vary in relation to their respective populations in such a way that each Member from a more populous Member State represents more citizens than each Member from a less populous Member State and conversely, but also that no less populous Member State has more seats than a more populous Member State[.]"

[17] This additional seat was added, on Italian intransigence, by the Lisbon Intergovernmental Council; see Declaration (No. 4) on the Composition of the European Parliament: "The additional seat in the European Parliament will be attributed to Italy."

[18] Article 14 (3) TEU.   [19] Article 1 (1) and (3) of the 1976 Election Act (supra n. 9).

traditionally British election method of first-past-the-post.[20] The specifics of the election procedure are however principally left to the Member States.[21] European parliamentary elections thus still do not follow "a uniform electoral procedure in all Member States", but are rather conducted "in accordance with principles common to all Member States".[22] The Treaties nonetheless insist on one common constitutional rule: "every citizen of the Union residing in a Member State of which he is not a national shall have the right to vote and to stand as a candidate in elections to the European Parliament in the Member State in which he resides, under the same conditions as nationals of that State".[23]

(b) Parliamentary powers

When the 1951 Paris Treaty set up the European Parliament, its sole function was to exercise "supervisory powers".[24] Parliament was indeed a passive onlooker on the decision-making process within the first Community. The 1957 Rome Treaty expanded Parliament's functions to "advisory and supervisory powers".[25] This recognized the active power of Parliament to be consulted on Commission proposals before their adoption by the Council.[26] After sixty years of evolution and numerous amendments, the Treaty on European Union today defines the powers of the European Parliament in Article 14 TEU as follows: "The European Parliament shall, jointly with the Council, exercise legislative and budgetary functions. It shall exercise functions of political control and consultation as laid down in the Treaties. It shall elect the President of the Commission."[27] This definition distinguishes

---

[20] This condition had not been part of the original 1976 Election Act, but was added through a 2002 amendment. This amendment was considered necessary as, hitherto, the British majority voting system "could alone alter the entire political balance in the European Parliament" (F. Jacobs et al., *The European Parliament* (Harper Publishing, 2005), 17). The best example of this distorting effect was the 1979 election to the European Parliament in which the British Conservatives won 60 out of 78 seats with merely 50 per cent of the vote (*ibid.*).

[21] Article 8 of the 1976 Election Act: "Subject to the provisions of this Act, the electoral procedure shall be governed in each Member State by its national provisions." Under the Act, Member States are free to decide whether to establish national or local constituencies for elections to the European Parliament (*ibid.*, Article 2), and whether to set a minimum threshold for the allocation of seats (*ibid.*, Article 3).

[22] Both alternatives are provided for in Article 223 (1) TFEU.   [23] Article 22 (2) TFEU.

[24] Article 20 ECSC.   [25] Article 137 EEC.

[26] *Roquette Frères* v. *Council* (*Isoglucose*), Case 138/79, [1980] ECR 3333.

[27] Article 14 (1) TEU.

between four types of powers: legislative and budgetary powers as well as supervisory and elective powers.

(i) Legislative powers

The European Parliament's primary power lies in the making of European laws. This involvement may take place at two moments in time. Parliament may informally propose new legislation.[28] However, it is not – unlike many national parliaments – entitled to formally propose bills. The task of making legislative proposals is, with minor exceptions, a constitutional prerogative of the Commission.[29]

The principal legislative involvement of Parliament starts therefore later, namely after the Commission has submitted a proposal to the European legislature. Like other federal legal orders, the European legal order acknowledges a number of different legislative procedures. The Treaties now textually distinguish between the "ordinary" legislative procedure and a number of "special" legislative procedures. The former is defined as "the joint adoption by the European Parliament and the Council" on a proposal from the Commission.[30] Special legislative procedures cover various degrees of parliamentary participation. Under the "consent procedure" Parliament must give its consent before the Council can adopt European legislation.[31] This is a cruder form of legislative participation that essentially grants a negative power. Parliament cannot suggest positive amendments, but must take-or-leave the Council's position. Under the "consultation procedure", by contrast, Parliament is not even entitled to do that. It merely needs to be consulted – a role that is closer to a supervisory function than to a legislative one.[32] Exceptionally, a

---

[28] Article 225 TFEU: "The European Parliament may, acting by a majority of its component Members, request the Commission to submit any appropriate proposal on matters on which it considers that a Union act is required for the purpose of implementing the Treaties. If the Commission does not submit a proposal, it shall inform the European Parliament of the reasons."

[29] On this power, see Chapter 2 – Section 1 (a) below.   [30] Article 289 (1) TFEU.

[31] For example: Article 19 TFEU, according to which "the Council, acting unanimously in accordance with a special legislative procedure and after obtaining the consent of the European Parliament, may take appropriate action to combat discrimination based on sex, racial or ethnic origin, religion or belief, disability, age or sexual orientation".

[32] For example: Article 22 (1) TFEU, which states: "Every citizen of the Union residing in a Member State of which he is not a national shall have the right to vote and to stand as a candidate at municipal elections in the Member State in which he resides, under the same conditions as nationals of that State. This right shall be exercised subject to detailed

special legislative procedure may make Parliament the dominant legislative chamber.[33]

Importantly, the Parliament's "legislative" powers may also extend to the external relations sphere. After Lisbon, Parliament has indeed become an important player in the conclusion of the Union's international agreements.

(ii) Budgetary powers

Parliaments have historically been involved in the adoption of national budgets. For they were seen as legitimating the *raising* of revenue. In the words of the American colonists: "No taxation, without representation". In the European Union, this picture is somewhat inverted. For since Union revenue is fixed by the Council and the Member States,[34] the European Parliament's budgetary powers have not focused on the income side but on the expenditure side. Its powers have consequently been described as the "reverse of those traditionally exercised by parliaments".[35]

Be that as it may, Parliament's formal involvement in the Union budget started with the 1970 and 1975 Budget Treaties. They distinguished between compulsory and non-compulsory expenditure, with the latter being expenditure that would not result from compulsory financial commitments flowing from the application of European law. Parliament's powers were originally confined to this second category. The Lisbon Treaty has however abandoned the distinction between compulsory and non-compulsory expenditure, and Parliament has thus become an equal partner, with the Council, in establishing the Union's annual budget.[36]

(iii) Supervisory powers

A third parliamentary power is that of holding the executive to account. Parliamentary supervisory powers typically involve the power to question, debate, and investigate.

A soft parliamentary power is the power to *debate*. To that effect, the European Parliament is entitled to receive the "general report on the activities of the Union" from the Commission,[37] which it "shall discuss in open

arrangements adopted by the Council, acting unanimously in accordance with a special legislative procedure and after consulting the European Parliament[.]"

[33] For example: Article 223 (2) TFEU – granting Parliament the power, with the consent of the Council, to adopt a Statute for its Members.

[34] See Article 311 TFEU on the "Union's own resources".

[35] D. Judge and D. Earnshaw, *The European Parliament* (Palgrave, 2008), 198.

[36] Article 314 TFEU.   [37] Article 249 (2) TFEU.

session".[38] And as regards the European Council, the Treaties require its President to "present a report to the European Parliament after each of the meetings of the European Council".[39] Similar obligations apply to the European Central Bank.[40] The power to *question* the European executive is formally enshrined only for the Commission: "The Commission shall reply orally or in writing to questions put to it by the European Parliament or by its Members."[41] However, both the European Council and the Council have confirmed their willingness to be questioned by Parliament.[42] Early on, Parliament introduced the institution of "Question Time" – modelled on the procedure within the British Parliament.[43] And under its own Rules of Procedure, Parliament is entitled to hold "an extraordinary debate" on "a matter of major interest relating to European Union Policy".[44]

Parliament also enjoys the formal power to *investigate*. It is constitutionally entitled to set up temporary Committees of Inquiry to investigate alleged contraventions or maladministration in the implementation of European law.[45] These (temporary) committees complement Parliament's standing committees. They have been used, inter alia, to investigate the (mis)handling of the BSE crisis.

Finally, European citizens have the general right to "petition" the European Parliament.[46] And according to a Scandinavian constitutional tradition, the European Parliament will also elect an "ombudsman". The European Ombudsman "shall be empowered to receive complaints" from any citizen or Union resident "concerning instances of maladministration in the activities of the Union institutions, bodies or agencies". S/he

---

[38] Article 233 TFEU.   [39] Article 15 (6) (d) TEU.   [40] Article 284 (3) TFEU.

[41] Article 230 TFEU – second indent.

[42] The Council accepted this political obligation in 1973; see Jacobs, *The European Parliament* (supra n. 20), 284.

[43] Rule 116 Parliament Rules of Procedure. For acceptance of that obligation by the Commission, see Framework Agreement on relations between the European Parliament and the European Commission, [2010] OJ L304/47, para. 46.

[44] Rule 141 Parliament Rules of Procedure.

[45] Article 226 (1) TFEU. For a good overview of the history of these committees, see M. Shackleton, "The European Parliament's New Committees of Inquiry: Tiger or Paper Tiger?", 36 (1998) *Journal of Common Market Studies*, 115.

[46] According to Article 227 TFEU, any citizen or Union resident has the right to petition the European Parliament "on any matter which comes within the Union's field or activity and which affects him, her or it directly". See also Article 20 (2) (d) TFEU.

"shall conduct inquiries" on the basis of complaints addressed to her or him directly or through a member of the European Parliament.[47]

(iv) Elective powers

Modern constitutionalism distinguishes between "presidential" and "parliamentary" systems. Within the former, the executive officers are independent from Parliament, whereas in the latter the executive is elected by Parliament. The European constitutional order sits somewhere "in between". Its executive was for a long time selected without any parliamentary involvement. However, as regards the Commission, the European Parliament has increasingly come to be involved in the appointment process. Today, Article 17 TEU describes the involvement of the European Parliament in the appointment of the Commission as follows:

> Taking into account the elections to the European Parliament and after having held the appropriate consultations, the European Council, acting by a qualified majority, shall propose to the European Parliament a candidate for President of the Commission. This candidate shall be elected by the European Parliament by a majority of its component members ... The Council, by common accord with the President-elect, shall adopt the list of the other persons whom it proposes for appointment as members of the Commission. They shall be selected, on the basis of the suggestions made by Member States ... The President, the High Representative of the Union for Foreign Affairs and Security Policy and the other members of the Commission shall be subject as a body to a vote of consent by the European Parliament. On the basis of this consent the Commission shall be appointed by the European Council, acting by a qualified majority.[48]

The appointment of the European executive thus requires a dual parliamentary consent. Parliament must – first – "elect" the President of the Commission. And it must – secondly – confirm the Commission as a collective body. (Apart from the President, the European Parliament has consequently not got the power to confirm each and every Commissioner.)[49] In light of this elective power given to Parliament, one

---

[47] Article 228 TFEU.   [48] Article 17 (7) TEU.

[49] However, Parliament may request each nominated Commissioner to appear before Parliament and to "present" his views. This practice thus comes close to "confirmation hearings" (Judge and Earnshaw, *The European Parliament* (supra n. 35), 205).

is indeed justified in characterizing the Union's governmental system as a "semi-parliamentary democracy".[50]

Once appointed, the Commission continues to "be responsible to the European Parliament".[51] Where this consent is lost, Parliament may vote on a motion of censure. If this vote of mistrust is carried, the Commission must resign as a body. The motion of collective censure mirrors Parliament's appointment power, which is also focused on the Commission *as a collective body*. This blunt "nuclear option" has never been used.[52] However, unlike the appointment power, Parliament has been able to sharpen its tools of censure significantly by concluding a political agreement with the Commission. Accordingly, if Parliament expresses lack of confidence in an *individual* member of the Commission, the President of the Commission "shall either require the resignation of that Member" or, after "serious" consideration, explain the refusal to do so before Parliament.[53] While this is a much "smarter sanction", it has also never been used due to the demanding voting requirements in Parliament.

Parliament is also involved in the appointment of other European officers. This holds true for the Court of Auditors,[54] the European Central Bank,[55] and the European Ombudsman.[56] However, it is not involved in the appointment of judges to the Court of Justice of the European Union.

2. The Council

The 1957 Rome Treaty had charged the Council with the task "to ensure that the objectives set out in this Treaty are attained".[57] This task involved the exercise of legislative as well as executive functions. And while other institutions would also be involved in these functions, the Council was to

---

[50] P. Dann, "European Parliament and Executive Federalism: Approaching a Parliament in a Semi-Parliamentary Democracy", 9 (2003) *European Law Journal*, 549.

[51] Article 17 (8) TEU.

[52] Once, however, the European Parliament came close to using this power when in 1999 it decided to censure the Santer Commission. However, that Commission chose collectively to resign instead.

[53] Framework Agreement (supra n. 43), para. 5. However, this rule had been contested by the Council; see Council Statement concerning the Framework Agreement on relations between the European Parliament and the Commission ([2010] OJ C287/1).

[54] Article 286 (2) TFEU.   [55] Article 283 (2) TFEU.   [56] Article 228 (2) TFEU.

[57] Article 145 EEC.

be the central institution within the European Union. This has dramatically changed with the rise of two rival institutions. On one side, the ascendancy of the European Parliament has limited the Council's legislative role within the Union. On the other side, the rise of the *European* Council has restricted the Council's executive powers. (Importantly: the European Council is not identical with the Council. It constitutes a separate Union institution composed of the Heads of State or Government of the Member States.)[58] Today, the Council is best characterized as the "federal" chamber within the Union legislature. It is the organ in which national governments meet.

What is the composition of this federal chamber, and what is its internal structure? How will the Council decide – by unanimity or qualified majority? And what are the powers enjoyed by the Council? This second section addresses these questions in four subsections.

(a) Composition and configurations

Within the European Union, the Council is the institution of the Member States. Its intergovernmental character lies in its composition. The Treaty on European Union defines it as follows: "The Council shall consist of a representative of each Member State at ministerial level, who may commit the government of the Member State in question and cast its vote."[59] Within the Council, each national minister thus represents the interests of "his" Member State. These interests may vary depending on the subject matter decided in the Council. And indeed, depending on the subject matter at issue, there are different Council configurations.[60] And for each configuration, a different national minister will be representing "his" State. While there is thus – legally – but one single Council, there are – politically – ten different Councils.

The existing Council configurations are as follows:

---

[58] Article 15 (2) TEU. For an analysis of the European Council, see Schütze, *European Constitutional Law* (supra n. 3), Chapter 3 – Section 3.

[59] Article 16 (2) TEU.

[60] Article 16 (6) TEU: "The Council shall meet in different configurations, the list of which shall be adopted in accordance with Article 236 of the Treaty on the Functioning of the European Union." While the European Council has not yet adopted the list, the Council was itself entitled to lay down the list (see Article 4 of the Protocol (No. 36) on Transitional Provisions). This happened with Council Decision 2009/878, [2009] OJ L315/46.

Table 3 Council configurations

Council Configurations
1 General Affairs
2 Foreign Affairs
3 Economic and Financial Affairs
4 Justice and Home Affairs
5 Employment, Social Policy, Health and Consumer Affairs
6 Competitiveness (Internal Market, Industry and Research)
7 Transport, Telecommunications and Energy
8 Agriculture and Fisheries
9 Environment
10 Education, Youth and Culture

What is the mandate of each Council configuration? The Treaties only define the tasks of the first two Council configurations.[61] The "General Affairs Council" is charged to "ensure consistency in the work of the different Council configurations" below the General Affairs Council.[62] The "Foreign Affairs Council", on the other hand, is required to "elaborate the Union's external action on the basis of strategic guidelines laid down by the European Council and ensure that the Union's action is consistent".[63] The thematic scope and functional tasks of the remaining Council configurations are constitutionally open. They will generally deal with the subjects falling within their nominal ambit.

(b) Internal structure and organs

The Council has developed committees to assist it. From the very beginning, a committee composed of representatives of the Member States would support the Council.[64] That committee was made permanent under the 1957 Rome Treaty.[65] The resultant "Committee of *Permanent* Representatives" became

---

[61] Article 16 (6) TEU.   [62] *Ibid.*   [63] *Ibid.*

[64] The Committee beneath the ECSC Council was called "Commission de Coordination du Conseil des Ministres" (Cocor). Its members were not permanently residing in Brussels.

[65] The Rome Treaty contained, unlike the 1951 Paris Treaty, an express legal basis for a Council Committee in Article 151 EEC. While the provision did not expressly mention that these representatives would be permanent representatives, this had been the intention of the Member States (E. Noel, "The Committee of Permanent Representatives", 5 (1967) *Journal of Common Market Studies*, 219). The Merger Treaty formally established the Committee of Permanent Representatives (*ibid.*, Article 4).

known under its French acronym: "Coreper". The Permanent Representative is the ambassador of a Member State at the European Union. S/he is based in the national "Permanent Representation to the European Union". Coreper has two parts: Coreper II represents the meeting of the ambassadors, while Coreper I – against all intuition – represents the meetings of their deputies. Both parts correspond to particular Council configurations. Coreper II prepares the first four Council configurations – that is the more important political decisions; whereas Coreper I prepares the more technical remainder.

The function of Coreper is vaguely defined in the Treaties: "A Committee of Permanent Representatives of the Governments of the Member States shall be responsible for preparing the work of the Council."[66] The abstract definition has been – somewhat – specified in the following way: "All items on the agenda for a Council meeting shall be examined in advance by Coreper unless the latter decides otherwise. Coreper shall endeavour to reach agreement at its level to be submitted to the Council for adoption."[67] In order to achieve that task, Coreper has set up "working parties" below it.[68] (These working parties are composed of national civil servants operating on instructions from national ministries.) Where Coreper reaches agreement, the point will be classed as an "A item" that will be rubber-stamped by the Council. Where it fails to agree in advance, a "B item" will need to be expressly discussed by the ministers in the Council. (But importantly, even for "A items" Coreper is not formally entitled to take decisions itself. It merely "prepares" and facilitates formal decision-making in the Council.)

(c) Decision-making and voting

The Council will – physically – meet in Brussels to decide. The meetings are divided into two parts: one dealing with legislative activities, the other with non-legislative activities. When discussing legislation, the Council must meet in public.[69] The Commission will attend Council meetings.[70] However,

---

[66] Article 16 (7) TEU and Article 240 (1) TFEU. See also Article 19 of the Council Rules of Procedure.

[67] Article 19 (2) Council Rules of Procedure.

[68] *Ibid.*, Article 19 (3). Under this paragraph, the General Secretariat is under an obligation to produce a list of these preparatory bodies. For a recent version of this list, see General Secretariat of the Council of the European Union, 20 July 2010, POLGEN 115.

[69] Article 16 (8) TEU.

[70] According to Article 5(2) Council Rules of Procedure, the Council may however decide to deliberate without the Commission.

it is not a formal member of the Council and is thus not entitled to vote. The quorum within the Council is as low as it is theoretical: a majority of the members of the Council are required to enable the Council to vote.[71]

Decision-making in the Council will take place in two principal forms: *unanimity* voting and *majority* voting. Unanimity voting requires the consent of all national ministers and is provided in the Treaties for sensitive political questions.[72] Majority voting however represents the constitutional norm. The Treaties here distinguish between a simple and a qualified majority. "Where it is required to act by a simple majority, the Council shall act by a majority of its component members."[73] This form of majority vote is rare.[74] The constitutional default is indeed the qualified majority: "The Council shall act by a qualified majority except where the Treaties provide otherwise."[75]

What constitutes a qualified majority of Member States in the Council? This has been one of the most controversial constitutional questions in the European Union. From the very beginning, the Treaties had instituted a system of *weighted votes*. Member States would thus not be "sovereign equals" in the

Table 4 Weighted votes system within the Council

Weighted Votes – Member States: Votes	
Germany, France, Italy, United Kingdom	29
Spain, Poland	27
Romania	14
Netherlands	13
Belgium, Czech Republic, Greece, Hungary, Portugal	12
Austria, Bulgaria, Sweden	10
Denmark, Ireland, Lithuania, Slovakia, Finland	7
Cyprus, Estonia, Latvia, Luxembourg, Slovenia	4
Malta	3
Qualified Majority: 255/345	

---

[71] *Ibid.*, Article 11 (4).

[72] Important examples of sensitive political issues still requiring unanimity are foreign affairs (see Article 31 TEU), and "the harmonisation of legislation concerning turnover taxes, excise duties and other forms of indirect taxation" (see Article 113 TFEU).

[73] Article 238 (1) TFEU.

[74] For example: Article 150 TFEU. Most matters that allow for simple majority are (internal) procedural or institutional matters.

[75] Article 16 (3) TEU.

Council, but would possess a number of votes that correlated with the size of their population. Table 4 shows the system of weighted votes that applies today.

The weighting of votes is to some extent "degressively proportional". The voting ratio between the biggest and the smallest State is ten to one – a ratio that is roughly similar to the degressively proportional system for the European Parliament. However, the voting system also represents a system of symbolic compromises. For example, the four biggest Member States are all given the same number of votes – despite Germany's significantly greater demographic magnitude.[76]

In the past, this system of weighted votes has been attacked from two sides: from the smaller Member States as well as the bigger Member States. The smaller Member States have claimed that it favours the bigger Member States and have insisted that the 255 votes must be cast by a majority of the States. The bigger Member States, by contrast, have complained that the weighting unduly favours smaller Member States and have insisted on the political safeguard that the 255 votes cast in the Council correspond to 62 per cent of the total population of the Union. With these two qualifications taken into account, decision-making in the Council demands a *triple* majority: a *majority* of the weighted votes must be cast by a *majority* of the Member States representing a *majority* of the Union population.

This triple majority system will govern decision-making in the Union until 2014. From 1 November 2014 a completely new system of voting is to apply in the Council. This revolutionary change is set out in Article 16 (4) TEU:

As from 1 November 2014, a qualified majority shall be defined as at least 55 % of the members of the Council, comprising at least fifteen of them and representing Member States comprising at least 65 % of the population of the Union. A blocking minority must include at least four Council members, failing which the qualified majority shall be deemed attained. The other arrangements governing the qualified majority are laid down in Article 238(2) of the Treaty on the Functioning of the European Union.[77]

---

[76] According to the Union's official census figures (see Council Decision 2010/795, [2010] OJ L338/47), the German population exceeds that of France – the second most populous State of the Union – by about 17 million people.

[77] The Treaty recognizes an express exception to this in Article 238 (2) TFEU which states: "By way of derogation from Article 16(4) of the Treaty on European Union, as from 1 November 2014 and subject to the provisions laid down in the Protocol on transitional provisions,

This new Lisbon voting system will abolish the system of weighted votes in favour of a system that grants each State a single vote. In a Union of twenty-seven States, 55 per cent of the Council members correspond to fifteen States. But this majority is again qualified from two sides. The bigger Member States have insisted on a relatively high population majority behind the State majority. The population threshold of 65 per cent of the Union population would mean that any three of the four biggest States of the Union could block a Council decision. The smaller Member States have thus insisted on a qualification of the qualification. A qualified majority will be "deemed attained", where fewer than four States try to block a Council decision.

The new Lisbon system of qualified majority voting is designed to replace the triple majority with a simpler double majority.[78] And yet the Member States – always fearful of abrupt changes – have agreed on two constitutional compromises that cushion the new system of qualified majority voting. First, the Member States have revived the "Ioannina Compromise".[79] The latter was envisaged in a "Declaration on Article 16 (4)",[80] and is now codified in a Council Decision.[81] According to the Ioannina Compromise, the Council is under an obligation – despite the formal existence of the double majority in Article 16 (4) TEU – to continue deliberations, where a fourth of the States or States representing a fifth of the Union population oppose a decision.[82] The Council is here under the procedural duty to "do all in its power" to reach – within a reasonable time – "a satisfactory solution" to address the concerns of the blocking Member States.[83]

This soft mechanism is complemented by a hard mechanism to limit qualified majority voting in the Council. For the Treaties also recognize – regionally

---

where the Council does not act on a proposal from the Commission or from the High Representative of the Union for Foreign Affairs and Security Policy, the qualified majority shall be defined as at least 72 % of the members of the Council, representing Member States comprising at least 65 % of the population of the Union."

[78] However, the "Protocol on transitional provisions" grants any Member State the right to choose between the "old" and the "new" Union system of voting in the period between 1 November 2014 and 31 March 2017 (ibid., Article 3 (2)). See also "Declaration (No. 7) on Article 16(4) of the Treaty on European Union and Article 238(2) of the Treaty on the Functioning of the European Union", in particular (draft) Articles 1–3.

[79] The compromise was negotiated by the Member States' foreign ministers in Ioannina (Greece) – from where it takes its name. The compromise was designed to smooth the transition from the Union of twelve to a Union of fifteen Member States.

[80] Declaration (No. 7) on Article 16(4) (supra n. 78) contains a draft Council Decision.

[81] The Council formally adopted the decision in 2007 (see Council Decision 2009/857, [2009] OJ L314/73).

[82] Ibid., Article 4.   [83] Ibid., Article 5.

limited – versions of the "Luxembourg Compromise".[84] A patent illustration of this can be found in the context of the Union's Common Foreign and Security Policy which contains the following provision: "If a member of the Council declares that, for vital and stated reasons of national policy, it intends to oppose the adoption of a decision to be taken by qualified majority, a vote shall not be taken."[85] A Member State can here unilaterally block a Union decision on what it deems to be its vital interest.

(d) Functions and powers

The Treaties summarize the functions and powers of the Council as follows: "The Council shall, jointly with the European Parliament, exercise legislative and budgetary functions. It shall carry out policy-making and coordinating functions as laid down in the Treaties."[86]

Let us look at each of these four functions. First, the Council has traditionally been at the core of the Union's legislative function. Prior to the rise of the European Parliament, the Council indeed was the Union "legislator". The Council is today only a co-legislator, that is: a branch of the bicameral Union legislature.[87] And like Parliament, it must exercise its legislative powers in public.[88] Second, Council and Parliament also share in the exercise of the budgetary function. Third, what about the policy-making function? In this respect, the *European* Council has overtaken the Council. The former now decides on the general policy choices, and the role of the Council has consequently been limited to specific policy choices that implement the general ones. Yet, these choices remain significant and the Council Presidency will set "its" agenda. Fourth, the Council has significant coordinating functions within the European Union. Thus, in the context of general economic policy, the Member States are required to "regard their economic policies as a matter of common concern and shall coordinate them within the Council".[89] The idea of an "open method of coordination" experienced a renaissance in the last decade.[90]

---

[84] On the "Luxembourg Compromise", see Schütze, *European Constitutional Law* (supra n. 3), Chapter 1 – Section 2(b).

[85] Article 31 (2) TEU.   [86] Article 16 (1) TEU.

[87] On this point, see Chapter 2 – Section 1(a) below.   [88] Article 16 (8) TEU.

[89] Article 121 (1) TFEU.

[90] On the "open method of coordination", see G. de Búrca, "The Constitutional Challenge of New Governance in the European Union", 28 (2003) *European Law Review*, 814.

3. The Commission

The technocratic character of the early European Union expressed itself in the name of a third institution: the Commission. The Commission constituted the centre of the European Coal and Steel Community, where it was "to ensure that the objectives set out in [that] Treaty [were] attained".[91] In the European Union, the role of the Commission was, however, gradually "marginalized" by the Parliament and the Council. With these two institutions constituting the Union legislature, the Commission is today firmly located in the executive branch. In guiding the European Union, it – partly – acts like the Union's government. This third section analyses the composition of the Commission first, before exploring the relationship between the President and "his" college. A final subsection looks at the functions and powers of the Commission.

(a) Composition and election

The Commission consists of one national of each Member State.[92] Its members are chosen "on the ground of their general competence and European commitment from persons whose independence is beyond doubt".[93] The Commission's term of office is five years.[94] During this term, it must be "completely independent". Its members "shall neither seek nor take instructions from any Government or other institution, body, office or entity".[95] The Member States are under a duty to respect

---

[91] Article 8 ECSC.

[92] Article 17 (4) TEU. The Lisbon Treaty textually limits this principle in a temporal sense: it will theoretically only apply from the date of entry into force of the Treaty of Lisbon to 31 October 2014. Thereafter, Article 17 (5) TEU states: "As from 1 November 2014, the Commission shall consist of a number of members, including its President and the High Representative of the Union for Foreign Affairs and Security Policy, corresponding to two thirds of the number of Member States, unless the European Council, acting unanimously, decides to alter this number." This provision had been a centrepiece of the Lisbon Treaty, as it was designed to increase the effectiveness of the Commission by decreasing its membership. However, after the failure of the first Irish ratification referendum, the European Council decided to abandon this constitutional reform in order to please the Irish electorate, see Presidency Conclusions of 11–12 December 2008 (Document 17271/1/08 Rev 1).

[93] Article 17 (3) TEU.   [94] *Ibid.*   [95] *Ibid.*

this independence.[96] Breach of the duty of independence may lead to a Commissioner being "compulsorily retired".[97]

But how is the Commission selected? Originally, the Commission was "appointed".[98] The appointment procedure has subsequently given way to an election procedure. This election procedure has two stages. In a first stage, the President of the Commission will be elected. The President will be nominated by the European Council "[t]aking into account the elections to the European Parliament", that is: in accordance with the latter's political majority.[99] The nominated candidate must then be "elected" by the European Parliament. If not confirmed by Parliament, a new candidate needs to be found by the European Council.[100] With the election of the Commission President begins the second stage of the selection process. In accord with the President, the Council will adopt a list of candidate Commissioners on the basis of suggestions made by the Member States.[101] With the list being agreed, the proposed Commission is subjected "as a body to a vote of consent by the European Parliament", and on the basis of this election, the Commission shall be appointed by the European Council.[102] This complex and compound selection process constitutes a mixture of "international" and "national" elements. The Commission's democratic legitimacy thus derives partly from the Member States, and partly from the European Parliament.

(b) The President and "his" College

The Commission President helps in the selection of "his" institution. This position as the "Chief" Commissioner *above* "his" college is clearly established by the Treaties.[103] "The Members of the Commission shall carry out the duties devolved upon them by the President *under his*

---

[96] Article 245 TFEU – first indent.

[97] Article 245 TFEU – second indent. See also Article 247 TFEU: "If any Member of the Commission no longer fulfils the conditions required for the performance of his duties or if he has been guilty of serious misconduct, the Court of Justice may, on application by the Council acting by a simple majority or the Commission, compulsorily retire him." On the replacement procedure, see Article 246 TFEU.

[98] Articles 9 and 10 ECSC.

[99] The term of the Commission runs in parallel with that of the Parliament.

[100] Article 17 (7) TEU – first indent.   [101] Article 17 (7) TEU – second indent.

[102] Article 17 (7) TFEU – third indent.

[103] N. Nugent, *The European Commission* (Palgrave, 2000), 68: "The Commission President used to be thought of as *primus inter pares* in the College. Now, however, he is very much *primus.*"

authority."[104] In light of this political authority, the Commission is typically named after its President.[105]

The powers of the President are identified in Article 17 (6) TEU, which reads:

The President of the Commission shall:

(a) lay down guidelines within which the Commission is to work;
(b) decide on the internal organisation of the Commission, ensuring that it acts consistently, efficiently and as a collegiate body;
(c) appoint Vice-Presidents, other than the High Representative of the Union for Foreign Affairs and Security Policy, from among the members of the Commission.

A member of the Commission shall resign if the President so requests. The High Representative of the Union for Foreign Affairs and Security Policy shall resign, in accordance with the procedure set out in Article 18(1), if the President so requests.

The three powers of the President mentioned above are formidable. First, s/he can lay down the political direction of the Commission in the form of strategic guidelines. The Presidential guidelines will subsequently be translated into the Commission's Annual Work Programme. Second, the President is entitled to decide on the internal organization of the Commission.[106] In the words of the Treaties: "[T]he responsibilities incumbent upon the Commission shall be structured and allocated among its members by its President." The President is authorized to "reshuffle the allocation of those responsibilities during the Commission's term of office",[107] and may even ask a Commissioner to resign. Third, the President can appoint Vice-Presidents from "within" the Commission. Finally, there is a fourth power not expressly mentioned in Article 17 (6) TEU: "The President shall represent the Commission."[108]

---

[104] Article 248 TFEU (emphasis added).

[105] For example: the current Commission is called the "Barroso Commission".

[106] Due to its dual constitutional role, some special rules apply to the High Representative of the Union. Not only do the Treaties determine the latter's role within the Commission, the President will not be able *unilaterally* to ask for her resignation. (See Article 18 (4) TEU: "The High Representative shall be one of the Vice-Presidents of the Commission. He shall ensure the consistency of the Union's external action. He shall be responsible within the Commission for responsibilities incumbent on it in external relations and for coordinating other aspects of the Union's external action.") On the role of the High Representative, see Schütze, *European Constitutional Law* (supra n. 3), Chapter 3 – Section 4 (b)(iii).

[107] Article 248 TFEU.   [108] Article 3 (5) Commission Rules of Procedure.

Table 5 Commission College: President and portfolios

President	
Agriculture and Rural Development	Health and Consumer Policy
Climate Action	Home Affairs
Competition	Industry and Entrepreneurship
Development	Inter-Institutional Relations and Administration
Digital Agenda	Internal Market and Services
Economic and Monetary Affairs	International Cooperation, Humanitarian Aid and Crisis Response
Education, Culture, Multilingualism and Youth	Justice, Fundamental Rights and Citizenship
Employment, Social Affairs and Inclusion	Maritime Affairs and Fisheries
Energy	Regional Policy
Enlargement and European Neighbourhood Policy	Research, Innovation and Science
Environment	Taxation and Customs Union, Audit and Anti-Fraud
Financial Programming and Budget	Trade
Foreign Affairs & Security Policy	Transport

What are the "ministerial" responsibilities into which the present Commission is structured? Due to the requirement of one Commissioner per Member State, the "Barroso Commission" had to divide the tasks of the European Union into twenty-six (!) "portfolios". Reflecting the priorities of the current President, they are as setout in Table 5.

Each Commissioner is thereby responsible for "his" portfolio, and will be assisted in this by his own cabinet.[109]

(c) Functions and powers

What are the functions and corresponding powers of the Commission in the governmental structure of the European Union? The Treaties provide a concise constitutional overview of its tasks in Article 17 TEU:

---

[109] Article 19 (1) Commission Rules of Procedure: "Members of the Commission shall have their own cabinet to assist them in their work and in preparing Commission decisions. The rules governing the composition and operation of the cabinets shall be laid down by the President."

The Commission shall promote the general interest of the Union and take appropriate initiatives to that end. It shall ensure the application of the Treaties, and of measures adopted by the institutions pursuant to them. It shall oversee the application of Union law under the control of the Court of Justice of the European Union. It shall execute the budget and manage programmes. It shall exercise coordinating, executive and management functions, as laid down in the Treaties. With the exception of the common foreign and security policy, and other cases provided for in the Treaties, it shall ensure the Union's external representation. It shall initiate the Union's annual and multiannual programming with a view to achieving interinstitutional agreements.[110]

The provision distinguishes six different functions. The first three functions constitute the Commission's core functions. First, the Commission is tasked to "*promote* the general interests of the Union" through initiatives. It is thus to act as a "motor" of European integration. In order to fulfil this – governmental – function, the Commission is given the (almost) exclusive right to *formally* propose legislative bills.[111] "Union acts may only be adopted on the basis of a Commission proposal, except where the Treaties provide otherwise."[112] The Commission's prerogative to propose legislation is a fundamental characteristic of the European constitutional order. The right of initiative extends to (multi)annual programming of the Union,[113] and embraces the power to make proposals for law reform.[114]

The second function of the Commission is to "*ensure* the application" of the Treaties. This function covers a number of powers – legislative and executive in nature. The Commission may thus be entitled to apply the Treaties by adopting secondary legislation. This secondary legislation may

---

[110] Article 17 (1) TEU.

[111] We saw above that the Parliament or the Council can informally suggest legislative bills to the Commission. Indeed, the great majority of Commission bills originate outside the Commission (see Nugent, *The European Commission* (supra n. 103), 236).

[112] Article 17 (2) TEU. For an exception, see Article 76 TFEU on legislative measures in the field of police and judicial cooperation in criminal matters.

[113] Under Article 314 (2) TFEU, the Commission is entitled to propose the draft budget: "The Commission shall submit a proposal containing the draft budget to the European Parliament and to the Council not later than 1 September of the year preceding that in which the budget is to be implemented."

[114] This is normally done through "White Papers" or "Green Papers". For a famous "White Paper", see EU Commission, Completing the Internal Market: White Paper from the Commission to the European Council (COM(85) 310). For a famous "Green Paper", see EU Commission, Damages Actions for Breach of the EC Antitrust Rules (COM(2005) 672).

be adopted directly under the Treaties;[115] or, under powers delegated to the Commission from the Union legislature.[116] In some areas the Commission may also be granted the executive power to apply the Treaties itself. The direct enforcement of European law can best be seen in the context of European competition law,[117] where the Commission enjoys significant powers to fine – private or public – wrongdoers. These administrative penalties sanction the non-application of European law.

The third function of the Commission is to act as guardian of the Union. It shall thus "*oversee* the application" of European law. The Treaties indeed grant the Commission significant powers to act as "police" and "prosecutor" of the Union. The policing of European law involves the power to monitor and to investigate infringements of European law. The powers are – again – best defined in the context of European competition law.[118] Where an infringement of European law has been identified, the Commission may bring the matter before the Court of Justice. The Treaties thus give the Commission the power to bring infringement proceedings against Member States,[119] and other Union institutions.[120]

4. The Court of Justice of the European Union

"Tucked away in the fairyland Duchy of Luxembourg",[121] and housed in its "palace", lies the Court of Justice of the European Union. The Court constitutes the judicial branch of the European Union. It is composed of various

---

[115] See Article 106 (3) TFEU: "The Commission shall ensure the application of the provisions of this Article and shall, where necessary, address appropriate directives or decisions to Member States."

[116] On delegated legislation, see Schütze, *European Constitutional Law* (supra n. 3), Chapter 7 – Section 2.

[117] See Article 105 (1) TFEU: "[T]he Commission shall ensure the application of the principles laid down in Articles 101 and 102. On application by a Member State or on its own initiative, and in cooperation with the competent authorities in the Member States, which shall give it their assistance, the Commission shall investigate cases of suspected infringement of these principles. If it finds that there has been an infringement, it shall propose appropriate measures to bring it to an end."

[118] See Regulation 1/2003 on the implementation of the rules on competition laid down in Articles 81 and 82 of the Treaty ([2003] OJ L1/1), Chapter V: "Powers of Investigation".

[119] Article 258 TFEU. For an extensive discussion of this, see Chapter 8 – Section 1 below.

[120] On this point, see Chapter 8 – Sections 2–4 below.

[121] E. Stein, "Lawyers, Judges, and the Making of a Transnational Constitution", 75 (1981) *American Journal of International Law*, 1.

courts that are linguistically roofed under the name "Court of Justice of the European Union" and includes the "Court of Justice", the "General Court" and "specialized courts".[122] The Court's task is to "ensure that in the interpretation and application of the Treaties the law is observed".[123] This fourth section starts by analysing the Union's judicial architecture, before surveying the judicial powers of the Court of Justice of the European Union.

(a) Judicial architecture: the European court system

When the European Union was born, its judicial branch consisted of a single court: the "Court of Justice". The (then) Court was a "one stop shop". All judicial affairs of the Union would need to pass through its corridors.

With its workload having risen to dizzying heights, the Court pressed the Member States to provide for a judicial "assistant". And the Member States agreed to create a second court in the Single European Act which granted the Council the power to "attach to the Court of Justice a court with jurisdiction to hear and determine at first instance", that was "subject to a right of appeal to the Court of Justice".[124] Thanks to this definition, the newly created court was baptized the "Court of First Instance".[125] With the Lisbon Treaty, the Court has now been renamed the "General Court". The reason for this change of name lies in the fact that the Court is no longer confined to first instance cases. Instead, "[t]he General Court shall have jurisdiction to hear and determine actions or proceedings brought against decisions of the specialized courts".[126] What are the "specialized courts" in the European Union? The Union has currently only one specialized court: the "Civil Service Tribunal".[127] And while the Commission had long proposed a European "Patent Court" as a second specialized court,[128] it has not yet been established.

---

[122] Article 19 (1) TEU.   [123] *Ibid.*   [124] Article 11 (1) Single European Act.

[125] The Court was set up by Council Decision 88/591 establishing a Court of First Instance of the European Communities ([1988] OJ L319/1).

[126] Article 256 (2) TFEU.

[127] Council Decision 2004/752 establishing the European Union Civil Service Tribunal ([2004] OJ L333/7). See also N. Lavranos, "The New Specialised Courts within the European Judicial System", 30 (2005) *European Law Review*, 261.

[128] Commission Proposal for a Council Decision establishing the Community Patent Court and concerning appeals before the Court of First Instance (COM(2003) 828 final). For a discussion of this proposal, see A. Arnull, *The European Court of Justice* (Oxford University Press, 2006), 151–2.

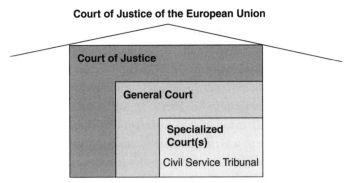

Figure 1.1 Structure of the Court of Justice of the European Union

The Court of Justice of the European Union thus represents a three-tiered system of courts.[129] The architecture of the Union's judicial branch can be seen in Figure 1.1.

(b) Jurisdiction and judicial powers

The traditional role of courts in modern societies is to act as independent arbitrators between competing interests. Their jurisdiction may be compulsory, or not. The jurisdiction of the Court of Justice of the European Union is compulsory "within the limits of the powers conferred on it in the Treaties".[130] While compulsory, the Court's jurisdiction is thus limited. Based on the principle of conferral, the Court has no "inherent" jurisdiction.

The functions and powers of the Court are classified in Article 19 (3) TEU:

The Court of Justice of the European Union shall, in accordance with the Treaties:

(a) rule on actions brought by a Member State, an institution or a natural or legal person;

(b) give preliminary rulings, at the request of courts or tribunals of the Member States, on the interpretation of Union law or the validity of acts adopted by the institutions;

(c) rule in other cases provided for in the Treaties.

---

[129] In terms of the European Union's judicial reports, there are thus three different prefixes before a case. Cases before the Court of Justice are C-Cases, cases before the General Court are T-Cases (as the French name for the General Court is "Tribunal"), and cases before the Civil Service Tribunal are F-Cases (stemming from the French "fonction publique" for civil service).

[130] Article 13 (2) TEU.

The provision classifies the judicial tasks by distinguishing between direct and indirect actions. The former are brought directly before the European Court. The latter arrive at the Court indirectly through preliminary references from national courts. The powers of the Court under the preliminary reference procedure are set out in a single Article.[131] By contrast, there exist a number of direct actions set out in the Treaty on the Functioning of the European Union. The TFEU distinguishes between enforcement actions brought by the Commission or a Member State,[132] judicial review proceedings for actions and inactions of the Union institutions,[133] damages actions for the (non-)contractual liability of the Union,[134] as well as a few minor jurisdictional heads.[135]

In light of its broad jurisdiction, the Court of Justice of the European Union can be characterized as a "constitutional", "administrative", and an "international" court as well as an "industrial tribunal". Its jurisdiction includes public and private matters. And while the Court claims to act like a "continental" civil law court, it has been fundamental in shaping the structure and powers of the European Union as well as the nature of European law. The (activist) jurisprudence of the Court will thus be regularly encountered in the subsequent chapters of this book.

---

[131] Article 267 TFEU. The provision is analysed in Chapter 7 – Sections 1 and 2 below.

[132] Articles 258–60 TFEU. The provisions are analysed in Chapter 8 – Section 1 below.

[133] Articles 263–6 TFEU. The provisions are analysed in Chapter 8 – Sections 2 and 3 below.

[134] Articles 268 and 340 TFEU. The provisions are analysed in Chapter 8 – Section 4 below.

[135] Articles 269–74 TFEU.

Introduction

British constitutionalism defines (primary) legislation as an act adopted by the Queen-in-Parliament. Behind this "compound" legislator stands a legislative procedure. This legal procedure links the House of Commons, the House of Lords and the monarchy. European constitutionalism also adopts a procedural definition of legislative power. However, unlike British constitutional law, the Treaties distinguish two types of legislative procedures: an ordinary legislative procedure and special legislative procedures. Article 289 TFEU states:

1. The ordinary legislative procedure shall consist in the joint adoption by the European Parliament and the Council of a regulation, directive or decision on a proposal from the Commission. This procedure is defined in Article 294.
2. In the specific cases provided for by the Treaties, the adoption of a regulation, directive or decision by the European Parliament with the participation of the

Council, or by the latter with the participation of the European Parliament, shall constitute a special legislative procedure.[1]

European "legislation" is thus – formally – defined as an act adopted by the bicameral Union legislator. According to the *ordinary* legislative procedure, the European Parliament and the Council act as co-legislators with *symmetric* procedural rights. European legislation is therefore seen as the product of a "joint adoption" by both institutions. But the Treaties also recognize *special* legislative procedures. The defining characteristic of these special procedures is that they abandon the institutional equality between the European Parliament and the Council. Logically, then, Article 289 (2) TFEU recognizes two variants. In the first variant, the European Parliament acts as the dominant institution, with the mere "participation" of the Council in the form of "consent".[2] The second variant inverts this relationship. The Council is here the dominant institution, with the Parliament either participating through its "consent",[3] or in the form of "consultation".[4]

Having analysed the various Union institutions in Chapter 1, this Chapter explores their interaction in the creation of European (secondary) law. Sections 1 and 2 respectively discuss the ordinary and special legislative procedures in more detail. Section 3 looks at the principle of subsidiarity – a constitutional principle that limits the Union legislator from exercising its competences where the Member States would be able to achieve the

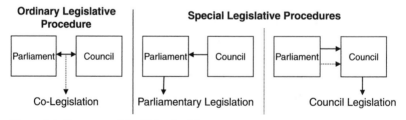

Figure 2.1 Structure of the Union legislator

---

[2] See Articles 223 (2), 226 and 228 TFEU. The procedure for the adoption of the Union budget is laid down in Art. 314 TFEU and will not be discussed here.
[3] See Articles 19 (1), 25, 86 (1), 223 (1), 311, 312 and 352 TFEU.
[4] See Articles 21 (3), 22 (1), 22 (2), 23, 64 (3), 77 (3), 81 (3), 87 (3), 89, 113, 115, 118, 126, 127 (6), 153 (2), 182 (4), 192 (2), 203, 262, 308, 311, 349 TFEU.

desirable social aim themselves. Within the Union legal order, this principle has been primarily understood as a procedural safeguard that – indirectly – involves the national parliaments prior to the adoption of a legislative act. An excursus finally looks at the procedure for the conclusion of international agreements. These agreements, while not formally concluded under a legislative procedure, nonetheless constitute a rich (external) source of European law.

1. The "ordinary" legislative procedure

(a) Constitutional theory: formal text

The ordinary legislative procedure has seven stages. Article 294 TFEU defines five stages; two additional stages are set out in Article 297 TFEU.

Proposal stage. Under the ordinary legislative procedure, the Commission enjoys – with minor exceptions – the exclusive right to submit a legislative proposal.[5] This (executive) prerogative guarantees a significant agenda-setting power to the Commission. The Treaties – partly – protect this power from "external" interferences by insisting that any amendment that the Commission dislikes will require unanimity in the Council – an extremely high decisional hurdle.[6]

First reading. The Commission proposal goes to the European Parliament. The Parliament will act by a majority of the votes cast,[7] that is: the majority of physically present parliamentarians. It can reject the proposal,[8] approve it, or – as a middle path – amend it. The bill then moves to the Council,

---

[5] Article 294 (2) TFEU. Paragraph 15 recognizes exceptions to this rule in cases provided for in the Treaties. The perhaps most significant exception is Article 76 TFEU referring to legislative measures in the field of police and judicial cooperation in criminal matters.

[6] Article 293 (1) TFEU, as well as Article 284 (9) TFEU. Moreover, until the conciliation stage the Commission may unilaterally alter or withdraw the proposal: Article 293 (2) TFEU.

[7] Article 294 (3) TFEU is silent on the voting regime within Parliament, and therefore Article 231 TFEU applies: "Save as otherwise provided in the Treaties, the European Parliament shall act by a majority of the votes cast. The rules of procedure shall determine the quorum."

[8] This option is not expressly recognized in the text of Article 294 (3) TFEU, but it is indirectly recognized in Rule 56 of the Parliament's Rules of Procedure.

which will act by a qualified majority of its members.[9] Where the Council agrees with Parliament's position, the bill is adopted after the first reading. Where it disagrees, the Council is called to provide its own position and communicate it, with reasons, to Parliament.

Second reading. The (amended) bill lies for the second time in Parliament's court; and Parliament has three choices as to what to do with it. Parliament may positively approve the Council's position by a majority of the votes cast;[10] or reject it by a majority of its component members.[11] Approval is thus easier than rejection. (This tendency is reinforced by assimilating passivity to approval.)[12] However, Parliament has a third choice: it may propose, by a majority of its component members, amendments to the Council position.[13] The amended bill will be forwarded to the Council and to the Commission (that must deliver an opinion on the amendments). The bill is thus back in the Council's court, and the Council has two options. Where it approves all (!) of Parliament's amendments, the legislative act is adopted.[14] (The Council thereby acts by a qualified majority, unless the Commission disagrees with any of the amendments suggested by the Council or the Parliament.)[15] But where the Council cannot approve all of Parliament's amendments, the bill enters into the conciliation stage.[16]

Conciliation stage. This stage presents the last chance to rescue the legislative bill. As agreement within the "formal" legislature has proved impossible, the Union legal order "delegates" the power to draft a "joint text" to a committee. This committee is called the "Conciliation Committee".[17] The

---

[9] Article 294 (4) and (5) TFEU are silent on the voting regime, and therefore Article 16 (4) TEU applies: "The Council shall act by a qualified majority except where the Treaties provide otherwise."

[10] Article 294 (7) (a) TFEU.   [11] Article 294 (7) (b) TFEU.

[12] According to Article 294 (7) (a) TFEU – second alternative, where the Parliament does not act within three months, "the act shall be deemed to have been adopted in the wording which corresponds to the position of the Council".

[13] Article 294 (7) (c) TFEU. For an (internal) limitation on what types of amendments can be made, see Rule 66 (2) of the Parliament's Rules of Procedure.

[14] Article 294 (8) (a) TFEU.   [15] Article 294 (9) TFEU.   [16] Article 294 (8) (b) TFEU.

[17] The Conciliation Committee is not a standing committee, but an ad hoc committee that "is constituted separately for each legislative proposal requiring conciliation" (European Parliament, "Codecision and Conciliation" at: http://www.europarl.europa.eu/code/information/guide_en.pdf, 15).

mandate of the Committee is restricted to reaching agreement on a joint text "on the basis of the positions of the European Parliament and the Council at second reading".[18] The Committee is composed of members representing the Council,[19] and an equal number of members representing the European Parliament.[20] (The Commission will take part "in" the committee, but is not a part "of" the Committee. Its function is to act as a catalyst for conciliation.)[21] The Committee thus represents a "miniature legislature"; and like its constitutional model, the Committee co-decides by a qualified majority of the Council representatives, and a majority of the representatives sent by Parliament. Where the Committee does not adopt a joint text, the legislative bill has failed. Where the Committee has managed to approve a joint text, the latter returns to the "formal" Union legislator for a third reading.

Third reading. The "formal" Union legislature must positively approve the joint text (without the power of amending it). The Parliament needs to endorse the joint text by a majority of the votes cast, whereas the Council must confirm the text by a qualified majority. Where one of the two chambers disagrees with the proposal made by the Conciliation Committee, the bill finally flounders. Where both chambers approve the text, the bill is adopted and only needs to be "signed" and "published".

Signing and publication. The last two stages before a bill becomes law are set out in Article 297 TFEU which states: "Legislative acts adopted under the ordinary legislative procedure shall be signed by the President of the European Parliament and by the President of the Council"; and they shall subsequently "be published in the Official Journal of the European

---

[18] Article 294 (10) TFEU. However, the Court of Justice has been flexible and allowed the Conciliation Committee to find a joint text that goes beyond the common position after the second reading (see *The Queen on the application of International Air Transport Association et al.* v. *Department of Transport*, Case C-344/04, [2006] ECR I-403).

[19] The Permanent Representative or his Deputy will typically represent the national ministers in the Council.

[20] The parliamentary delegation must reflect the political composition of the formal Parliament (see Rule 68 (2) of the Parliament's Rules of Procedure). It will normally include the three Vice-Presidents responsible for conciliation, the Rapporteur and Chair of the responsible parliamentary committee.

[21] Article 294 (11) TFEU. Formally, it will be the Commissioner responsible for the subject matter of the legislative bill who will take part in the Conciliation Committee.

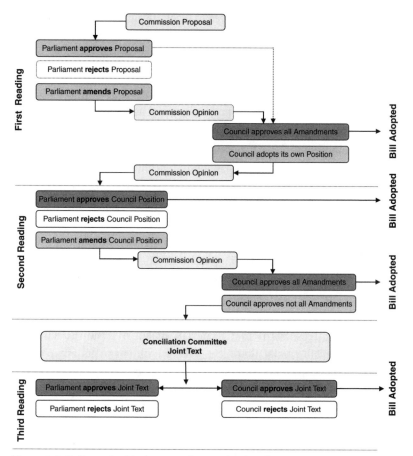

Figure 2.2 Ordinary legislative procedure under Article 294

Union".[22] The publication requirement is a fundamental element of modern societies governed by the rule of law. Only "public" legislative acts will have the force of law. The Union legal order also requires that all legislative acts "shall state the reasons on which they are based and shall refer to any proposals, initiatives, recommendations, request or opinions required by the Treaties".[23] This formal "duty to state reasons" can be judicially reviewed, and represents a hallmark of legislative rationality.

---

[22] Article 297 (1) TFEU. For legislation, this will be the "L" Series.
[23] Article 296 TFEU – second indent.

(b) Constitutional practice: informal trilogues

Constitutional texts often only provide a stylized sketch of the formal relations between institutions. And this formal picture will need to be coloured and revised by informal constitutional practices. This is very much the case for the constitutional text governing the ordinary legislative procedure. The rudimentary status of the constitutional text is indeed recognized by the Treaties themselves,[24] and the importance of informal practices has been expressly acknowledged by the European institutions.[25] The primary expression of these informal institutional arrangements are tripartite meetings ("trilogues"). They combine the representatives of the three institutions in an "informal framework".[26]

What is the task of institutional trilogues? The trilogues system is designed to create informal bridges during the formal co-decision proce- dure that open up "possibilities for agreements at first and second reading stages, as well as contributing to the preparation of the work of the Conciliation Committee".[27] Trilogues may thus be held "at all stages of the [ordinary legislative] procedure".[28] Indeed, a "Joint Declaration" of the Union institutions contains respective commitments for each procedural stage. In order to facilitate a formal agreement within the Union legislator during the first reading, informal agreements between the institutional representatives will thus be forwarded to Parliament or Council respec- tively.[29] This equally applies to the second reading,[30] and to the conciliation stage.[31] The strategy of informality has proved extremely successful.[32]

---

[24] Article 295 TFEU states: "The European Parliament, the Council and the Commission shall consult each other and by common agreement make arrangements for their cooper- ation. To that end, they may, in compliance with the Treaties, conclude interinstitutional agreements which may be of a binding nature."

[25] See "Joint Declaration on Practical Arrangements for the Codecision Procedure", [2007] OJ C145/5.

[26] *Ibid.*, para. 8.   [27] *Ibid.*, para. 7.   [28] *Ibid.*, para. 8.

[29] *Ibid.*, para. 14: "Where an agreement is reached through informal negotiations in trilogues, the chair of Coreper shall forward, in a letter to the chair of the relevant parliamentary committee, details of the substance of the agreement, in the form of amendments to the Commission proposal. That letter shall indicate the Council's willingness to accept that outcome, subject to legal-linguistic verification, should it be confirmed by the vote in plenary. A copy of that letter shall be forwarded to the Commission." For the inverted obligation, see para. 18.

[30] *Ibid.*, para. 23.   [31] *Ibid.*, paras. 24–5.

[32] According to the European Parliament, "Co-decision and Conciliation" (supra n. 17), 14, in the period between 2004 and 2009, 72 per cent of legislative acts were agreed at first

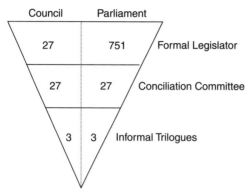

Figure 2.3 Declining democratic representation

And yet, there are serious constitutional problems. For informal trilogues should not be allowed to short-circuit the formal legislative procedure. Were this to happen, democratic deliberation within a fairly representative European Union would be replaced by the informal government of a dozen representatives of the three institutions. And indeed, the democratic deficit of the Union would not lie in the *formal* structure of the Union legislator, but in its *informal* bypassing.

2. The "special" legislative procedures

In addition to the ordinary legislative procedure, the Treaties recognize three special legislative procedures. Unlike the ordinary procedure, the Union act will here not be the result of a "joint adoption" of the European Parliament and the Council. It will be adopted by *one* of the two institutions. In the first variant of Article 289 (2) TFEU, this will be the Parliament; yet the Treaties generally require the "consent" of the Council. In the second variant of Article 289 (2) TFEU, the Council will adopt the legislative act; yet the Treaties require either the "consent" or "consultation" of the Parliament. The first two special procedures may be characterized as the "consent procedure", the third special procedure can be referred to as the "consultation procedure".

What are the characteristics of the "consent procedure" and the "consultation procedure"? The former requires one institution to consent to the

reading, and 23 per cent at second reading. This leaves only 5 per cent to pass through conciliation and the third reading.

legislative bill of the other. Consent is less than co-decision, for only the dominant institution will be able to determine the substantive content of the bill. The non-dominant institution will be forced to "take-it-or-leave-it". But this veto power is still – much – stronger than mere consultation. For while the Court has recognized that consultation is "an essential factor in the institutional balance intended by the Treaty",[33] consultation is nonetheless a mere "formality".[34] The formal obligation to consult will *not* mean that the adopting institution must take into account the substantive views of the other.[35]

3. The principle of subsidiarity

Subsidiarity – the quality of being "subsidiary" – derives from *subsidium*. The Latin concept evolved in the military context. It represented an "assistance" or "aid" that stayed in the background. Figuratively, an entity is subsidiary where it provides a "subsidy" – an assistance of subordinate or secondary importance. In political philosophy, the principle of subsidiarity came to represent the idea "that a central authority should have a subsidiary function, performing only those tasks which cannot be performed effectively at a more immediate or local level".[36] The principle thus has a positive and a negative aspect.[37] It positively encourages "large associations" to assist smaller ones, where they need help; and it negatively discourages "to assign to a greater and higher association what lesser and subordinate organizations can do". It is this dual character that has given the principle of subsidiarity its "Janus-like" character.[38]

---

[33] *Roquette Frères* v. *Council (Isoglucose)*, Case 138/79, [1980] ECR 3333, para. 33.

[34] The "formality" still requires that the Council has to wait until Parliament has provided its opinion (see *ibid.*, para. 34): "In that respect it is pertinent to point out that observance of that requirement implies that the Parliament has expressed its opinion. It is impossible to take the view that the requirement is satisfied by the Council's simply asking for the opinion." On this point, see also *Parliament* v. *Council*, Case C-65/93, [1995] ECR I-643; however, this case also established implied limitations on Parliament's prerogative (*ibid.*, paras. 27–28).

[35] This was confirmed in *Parliament* v. *Council*, Case C-417/93, [1995] ECR I-1185, esp. paras. 10 and 11.

[36] See *Oxford English Dictionary*: "subsidiary" and "subsidiarity".

[37] C. Calliess, *Subsidiaritäts- und Solidaritätsprinzip in der Europäischen Union* (Nomos, 1999), 26.

[38] V. Constantinesco, "Who's Afraid of Subsidiarity?," 11 (1991) *Yearbook of European Law*, 33 at 35.

When did the subsidiarity principle become a constitutional principle of the European Union? The principle of subsidiarity surfaced in 1975,[39] but it would only find official expression in the context of the Union's environmental policy after the Single European Act (1986).[40] The Maastricht Treaty on European Union (1992) finally lifted the subsidiarity principle beyond its environmental confines. It became a general constitutional principle of the European Union. Today, the Treaty on European Union defines it in Article 5, whose third paragraph states:

> Under the principle of subsidiarity, in areas which do not fall within its exclusive competence, the Union shall act only if and in so far as the objectives of the proposed action cannot be sufficiently achieved by the Member States, either at central level or at regional and local level, but can rather, by reason of the scale or effects of the proposed action, be better achieved at Union level.

The definition clarifies that subsidiarity is only to apply within the sphere of non-exclusive powers and thus confirms that the European principle of subsidiarity is a principle of *cooperative* federalism.[41] The Treaty definition of subsidiarity recognizes *two* tests. The first may be called the *national insufficiency test*. The Union can only act where the objectives of the proposed action could not be sufficiently achieved by the Member States (centrally or regionally). This appears to be an absolute standard. But how can this test be squared with the second test in Article 5(3) TEU? That test is a *comparative efficiency test*. The Union should not act unless it can *better* achieve the objectives of the proposed action. Will the combination of these two tests mean that the Union would not be entitled to act where it is – in relative terms – better able to tackle a social problem, but where the Member States could – in absolute terms – still achieve the desired result? Worse, the formulation 'if and in so far' potentially offered *two* versions of the subsidiarity principle. The first version concentrates on the 'if' question by asking *whether* the Union should act. This has been defined as the principle of subsidiarity *in a strict sense*. The second version concentrates

---

[39] For a detailed textual genealogy of the subsidiarity principle in the European legal order, see R. Schütze, *From Dual to Cooperative Federalism: The Changing Structure of European Law* (Oxford University Press, 2009), 247 et seq.

[40] The (then) newly inserted Article 130 r (4) EEC restricted Community environmental legislation to those actions whose objectives could "be attained better at Community level than at the level of the individual Member States".

[41] On the meaning of that concept, see Schütze, *From Dual to Cooperative Federalism* (supra n. 39), 4 et seq.

on the 'in-so-far' question by asking *how* the Union should act. This has been referred to as the principle of subsidiarity *in a wide sense.*[42]

The wording of Article 5(3) TEU is indeed a textual failure. And in the past two decades, two – parallel – approaches evolved to give meaning to the subsidiarity principle. The first approach concentrates on the political safeguards of federalism. The second approach focuses on subsidiarity as an objective judicial standard.

(a) Subsidiarity as a political safeguard

Despite its literary presence,[43] the principle of subsidiarity has remained a subsidiary principle of European constitutionalism. The reason for its shadowy existence has been its lack of conceptual contours. If subsidiarity was everything to everyone, how should the Union apply it? To limit this semantic uncertainty, constitutional clarifications have tried to "proceduralize" the principle. This attempt to develop subsidiarity into a political safeguard of federalism can be seen in Protocol (No. 2) "On the Application of the Principles of Subsidiarity and Proportionality". Importantly, the Protocol only applies to "draft legislative acts",[44] that is: acts to be adopted under the ordinary or a special legislative procedure.

The Protocol aims to establish "a system of monitoring" the application of the principle. Each Union institution is called upon to ensure constant respect for the principle of subsidiarity.[45] And this means in particular that they must forward draft legislative acts to national parliaments.[46] These draft legislative acts must "be justified" with regard to the principle of subsidiarity and proportionality.[47] This (procedural) duty to provide reasons is defined as follows:

Any draft legislative act should contain a detailed statement making it possible to appraise compliance with the principles of subsidiarity and proportionality. This

---

[42] K. Lenaerts, "The Principle of Subsidiarity and the Environment in the European Union: Keeping the Balance of Federalism", 17 (1994) *Fordham International Law Journal*, 846 at 875.

[43] From the – abundant – literature, see G. Berman, "Taking Subsidiarity Seriously: Federalism in the European Community and the United States", 94 (1994) *Columbia Law Review*, 331; G. de Búrca, "Reappraising Subsidiarity Significance after Amsterdam", Harvard Jean Monnet Working Paper 1999/07; D. Z. Cass, "The Word that Saves Maastricht? The Principle of Subsidiarity and the Division of Powers within the European Community", 29 (1992) *Common Market Law Review*, 1107; Constantinesco, "Who's Afraid" (supra n. 38).

[44] Article 3 of the Protocol.   [45] *Ibid.*, Article 1.   [46] *Ibid.*, Article 4.   [47] *Ibid.*, Article 5.

statement should contain some assessment of the proposal's financial impact and, in the case of a directive, of its implications for the rules to be put in place by Member States, including, where necessary, the regional legislation. The reasons for concluding that a Union objective can be better achieved at Union level shall be substantiated by qualitative and, wherever possible, quantitative indicators. Draft legislative acts shall take account of the need for any burden, whether financial or administrative, falling upon the Union, national governments, regional or local authorities, economic operators and citizens, to be minimised and commensurate with the objective to be achieved.[48]

But how is this duty enforced? One solution would point to the European Court;[49] yet, the Protocol prefers a second solution: the active involvement of national parliaments in the legislative procedure of the European Union.[50] The makers of the Lisbon Treaty hoped that this idea would kill two birds with one stone. The procedural involvement of national parliaments promised to strengthen the federal *and* the democratic safeguards within Europe.

But if national parliaments are to be the Union's "watchdogs of subsidiarity",[51] would they enjoy a veto right (hard constitutional solution) or only a monitoring right (soft constitutional solution)? According to the Subsidiarity Protocol, each national parliament may within eight weeks produce a reasoned opinion stating why it considers that a European legislative draft does not comply with the principle of subsidiarity.[52] Each Parliament will thereby have two votes.[53] Where the negative votes amount to one-third of all the votes allocated to the national parliaments, the European Union draft "must be reviewed". This is called the "yellow card"

---

[48] *Ibid.*

[49] *Ibid.*, Article 8: "The Court of Justice of the European Union shall have jurisdiction in actions on grounds of infringement of the principle of subsidiarity by a legislative act, brought in accordance with the rules laid down in Article 263 of the Treaty on the Functioning of the European Union by Member States, or notified by them in accordance with their legal order on behalf of their national Parliament or a chamber thereof." For a discussion of the Court's deferential stance, see Section 3(b) below.

[50] This function is acknowledged in Article 12 (b) TEU, which requests national parliaments to contribute to the good functioning of the Union "by seeing to it that the principle of subsidiarity is respected in accordance with the procedures provided for in the Protocol on the application of the principles of subsidiarity and proportionality".

[51] I. Cooper, "The Watchdogs of Subsidiarity: National Parliaments and the Logic of Arguing in the EU", 44 (2006) *Journal of Common Market Studies*, 281.

[52] Article 6 Protocol (No. 2) "On the Application of the Principles of Subsidiarity and Proportionality".

[53] *Ibid.*, Article 7 (1).

mechanism, since the Union legislator "may decide to maintain, amend or withdraw the draft".[54]

The yellow card mechanism is slightly strengthened in relation to proposals under the ordinary legislative procedure; albeit, here, only a majority of the votes allocated to the national parliaments will trigger it.[55] Under this "orange card" mechanism, the Commission's justification for maintaining the proposal, as well as the reasoned opinions of the national parliaments, will be submitted to the Union legislator. And the Union legislator will have to consider whether the proposal is compatible with the principle of subsidiarity. Where one of its chambers finds that the proposal violates the principle of subsidiarity, the proposal is rejected.[56] While this arrangement makes it – slightly – easier for the European Parliament to reject a legislative proposal on subsidiarity grounds, it makes it – ironically – more difficult for the Council to block a proposal on the basis of subsidiarity than on the basis of a proposal's lack of substantive merit.[57]

The Subsidiarity Protocol has rejected the idea of a "red card" mechanism. This rejection has been bemoaned. The proposed procedural safeguards are said to "add very little" to the federal control of the Union legislator.[58] Others have – rightly – greeted the fact that the subsidiarity mechanism will leave the political decision to adopt the legislative act ultimately to the *European* legislator. "[T]o give national parliaments what would amount to a veto over proposals would be incompatible with the Commission's constitutionally protected independence."[59] "[A] veto power vested in national Parliaments would distort the proper distribution of power and

---

[54] *Ibid.*, Article 7 (2). The threshold is lowered to one-quarter for European laws in the area of freedom, security, and justice.

[55] *Ibid.*, Article 7(3).

[56] *Ibid.*, Article 7 (3) (b): "if, by a majority of 55% of the members of the Council or a majority of the votes cast in the European Parliament, the legislator is of the opinion that the proposal is not compatible with the principle of subsidiarity, the legislative proposal shall not be given further consideration".

[57] For an analysis of this point, see G. Barrett, "'The King is Dead, Long live the King': the Recasting by the Treaty of Lisbon of the Provisions of the Constitutional Treaty concerning National Parliaments", 33 (2008) *European Law Review*, 66 at 80–1. In the light of the voting threshold, "it seems fair to predict that blockade of legislative proposals under Article 7(2) is likely to be a highly exceptional and unusual situation".

[58] See House of Commons, European Scrutiny Committee (Thirty-third Report: 2001–02): Subsidiarity, National Parliaments and the Lisbon Treaty, www.parliament.the-stationery-office.com/pa/cm200708/cmselect/cmeuleg/563/563.pdf, para. 35.

[59] A. Dashwood, "The Relationship between the Member States and the European Union/ Community", 41 (2004) *Common Market Law Review*, 355 at 369.

responsibility in the EU's complex but remarkably successful system of transnational governance by conceding too much to State control."[60] Indeed, to have turned national parliaments into "co-legislators" in the making of European law would have aggravated the "political interweaving" of the European and the national level and thereby deepened joint-decision traps.[61] The rejection of the hard veto solution is thus to be welcomed. The soft constitutional solution will indeed allow national parliaments to channel their scrutiny to where it can be most useful and effective: on their respective national governments.

(b) Subsidiarity as a judicial safeguard

Any substantive meaning of the subsidiarity principle is in the hands of the European Court of Justice. How has the Court defined the relationship between the national insufficiency test and the comparative efficiency test? And has the Court favoured the restrictive or the wide meaning of subsidiarity?

There are surprisingly few judgments that address the principle of subsidiarity. In *United Kingdom* v. *Council (Working Time)*,[62] the United Kingdom had applied for the annulment of the Working Time Directive. The applicant claimed "that the [Union] legislature neither fully considered nor adequately demonstrated whether there were transnational aspects which could not be satisfactorily regulated by national measures, whether such measures would conflict with the requirements of the [Treaties] or significantly damage the interests of Member States or, finally, whether action at [European] level would provide clear benefits compared with action at national level". The principle of subsidiarity would "not allow the adoption of a directive in such wide and prescriptive terms as the contested directive, given that the extent and the nature of legislative regulation of working time vary very widely between Member States".[63]

How did the Court respond? The Court offered an interpretation of subsidiarity that has structured the judicial vision of the principle ever since:

---

[60] S. Weatherill, "Using National Parliaments to Improve Scrutiny of the Limits of EU Action", 28 (2003) *European Law Review*, 909 at 912.

[61] On the concept and shortfalls of "political interweaving" (*Politikverflechtung*), see: F. Scharpf, "The Joint-Decision Trap: Lessons from German Federalism and European Integration", 66 (1988), *Public Administration*, 239.

[62] *United Kingdom* v. *Council*, Case C-84/94, [1996] ECR I-5755.   [63] *Ibid.*, para. 46.

Once the Council has found that it is necessary to improve the existing level of protection as regards the health and safety of workers and to harmonize the conditions in this area while maintaining the improvements made, achievement of that objective through the imposition of minimum requirements necessarily presupposes [Union]-wide action, which otherwise, as in this case, leaves the enactment of the detailed implementing provisions required largely to the Member States. The argument that the Council could not properly adopt measures as general and mandatory as those forming the subject-matter of the directive will be examined below in the context of the plea alleging infringement of the principle of proportionality.[64]

This judicial definition contained two fundamental choices. First, the Court assumed that where the Union had decided to "harmonize" national laws, that objective necessarily presupposed Union legislation. This view answers the national insufficiency test with a mistaken tautology: only the Union can harmonize laws, and therefore the Member States already fail the first test. But assuming the "whether" of European action had been affirmatively established, could the European law go "as far" as it had? This was the second crucial choice of the Court. It decided against the idea of subsidiarity in a wider sense. Instead of analysing the intensity of the European law under Article 5(3) TEU, it chose to review it under the auspices of the principle of proportionality under Article 5(4) TEU. It is there that the Court made a third important choice. In analysing the proportionality of the European law, it ruled that "the Council must be allowed a wide discretion in an area which, as here, involves the legislature in making social policy choices and requires it to carry out complex assessments". Judicial review would therefore be limited to examining "whether it has been vitiated by *manifest error or misuse of powers, or whether the institution concerned has manifestly exceeded the limits of its discretion*".[65] The Court would thus apply a *low* degree of judicial scrutiny.

In subsequent jurisprudence, the Court drew a fourth – procedural – conclusion from choices one and three. In *Germany* v. *Parliament and Council (Deposit Guarantee Scheme)*,[66] the German Government had claimed that the Union act violated the *procedural* obligation to state reasons.[67] The

---

[64] *Ibid.*, para. 47.   [65] *Ibid.*, para. 58 (emphasis added).

[66] *Germany* v. *Parliament and Council (Deposit Guarantee Scheme)*, Case C-233/94, [1997] ECR I-2405.

[67] On that duty to give reasons, see Section 1(a) above. Germany made it an express point that it was this provision – and not the principle of subsidiarity as such – that it claimed had been violated (*ibid.*, para. 24).

European law had not explained how it was compatible with the principle of subsidiarity; and Germany insisted that it was necessary that "the [Union] institutions must give detailed reasons to explain why only the [Union], to the exclusion of the Member States, is empowered to act in the area in question". "In the present case, the Directive does not indicate in what respects its objectives could not have been sufficiently attained by action at Member State level or the grounds which militated in favour of [Union] action."[68]

The Court gave short shrift to that accusation. Looking at the recitals of the European law, it found that the Union legislator had given some "consideration" to the principle of subsidiarity. Believing previous actions by the Member States insufficient, the European legislator had found it indispensable to ensure a harmonized minimum level. This was enough to satisfy the procedural obligations under the subsidiarity enquiry.[69] It was a low explanatory threshold indeed.

Choices one, three, and four have been confirmed in subsequent jurisprudence. By concentrating on the national insufficiency test, the Court has thus short-circuited the comparative efficiency test.[70] It has not searched for qualitative or quantitative benefits of European laws,[71] but confirmed its manifest error test – thus leaving subsidiarity to the political safeguards of federalism.[72] This is reflected in the low justificatory standard imposed on the Union legislator.[73] By contrast, as regards the second choice,

---

[68] *Ibid.*, para. 23.   [69] *Ibid.*, paras. 26–8.

[70] See *The Queen* v. *Secretary of State for Health, ex parte British American Tobacco (Investments) Ltd and Imperial Tobacco Ltd*, Case C-491/01, [2002] ECR I-11453, paras. 181–3: "[T]he Directive's objective is to eliminate the barriers raised by the differences which still exist between the Member States' laws, regulations and administrative provisions on the manufacture, presentation and sale of tobacco products, while ensuring a high level of health protection, in accordance with Article [114 (3) TFEU]. Such an objective cannot be sufficiently achieved by the Member States individually and calls for action at [European] level, as demonstrated by the multifarious development of national laws in this case." See also *Netherlands* v. *Parliament and Council*, Case C-377/98, [2001] ECR I-7079, para. 32; *Commission* v. *Germany*, Case C-103/01, [2003] ECR I-5369, paras. 46–7; as well as *The Queen, ex parte National Association of Health Stores and others* v. *Secretary of State for Health*, Joined Cases C-154 and 155/04, [2005] ECR I-6451, paras. 104–8.

[71] See Article 5 Protocol (No. 2) "On the Application of the Principles of Subsidiarity and Proportionality".

[72] See *Germany* v. *Parliament*, Case C-233/94 (supra n. 66), para. 56; as well as *Belgium* v. *Commission*, Case C-110/03, [2005] ECR I-2801, para. 68.

[73] See *Netherlands* v. *Parliament*, Case C-377/98 (supra n. 70), para. 33: "Compliance with the principle of subsidiarity is necessarily implicit in the fifth, sixth and seventh recitals of the preamble to the Directive, which state that, in the absence of action at [European] level, the development of the laws and practices of the different Member States impedes

the Court has remained ambivalent. While in some cases it has incorporated the intensity question into its subsidiarity analysis,[74] other jurisprudence has kept the subsidiarity and the proportionality principles at arm's length.[75]

What is the better option here? It has been argued that subsidiarity should be understood "in a wider sense".[76] For it is indeed impossible to reduce subsidiarity to "whether" the Union should exercise one of its competences. The distinction between "competence" and "subsidiarity" – between Article 5(2) and 5(3) TEU – will only make sense if the subsidiarity principle concentrates on the "whether" of *the specific act at issue*. But the "whether" and the "how" of the specific action are inherently tied together. The principle of subsidiarity will thus ask *whether* the European legislator has *unnecessarily* restricted national autonomy. A subsidiarity analysis that will not question the *federal* proportionality of a European law is bound to remain an empty formalism. Subsidiarity properly understood *is* federal proportionality.[77] In order to give substantive meaning to subsidiarity, the Court should therefore analyse the "in-so-far" aspect within its subsidiarity calculus.

4. Excursus: the (ordinary) treaty-making procedure

How will the Union act externally, and through which procedures? This depends on the type of act adopted. An analysis of decision-making procedures within the Union's external powers must distinguish between unilateral acts and international agreements.[78] International agreements concluded by the Union have come to constitute a rich source of European

---

the proper functioning of the internal market. It thus appears that the Directive states sufficient reasons on that point."

[74] In *The Queen* v. *Secretary of State for Health*, Case C-491/01, the Court identified the "intensity of the action undertaken by the [Union]" with the principle of subsidiarity and not the principle of proportionality (supra n. 70, para. 184). This acceptance of subsidiarity *sensu lato* can also be seen at work in *Arcor* v. *Germany*, Case C-55/06, [2008] ECR I-2931, where the Court identified the principle of subsidiarity with the idea that "the Member States retain the possibility to establish specific rules on the field in question" (ibid., para. 144).

[75] See *United Kingdom* v. *Council (Working Time Directive)*, Case C-84/94 (supra n. 62); as well as *Commission* v. *Germany*, Case C-103/01 (supra n. 70), para. 48.

[76] Schütze, *From Dual to Cooperative Federalism* (supra n. 39), 263 et seq.

[77] On the – liberal – principle of proportionality, see Chapter 8 – Section 3(b/ii) below.

[78] For an analysis of this point, see R. Schütze, *European Constitutional Law* (Cambridge University Press, 2012), Chapter 6 – Section 3.

law. The "ordinary" treaty-making procedure for them is found in Article 218 TFEU.[79]

What is the inter-institutional balance within this procedure? The central institution within this procedure is the Council – not just as primus inter pares with Parliament, but simply as primus. Article 218 acknowledges the central role of the Council in all stages of the procedure: "The Council shall authorize the opening of negotiations, adopt negotiating directives, authorize the signing of agreements and conclude them."[80] The Council hereby acts by a qualified majority, except in four situations. It shall act unanimously: when the agreement covers a field for which unanimity is required; for association agreements; with regard to Article 212 agreements with States that are candidates for Union accession; and, in respect of the Union's accession agreement to the European Convention on Human Rights (ECHR).[81]

Having recognized the primary role of the Council, Article 218 then defines the secondary roles of the other EU institutions in the various procedural stages of treaty-making. The provision distinguishes between the initiation and negotiation of the agreement, its signing and conclusion, and also provides special rules for its modification and suspension. Exceptionally, the Union can even become a party to an international agreement without having concluded it. This – rare – phenomenon occurs where the Union "inherits" international agreements from its Member States through the doctrine of functional succession.

(a) Initiation and negotiation

Under Article 218 (3), the Commission holds the exclusive right to make recommendations for agreements that principally deal with matters that do not fall within the Common Foreign and Security Policy (CFSP). By contrast, as regards subjects that exclusively or principally fall into the CFSP, it is the High Representative who will submit recommendations to the Council. For matters falling partly within the CFSP and partly outside it, there is also the possibility of "joint proposals".[82]

---

[79] Two special procedures are found in Articles 207 and 219 TFEU. The former deals with trade agreements within the context of the Union's common commercial policy. The latter expresses a derogation from the "ordinary" procedure for "formal agreements on an exchange-rate system for the euro in relation to the currencies of third states" (see Article 219 (1) TFEU).

[80] Article 218 (2) TFEU.   [81] Article 218 (8) TFEU.   [82] See Articles 22 (2) and 30 (1) TEU.

On the recommendation, the Council may decide to open negotiations and nominate the Union negotiator "depending on the subject matter of the agreement envisaged".[83] This formulation is ambivalent. Textually, the phrase suggests a liberal meaning. The Council can – but need not necessarily – appoint the Commission as Union negotiator for an agreement. According to this reading the Commission will not enjoy a prerogative to be the Union's negotiator. However, a systematic reading of the phrase leads to a different meaning. For if read in light of the jurisdictional division between the Commission and the High Representative at the recommendation stage, the Commission should be constitutionally entitled to be the Union negotiator for all Union agreements that "exclusively or principally" fall into the Treaty on the Functioning of the European Union.[84]

The Council will be able to address directives to the negotiator and subject its powers to consultation with a special committee. Where the Commission is chosen as Union negotiator, it thus still needs to be "authorized" by the Council and would conduct the negotiations under the control of the Council. The Commission's powers here are therefore between "autonomous" and "delegated" powers. The lower degree of institutional autonomy is justified by the fact that third parties are involved. (The subsequent rejection of a negotiated agreement by the Council would indeed have "external" negative repercussions, and for that reason the ex ante involvement of the Council is a useful constitutional device.) On the other hand, the existence of an internal safeguard checking the Union negotiator creates, to some extent, a "two-front war". For the Union negotiator has not only to negotiate externally with the third party, but it also needs to deal internally with the Council.

Parliament is not formally involved in the negotiation. However, Article 218 (10) constitutionalizes its right to be informed during all stages of the procedure. And this right has the potential of becoming an informal political safeguard that anticipates the interest of Parliament at the negotiation stage.[85]

---

[83] Article 218 (3) TFEU.

[84] In this sense see also P. Eeckhout, *EU External Relations Law* (Oxford University Press, 2011), 196.

[85] See Framework Agreement on Relations between the European Parliament and the European Commission, especially Annex III. According to para. 3 of the Annex, "[t]he Commission shall take due account of Parliament's comments throughout the negotiations".

Finally, any Union institution and the Member States are entitled to challenge the "constitutionality" of a draft agreement *prior* to its conclusion. This judicial safeguard can be found in Article 218 (11), which creates the jurisdiction of the Court for an "Opinion".[86] Where this "Opinion" leads to a finding that the envisaged agreement is not compatible with the Treaties, the agreement may not enter into force – unless the Treaties themselves are amended.[87] The possibility of an ex ante "review" of a draft agreement contrasts with the Court's ordinary ex post review powers.[88] However, the exception is – again – justified by the fact that third party rights under international law are involved. Indeed, it is a rule of international law that, once an agreement is validly concluded under international law, a contracting party generally cannot subsequently invoke internal constitutional problems to deny its binding effect.[89] Ex post review of an international agreement will thus be too late to negate the external effects of an international agreement.

(b) Signing and conclusion

The Council will sign and conclude the agreement on a proposal by the negotiator.[90]

Prior to the formal conclusion of the agreement, the European Parliament must be actively involved, except where the agreement *exclusively* relates to the CFSP. (When compared with the Commission's involvement at the proposal stage,[91] the TFEU is here more generous, for it expands

---

[86] Article 218 (11) TFEU. The Court has so far delivered fifteen Opinions on international agreements: see Table of Cases.

[87] This happened, for example, with regard to the European Convention on Human Rights in 1996; see *Opinion 2/94 (Accession to ECHR)*, [1996] ECR I-1759. Prior to the Lisbon Treaty, accession to the Convention was thus unconstitutional. The Lisbon Treaty has amended the original Treaties, which now contain an express competence to accede to the ECHR in Article 6(2) TEU.

[88] On (ex post) judicial review in the Union legal order, see Chapter 8 – Section 3 below.

[89] See Article 46 Vienna Convention of the Law of Treaties: "(1) A State may not invoke the fact that its consent to be bound by a treaty has been expressed in violation of a provision of its internal law regarding competence to conclude treaties as invalidating its consent unless that violation was manifest and concerned a rule of its internal law of fundamental importance. (2) A violation is manifest if it would be objectively evident to any State conducting itself in the matter in accordance with normal practice and in good faith."

[90] Article 218 (5) and (6) TFEU. The conclusion will usually be done by means of a Council Decision.

[91] Article 218 (3) TFEU: agreements relating "exclusively *or principally*" to the CFSP.

parliamentary involvement to agreements that even principally relate to CFSP matters.) Article 218 (6) thereby distinguishes between two forms of parliamentary participation in the conclusion procedure: consultation and consent. The former is the residual category and applies to all agreements that do not require consent. The types of agreements where the Council needs to obtain parliamentary consent are enumerated in the form of five situations listed under Article 218 (6) (a): (i) association agreements; (ii) the agreement on Union accession to the European Convention on Human Rights; (iii) agreements establishing a specific institutional framework; (iv) agreements with important budgetary implications for the Union; (v) agreements covering fields to which either the ordinary legislative procedure applies, or the special legislative procedure where consent by the European Parliament is required.

The first, second and third categories may be explained by the constitutional idea of "political treaties".[92] For association agreements as well as institutional framework agreements, such as the ECHR, will by definition express an important *political* choice with long-term consequences. For these fundamental political choices Parliament – the representative of the European citizens – must give its democratic consent. The fourth category represents a constitutional reflex that protects the special role the European Parliament enjoys in establishing the Union budget.[93] The fifth category makes profound sense from the perspective of procedural parallelism. Under paragraph 6 (a) (v), Parliament is entitled to veto "agreements covering fields" that internally require parliamentary co-decision or consent. The parallelism between the internal and external sphere is however not complete: Parliament will indeed *not* enjoy the power of co-conclusion in areas in which the "ordinary" legislative procedure applies. Its internal power to co-decision is here reduced to a mere power of "consent". It must "take-or-leave" the negotiated international agreement. This structural "democratic deficit" in the procedural regime for international agreements is not a *sui generis* characteristic of the European Union, but can be found in other constitutional orders of the world.[94] It is generally justified by reference to

---

[92] R. Jennings and S. Watts (eds.), *Oppenheim's International Law* (Oxford University Press, 2008), 211.

[93] For an extensive discussion of this category, see *Parliament* v. *Council (Mauritania Fisheries Agreement)*, Case 189/97, [1999] ECR I-4741.

[94] For example: in the United States. According to Article II – Section 2 of the US Constitution, it is the President that "shall have Power, by and with the Advice and Consent of the Senate,

the "exceptional" nature of foreign affairs and, in particular: their "volatile" and "secretive" nature.

(c) Modification and suspension (termination)

Article 218 (7) deals with modifications of international agreements that have been successfully concluded. The Council may "authorize the negotiator to approve on the Union's behalf modifications to the agreement where it provides for them to be adopted by a simplified procedure or by a body set up by the agreement". (The Council can attach specific conditions to such an authorization.) In the absence of such a specific authorization for a simplified revision procedure, the ordinary treaty-making procedure will apply. This follows from a constitutional principle called *actus contrarius*. In order to modify an act or international agreement the same procedure needs to be followed that led to the conclusion of the international agreement in the first place.

Article 218 (9) deals with the suspension of an international agreement. The provision specifies that the Commission or the High Representative may propose to the Council the suspension of the agreement. (And while the provision does not expressly refer to the jurisdictional division between the two actors, as mentioned in Article 218 (3) for the proposal stage, we should assume that this rule would apply analogously. The High Representative should thus solely be entitled to recommend the suspension for international agreements that relate "exclusively or principally" to the CFSP.) Parliament is not expressly mentioned and will thus only have to be informed of the Council decision. This truncated procedure allows the Union quickly to decide on the (temporary) suspension of an agreement. However, this "executive" decision without parliamentary consent distorts to some extent the institutional balance in the external relations field.

How are Union agreements terminated? Unfortunately, Article 218 does not expressly set out a procedural regime for the termination of a Union agreement. Two views are possible. The first view is again based on the idea of *actus contrarius*: the termination of an agreement would need to follow the very same procedure for its conclusion. This procedural parallelism has been contested by reference to the common constitutional traditions of the

to make Treaties, provided two thirds of the Senators present concur". The American Parliament – the House of Representatives – is not formally involved.

Union's Member States, which leave the termination decision principally in the hands of the executive.[95] A second view therefore reverts to the suspension procedure applied analogously.

(d) Union succession to Member State agreements

Can the Union be bound by agreements that it has not formally concluded? The counterintuitive answer is positive: under European law, the Union can be bound by agreements of its Member States where the Union has succeeded the latter.[96]

The doctrine of Union succession to international agreements of the Member States is thereby a doctrine of *functional* succession.[97] It is not based on a transfer of territory, but on a transfer of *functions*. The European Court announced this European doctrine in relation to the General Agreement on Tariffs and Trade in *International Fruit*.[98] Formally, the Union was not a party to the international treaty, but the Court found that "in so far as under the [European] Treat[ies] the [Union] has *assumed the powers previously exercised by Member States* in the area covered by the General Agreement, the provisions of that agreement have the effect of binding the [Union]".[99] Functional succession thus emanated from the exclusive nature of the Union's powers under the Common Commercial Policy (CCP). Since the Union had assumed the "functions" previously exercised by the Member States in this area, it was entitled and obliged to also assume their international obligations.

For a long time after *International Fruit*, the succession doctrine remained quiet. But in the last decade it has experienced a constitutional

---

[95] C. Tomuschat, "Artikel 300 EG" in H. von der Groeben and J. Schwarze (eds.), *Kommentar zum Vertrag über die Europäische Union und zur Gründung der Europäischen Gemeinschaft* (Nomos, 2004), vol. IV, para. 61.

[96] For an overview, see R. Schütze, "The 'Succession Doctrine' and the European Union" in A. Arnull et al. (eds.), *A Constitutional Order of States?: Essays in EU Law in honour of Alan Dashwood* (Hart, 2011), 459.

[97] See P. Pescatore, *L'ordre juridique des Communautés Européennes* (Presse universitaire de Liège, 1975), 147–8 (my translation): "[B]y taking over, by virtue of the Treaties, certain competences and certain powers previously exercised by the Member States, the [Union] equally had to assume the international obligations that controlled the exercise of these competences and powers[.]"

[98] *International Fruit Company NV* v. *Produktschap voor Groenten en Fruit*, Joined Cases 21–24/72, [1972] ECR 1219.

[99] *Ibid.*, paras. 14–18 (emphasis added).

revival. This allowed the Court better to define the doctrine's contours. Three principles seem to govern functional succession in the European legal order. First, for the succession doctrine to come into operation *all* the Member States must be parties to an international treaty.[100] Second, *when* the international treaty is concluded is irrelevant. It will thus not matter whether the international treaty was concluded before or after the creation of the European Community in 1958.[101] Third, the Union will only succeed to international treaties, where there is a "*full transfer of the powers* previously exercised by the Member States".[102] The Union will thus not succeed to all international agreements concluded by all the Member States, but only to those where it has assumed an exclusive competence. Would the European succession doctrine thereby be confined to the sphere of the Union's *constitutionally* exclusive powers; or would *legislative* exclusivity generated by Article 3 (2) TFEU be sufficient?[103] The Court has shown a preference for a succession doctrine that includes legislative exclusivity. In *Bogiatzi*,[104] the Court indeed found that a "full transfer" could take place where European legislation completely preempted the Member States from the substantive scope of the international treaty.

---

[100] *Commune de Mesquer* v. *Total*, Case C-188/07, [2008] ECR I-4501.
[101] *Intertanko and others* v. *Secretary of State for Transport*, Case 308/06, [2008] ECR I-4057.
[102] *Ibid.*, para. 4 (emphasis added).
[103] On the idea of legislative exclusivity, see: Chapter 3 – Section 4(a).
[104] *Bogiatzi* v. *Deutscher Luftpool and others*, Case C-301/08, [2009] ECR I-10185.

Introduction

When the British Parliament legislates, it need not "justify" its acts. It is traditionally considered to enjoy a competence to do all things.[1] This "omnipotence" was inherent in the idea of a sovereign parliament in a "sovereign state". The European Union is neither "sovereign" nor a "state". Its powers are *not inherent* powers. They must be *conferred* by its foundational charter: the European Treaties. This constitutional principle is called the "principle of conferral". The Treaty on European Union defines it as follows:

Under the principle of conferral, the Union shall act only within the limits of the competences conferred upon it by the Member States in the Treaties to attain the

---

[1] In the words of A. V. Dicey, *Introduction to the Study of the Law of the Constitution* (Liberty Fund, 1982), 37–8: "The principle of Parliamentary sovereignty means neither more nor less than this, namely that Parliament thus defined has, under the English constitution, the right to make or unmake any law whatever: and, further, that no person or body is recognized by the law of England as having a right to override or set aside the legislation of Parliament."

ᴄs set out therein. Competences not conferred upon the Union in the Treaties remain with the Member States.[2]

The Treaties employ the notion of competence in various provisions. Nevertheless, there is no positive definition of the concept. So what is a legislative competence? The best definition is this: a legislative competence is the *material field* within which an authority is entitled to legislate. What are these material fields in which the Union is entitled to legislate? The Treaties do *not* enumerate the Union's "competences" in a single list. Instead, the Treaties pursue a different technique: they attribute legal competence for each and every Union activity in the respective Treaty title. Each policy area contains a provision – sometimes more than one – on which Union legislation can be based. The various "Union policies and internal actions" of the Union are set out in Part III of the Treaty on the Functioning of the European Union.[3]

The Treaties thus present a picture of thematically limited competences in distinct policy areas. This picture is however – partly – misleading. Three legal developments have posed serious threats to the principle of conferral. First, the rise of teleological interpretation (see Section 1 below). The Union's competences are interpreted in such a way that they potentially "spill over" into other policy areas. This "spillover" effect can be particularly observed with regard to a second development: the rise of the Union's general competences. For in addition to its thematic competences in specific areas, the Union enjoys two legal bases that horizontally cut across the various policy titles within the Treaties. These two competences are Articles 114 and 352 TFEU (see Section 2 below). Lastly, a third development that would qualify the principle of conferral significantly: the doctrine of implied external powers (see Section 3 below).

What types of competences are recognised by the Treaties? The original Treaties did not specify the relationship between European and national competences.[4] They betrayed no sign of a distinction between different competence categories. This has however changed. Different competence categories were first "discovered" by the European Court of Justice, and the

---

[2] Article 5 (2) TEU.

[3] And yet, there exist some legal bases outside Part III of the TFEU, such as Article 16 (2) TFEU "on rules relating to the protection of individuals with regard to the processing of personal data by Union institutions", and Article 352 TFEU – the Union's most famous legal base.

[4] J. V. Louis, "Quelques Réflexions sur la répartition des compétences entre la communauté européenne et ses états membres", 2 (1979) *Revue d'Intégration Européenne*, 355, 357.

Table 6 Union policies and internal actions

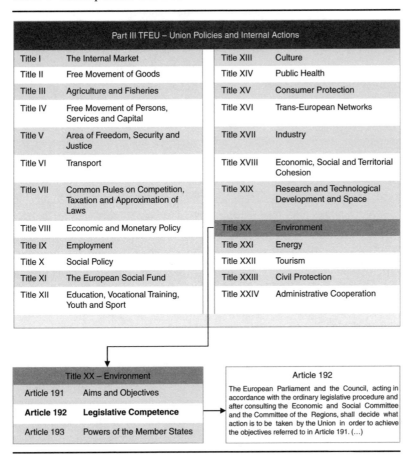

Part III TFEU – Union Policies and Internal Actions			
Title I	The Internal Market	Title XIII	Culture
Title II	Free Movement of Goods	Title XIV	Public Health
Title III	Agriculture and Fisheries	Title XV	Consumer Protection
Title IV	Free Movement of Persons, Services and Capital	Title XVI	Trans-European Networks
Title V	Area of Freedom, Security and Justice	Title XVII	Industry
Title VI	Transport	Title XVIII	Economic, Social and Territorial Cohesion
Title VII	Common Rules on Competition, Taxation and Approximation of Laws	Title XIX	Research and Technological Development and Space
Title VIII	Economic and Monetary Policy	Title XX	Environment
Title IX	Employment	Title XXI	Energy
Title X	Social Policy	Title XXII	Tourism
Title XI	The European Social Fund	Title XXIII	Civil Protection
Title XII	Education, Vocational Training, Youth and Sport	Title XXIV	Administrative Cooperation

Title XX – Environment	
Article 191	Aims and Objectives
Article 192	**Legislative Competence**
Article 193	Powers of the Member States

Article 192

The European Parliament and the Council, acting in accordance with the ordinary legislative procedure and after consulting the Economic and Social Committee and the Committee of the Regions, shall decide what action is to be taken by the Union in order to achieve the objectives referred to in Article 191. (...)

Lisbon Treaty has now codified them. These competence categories will be discussed in Section 4.

1. Union competences: teleological interpretation

The Union must act "within the limits of the competences conferred upon it *by the Member States*".[5] Did this mean that the Member States would be able to determine the scope of the Union's competences? A *strict* principle

---

[5] Article 5 (2) TEU (emphasis added).

of conferral would indeed deny the Union the power autonomously to interpret its competences. But this solution encounters serious practical problems: how is the Union to work if every legislative bill would need to gain the consent of every national parliament? Classic international organizations solve this dilemma between theory and practice by insisting that the interpretation of international treaties must be in line with the clear intentions of the Member States.[6] Legal competences will thus be interpreted restrictively. This restrictive interpretation is designed to preserve the sovereign rights of the States by preserving the historical meaning of the founding treaty.

By contrast, a *soft* principle of conferral allows for teleological interpretation of competences. Instead of looking at the historical will of the founders, teleological interpretation asks what is the purpose – or *telos* – of a rule. It thus looks behind the legal text in search of a legal solution to a social problem that may not have been anticipated when the text was drafted. Teleological interpretation can therefore – partly – constitute a "small" amendment of the original rule. It is potentially a method of incremental change that complements the – rare – qualitative changes following "big" Treaty amendments.

Has the Union been able autonomously to interpret the scope of its competences, and if so how? After a brief period of following international law logic,[7] the Union embraced the constitutional technique of teleological interpretation. This technique can be seen in relation to the interpretation of the Union's *competences*, as well as in relation to the interpretation of European *legislation*. The first situation is famously illustrated in the controversy surrounding the adoption of the (first) Working Time Directive.[8] The Directive had been based on a provision within Title X on "Social Policy". That provision allowed the Union to "encourage improvements, especially in the working environment, as regards the health and safety of workers".[9] Would this competence entitle the Union to adopt legislation on

---

[6] In international law, this principle is called the "in dubio mitius" principle. In case of doubt, the "milder" interpretation should be preferred.

[7] See *Fédération Charbonnière de Belgique* v. *High Authority of the European Coal and Steel Community*, Case 8/55, [1954–56] ECR 245.

[8] *United Kingdom of Great Britain and Northern Ireland* v. *Council*, Case C-84/94, [1996] ECR I-5755.

[9] Ex-Article 118a (1) EEC. This competence is today Article 153 (1) (a) TFEU, which allows the Union to support and implement the activities of the Member States as regards the "improvement in particular of the working environment to protect workers' health and safety".

the general organization of working time?[10] The United Kingdom strongly contested this teleological reading. It claimed that there was no thematic link to health and safety, and that the Union legislator had therefore acted *ultra vires*. The Court, however, backed up the Union legislator. Its teleological reasoning was as follows:

> There is nothing in the wording of Article [153 TFEU] to indicate that the concepts of "working environment", "safety" and "health" as used in that provision should, in the absence of other indications, be interpreted restrictively, and not as embracing all factors, physical or otherwise, capable of affecting the health and safety of the worker in his working environment, including in particular certain aspects of the organization of working time.[11]

With one famous exception,[12] the European Court has indeed accepted all the teleological interpretations of Union competences by the Union legislator.

But more than that, the Court itself interprets Union legislation in a teleological manner. The classic case in this context is *Casagrande*.[13] In order to facilitate the free movement of persons in the internal market, the Union had adopted legislation designed to abolish discrimination between workers of different Member States as regards employment, remuneration, and other conditions of work.[14] And to facilitate the integration of the worker and his family into the host state, the Union legislation contained the following provision:

---

[10] Section II of Directive 93/104 regulated minimum rest periods. Member States were obliged to introduce national laws to ensure that every worker is entitled to a minimum daily rest period of eleven consecutive hours per twenty-four hour period (*ibid.*, Article 3) and to a rest break where the working day is longer than six hours (*ibid.*, Article 4). Article 5 granted a minimum uninterrupted rest period of twenty-four hours in each seven-day period and determined that this period should in principle include Sunday. Article 6 established a maximum weekly working time of 48 hours; and finally, the Directive established a four weeks' paid annual leave (*ibid.*, Article 7).

[11] *United Kingdom* v. *Council*, Case C-84/94 (supra n. 8), para. 15. The Court, however, annulled the second sentence of Article 5 of the Directive that had tried to protect, in principle, Sunday as a weekly rest period. In the opinion of the Court, the Council had "failed to explain why Sunday, as a weekly rest day, is more closely connected with the health and safety of workers than any other day of the week" (*ibid.*, para. 37).

[12] *Germany* v. *Parliament and Council (Tobacco Advertising)*, Case C-376/98, [2000] ECR I-8419. This exception will be discussed below in the context of the Union's "harmonization competence".

[13] *Casagrande* v. *Landeshauptstadt München*, Case 9/74, [1974] ECR 773.

[14] Regulation 1612/68 on freedom of movement for workers within the Community, [1968] OJ (Special English Edition) 475.

The children of a national of a Member State who is or has been employed in the territory of another Member State *shall be admitted* to that State's general educational, apprenticeship and vocational training courses under the same conditions as the nationals of that State, if such children are residing in its territory. Member States shall encourage all efforts to enable such children to attend these courses under the best possible conditions.[15]

Would this provision entitle the son of an Italian worker employed in Germany to receive an educational grant for his studies? Literally interpreted, the provision exclusively covers the "admission" of workers' children to the educational system of the host state. But the Court favoured a teleological interpretation that would maximize the useful effect behind the Union legislation. And since the purpose of the provision was "to ensure that the children may take advantage on an equal footing of the educational and training facilities available", it followed that the provision referred "*not only to rules relating to admission*, but also to general measures intended to facilitate educational attendance".[16] Thus, despite the fact that the (then) Treaties did not confer an express competence in educational matters on the Union, the Court considered that national educational grants fell within the scope of European legislation. The teleological interpretation of Union legislation had thus "spilled over" into spheres that the Member States had believed to have remained within their exclusive competences.

2. The general competences of the Union

In principle, the Treaties grant special competences within each policy area.[17] Yet in addition to these thematic competences, the Union legislator enjoys two general competences: Article 114 and Article 352 TFEU. The former represents the Union's "harmonization competence"; the latter constitutes its "residual competence". Both competences cut – horizontally – through the Union's sectoral policies, and have even been used – or some might say: abused – to develop policies not expressly mentioned in the Treaties.

---

[15] *Ibid.*, Article 12 (emphasis added).

[16] *Casagrande* v. *Landeshauptstadt München*, Case 9/74, (supra n. 13) paras. 8–9 (emphasis added).

[17] We thus find the Union's competence on environmental protection (Article 192 TFEU), in the Treaties' title dedicated to the environment (Title XX of Part III of the TFEU). On this point, see Table 6 above.

(a) The harmonization competence: Article 114

On the basis of Article 114 TFEU, the European Union is entitled to adopt measures for the approximation of national laws "which have as their object the establishment and functioning of the internal market". The Union's competence to harmonize national laws thus applies where national laws affect the establishment *or* functioning of the internal market. The former alternative concerns obstacles to the four freedoms of movement; the latter alternative captures distortions of competition resulting from disparities between national laws.

What is the scope of Article 114? In the past, the Union legislator has employed an extremely wide reading of this general competence. Its potentially unlimited scope is illustrated by *Spain* v. *Council*.[18] The European legislator had created a supplementary protection certificate for medicinal products, which could be granted under the same conditions as national patents by each of the Member States.[19] Three major constitutional hurdles seemed to oppose the constitutionality of this European law. First, Article 114 could theoretically not be used to create *new European* rights as it should only harmonize *existing national* rights. Secondly, the European law should theoretically further the creation of a single European market; yet, the supplementary certificate extended the duration of national patents and thus prolonged the compartmentalization of the common market into distinct national markets. Finally, at the time of its adoption only *two* Member States had legislation concerning a supplementary certificate. Was this enough to trigger the Union's *harmonization* power?

The Court took the first hurdle by force. It simply rejected the claim that the European law created a new right.[20] The same blind force would be applied to the second argument. The Court did not discuss whether the European law hindered the free circulation of pharmaceutical goods between Member States. Instead, the Court concentrated on the third hurdle in the form of the question, whether Article 114 required the *pre*-existence of diverse national laws. In the eyes of the Court, this was not the case. The Court accepted that the contested law aimed "*to prevent the heterogeneous*

---

[18] *Spain* v. *Council*, Case C-350/92, [1995] ECR I-1985.

[19] Regulation 1768/92 concerning the creation of a supplementary protection certificate for medicinal products, [1992] OJ L182/1.

[20] *Spain* v. *Council*, Case C-350/92, (supra n. 18) para. 27.

development of national laws leading to further disparities which would be likely to create obstacles to the free movement of medicinal products within the [Union] and thus directly affect the establishment and the functioning of the internal market".[21] The European legislator was thus entitled to use its harmonization power to prevent *future* obstacles to trade or a *potential* fragmentation of the internal market.

For a long time, the scope of the Union's harmonization power appeared devoid of constitutional boundaries. Yet, the existence of constitutional limits was confirmed in *Germany* v. *Parliament and Council (Tobacco Advertising).*[22] The bone of contention had been a European law that banned the advertising and sponsorship of tobacco products.[23] Could a prohibition or ban be based on the Union's internal market competence? Germany objected to the idea. It argued that the Union's harmonization power could only be used to promote the internal market; and this was not so in the event, where the Union legislation constituted, in practice, a total prohibition of tobacco advertising.[24] The Court accepted – to the surprise of many – the argument. And it annulled, for the first time in its history, a European law on the ground that it went beyond the Union's harmonization power. Emphatically, the Court pointed out that the harmonization power could not grant the Union an unlimited power to regulate the internal market:

> To construe that article as meaning that it vests in the [Union] legislature a general power to regulate the internal market would not only be contrary to the express wording of the provisions cited above but would also be incompatible with the principle embodied in Article [5 TEU] that the powers of the [Union] are limited to those specifically conferred on it. Moreover, a measure adopted on the basis of Article [114] of the [FEU] Treaty must genuinely have as its object the improvement of the conditions for the establishment and functioning of the internal market. If a mere finding of disparities between national rules and of the abstract risk of obstacles to the exercise of fundamental freedoms or of distortions of competition liable to result therefrom were sufficient to justify the choice of Article [114] as a

---

[21] *Ibid*, para. 35 (emphasis added).

[22] *Germany* v. *Parliament and Council (Tobacco Advertising)*, Case C-376/98 (supra n. 12).

[23] Directive 98/43/EC on the approximation of the laws, regulations and administrative provisions of the Member States relating to the advertising and sponsorship of tobacco products, [1998] OJ L213/9.

[24] Germany had pointed out that the sole form of advertising allowed under the Directive was advertising at the point of sale, which only accounted for 2 per cent of the tobacco industry's advertising expenditure (*Tobacco Advertising*, (supra n. 12) para. 24).

legal basis, judicial review of compliance with the proper legal basis might be rendered nugatory.[25]

With *Tobacco Advertising*, the Court insisted on *three* constitutional limits to the Union's harmonization power. First, the European law must *harmonize* national laws. Thus Union legislation "which leaves unchanged the different national laws already in existence, cannot be regarded as aiming to approximate the laws of the Member States".[26] Secondly, a simple disparity in national laws will not be enough to trigger the Union's harmonization competence. The disparity must give rise to obstacles in trade or appreciable distortions in competition. Thus: while Article 114 can be used to "harmonize" *future* disparities in national laws, it must be "likely" that the divergent development of national laws will lead to obstacles in trade.[27] Thirdly, the Union legislation must actually contribute to the elimination of obstacles to free movement or distortions of competition.[28] These three constitutional limits to the Union's "harmonization power" have been confirmed *in abstracto*;[29] yet subsequent jurisprudence has led to fresh accusations that Article 114 grants the Union an (almost) unlimited competence.[30]

---

[25] *Ibid.*, paras. 83–4.

[26] *Parliament & Council*, Case C-436/03, [2006] ECR I-3733, para. 44. The Court here confirmed and extended the point made in relation to intellectual property law (see *Spain* v. *Council*, Case C-350/92 (supra n. 18); as well as *Netherlands* v. *Council and Parliament*, Case C-377/98, [2001] ECR I-7079).

[27] *Germany* v. *Parliament and Council (Tobacco Advertising)*, Case C-376/98, (supra n. 12) para. 86.

[28] *British American Tobacco*, Case C-491/01, [2002] ECR I-11453, para. 60.

[29] On this point, see *ibid.*, as well as *Swedish Match*, Case C-210/03, [2004] ECR I-11893; and *Germany* v. *Parliament and Council (Tobacco Advertising II)*, Case C-380/03, [2006] ECR I-11573.

[30] See *Tobacco Advertising II* (supra n. 29), para. 80: "Recourse to Article [114 TFEU] as a legal basis does not presuppose the existence of an actual link with free movement between the Member States in every situation covered by the measure founded on that basis. As the Court has previously pointed out, to justify recourse to Article [114 TFEU] as the legal basis what matters is that the measure adopted on that basis must actually be intended to improve the conditions for the establishment and functioning of the internal market." This statement explains why a total ban on the marketing of a product may still be justified under Article [114 TFEU] (see *Swedish Match* supra n. 29). This has led D. Wyatt, "Community Competence to Regulate the Internal Market", Oxford Faculty of Law Research Paper 9/2007, to query whether *Tobacco Advertising* was a "false dawn" (*ibid.* 23). For a recent confirmation of this thesis, see: *The Queen, ex parte Vodafone et al.* v. *Secretary of State*, Case C-58/08 [2010] ECR I-4999.

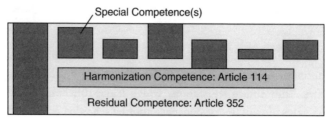

Figure 3.1 General and special competences

(b) The residual competence: Article 352

Article 352 TFEU constitutes the most general competence within the Treaties. Comparable to the "Necessary and Proper Clause" in the American Constitution,[31] it allows the Union to legislate or act where it is "necessary, within the framework of the policies defined in the Treaties, to attain one of the objectives set out in the Treaties, and the Treaties have not provided the necessary powers".

The legislative competence under Article 352 may be used in two ways. First, it can be employed in a policy title in which the Union is already given a specific competence, but where the latter is deemed insufficient to achieve a specific objective. Second, the residual competence can be used to develop a policy area that has no specific title within the Treaties. The textbook illustration for the second – and more dangerous – potential of Article 352 is provided by the development of a Union environmental policy *prior* to the Single European Act. For, stimulated by the political enthusiasm to develop such a European policy after the 1972 Paris Summit, the Commission and the Council faced the legal problem that environmental policy was not an official Union policy. There was therefore no specific legal title offered by the Treaties! And the way out of this dilemma was suggested by the Member States themselves. They called on the Union institutions to make the widest possible use of all provisions of the Treaties, especially Article 352.[32] The Member States thus favoured an extensive interpretation of the provision to cause a "small amendment" of the Treaties. And the

---

[31] According to Article I, Section 8, Clause 18 of the US Constitution, the American Union shall have the power "[t]o make all Laws which shall be necessary and proper for carrying into Execution the foregoing Powers, and all other Powers vested by this Constitution in the Government of the United States, or in any Department or Officer thereof".

[32] European Council, *First Summit Conference of the Enlarged Community*; Bulletin of the European Communities, EC 10–1972, 9 at 23.

"indirect" development of a European environmental competence was indeed impressive.[33]

Are there constitutional limits to Article 352? The provision expressly mentions two limitations. First, "[m]easures based on this Article shall not entail harmonization of Member States' laws or regulations in cases where the Treaties exclude such harmonization".[34] This precludes the use of the Union's residual competence in policy areas in which the Union is limited to merely "complementing" national action.[35] Second, Article 352 "cannot serve as a basis for attaining objectives pertaining to the common foreign and security policy".[36] This codifies past jurisprudence,[37] and is designed to protect the constitutional boundary drawn between the Treaty on European Union and the Treaty on the Functioning of the European Union.[38]

In addition to these two express boundaries, the European Court has also recognized an *implied* limitation to the Union's residual competence. While Article 352 could be used for "small" amendments to the Treaties, it could not be used to effect "qualitative leaps" that would change the constitutional identity of the European Union.[39] The Court confirmed this implied restriction in Opinion 2/94.[40] The European Court had been requested to preview the Union's power to accede to the European Convention on Human Rights ("ECHR") – at a time when there was no express power to do so in the Treaties.[41] The Court characterized the relationship between the Union's residual competence and the principle of conferral as follows:

---

[33] Prior to the entry into force of the Single European Act (SEA), a significant number of environment-related measures were adopted on the basis of Articles [115] and [352], thus "laying the foundation for the formation of a very specific [Union] environmental policy" (see F. Tschofen, "Article 235 of the Treaty Establishing the European Economic Community: Potential Conflicts between the Dynamics of Lawmaking in the Community and National Constitutional Principles", 12 (1991) *Michigan Journal of International Law*, 471 at 477).

[34] Article 352 (3) TFEU.

[35] On "complementary" competences in the Union legal order that exclude all harmonization, see Section 4 (d) below.

[36] Article 352 (4) TFEU.

[37] See *Kadi* v. *Council and Commission*, Case C-402/05P, [2008] ECR I-6351, paras. 198–9.

[38] See Art. 40 TEU – second indent.

[39] A. Tizzano, "The Powers of the Community", in Commission (ed.), *Thirty Years of Community Law* (Office for Official Publications of the EC, 1981), 43.

[40] Opinion 2/94 (*Accession by the European Community to the European Convention on Human Rights*), [1996] ECR I-1759.

[41] After the Lisbon Treaty, the Union is now given the express competence to accede to the Convention (see Art. 6 (2) TEU). On this point, see Chapter 4 – Section 4 below.

Article [352] is designed to fill the gap where no specific provisions of the Treaty confer on the [Union] institutions express or implied powers to act, if such powers appear none the less to be necessary to enable the [Union] to carry out its functions with a view to attaining one of the objectives laid down by the Treaty. That provision, being an integral part of an institutional system based on the principle of conferred powers, cannot serve as a basis for widening the scope of [Union] powers *beyond the general framework* created by the provisions of the Treaty as a whole and, in particular, by those that define the *tasks* and the *activities* of the [Union]. On any view, Article [352] cannot be used as a basis for the adoption of provisions whose effect would, in substance, be to amend the Treaty without following the procedure which it provides for that purpose.[42]

The framework of the Treaty was thus defined by the Union's tasks and activities. They would form the outer jurisdictional circle within which any legislative activity of the Union had to take place. However, instead of clarifying whether the protection of human rights constituted an "objective" of the European Union, the Court – prudently to some, cowardly to others – concentrated on the *external* constitutional limits which any interpretation of Article 352 would encounter. The judicial reasoning in the second part of the judgment was as follows: the accession of the Union to the ECHR would not cause a small (informal) amendment of the Union legal order, but one with "*fundamental institutional implications* for the [Union] and for the Member States, [which] would be of *constitutional significance* and would therefore be such as to go beyond the scope of Article [352]". "It could be brought about only by way of Treaty amendment."[43] Article 352 would thus encounter an external border in the constitutional identity of the European legal order.

3. The doctrine of implied (external) powers

The European Treaties do acknowledge the international personality of the European Union.[44] But what about the Union's treaty-making powers? The powers of the Union are enumerated powers; and under the 1957 Rome Treaty, these treaty-making powers were originally confined to international agreements under the Common Commercial Policy and Association

---

[42] Opinion 2/94, paras. 29–30 (emphasis added).   [43] Opinion 2/94, para. 35.

[44] Article 47 TEU: "The Union shall have legal personality."

Agreements with third countries or international organizations.[45] This restrictive attribution of treaty-making powers to the Union protected a status quo in which the Member States were to remain the protagonists on the international relations scene. This picture has changed dramatically through the doctrine of implied external powers. In the past four decades, the European Court has led – and won – a remarkable campaign to expand the Union's treaty-making powers.[46]

The battle over external competences began with *ERTA*.[47] The European Road Transport Agreement ("ERTA") had been drafted to harmonize certain social aspects of international road transport and involved a number of Member States as potential signatories. The negotiations were conducted without formal involvement of the Union. The Commission felt excluded from its role as Europe's external broker. It unsuccessfully insisted on being involved in the negotiations and eventually brought the matter before the European Court. There, the Commission argued that the Union competence under its transport policy included a treaty-making power (and that this power had become exclusive after the adoption of Union legislation).[48]

With regard to the scope of the Union's external powers, the Commission argued as follows. Article 91 TFEU "conferred on the [Union] powers defined in wide terms with a view to implementing the common transport policy [which] must apply to external relations just as much as to domestic measures".[49] This wide teleological interpretation of the wording of the Union's transport competence was justified, for "the full effect of this provision would be jeopardized if the powers which it confers, particularly that of laying down 'any appropriate provisions', within the meaning of subparagraph (1) [d] of the article cited, did not extend to the conclusion of agreements with third countries".[50] The Council opposed this *effet utile* interpretation, contending that "Article [91] relates only to measures *internal* to the [Union], and cannot be interpreted as authorizing the conclusion of international agreements". The power to enter into agreements with third countries "cannot be assumed in the absence of an express provision in the Treaty".[51]

---

[45] See Articles 207 and 217 TFEU.

[46] R. Schütze, "Parallel External Powers in the European Community: From 'Cubist' Perspectives Towards 'Naturalist' Constitutional Principles?", 23 (2004) *Yearbook of European Law*, 225.

[47] *Commission* v. *Council (ERTA)*, Case 22/70, [1971] ECR 263.

[48] On this point, see Section 4 (a) below.   [49] *ERTA* (supra n. 47), para. 6.

[50] *Ibid.*, para. 7.   [51] *Ibid.*, paras. 9–10 (emphasis added).

In its judgment, the European Court famously sided with the Commission's extensive stance:

> To determine in a particular case the [Union's] authority to enter into international agreements, regard must be had to the whole scheme of the Treaty no less than to its substantive provisions. Such authority arises not only from an express conferment by the Treaty – as is the case with [Article 207] and [ex-] Article 114 for tariff and trade agreements and with [Article 217] for association agreements – but may equally flow from other provisions of the Treaty and from measures adopted, within the framework of those provisions, by the [Union] institutions ...
>
> According to [Article 90], the objectives of the Treaty in matters of transport are to be pursued within the framework of a common policy. With this in view, [Article 91 (1)] directs the Council to lay down common rules and, in addition, "any other appropriate provisions". By the terms of subparagraph (a) of the same provision, those common rules are applicable "to international transport to or from the territory of a Member State or passing across the territory of one or more Member States". This provision is equally concerned with transport from or to third countries, as regards that part of the journey which takes place on [Union] territory. It thus assumes that the powers of the [Union] extend to relationships arising from international law, and hence involve the need in the sphere in question for agreements with the third countries concerned.[52]

The passage spoke the language of teleological interpretation: in the light of the general scheme of the Treaty, the Union's power to adopt "any other appropriate provision" to give effect to the Union's transport policy objectives was interpreted to include the legal power to conclude international agreements.[53]

This doctrine of implied external powers was confirmed in *Opinion 1/76*.[54] However, its ultimate triumph would be celebrated in *Opinion 2/91*.[55] The European Court had been requested to give an opinion on the conclusion of Convention No. 170 of the International Labour Organization. The Court's brief syllogistic reasoning was as follows: the field covered by the relevant Convention fell within the Union's internal competence, "[c]onsequently", the adoption of Convention No. 170 "falls

---

[52] *Ibid.*, paras. 15–16 and 23–7.

[53] In the words of the *ERTA* Court: "With regard to the implementation of the Treaty the system of internal Community measures may not therefore be separated from that of external relations" (*ibid.*, para. 19).

[54] Opinion 1/76 (*Laying-up Fund*), [1977] ECR 741.

[55] Opinion 2/91 (*ILO Convention No. 170*) [1993] ECR I-1061.

within the [Union's] area of [external] competence".[56] From the very fact that the Union has an internal power – in this case the competence to adopt social provisions – the Court implied an external power to conclude international treaties for all matters falling within the scope of the Union's internal competence. The reasoning of the Court was based on the idea of a parallel treaty-making power running alongside internal legislative power. The European Court here confirmed a doctrine according to which "treaty power is coextensive with its internal domestic powers", and which thus "cuts across all areas of its internal domestic competence".[57]

The Lisbon Treaty has tried to codify the implied powers doctrine in Article 216 TFEU.[58] The provision states:

The Union may conclude an agreement with one or more third countries or international organizations where the Treaties so provide or where the conclusion of an agreement is necessary in order to achieve, within the framework of the Union's policies, one of the objectives referred to in the Treaties, or is provided for in a legally binding Union act or is likely to affect common rules or alter their scope.[59]

While recognizing the express treaty-making competences of the Union elsewhere conferred by the Treaties, the provision grants the Union a residual competence to conclude international agreements in three situations.

The first alternative mentioned in Article 216 confers a treaty power to the Union "where the conclusion of an agreement is necessary in order to achieve, within the framework of the Union's policies, one of the objectives referred to in the Treaties". This formulation is – strikingly – similar to the one found in the Union's general competence in Article 352. And if the Court decides to confirm this parallelism, the Union will have a residual competence to conclude international agreements that cuts across the jurisdictional scope of the entire Treaty on the Functioning of the Union.[60] This competence

---

[56] *Ibid.*, paras. 15–17.

[57] E. Stein, "External Relations of the European Community: Structure and Process" in *Collected Courses of the Academy of European Law* (The Hague: Martinus Nijhoff, 1990), vol. I-1, 115 at 146.

[58] See European Convention, Final Report Working Group VII – External Action (CONV 459/ 02), para. 18: "The Group saw merit in making explicit the jurisprudence of the Court[.]"

[59] Article 216 (1) TFEU.

[60] It is true that Article 216 TFEU – unlike Article 352 TFEU – has no fourth paragraph excluding its use "for attaining objectives pertaining to the Common Foreign and Security Policy". The problem therefore has been raised whether Article 216 is even wider than Article 352 in that it may also be used to pursue a CFSP objective (see M. Cremona, "External

would even be wider than the judicial doctrine of parallel external powers. For past doctrine insisted that an implied external competence derived from an internal *competence* – and thus did not confer a treaty power to pursue any internal *objective*.[61] Yet the first alternative in Article 216 textually disconnects the Union's external competences from its internal competences. The latter might therefore no longer represent a constitutional limit to the Union's treaty powers.

Regardless of what the Court will eventually make of this first alternative, Article 216 mentions two additional situations. The Union will also be entitled to conclude international agreements, where this "is provided for in a legally binding act or is likely to affect common rules or alter their scope". Both alternatives make the existence of an external competence dependent on the existence of secondary Union law. Two objections may be launched against this view. Theoretically, it is difficult to accept that the Union can expand its competences without Treaty amendment through the simple adoption of internal Union acts. Practically, it is hard to see how either alternative will ever go beyond the first alternative.[62] And in any event, as we shall see below, it is likely that alternatives two and three were the result of a fundamental confusion within the Constitutional Convention drafting the text behind Article 216 TFEU.

Relations and External Competence of the European Union: the Emergence of an Integrated Policy" in P. Craig and G. de Búrca, *The Evolution of EU Law* (Oxford University Press, 2011), 217 at 226). However, even in the absence of an express limitation, Article 40 TEU should – in theory – operate as an implied limitation to the scope of Article 216 (1) TFEU.

[61] The classic doctrine of implied external powers, as defined in *Opinion 1/76*, thus stated that "whenever [European] law has created for the institutions of the [Union] *powers* within its internal system for the purposes of attaining a specific objective, the [Union] has authority to enter into the international commitments necessary for the attainment of that objective even in the absence of an express provision in that connexion" (Opinion 1/ 76 (*Laying-up Fund*), [1977] ECR 741, para. 3 – emphasis added). And to make it even clearer, the Court went on to state that the external powers flowed "by implication from the provisions of the Treaty creating the internal *power*" (*ibid.*, para. 4 – emphasis added).

[62] In any event, the existence of the first alternative next to the second alternative should now – finally – put to rest the idea that the existence of (implied) treaty power depends on the existence of internal legislation. For a long time, however, the European Court was undecided whether implied external powers were automatically implied from internal powers; or, whether they were contingent on the actual exercise of these internal powers through the adoption of internal legislation. The better view had always insisted on parallel external powers running alongside the (Union's) internal powers without regard to European legislation (see E. Stein, "External Relations of the European Community: Structure and Process" (supra n. 57) at 146).

4. The categories of Union competences

Different types of competences constitutionally pitch the *relative degree of responsibility* of public authorities within a material policy field. The respective differences are thus of a relational kind: exclusive competences "exclude" the other authority from acting within the same policy area, while non-exclusive competences permit the co-existence of two legislators. Importantly, in order to provide a clear picture of the federal division of powers, each policy area should ideally correspond to one competence category.

What then are the competence categories developed in the European legal order? The distinction between exclusive and non-exclusive competences had emerged early on.[63] The Treaties today distinguish between various categories of Union competence in Article 2 TFEU. The provision reads as follows:

1. When the Treaties confer on the Union exclusive competence in a specific area, only the Union may legislate and adopt legally binding acts, the Member States being able to do so themselves only if so empowered by the Union or for the implementation of Union acts.

2. When the Treaties confer on the Union a competence shared with the Member States in a specific area, the Union and the Member States may legislate and adopt legally binding acts in that area. The Member States shall exercise their competence to the extent that the Union has not exercised its competence. The Member States shall again exercise their competence to the extent that the Union has decided to cease exercising its competence.

3. The Member States shall coordinate their economic and employment policies within arrangements as determined by this Treaty, which the Union shall have competence to provide.

4. The Union shall have competence, in accordance with the provisions of the Treaty on European Union, to define and implement a common foreign and security policy, including the progressive framing of a common defence policy.

5. In certain areas and under the conditions laid down in the Treaties, the Union shall have competence to carry out actions to support, coordinate or supplement

---

[63] See R. Schütze, "Dual Federalism Constitutionalised: The Emergence of Exclusive Competences in the EC Legal Order", 32 (2007) *European Law Review*, 3.

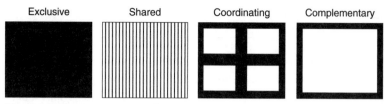

Figure 3.2 Competence categories

the actions of the Member States, without thereby superseding their competence in these areas. Legally binding acts of the Union adopted on the basis of the provisions of the Treaties relating to these areas shall not entail harmonization of Member States' laws or regulations.

Outside the Common Foreign and Security Policy,[64] the Treaties thus expressly recognize four general competence categories: exclusive competences, shared competences, coordinating competences, and complementary competences. And Articles 3 to 6 TFEU correlate the various Union policies to a particular competence category.

Let us look at each competence category in turn.

(a) Exclusive competences: Article 3

Exclusive powers are constitutionally guaranteed monopolies. Only one governmental level is entitled to act autonomously. Exclusive competences are thus double-edged provisions. Their positive side entitles one authority to act, while their negative side 'excludes' anybody else from acting autonomously within its scope. For the European legal order, exclusive competences are defined as areas in which "only the Union may legislate and adopt legally binding acts". The Member States will only be enabled to act "if so empowered by the Union or for the implementation of Union acts".[65]

What are the policy areas of constitutional exclusivity? In the past, the Court has accepted a number of competences to qualify under this type. The first exclusive competence was discovered in the context of the Common

---

[64] For an analysis of this sui generis category, see R. Schütze, *European Constitutional Law* (Cambridge University Press, 2012), Chapter 6 – Section 2(a).
[65] Article 2(1) TFEU.

Commercial Policy (CCP). In *Opinion 1/75,*[66] the Court found that the existence of a merely shared competence within the field would "compromise[] the effective defence of the common interests of the [Union]".[67] A second area of exclusive competence was soon discovered in relation to the conservation of biological resources of the sea. In *Commission* v. *United Kingdom,*[68] the Court found that Member States would be "no longer entitled to exercise any power of their own in the matter of conservation measures in the waters under their jurisdiction".[69] Article 3 (1) TFEU now expressly mentions five policy areas: (a) the customs union; (b) the establishment of the competition rules necessary for the functioning of the internal market; (c) monetary policy for the Member States whose currency is the euro; (d) the conservation of marine biological resources under the common fisheries policy; and (e) the common commercial policy. In light of the judicial status quo, this enumeration poses some definitional problems.[70]

Much greater constitutional confusion is however created by Article 3(2) TFEU which states:

The Union shall also have exclusive competence for the conclusion of an international agreement when its conclusion is provided for in a legislative act of the Union or is necessary to enable the Union to exercise its internal competence, or in so far as its conclusion may affect common rules or alter their scope.

In addition to the constitutionally fixed exclusive competences – mentioned in Article 3 (1) – the Union legal order thus acknowledges the possibility of a *dynamic* growth of its exclusive competences in the external sphere. According to Article 3 (2), the Union may subsequently obtain exclusive treaty-making power, where one of three situations is fulfilled. These three situations are said to codify three famous judicial doctrines. These doctrines were developed in the jurisprudence of the European Court prior to the Lisbon Treaty.[71]

According to the first situation, the Union will obtain a subsequently exclusive treaty-making power when the conclusion of an international agreement "is provided for in a legislative act". This formulation

---

[66] Opinion 1/75 (*Draft Understanding on a Local Cost Standard*), [1975] ECR 1355.
[67] *Ibid.*, para. 13.   [68] *Commission* v. *United Kingdom,* Case 804/79, [1981] ECR 1045.
[69] *Ibid.*, para. 18.   [70] See Schütze, "Dual Federalism Constitutionalised" (supra n. 63).
[71] On the three judicial doctrines, see Schütze, "Parallel External Powers" (supra n. 46).

corresponds to the "WTO Doctrine". In *Opinion 1/94* on the compatibility of the WTO Agreement with the Treaties,[72] the Court had indeed stated: "[w]henever the [Union] has concluded in its internal legislative acts provisions relating to the treatment of nationals of non-member countries or expressly conferred on the institutions powers to negotiate with non-member countries, it acquires exclusive external competence in the spheres covered by those acts".[73] Article 3 (2) codifies this judicial doctrine. However, the codification is more restrictive, as it excludes the first alternative ("provisions relating to the treatment of nationals of non-member countries") from its scope.

The second situation mentioned in Article 3 (2) grants the Union an exclusive treaty power, where this "is necessary to enable the Union to exercise its internal competence". This formulation appears to codify the "Opinion 1/76 Doctrine",[74] albeit in a much *less* restrictive form. In its jurisprudence the Court had confined this second line of subsequent exclusivity to situations "where the conclusion of an international agreement is necessary in order to achieve Treaty objectives *which cannot be attained by the adoption of autonomous rules*",[75] and where the achievement of an internal objective is "inextricably linked" with the external sphere.[76] None of these restrictions can be found in Article 3 (2). And in its unqualified openness, the second situation comes close to the wording of the Union's "residual" legislative competence: Article 352 TFEU. The almost identical wording of Article 3 (2) and Article 216 TFEU moreover suggests that "implied shared competence would disappear"; yet, this would be "a wholly undesirable departure from the case law".[77]

Finally, the third situation in Article 3 (2) appears to refer to the Court's "ERTA doctrine". Under the *ERTA* doctrine,[78] the Member States are deprived of their treaty-making power to the extent that their exercise affects internal European law. Each time the Union "adopts provisions

[72] Opinion 1/94 (*WTO Agreement*), [1994] ECR I-5267.   [73] *Ibid.*, para. 95.

[74] Opinion 1/76 (*Laying-Up Fund*), [1977] ECR 741. On the evolution of the "Opinion 1/76 Doctrine", see Schütze, "Parallel External Powers" (supra n. 46), 250 et seq.

[75] Opinion 2/92 (*Third Revised Decision of the OECD on National Treatment*), [1995] ECR I-521, Part V – para. 4 (emphasis added).

[76] *Commission* v. *Germany* (*Open Skies*), Case C-476/98, [2002] ECR I-9855, para. 87.

[77] M. Cremona, "A Constitutional Basis for Effective External Action? An Assessment of the Provisions on EU External Action in the Constitutional Treaty", EUI Working Paper 2006/30, 10.

[78] *Commission* v. *Council (ERTA)* (supra n. 47).

laying down common rules, whatever form these may take, the Member States no longer have the right, acting individually or even collectively, to undertake obligations with third countries *which affect those rules*".[79] The principle behind *ERTA* is to prevent an international agreement concluded by the Member States from undermining "the uniform and consistent application of the [Union] rules and the proper functioning of the system which they establish".[80] Has Article 3 (2) properly codified this third judicial line of subsequently exclusive powers? The third alternative in Article 3 (2) – strangely – breaks the link between a *Member State* agreement and internal European law, and replaces it with an analysis of the effect of a *Union* agreement on European rules. This simply must be an "editorial mistake" on the part of the Treaty-makers, and it is hoped that the Court will correct this as soon as possible.

(b) Shared competences: Article 4

Shared competences are the "ordinary" competences of the European Union. Unless the Treaties expressly provide otherwise, a Union competence will be shared.[81]

Within a shared competence, "the Union and the Member States may legislate".[82] However, according to the formulation in Article 2 (2) TFEU both appear to be prohibited from acting at the same time: "[t]he Member States shall exercise their competence to the extent that the Union has not exercised its competence". This formulation invokes the geometrical image of a divided field: the Member States may only legislate in that part which the European Union has not (yet) entered. Within one field, *either* the European Union *or* the Member States can exercise their shared competence.[83]

When viewed against the constitutional status quo ante, this is a mystifying conception of shared competences. For in the past fifty years, shared

---

[79] *Ibid.*, para. 18 (emphasis added).

[80] Opinion 1/03 (*Lugano Convention*), [2006] ECR I-1145, para. 133.

[81] Article 4 TFEU states that EU competences will be shared "where the Treaties confer on it a competence which does not relate to the areas referred to in Articles 3 and 6", that is: areas of exclusive or complementary EU competence.

[82] Article 2 (2) TFEU.

[83] The Union may, however, decide to "cease exercising its competence". This re-opening of legislative space arises "when the relevant EU institutions decide to repeal a legislative act, in particular better to ensure constant respect for the principles of subsidiarity and proportionality". See Declaration (No. 18) "In Relation to the Delimitation of Competences".

competences allowed the Union and the Member States to act in the same field at the same time. The (exceptional) exception to that rule concerned situations where the Union field preempted the Member States.[84] The formulation in Article 2(2) TFEU is – sadly – based on that exception. It appears to demand "automatic [field] pre-emption of Member State action where the Union has exercised its power".[85] Will the technique of European minimum harmonization – allowing for higher national standards – thus be in danger? This seems doubtful, since the Treaties expressly identify minimum harmonization competences as shared competences.[86]

This preemption problem is not the only textual problem. For Article 4 TFEU recognizes a special type of shared competence in paragraphs 3 and 4. Both paragraphs separate the policy areas of research, technological development and space, as well as development cooperation and humanitarian aid from the "normal" shared competences. What is so special about these areas? According to paragraphs 3 and 4, the "exercise of that competence shall not result in Member States being prevented from exercising theirs". But since that qualification actually undermines the very essence of what constitutes a "shared" competence, set out in Article 2(2) TFEU, these policy areas should never have been placed there. This special type of shared competence has been described as parallel competence.

(c) Coordinating competences: Article 5

Coordinating competences are defined in the third paragraph of Article 2 TFEU; and Article 5 TFEU places "economic policy", "employment policy" and "social policy" within this category. The inspiration for this third competence category was the absence of a political consensus in the European Convention. Whereas one group wished to place economic and employment coordination within the category of shared competences,

---

[84] On the various preemption types, see Schütze, *European Constitutional Law* (supra n. 64), Chapter 10 – Section 3.

[85] P. Craig, "Competence: Clarity, Conferral, Containment and Consideration", 29 (2004) *European Law Review* 323, 334. The Treaties, however, clarify that such field preemption would "only" be in relation to the legislative act at (see Protocol (No. 25) "On the Exercise of Shared Competence": "With reference to Article 2 of the Treaty on the Functioning of the European Union on shared competence, when the Union has taken action in a certain area, the scope of this exercise of competence only covers those elements governed by the Union act in question and therefore does not cover the whole [competence] area.")

[86] See Article 4 (2) (e) TFEU on the shared "environment" competence.

an opposing view advocated their classification as complementary competence. The Presidium thus came to feel that "the specific nature of the coordination of Member States' economic and employment policies merits a separate provision".[87]

The constitutional character of coordinating competences remains largely undefined. From Articles 2 and 5 TFEU, we may solely deduce that the European Union has a competence to provide "arrangements" for the Member States to exercise their competences in a coordinated manner. The Union's coordination effort may include the adoption of "guidelines" and "initiatives to ensure coordination". It has been argued that the political genesis for this competence category should place it, on the normative spectrum, between shared and complementary competences.[88] If this systematic interpretation is accepted, coordinating competences would have to be normatively stronger than complementary competences. This would imply that the adoption of Union acts resulting in *some* degree of harmonization would be constitutionally permitted under these competences.

(d) Complementary competences: Article 6

The term "complementary competence" is not used in Article 2 (5) TFEU. However, it appears to be the best way generically to refer to "actions to support, coordinate or supplement the actions of the Member States".[89] Article 6 TFEU lists seven areas: the protection and improvement of human health; industry; culture; tourism; education, vocational training, youth, and sport; civil protection; and administrative co-operation. Is this an exhaustive list? This should be the case in the light of the residual character of shared competences.

The contours of this competence type are – again – largely unexplored by jurisprudence. However, after the Lisbon reform, it appears to be a defining characteristic of complementary competences that they do "not entail harmonization of Member States' laws or regulations".[90] But what exactly is the prohibition of "harmonization" supposed to mean? Two views can be

---

[87] The Presidium CONV 724/03 (Annex 2), 68. Arguably, the addition of a new competence type was unnecessary in the light of Article 2(6) TFEU. That provision states: "The scope of and arrangements for exercising the Union's competences shall be determined by the provisions of the Treaties relating to each area."

[88] See in this sense, Craig, "Competence" (supra n. 85), 338.   [89] Article 2 (5) TFEU.

[90] Article 2 (5) TFEU – second indent.

put forward. According to the first, the exclusion of harmonization means that Union legislation must not modify *existing* national legislation. However, considering the wide definition given to the concept of "harmonization" by the Court of Justice in *Spain* v. *Council*, any legislative intervention on the part of the Union will unfold a de facto harmonizing effect within the national legal orders.[91] From this strict reading, the exclusion of harmonization would consequently deny all pre-emptive effect to European legislation.[92] A second, less restrictive, view argues that the Union's legislative powers are only trimmed so as to prevent the de jure harmonization of national legislation.[93]

---

[91] *Spain* v. *Council*, Case C-350/92, [1995] ECR I-1985. In that judgment, the Court found the adoption of a Regulation not beyond the scope of Article [114 TFEU] because it aimed "to prevent the heterogeneous development of national laws leading to further disparities" in the internal market (*ibid.*, para. 35). The case was discussed in Section 2 (a) above.

[92] See A. Bardenhewer-Rating and F. Niggermeier, "Artikel 152", para. 20, in H. von der Groeben and J. Schwarze, *Kommentar zum Vertrag über die EU* (Nomos, 2003).

[93] For K. Lenaerts "incentive measures can be adopted in the form of Regulations, Directives, Decisions or atypical legal acts and are thus normal legislative acts of the [Union]". "[T]he fact that a [European] incentive measure may have the indirect effect of harmonizing ... does not necessarily mean that it conflicts with the prohibition on harmonization" (K. Lenaerts, "Subsidiarity and Community Competence in the Field of Education", 1 (1994–1995) *Columbia Journal of European Law*, 1 at 13 and 15).

Fundamental rights 4

Introduction

The protection of human rights is a central task of many modern constitutions.[1] This protective task is principally transferred onto the judiciary and involves the judicial review of governmental action.[2] The protection of human rights may be limited to judicial review of the executive.[3] But in its expansive form, it extends to the review of parliamentary legislation. And where this is the case, human rights will set "substantive" limits within which democratic government must take place.[4]

---

[1] On human rights as constitutional rights, see A. Sajó, *Limiting Government* (Central European University Press, 1999), Chapter 8.

[2] See M. Cappelletti, *Judicial Review in the Contemporary World* (Bobbs-Merrill, 1971).

[3] For the classic doctrine of parliamentary sovereignty in the United Kingdom, see A. V. Dicey, *Introduction to the Study of the Law of the Constitution* (Liberty Fund, 1982).

[4] On the idea of human rights as "outside" majoritarian (democratic) politics, see Sajó, *Limiting Government* (supra n. 1), Chapter 2, esp. 57 et seq.

The European Union follows this second constitutional tradition.[5] It considers itself to be "founded on the values of respect for human dignity, freedom, democracy, equality, the rule of law and respect for human rights".[6] Human rights are thus given a "foundational" place in the Union. They are – literally – "fundamental" rights, which constitutionally limit the exercise of all Union competences.

What are the sources of human rights in the Union legal order? While there was no "Bill of Rights" in the original Treaties, three sources for European fundamental rights were subsequently developed. The European Court first began distilling general principles protecting fundamental rights from the constitutional traditions of the Member States. This *unwritten* bill of rights was inspired and informed by a second bill of rights: the European Convention on Human Rights. This *external* bill of rights was, decades later, matched by a *written* bill of rights specifically for the European Union: the Charter of Fundamental Rights. These three sources of European human rights are now expressly referred to – in reverse order –in Article 6 of the Treaty on European Union:

1. The Union recognises the rights, freedoms and principles set out in the Charter of Fundamental Rights of the European Union of 7 December 2000, as adapted at Strasbourg, on 12 December 2007, which shall have the same legal value as the Treaties . . .
2. The Union shall accede to the European Convention for the Protection of Human Rights and Fundamental Freedoms. Such accession shall not affect the Union's competences as defined in the Treaties.
3. Fundamental rights, as guaranteed by the European Convention for the Protection of Human Rights and Fundamental Freedoms and as they result from the constitutional traditions common to the Member States, shall constitute general principles of the Union's law.

What is the nature and effect of each source of fundamental rights? And to what extent will they limit the Union? This Chapter investigates the three bills of rights of the Union. Section 1 starts with the discovery of an "unwritten" bill of rights in the form of general principles of European

---

[5] On this point, see *Parti Écologiste "Les Verts"* v. *European Parliament*, Case 294/83 [1986] ECR 1339, para. 23: "a [Union] based on the rule of law, inasmuch as neither its Member States nor its institutions can avoid a review of the question whether the measures adopted by them are in conformity with the basic constitutional charter, the Treaty". For an extensive discussion of judicial review in the Union legal order, see Chapter 8 – Section 3.

[6] Article 2 (1) TEU.

law. Section 2 subsequently discusses possible structural limits to European human rights in the form of international obligations flowing from the United Nations Charter. Section 3 analyses the Union's "written" bill of rights in the form of its Charter of Fundamental Rights. Finally, Section 4 explores the European Convention on Human Rights as an external bill of rights for the European Union.

1. The birth of European fundamental rights

Originally, the European Treaties contained no express reference to human rights.[7] Nor did the birth of European fundamental rights happen overnight. The Court had been invited – as long ago as 1958 – to review the constitutionality of a European act in light of fundamental rights. In *Stork*,[8] the applicant challenged a European decision on the ground that the Commission had infringed *German* fundamental rights. In the absence of a European bill of rights, this claim drew on the so-called "mortgage theory". According to this theory, the powers conferred on the European Union were tied to a human rights "mortgage". *National* fundamental rights would bind the *European* Union, since the Member States could not have created an organization with more powers than themselves.[9] This argument was – correctly[10] – rejected by the Court. The task of the European institutions was to apply European laws "without regard for their validity under national law".[11] National fundamental rights could be *no direct* source of European human rights.

---

[7] For speculations on the historical reasons for this absence, see P. Pescatore, "The Context and Significance of Fundamental Rights in the Law of the European Communities", 2 (1981) *Human Rights Journal*, 295; as well as M. A. Dauses, "The Protection of Fundamental Rights in the Community Legal Order", 10 (1985), *European Law Review*, 399. For a new look at the historical material, see also G. de Búrca "The Evolution of EU Human Rights Law" in P. Craig and G. de Búrca (eds.), *The Evolution of EU Law* (Oxford University Press, 2011), 465.

[8] *Stork & Cie* v. *High Authority of the European Coal and Steel Community*, Case 1/58, [1958] ECR (English Special Edition) 17.

[9] In Latin the legal proverb is clear: "Nemo dat quod non habet".

[10] For a criticism of the "mortgage theory", see H. G. Schermers, "The European Communities Bound by Fundamental Rights", 27 (1980) *Common Market Law Review*, 249 at 251; as well as R. Schütze, "EC Law and International Agreements of the Member States – An Ambivalent Relationship?", 9 (2006–07) *Cambridge Yearbook of European Legal Studies*, 387 at 399–402.

[11] *Stork* v. *High Authority*, Case 1/58 (supra n. 8), 26: "Under Article 8 of the [ECSC] Treaty the [Commission] is only required to apply Community law. It is not competent to apply the national law of the Member States. Similarly, under Article 31 the Court is only required to ensure that in the interpretation and application of the Treaty, and of rules laid down for implementation thereof, the law is observed. It is not normally required to rule on provisions

This position of the European Union towards national fundamental rights never changed. However, the Court's view evolved with regard to the existence of implied *European* fundamental rights. Having originally found that European law did "not contain any general principle, *express or otherwise*, guaranteeing the maintenance of vested rights",[12] the Court subsequently discovered "fundamental human rights enshrined in the general principles of [European] law".[13]

This new position was spelled out in *Internationale Handelsgesellschaft*.[14] The Court here – again – rejected the applicability of national fundamental rights to European law. But the judgment now confirmed the existence of an "analogous guarantee inherent in [European] law".[15] Accordingly, "respect for fundamental rights forms an integral part of the general principles of law protected by the Court of Justice".[16] Whence did the Court derive these fundamental rights? The famous answer was that the Union's (unwritten) bill of rights would be "*inspired* by the constitutional traditions *common* to the Member States".[17] While thus not a direct source, national constitutional rights constituted an *indirect* source for the Union's fundamental rights.

What was the nature of this indirect relationship between national rights and European rights? How would the former influence the latter? A constitutional clarification was offered in *Nold*.[18] Drawing on its previous jurisprudence, the Court held:

[F]undamental rights form an integral part of the general principles of law, the observance of which it ensures. In safeguarding these rights, the Court is bound to draw *inspiration* from constitutional traditions common to the Member States, and it cannot therefore uphold measures which are incompatible with fundamental rights recognized and protected by the constitutions of those States. Similarly, international treaties for the protection of human rights on which the Member States have

---

of national law. Consequently, the [Commission] is not empowered to examine a ground of complaint which maintains that, when it adopted its decision, it infringed principles of German constitutional law (in particular Articles 2 and 12 of the Basic Law)." And see also *Geitling Ruhrkohlen-Verkaufsgesellschaft mbH, Mausegatt Ruhrkohlen-Verkaufsgesellschaft mbH and I. Nold KG v. High Authority of the European Coal and Steel Community*, Joined Cases 36, 37, 38/59 and 40/59, [1959] ECR (English Special Edition) 423.

[12] *Ibid.*, 439 (emphasis added).

[13] *Stauder* v. *City of Ulm*, Case 29/69, [1969] ECR 419, para. 7.

[14] *Internationale Handelsgesellschaft mbH* v *Einfuhr- und Vorratsstelle für Getreide und Futtermittel*, Case 11/70, [1979] ECR 1125.

[15] *Ibid.*, para. 4.   [16] *Ibid.*   [17] *Ibid.* (emphasis added).

[18] *Nold* v. *Commission*, Case 4/73, [1974] ECR 491.

collaborated or of which they are signatories, can supply *guidelines* which should be followed within the framework of [European] law.[19]

In searching for fundamental rights inside the general principles of European law, the Court would thus draw "inspiration" from the common constitutional traditions of the Member States. One – ingenious – way of identifying a common "agreement" between the various national constitutional traditions was to use international *agreements* of the Member States. And one such international agreement was the European Convention on Human Rights. Having been ratified by all Member States and dealing specially with human rights,[20] the Convention would soon assume a "particular significance" in identifying fundamental rights for the European Union.[21] And yet none of this conclusively characterized the legal relationship between European human rights, national human rights and the European Convention on Human Rights.

Let us therefore look at the question of the Union human rights standard first, before analysing the constitutional doctrines on limits to European human rights.

(a) The European standard – an "autonomous" standard

Human rights express, together with the institutional structures of a polity, the fundamental values of a society. Each society may wish to protect distinct values and give them a distinct level of protection.[22] Not all

---

[19] *Ibid.*, para. 13 (emphasis added).

[20] When the EC Treaty entered into force on 1 January 1958, five of its Member States were already parties to the European Convention for the Protection of Human Rights and Fundamental Freedoms, signed in Rome on 4 November 1950. Ever since France joined the Convention system in 1974, all EC Member States have also been members of the European Convention legal order. For an early reference to the Convention in the jurisprudence of the Court, see *Rutili* v. *Ministre de l'intérieur*, Case 36/75, [1975] ECR 1219, para. 32.

[21] See *Höchst* v. *Commission*, Joined Cases 46/87 and 227/88, [1989] ECR 2859, para. 13: "The Court has consistently held that fundamental rights are an integral part of the general principles of law the observance of which the Court ensures, in accordance with constitutional traditions common to the Member States, and the international treaties on which the Member States have collaborated or of which they are signatories. The European Convention for the Protection of Human Rights and Fundamental Freedoms of 4 November 1950 (hereinafter referred to as 'the European Convention on Human Rights') is of particular significance in that regard."

[22] "Constitutions are not mere copies of a universalist ideal, they also reflect the idiosyncratic choices and preferences of the constituents and are the highest legal expression of the country's value system." See B. de Witte, "Community Law and National Constitutional Values", 2 (1991/2) *Legal Issues of Economic Integration*, 1 at 7.

societies may thus choose to protect a constitutional "right to work",[23] while most liberal societies will protect "liberty"; yet, the level at which liberty is protected might vary.[24]

Which fundamental rights exist in the European Union, and what is their level of protection? From the very beginning, the Court of Justice was not completely free to invent an unwritten bill of rights. Instead, and in the words of the famous *Nold* passage, the Court was "*bound to* draw inspiration from constitutional traditions *common* to the Member States".[25] But how binding would that inspiration be? Could the Court discover human rights that not all Member States recognize as a national human right? And would the Court consider itself under the obligation to use a particular standard for a human right, where a right's "scope and the criteria for applying it vary"?[26]

The relationship between the European and the various national standards is not an easy one. Would the obligation to draw inspiration from the constitutional traditions *common* to the States imply a common *minimum* standard? Serious practical problems follow from this view. For if the European Union consistently adopted the lowest common denominator to assess the legality of its acts, it would run the risk of undermining its legitimacy. This would inevitably lead to charges that the European Court refuses to take human rights seriously. Should the Union thus favour the *maximum* standard among the Member States,[27] as "the most liberal interpretation must prevail"?[28] This time, there are serious theoretical problems with this view. For the maximalist approach assumes that courts always balance private rights against public interests. But this is not necessarily the case;[29] and, in

---

[23] Article 4 of the Italian Constitution states: "The Republic recognises the right of all citizens to work and promotes those conditions which render this right effective."

[24] To illustrate this point with a famous joke: "In Germany everything is forbidden, unless something is specifically allowed, whereas in Britain everything which is not specifically forbidden, is allowed." (The joke goes on to claim that: "In France everything is allowed, even if it is forbidden; and in Italy everything is allowed, especially when it is forbidden.")

[25] *Nold* (supra n. 18), para. 13 (emphasis added).

[26] *AM & S Europe Limited* v. *Commission*, Case 155/79, [1982] ECR 1575, para. 19.

[27] In favour of a maximalist approach, see L. Besselink, "Entrapped by the Maximum Standard: On Fundamental Rights, Pluralism and Subsidiarity in the European Union", 35 (1998) *Common Market Law Review*, 629.

[28] This "Dworkinian" language comes from Stauder (supra n. 13), para. 4.

[29] The Court of Justice was faced with such a right-right conflict in *Society for the Protection of Unborn Children Ireland Ltd* v. *Stephen Grogan and others*, Case C-159/90, [1991] ECR I-4685, but (in)famously refused to decide the case for lack of jurisdiction.

any event, the maximum standard is subject to a communitarian critique.[30] Worse: *both* the minimalist and the maximalist approach suffer from a fatal flaw: they subject the Union legal order "to the constitutional dictate of individual Member States",[31] and the Court has consequently rejected both approaches.[32]

What about the European Convention on Human Rights as a Union standard? The Convention has indeed developed into a standard that is (partly) independent from what the Court sees as the constitutional traditions of the Member States.[33] But what is the status of the Convention in the Union legal order? The relationship between the Union and the European Convention has remained ambivalent. The Court of Justice has not applied the "succession theory" to the ECHR – and that for good reasons.[34] And in implicitly rejecting the "succession theory", the European Court has never considered itself materially bound by the interpretation given to the Convention by the European Court of Human Rights. This interpretative freedom has created the possibility of a distinct *Union* standard.[35]

Have subsequent Treaty amendments transformed the indirect relationship between Union fundamental rights and the ECHR into a direct relationship? The argument had been made following the Maastricht Treaty. The (old) Article 6(2) EU expressly called on the Union to respect fundamental

---

[30] J. Weiler, "Fundamental Rights and Fundamental Boundaries: On Standards and Values in the Protection of Human Rights" in N. Neuwahl and A. Rosas (eds.), *The European Union and Human Rights* (Brill, 1995), 51 at 61: "If the ECJ were to adopt a maximalist approach this would simply mean that for the [Union] in each and every area the balance would be most restrictive on the public and general interest. A maximalist approach to human rights would result in a minimalist approach to [Union] government."

[31] *Ibid.*, 59.

[32] For the early (implicit) rejection of the minimalist approach, see *Hauer* v. *Land Rheinland-Pfalz*, Case 44/79, [1979] ECR 3727, para. 32 – suggesting that a fundamental right only needs to be protected in "*several* Member States" (emphasis added).

[33] For example: in *Hauer* (supra n. 32), the Court began by looking at the ECHR (paras. 17–19) and only after a finding that the Convention would not generate a sufficiently precise standard would the Court turn to the "constitutional rules and practices of the nine Member States" (paras. 20–1).

[34] On the succession theory, see Chapter 2 – Section 4(d) above.

[35] Yet it equally entailed the danger of diverging interpretations of the European Convention in Strasbourg and Luxembourg; see in particular: *Höchst AG* v. *Commission* (supra n. 21). For an excellent analysis see: R. Lawson, "Confusion and Conflict? Diverging Interpretations of the Europe Convention on Human Rights in Strasbourg and Luxembourg" in R. Lawson and M. de Blois (eds.), *The Dynamics of the Protection of the Rights in Europe* (Martinus Nijhoff, 1994), vol. III, 219 and esp. 234–50.

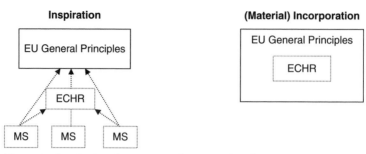

Figure 4.1 Inspiration theory versus incorporation theory

rights "as guaranteed by the European Convention for the Protection of Human Rights and Fundamental Freedoms". Some commentators consequently began to argue that "[t]he ECHR is now *formally* integrated into EC law".[36] More moderate voices limited the binding effect to its material de facto dimension.[37] However, neither view was accepted by the Court.[38] Yet the Lisbon amendments might have changed this overnight. Today, there are strong textual reasons for claiming that the European Convention is *materially* binding on the Union. For according to the (new) Article 6(3) TEU, fundamental rights as guaranteed by the Convention "shall constitute general principles of the Union's law". Will this formulation not mean that all Convention rights *are* general principles of Union law? If so, the Convention standard would henceforth provide a direct standard for the Union. But if this route were chosen, the Convention standard would – presumably – only provide a *minimum* standard for the Union's general principles.

In conclusion, the Union standard for the protection of fundamental rights is an *autonomous* standard. While drawing inspiration from the constitutional traditions common to the Member States and the European Convention on Human Rights, the Court of Justice has – so far – not

---

[36] L. B. Krogsgaard, "Fundamental Rights in the European Community after Maastricht", 19 (1993) *Legal Issues of European Economic Integration*, 99 at 108 (emphasis added).

[37] F. G. Jacobs, "European Community Law and the European Convention on Human Rights" in D. Curtin and T. Heukels (eds.), *Institutional Dynamics of European Integration* (Martinus Nijhoff, 1994), vol. II, 561 at 563 (emphasis added): "As a result of the development of the case-law, now confirmed by the Single European Act and the Treaty on European Union, the [Union] can be said to be subject *in effect* to, if not bound formally by, the European Convention on Human Rights."

[38] See *Schmidberger, Internationale Transporte und Planzüge* v. *Austria*, Case C–112/00, [2003] ECR I–5659.

considered itself directly bound by a particular national or international standard. The Court has thus been free to distil and protect what it sees as the shared values among the majority of people(s) within the Union and has thereby assisted – dialectically – in the establishment of a shared identity for the people(s) of Europe.[39]

(b) Limitations, and "limitations on limitations"

Within the European philosophical tradition, certain rights are absolute rights. They cannot – under any circumstances – be legitimately limited.[40] However, with the exception of the most fundamental of fundamental rights, human rights are *relative* rights that may be limited in accordance with the public interest. Private property may thus be taxed and individual freedom be restricted – *if* such actions are justified by the common good.

Nonetheless, liberal societies would cease to be liberal if they permitted unlimited limitations to human rights in pursuit of the public interest. Many legal orders consequently recognize limitations on public interest limitations. These "limitations on limitations" to fundamental rights can be relative or absolute in nature. According to the principle of proportionality, each restriction of a fundamental right must be "proportionate" in relation to the public interest pursued.[41] The principle of proportionality is thus a relative principle. It balances interests: the greater the public interest protected, the greater the right restrictions permitted. And in order to limit this relativist logic, a second principle may come into play. According to the "essential core" doctrine,[42] any limitation of human rights – even proportionate ones – must never undermine the "very substance" of a

---

[39] T. Tridimas, "Judicial Federalism and the European Court of Justice", in J. Fedtke and B. S. Markesinis (eds.), *Patterns of Federalism and Regionalism: Lessons for the UK* (Hart, 2006), 149 at 150 – referring to the contribution of the judicial process "to the emergence of a European *demos*".

[40] The European Court of Justice followed this tradition and recognized the existence of absolute rights in *Schmidberger* (supra n. 38, para. 80): "the right to life or the prohibition of torture and inhuman or degrading treatment or punishment, which admit of no restriction".

[41] *Hauer*, Case 44/79 (supra n. 32), para. 23. On the proportionality principle in the Union legal order, see Chapter 8 – Section 3 (b/ii) below.

[42] For the German constitutional order, see Article 19 (2) German Constitution: "The essence of a basic right must never be violated."

fundamental right. This sets an absolute limit to all governmental power by identifying an "untouchable" core.

Has the European legal order recognized limits to human rights? From the very beginning, the Court clarified that human rights are "far from constituting unfettered prerogatives",[43] and that they may thus be subject "to limitations laid down in accordance with the public interest".[44] Yet the Court equally recognized "limitations on limitations". Indeed, the principle of proportionality is almost omnipresent in the jurisprudence of the Court.[45]

By contrast, the existence of an "essential core" doctrine is still unclear. True, the Court has used formulations that come – very – close to the doctrine,[46] but its relationship to the proportionality principle has remained ambivalent.[47] The Court may however have recently confirmed the existence of the doctrine by recognizing an "untouchable" core of European citizenship rights in *Zambrano*.[48] Two Colombian parents had challenged the rejection of their Belgian residency permits on the ground that their children had been born in Belgium and thereby assumed Belgian and – thus – European citizenship.[49] The Court held that even if the Belgian measures were proportionate as such, they would "have the effect of

---

[43] *Nold* v. *Commission*, Case 4/73 (supra n. 18), para. 14 (emphasis added).   [44] *Ibid.*

[45] On the proportionality principle, see T. Tridimas, *The General Principles of EU Law* (Oxford University Press, 2007), Chapters 3–5.

[46] The European Courts appear to accept the doctrine implicitly; see e.g., *Nold* (supra n. 18, para. 14): "Within the [Union] legal order it likewise seems legitimate that these rights should, of necessity, be subject to certain limits justified by the overall objectives pursued by the [Union], on condition that the substance of these rights is left untouched"; as well as *Wachauf* v. *Bundesamt für Ernährung und Forstwirtschaft*, Case 5/88, [1989] ECR 2609, para. 18: "[R]estrictions may be imposed on the exercise of those rights, in particular in the context of a common organization of a market, provided that those restrictions in fact correspond to objectives of general interest pursued by the [Union] and do not constitute, with regard to the aim pursued, a disproportionate and intolerable interference, impairing the very substance of those rights."

[47] This point is made by P. Craig, *The Lisbon Treaty: Law, Politics, and Treaty Reform* (Oxford University Press, 2010), 224, who points out that the Court often merges the doctrine of proportionality and the "essential core" doctrine.

[48] *Zambrano* v *Office national de l'emploi*, Case C-34/09 (nyr). Admittedly, there are many questions that this – excessively – short case raises (see "Editorial: Seven Questions for Seven Paragraphs", 36 (2011) *European Law Review* 161). For a first analysis of this case, see K. Hailbronner and D. Thym, "Case Comment", 48 (2011) *Common Market Law Review*, 1253.

[49] According to Article 20 (1) TFEU: "Citizenship of the Union is hereby established. Every person holding the nationality of a Member State shall be a citizen of the Union. Citizenship of the Union shall be additional to and not replace national citizenship."

depriving citizens of the Union of the genuine enjoyment of the substance of the rights conferred by virtue of their status as citizens of the Union".[50]

2. United Nations law: external limits to European human rights?

The European legal order is a constitutional order based on the rule of law.[51] This implies that an individual, where legitimately concerned,[52] must be able to challenge the legality of a European act on the basis that his or her human rights have been violated. Should there be exceptions to this constitutional rule? This question is controversially debated in comparative constitutionalism.[53] And it has lately received much attention in a special form: will European fundamental rights be limited by international obligations flowing from the United Nations Charter?

The classic answer to this question was offered by *Bosphorus*.[54] The case dealt with a European regulation implementing the United Nations embargo against the Federal Republic of Yugoslavia.[55] Protesting that its fundamental right to property was violated, the plaintiff challenged the European legislation. And the Court had no qualms in judicially reviewing the European legislation – even if a lower review standard was applied.[56] The constitutional message behind the classic approach was clear: where the Member States decided to fulfil their international obligations

---

[50] *Zambrano* (supra n. 48), para. 42; and see also para. 44: "In those circumstances, those citizens of the Union would, as a result, be unable to exercise the substance of the rights conferred on them by virtue of their status as citizens of the Union."

[51] See *Parti Écologiste*, Case 294/83 (supra n. 5).

[52] On the judicial standing of private parties in the Union legal order, see Chapter 8 – Section 3 (c).

[53] For discussion of the idea of an "emergency constitution" in a comparative constitutional perspective, see C. L. Rossiter, *Constitutional Dictatorship: Crisis Government in the Modern Democracies* (Harcourt, Brace & World, 1963).

[54] *Bosphorus Hava Yollari Turizm ve Ticaret AS* v. *Minister for Transport, Energy and Communications and others*, Case C-84/95, [1996] ECR I-3953.

[55] Council Regulation (EEC) No. 990/93 of 26 April 1993 concerning trade between the European Economic Community and the Federal Republic of Yugoslavia (Serbia and Montenegro) (OJ 1993 L102, 14) was based on UN Security Council Resolution 820 (1993).

[56] For a critique of the standard of review, see I. Canor, "'Can Two Walk Together, Except They Be Agreed?' The Relationship between International Law and European Law : The Incorporation of United Nations Sanctions against Yugoslavia into European Community Law through the Perspective of the European Court of Justice", 35 (1998) *Common Market Law Review*, 137 at 162.

under the United Nations *qua* European law, they would have to comply with the constitutional principles of the Union legal order, and in particular: European human rights.

This classic approach was challenged by the General Court in *Kadi*.[57] The applicant was a suspected Taliban terrorist, whose financial assets had been frozen as a result of European legislation that reproduced United Nations Security Council Resolutions.[58] Kadi claimed that his fundamental rights of due process and property had been violated. The Union organs intervened in the proceedings and argued – to the surprise of many – that "the Charter of the United Nations prevail[s] over every other obligation of international, [European] or domestic law" with the effect that European human rights should be inoperative.[59] To the even greater surprise – if not shock – of European constitutional scholars,[60] the General Court accepted this argument. How did the Court come to this conclusion? It had recourse to a version of the "succession doctrine",[61] according to which the Union may be bound by the international obligations of its Member States.[62] While this conclusion was in itself highly controversial, the dangerous part of the judgment related to the consequences of that conclusion. For the General Court recognized "structural limits, imposed by general international law" on the judicial review powers of the European Court.[63] In the words of the Court:

Any review of the internal lawfulness of the contested regulation, especially having regard to the provisions or general principles of [European] law relating to the protection of fundamental rights, would therefore imply that the Court is to consider, indirectly, the lawfulness of those [United Nations] resolutions. In that hypothetical

---

[57] *Kadi* v. *Council and Commission*, Case T-315/01, [2005] ECR II-3649.

[58] The challenge principally concerned Council Regulation (EC) 881/2002 imposing certain specific restrictive measures directed against certain persons and entities associated with Osama bin Laden, the Al-Qaeda network and the Taliban, and repealing Regulation 467/2001, [2002] OJ L139/9. The Regulation aimed to implement UN Security Council Resolution 1390 (2002) laying down the measures to be directed against Osama bin Laden, members of the Al-Qaeda network and the Taliban and other associated individuals, groups, undertakings, and entities.

[59] *Kadi*, Case T-315/01 (supra n. 57), paras. 156 and 177.

[60] P. Eeckhout, *Does Europe's Constitution Stop at the Water's Edge? Law and Policy in the EU's External Relations* (Europa Law Publishing, 2005); as well as R. Schütze, "On 'Middle Ground': The European Community and Public International Law", *EUI Working Paper* 2007/13.

[61] *Kadi*, Case T-315/01 (supra n. 57), paras. 193 et seq.

[62] On the doctrine, see Chapter 2 – Section 4(d) above.

[63] *Kadi*, Case T-315/01 (supra n. 57), para. 212.

situation, in fact, the origin of the illegality alleged by the applicant would have to be sought, not in the adoption of the contested regulation but in the resolutions of the Security Council which imposed the sanctions. In particular, if the Court were to annul the contested regulation, as the applicant claims it should, although that regulation seems to be imposed by international law, on the ground that that act infringes his fundamental rights which are protected by the [Union] legal order, such annulment would indirectly mean that the resolutions of the Security Council concerned themselves infringe those fundamental rights.[64]

The General Court thus declined jurisdiction to directly review European legislation *because it would entail an indirect review of the United Nations resolutions.* The justification for this self-abdication was that United Nations law was binding on all Union institutions, including the European Courts.

From a constitutional perspective, this reasoning was prisoner to a number of serious mistakes.[65] And in its appeal judgment,[66] the Court of Justice remedied these constitutional blunders and safely returned to the traditional *Bosphorus* approach. The Court held:

[T]he obligations imposed by an international agreement cannot have the effect of prejudicing the constitutional principles of the [European Treaties], which include the principle that all [Union] acts must respect fundamental rights, that respect constituting a condition of their lawfulness which it is for the Court to review in the framework of the complete system of legal remedies established by the Treat[ies].[67]

The United Nations Charter, while having special importance within the European legal order,[68] would – in this respect – not be different from other international agreements.[69] Like "ordinary" international agreements, the United Nations Charter might – if materially binding – have primacy over

---

[64] *Ibid.*, paras. 215–16 (references omitted).

[65] First, even if one assumes that the Union succeeded the Member States and was thus bound by United Nations law, the hierarchical status of international agreements is *below* the European Treaties. It would thus be European human rights that limit international agreements – not the other way around. The Court's position was based on a second mistake: the General Court believed the United Nations Charter prevails over every international and domestic obligation (*ibid.*, para. 181). But this is simply wrong with regard to the "domestic law" part. The United Nations has never claimed "supremacy" within domestic legal orders, and after the constitutionalization of the European Union legal order, the latter now constitutes such a "domestic" legal order vis-à-vis international law.

[66] *Kadi and Al Barakaat International Foundation* v. *Council and Commission*, Case C-402/05P, [2008] ECR I-6351.

[67] *Ibid.*, para. 285.   [68] *Ibid.*, para. 294 ("special importance").   [69] *Ibid.*, para. 300.

European legislation but "[t]hat primacy at the level of [European] law would not, however, extend to primary law, in particular to the general principles of which fundamental rights form part".[70] European human rights would thus *not* find an external structural limit in the international obligations stemming from the United Nations.[71] The Union was firmly based on the rule of law, and this meant that all European legislation – regardless of its "domestic" or international origin – would be limited by the respect for fundamental human rights.[72]

3. The Charter of Fundamental Rights

The desire for a *written* bill of rights for the European Union first expressed itself in arguments favouring accession to the European Convention on Human Rights.[73] Yet an alternative strategy became prominent in the late twentieth century: the Union's own bill of rights. The initiative for a "Charter of Fundamental Rights" came from the European Council, which transferred the drafting mandate to a "European Convention".[74] The idea behind an internal codification was to strengthen the protection of fundamental rights in Europe "by making those rights more visible in a Charter".[75] The Charter was proclaimed in 2000, but it was *not* legally binding. Its status was similar to the European Convention on Human Rights: it provided a valuable *inspiration* but imposed no formal obligation on the European institutions.[76] This ambivalent status was immediately perceived as a constitutional problem.[77] But it took almost a decade before the Lisbon Treaty recognized the Charter as having "the same legal value as the Treaties".

---

[70] *Ibid.*, para. 308.   [71] *Ibid.*, para. 327.

[72] The Court in fact identified a breach of the right of defence, especially the right to be heard (*ibid.*, para. 353), as well as an unjustified violation of the right to property (*ibid.*, para. 370).

[73] Commission, Memorandum on the Accession of the European Communities to the European Convention for the Protection of Human Rights and Fundamental Freedoms, [1979] Bulletin of the European Communities – Supplement 2/79, especially: 11 et seq.

[74] On the drafting process, see G. de Búrca, "The Drafting of the European Union Charter of Fundamental Rights", 26 (2001) *European Law Review*, 126.

[75] Charter, Preamble 4. For a criticism of the idea of codification, see J. Weiler, "Does the European Union Truly Need a Charter of Rights?", 6 (2000) *European Law Journal*, 95 at 96.

[76] See *Parliament* v. *Council*, Case C-540/03, [2006] ECR I-5769, para. 38: "the Charter is not a legally binding instrument".

[77] The Charter was announced at the Nice European Council, and its status was one of the questions in the 2000 Nice "Declaration on the Future of the Union".

The Charter "reaffirms" the rights that result "in particular" from the constitutional traditions common to the Member States, the European Convention on Human Rights and the general principles of European law.[78] This formulation suggested two things. First, the Charter aims to codify existing fundamental rights and was thus not intended to create "new" ones.[79] And, second, it codified European rights from *various* sources – and thus not solely the general principles found in the European Treaties. To help identify the sources behind individual Charter articles, the Member States decided to give the Charter its own commentary. These "Explanations" are not strictly legally binding, but they must be given "due regard" in the interpretation of the Charter.[80]

The Charter divides the Union's fundamental rights into six classes. The classic liberal rights are covered by Titles I to III as well as Title VI. The controversial Title IV codifies the rights of workers; yet, provision is also made for the protection of the family and the right to health care.[81]

Table 7. Structure of the Charter of Fundamental Rights

Preamble	
Title I – Dignity	Title IV – Solidarity
Title II – Freedoms	Title V – Citizens' Rights
Title III – Equality	Title VI – Justice

Title VII – General Provisions
Article 51 – Field of Application
Article 52 – Scope and Interpretation of Rights and Principles
Article 53 – Level of Protection
Article 54 – Prohibition of Abuse of Rights

Protocol No. 30 on Poland and the United Kingdom
Explanations

---

[78] Charter, Preamble 5.

[79] See Protocol (No. 30) "On the Application of the Charter of Fundamental Rights of the European Union to Poland and to the United Kingdom," Preamble 6: "the Charter reaffirms the rights, freedoms and principles recognised in the Union and makes those rights more visible, but does not create new rights or principles".

[80] Article 6 (1) TEU, and Article 52 (7) Charter: "The explanations drawn up as a way of providing guidance in the interpretation of this Charter shall be given due regard by the courts of the Union of the Member States." These "Explanations" are published in [2007] OJ C303/17.

[81] See, respectively, Articles 33 and 35 of the Charter.

Title V deals with "citizens' rights", that is: rights that a polity provides exclusively to its members.[82] This includes the right to vote and to stand as a candidate in elections.[83] The general principles on the interpretation and application of the Charter are finally set out in Title VII. These general provisions establish four fundamental principles. First, the Charter is addressed to the Union and will only exceptionally apply to the Member States.[84] Second, not all provisions within the Charter are "rights"; that is: directly effective entitlements to individuals.[85] Third, the rights within the Charter can, within limits, be restricted by Union legislation.[86] Fourth, the Charter tries to establish harmonious relations with the European Treaties and the European Convention, as well as with constitutional traditions common to the Member States.[87]

In the context of the present section, only principles two and three warrant special attention.

(a) (Hard) rights and (soft) principles

It is important to note that the Charter makes a distinction between (hard) rights and (soft) principles.[88] Hard rights are rights that will have direct effect and can, as such, be invoked before a court. Not all provisions within the Charter are rights in this strict sense. Indeed, the Charter also recognizes the existence of "principles" in its Title VII.[89]

What are these principles in the Charter, and what is their effect? The "Explanations" offer a number of illustrations, in particular Article 37 of the Charter dealing with "Environmental Protection". The provision reads:

---

[82] Not all rights in this title appear to be citizens' rights. For example, Article 41 of the Charter protecting the "right to good administration" states (emphasis added): "*Every person* has the right to have his or her affairs handled impartially, fairly and within a reasonable time by the institutions, bodies, offices and agencies of the Union."

[83] Article 39 Charter.

[84] Article 51 Charter. On the application of the Charter to the Member States, see R. Schütze, "The American Incorporation Doctrine and the European Union", 14 (2011/12) *Cambridge Yearbook of European Legal Studies* (forthcoming).

[85] Article 51 (1) and 52 (5) Charter.   [86] Article 52 (1) Charter.

[87] Article 52 (2)–(4) as well as (6) of the Charter. But see also Article 53 on the "Level of Protection".

[88] The distinction seems to contradict the jurisprudence of the Court with regard to fundamental *rights* as general *principles* in the context of the European Treaties. However, the best way to understand the distinction between "rights" and "principles" is not to see them as mutually exclusive; see Dauses, "Protection of Fundamental Rights" (supra n. 7) 406 and below.

[89] Articles 51 (1) and 52 (5) of the Charter.

"A high level of environmental protection and the improvement of the quality of the environment *must be integrated into the policies of the Union* and ensured in accordance with the principle of sustainable development."[90] This wording contrasts strikingly with that of a classic right provision.[91] For it constitutes less a *limit* to governmental action than an *aim* for governmental action. Principles indeed come close to orienting objectives, which "do not however give rise to direct claims for positive action by the Union institutions".[92] They are not subjective rights, but objective guidelines. Thus: "The provisions of this Charter which contain principles may be implemented by legislative and executive acts taken by institutions ... They shall be judicially cognisable only in the interpretation of such acts and in the ruling on their legality."[93] The difference between rights and principles is thus between a hard and a soft judicial claim. An individual will not have an (individual) right to a high level of environmental protection, but may claim that the Union violated the (governmental) principle when adopting too low a standard. In line with the classic task of legal principles,[94] the courts must thus generally draw "inspiration" from Union principles when interpreting European law.

But how is one to distinguish between "rights" and "principles"? Sadly, the Charter offers no catalogue of principles. Nor are its principles neatly grouped into a section within each substantive title. And even the wording of a particular article will not conclusively reveal whether it contains a right

Family and professional life

1. The family shall enjoy legal, economic and social protection.

2. To reconcile family and professional life, everyone shall have the right to protection from dismissal for a reason connected with maternity and the right to paid maternity leave and to parental leave following the birth or adoption of a child.

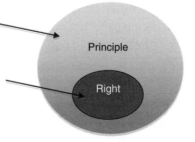

Figure 4.2 Principles and rights within the Charter

---

[90] Emphasis added.   [91] See Article 2 of the Charter: "Everyone has the right to life."
[92] "Explanations" (supra n. 80), 35.   [93] Article 52 (5) of the Charter.
[94] See R. Dworkin, *Taking Rights Seriously* (Duckworth, 1996).

or a principle. But, most confusingly, even a single article "may contain both elements of a right and of a principle".[95] How is this possible? The best way to make sense of this is to see rights and principles not as mutually exclusive concepts, but as distinct but overlapping legal constructs.[96] "Rights" are situational crystallizations of principles, and therefore derive from principles. A good illustration may be offered by Figure 4.2 and Article 33 of the Charter on the status of the family and its relation to professional life.

(b) Limitations, and "limitations on limitations"

Every legal order protecting fundamental rights recognizes that some rights can be limited to safeguard the general interest. For written bills of rights, these limitations are often recognized for each constitutional right. While the Charter follows this technique for some articles,[97] it also contains a provision that defines legitimate limitations to all fundamental rights. The "limitations on limitations" are set out in Article 52 of the Charter. The provision states:

> Any limitation on the exercise of the rights and freedoms recognised by this Charter must be *provided for by law* and *respect the essence of those rights and freedoms.* Subject to the principle of *proportionality*, limitations may be made only if they are necessary and genuinely meet objectives of general interest recognised by the Union or the need to protect the rights and freedoms of others.[98]

The provision presumes that each right within the Charter can be limited – a presumption that may be incorrect.[99] But be that as it may, any legitimate limitation must be provided for "by law". This (new) requirement seems to outlaw autonomous executive interventions into fundamental rights.[100] But the problem still is this: will a limitation of someone's fundamental rights require the (democratic) legitimacy behind formal legislation, that is:

---

[95]   "Explanations" (supra n. 80), 35.

[96]   In this sense see R. Alexy, *A Theory of Constitutional Rights* (Oxford University Press, 2002), 47 – using the Wittgensteinian concept of "family resemblance" to describe the relation between "rights" and "principles".

[97]   Article 17 (Right to Property) of the Charter states in paragraph 1: "No one may be deprived of his or her possessions, except in the public interest and in the cases and under the conditions provided for by law, subject to fair compensation being paid in good time for their loss. The use of property may be regulated by law in so far as is necessary for the general interest."

[98]   Article 52 (1) Charter (emphasis added).

[99]   Article 1 expressly states: "Human dignity is inviolable."

[100]   See *Knauf Gips* v. *Commission*, Case C-407/08 P (nyr).

a European law adopted under a "legislative procedure"?[101] This view would significantly shift the balance between fundamental rights and the pursuit of the common good of the Union. The Court thus appears to favour a material concept of "law" so as to widen the scope of legitimate limitations of fundamental rights.[102]

In any event, Article 52 (1) of the Charter expressly mentions two constitutional limitations on right limitations. One limitation is relative, while the other is absolute in nature. According to the principle of proportionality, each restriction of fundamental rights must be necessary in light of the general interest of the Union or the rights of others. And the provision now also confirms – it seems – the independent existence of an absolute limit by insisting that each public limitation must always "respect the essence" of the individual right in question.

4. The "external" bill of rights: the European Convention on Human Rights

The discovery of an unwritten bill of rights and the creation of a written bill of rights for the Union had been "internal" achievements. They did "not result in any form of external supervision being exercised over the Union's institutions".[103] And by preferring *its* internal human rights over any external international standard, the Court has even been accused of a "chauvinist" and "parochial" attitude.[104] This bleak picture *is* distorted – at the very least, when it comes to one international human rights treaty that has always provided an external standard to the European Union: the European Convention on Human Rights. From the very beginning, the Court of Justice took the Convention very seriously,[105] sometimes even too

---

[101] In favour of this view see D. Triantafyllou, "The European Charter of Fundamental Rights and the 'Rule of Law': Restricting Fundamental Rights by Reference", 39 (2002) *Common Market Law Review*, 53–64 at 61: "Accordingly, references to 'law' made by the Charter should ideally require a co-deciding participation of the European Parliament[.]"

[102] See *Schecke and Eifert*, Cases C-92 and 93/09 (nyr).

[103] I. de Jesús Butler and O. de Schutter, "Binding the EU to International Human Rights Law", 27 (2008) *Yearbook of European Law*, 277 at 278. This statement is correct only if limited to *direct* external supervision.

[104] G. de Búrca, "The European Court of Justice and the International Legal Order After *Kadi*", 51 (2010) *Harvard International Law Journal*, 1 at 4.

[105] See S. Douglas-Scott, "A Tale of Two Courts: Luxembourg, Strasbourg and the Growing European Human Rights Acquis", 43 (2006) *Common Market Law Review*, 629.

seriously.[106] This final section will look at the external standard imposed by the Convention prior to and after an eventual accession by the Union.

(a) Before accession: (limited) indirect review of Union law

The Union is (still) not a formal party to the European Convention. Could the Member States thus escape their international obligations under the Convention by transferring decision-making powers to the European Union? In order to avoid a normative vacuum, the European Convention system has accepted the *indirect* review of Union acts by establishing the doctrine of (limited) direct responsibility of Member States for acts of the Union.

Having originally found that the Union constituted an autonomous subject of international law whose actions could not be attributed to its Member States,[107] the European Commission on Human Rights and its Court subsequently changed views. In *M & Co* v. *Germany*,[108] the Commission found that, whereas "the Convention does not prohibit a Member State from transferring powers to international organisations", "a transfer of powers does not necessarily exclude a State's responsibility under the Convention with regard to the exercise of the transferred powers".[109] This would not, however, mean that the State was to be held responsible for all actions of the Union: "it would be contrary to the very idea of transferring powers to an international organisation to hold the Member States responsible for examining [possible violations] in each individual case".[110]

What, then, were the conditions for this limited indirect review of Union acts? Consistent with its chosen emphasis on state responsibility, the Convention system would not concentrate on the concrete decision of the Union, but on the State's decision to transfer powers to the Union. This transfer of powers was deemed "not incompatible with the Convention provided that within that organisation fundamental rights will receive an *equivalent protection*".[111] Member States would consequently not be responsible for every – compulsory – European Union act that violated the European Convention.

---

[106] See *Spain* v. *United Kingdom*, Case C-145/04, [2006] ECR I-7917.

[107] *Ibid.* The Convention Commission held that the complaint was "outside its jurisdiction ratione personae since the [Member] States by taking part in the decision of the Council of the European [Union] had not in the circumstances of the instant case exercised their 'jurisdiction' within the meaning of Art 1 of the Convention".

[108] *M & Co* v. *Federal Republic of Germany* (1990) 64 DR 138.   [109] *Ibid.*, 145.

[110] *Ibid.*, 146.   [111] *Ibid.*, 145 (emphasis added).

This was confirmed in *Bosphorus*.[112] Where the Union protected human rights in an "equivalent" manner to that of the Convention, the European Court of Human Rights would operate a "presumption" that the States had not violated the Convention by transferring powers to the European Union. This presumption translates into a lower review standard for acts adopted by the European Union,[113] since the presumption of equivalent protection could only be rebutted where the actual treatment of human rights within the Union was "manifestly deficient".[114] The lower review standard represented a compromise between two extremes: no control, as the Union was not a member, and full control even in situations in which the Member States acted as mere agents of the Union. This compromise was "the price for Strasbourg achieving a level of control over the EU, while respecting its autonomy as a separate legal order".[115]

(b) After accession: (full) direct review of Union law

The present Strasbourg jurisprudence privileges the Union legal order in not subjecting it to the full external review by the European Court of Human Rights. However, this privilege is not the result of the Union being a "model" member. Instead it results from the Union *not* being a formal member of the European Convention system.

Will the presumption that the Union – in principle – complies with the European Convention on Human Rights disappear with accession? It seems compelling that the *Bosphorus* presumption will cease once the Union accedes to the Convention. For "[b]y acceding to the Convention, the European Union will have agreed to have its legal system measured by the human rights standards of the ECHR", and will "therefore no longer deserve special treatment".[116] The replacement of an *indirect* review by a *direct* review should also – at least in theory – lead to the replacement of a *limited*

---

[112] *Bosphorus Hava* v. *Minister*, Case 84/95 (supra n. 54).

[113] J. Callewaert, "The European Convention on Human Rights and European Union Law: A Long Way to Harmony", (2009) *European Human Rights Law Review* 768, 773: "through the Bosphorus-presumption and its tolerance as regards 'non manifest' deficiencies, the protection of fundamental rights under [European] law is policed with less strictness than under the Convention".

[114] *Bosphorus Hava* v. *Minister*, Case 84/95 (supra n. 54), paras. 156–7.

[115] Douglas-Scott, "A Tale of Two Courts" (supra n. 105), 639.

[116] T. Lock, "EU Accession to the ECHR: Implications for Judicial Review in Strasbourg", 35 (2010) *European Law Review*, 777 at 798.

review by a *full* review. Yet the life of law is not always logic, and the Strasbourg Court may well decide to cherish past experiences by applying a lower review standard to the (acceded) European Union. We must wait and see whether or not logic will trump experience.

However, what is certain already is that accession will widen the scope of application of the European Convention to include direct Union action. For in the past, the indirect review of Union acts was based on the direct review of Member State acts implementing Union acts. And this, by definition, required that a *Member State* had acted in some way.[117] Thus in situations where the Union institutions had acted directly upon an individual without any mediating Member State measures, this Union act could not – even indirectly – be reviewed.[118] In the absence of a connecting factor to one of the signatory States, the Union act was thus outside the Convention's jurisdiction. This will definitely change once the Union accedes to the Convention. Henceforth all *direct* Union actions would fall within the jurisdiction of the Strasbourg Court. Thus even if a lower external standard were to continue, it would henceforth apply to all Union acts – and not just acts executed by the Member States.

---

[117] *Ibid.*, 779.

[118] See *Connolly* v. *Fifteen Member States of the European Union* (Application No. 73274/01).

Part II

European Law: Enforcement

This Part concentrates on the "enforcement" of European law in the courts. We shall see that European law establishes rights and obligations that directly affect individuals. The direct effect of European law in the national legal orders will be discussed in Chapter 5. Where a European norm is directly effective, it will also be "supreme" over national law. The "supremacy" of European law is the subject of Chapter 6. How will individuals enforce their "supreme" European rights? Chapters 7 and 8 look at the dual enforcement machinery within the Union legal order. Individuals will typically enforce their European rights in national courts. And in order to assist these courts in the interpretation and application of European law, the Union envisages a preliminary reference procedure. But the Union legal order has equally required national courts to provide effective remedies for the enforcement of European rights, and has even created a European remedy of state liability. Having the indirect enforcement of European law through the national courts discussed in Chapter 7, the direct enforcement of European law in the European Courts will be explored in Chapter 8.

Chapter 5 Direct effect

Chapter 6 (Legal) Supremacy

Chapter 7 National actions

Chapter 8 European actions

Introduction

Classic international law holds that each State can choose the relationship between its "domestic" law and "international" law. Two – constitutional – theories thereby exist: monism and dualism.[1] Monist States make international law part of their domestic legal order. International law will directly

---

[1] The choice between monism and dualism is a "national" choice. Thus, even where a State chooses the monist approach, monism in this sense only means that international norms are *constitutionally* recognized as an autonomous legal source of domestic law. Dualism, by contrast, means that international norms will not automatically, that is: through a constitutional incorporation, become part of the national legal order. Each international treaty demands a separate legislative act "incorporating" the international norm into domestic law. The difference between monism and dualism thus boils down to whether international law is incorporated via the constitution – such as in the United States; or whether international treaties need to be validated by a special parliamentary command – as in the United Kingdom. The idea that monism means that States have no choice but to apply international law is not accepted in international law.

Figure 5.1 Monism and dualism

apply *as if* it were domestic law.[2] By contrast, dualist States consider international law separate from domestic law. International law is viewed as the law *between* States; national law is the law *within* a State. While international treaties are thus binding "on" States, they cannot be binding "in" States. International law here needs to be "transposed" or "incorporated" into domestic law and will thus only have *indirect* effects through the medium of national law. The dualist theory is based on a basic division of labour: international institutions apply international law, while national institutions apply national law.

Did European law leave the choice between monism and dualism to its Member States? Section 1 examines this question in greater detail, before the remainder of this Chapter explores the doctrine of direct effect for European law. Section 2 starts out with the direct effect of the European Treaties. The European Court indeed confirmed that some Treaty provisions would be self-executing in the national legal orders. Nonetheless, the European Treaties are framework treaties; that is: they primarily envisage the adoption of European *secondary* law. This secondary law may take various forms. These forms are set out in Article 288 TFEU.[3] The provision defines the Union's legal instruments, and states:

[1] To exercise the Union's competences, the institutions shall adopt regulations, directives, decisions, recommendations and opinions.
[2] A regulation shall have general application. It shall be binding in its entirety and directly applicable in all Member States.

---

[2] Article VI, Clause 2 of the United States Constitution (emphasis added): "[A]ll Treaties made, or which shall be made, under the Authority of the United States, *shall be the supreme Law of the Land*; and the Judges in every State shall be bound thereby, any Thing in the Constitution or Laws of any State to the Contrary notwithstanding."

[3] The institutional practice of Union decision-making has created a number of "atypical" acts. For a discussion of atypical acts, see J. Klabbers, "Informal Instruments before the European Court of Justice", 31 (1994) *Common Market Law Review*, 997. But see now Article 296 TFEU – third indent: "When considering draft legislative acts, the European Parliament and the Council shall refrain from adopting acts not provided for by the relevant legislative procedure in the area in question."

[3] A directive shall be binding, as to the result to be achieved, upon each Member State to which it is addressed, but shall leave to the national authorities the choice of form and methods.

[4] A decision shall be binding in its entirety. A decision which specifies those to whom it is addressed shall be binding only on them.

[5] Recommendations and opinions shall have no binding force.

The provision acknowledges three binding legal instruments – regulations, directives, and decisions – and two non-binding instruments.[4] Why was there a need for three distinct binding instruments? The answer seems to lie in their specific – direct or indirect – effects in the national legal orders. While regulations and decisions were considered to be Union acts that would contain directly effective legal norms, directives appeared to lack this capacity. Much of the constitutional discussion on the direct effect of European secondary law has consequently concentrated on the direct effect of directives. Section 3 will therefore look at them in much detail. Finally, Section 4 analyses the doctrine of indirect effects within the Union legal order.

1. Direct applicability and direct effect

Would the Union legal order permit a dualist approach towards European law on the part of the Member States? The European Treaties contained a signal in favour of this permissive approach. For there existed an "international" enforcement machinery in the form of infringement actions before the Court of Justice.[5] However, the Treaties also contained strong signals against the "ordinary" international reading of European law. Not only was the Union entitled to adopt legal acts that were to be "directly applicable *in* all Member States".[6] From the very beginning, the Treaties also established

---

[4] Logic would dictate that non-binding acts are not binding. Yet, the European Court has accepted the possibility of their having some "indirect" legal effect. In *Grimaldi* v. *Fonds des maladies professionelles*, Case 322/88, [1989] ECR 4407, para. 18, the Court held that recommendations "cannot be regarded as having no legal effect" as they "supplement binding [European] provisions". "Non-binding" Union acts may, therefore, have legal "side effects". For an interesting overview, see L. Senden, *Soft Law in European Community Law: Its Relationship to Legislation* (Hart, 2004).

[5] On this point, see Chapter 8 – Section 1 below.   [6] Article 288 (2) TFEU.

a constitutional mechanism that envisaged the direct application of European law by the national courts.[7]

But regardless of whether a monist view had or had not been intended by the founding Member States, the European Court discarded any dualist leanings in the most important case of European law: *Van Gend en Loos*.[8] The Court here expressly cut the umbilical cord with classic international law by insisting that the European legal order was a "new legal order". In the famous words of the Court:

> The objective of the E[U] Treaty, which is to establish a common market, the functioning of which is of direct concern to interested parties in the [Union], implies that this Treaty is *more than an agreement which merely creates mutual obligations between the contracting States*. This view is confirmed by the preamble to the Treaty which refers not only to the governments but to peoples. It is also confirmed more specifically by the establishment of institutions endowed with sovereign rights, the exercise of which affects Member States and also their citizens. Furthermore, it must be noted that the nations of the States brought together in the [Union] are called upon to cooperate in the functioning of this [Union] through the intermediary of the European Parliament and the Economic and Social Committee.
>
> In addition the task assigned to the Court of Justice under Article [267], the object of which is to secure uniform interpretation of the Treaty by national courts and tribunals, confirms that the States have acknowledged that [European] law has an authority which can be invoked by their nationals before those courts and tribunals. The conclusion to be drawn from this is that the [Union] constitutes a *new legal order of international law* for the benefit of which the States have limited their sovereign rights, albeit within limited fields, and the subjects of which comprise not only Member States but also their nationals. *Independently of the legislation of Member States*, [European] law therefore not only imposes obligations on individuals but is also intended to confer upon them rights which become part of their legal heritage.[9]

All judicial arguments here marshalled to justify a monistic reading of European law are debatable.[10] But with a stroke of the pen, the Court confirmed the independence of the European legal order from classic international law. Unlike ordinary international law, the European Treaties

---

[7] Article 267 TFEU. On the provision, see Chapter 7 – Sections 1&2 below.

[8] *Van Gend en Loos* v. *Netherlands Inland Revenue Administration*, Case 26/62, [1963] ECR (Special English Edition) 1.

[9] *Ibid.*, 12.

[10] For a critical overview, see T. Arnull, *The European Union and its Court of Justice* (Oxford University Press, 2006), 168 et seq.

were more than agreements creating mutual obligations between States. Individuals were subjects of European law and their rights and obligations would derive *directly* from European law. European law would thus be *directly* applicable in the national legal orders. And it was to be enforced in national courts – despite the parallel existence of an international enforcement machinery.[11] And because European law was directly applicable law, the European legal order could *itself* determine the nature and effect of European law within the national legal orders. The direct applicability of European law thus allowed the Court *centrally* to develop two foundational doctrines of the European legal order: the doctrine of direct effect and the doctrine of supremacy. The present Chapter analyses the doctrine of direct effect; Chapter 6 deals with the doctrine of supremacy.

What is the relationship between direct applicability and direct effect? It is vital to understand that the Court's decision in favour of a monistic relationship between the European and the national legal orders did not mean that all European law could be enforced by national courts. To be enforceable, a norm must be "justiciable" or "executable";[12] that is, it must be capable of being applied by a public authority in a specific case. But not all legal norms have this quality. For example, where a European norm requires Member States to establish a public fund to guarantee unpaid wages for insolvent private companies, yet leaves a wide margin of discretion to the Member States on how to achieve that end, this norm is not

---

[11] *Van Gend en Loos*, Case 26/62 (supra n. 8), 13: "In addition the argument based on Articles [258] and [259] of the [FEU] Treaty put forward by the three Governments which have submitted observations to the Court in their statements of case is misconceived. The fact that these Articles of the Treaty enable the Commission and the Member States to bring before the Court a State which has not fulfilled its obligations does not mean that individuals cannot plead these obligations, should the occasion arise, before a national court, any more than the fact that the Treaty places at the disposal of the Commission ways of ensuring that obligations imposed upon those subject to the Treaty are observed, precludes the possibility, in actions between individuals before a national court, of pleading infringements of these obligations. A restriction of the guarantees against an infringement of [ex] Article 12 [EEC] by Member States to the procedures under Articles [258 and 259] would remove all direct legal protection of the individual rights of their nationals. There is the risk that recourse to the procedure under these Articles would be ineffective if it were to occur after the implementation of a national decision taken contrary to the provisions of the Treaty. The vigilance of individuals concerned to protect their rights amounts to an effective supervision in addition to the supervision entrusted by Articles [258 and 259] to the diligence of the Commission and of the Member States."

[12] On the application of the doctrine of direct effect to the national executive branch, see R. Schütze, *European Constitutional Law* (Cambridge University Press, 2012), Chapter 9 – Conclusion.

intended to have direct effects in a specific situation. While it binds the national legislator, the norm is not self-executing. The concept of direct applicability is thus wider than the concept of direct effect. Whereas the former refers to the *internal* effect of a European norm within national legal orders, the latter refers to the *individual* effect of a binding norm in specific cases.[13] Direct effect requires direct applicability, but not the other way around. The direct applicability of a norm makes its direct effect *possible*.

2. Direct effect of primary law

The European Treaties are framework treaties. They establish the objectives of the European Union, and endow it with the powers to achieve these objectives. Many of the European policies in Part III of the TFEU thus simply set out the competences and procedures for future Union secondary law. The Treaties, as primary European law, thereby offer the constitutional bones. But could this constitutional "skeleton" itself have direct effect? Would there be Treaty provisions that were sufficiently precise to give rise to rights or obligations that national courts could apply in specific situations?

The European Court affirmatively answered this question in *Van Gend en Loos*.[14] The case concerned a central objective of the European Union: the internal market. According to that central plank of the Treaties, the Union was to create a customs union between the Member States. Within a customs union, goods can move freely without any pecuniary charges being levied when crossing borders. The Treaties had chosen to establish the customs union gradually; and to this effect ex-Article 12 EEC contained a standstill obligation: "Member States shall refrain from introducing between themselves any new customs duties on imports or exports or any charges having equivalent effect, and from increasing those which they already apply in their trade with each other."[15] The Netherlands appeared to

---

[13] In this sense direct applicability is a "federal" question as it relates to the effect of a "foreign" norm in a domestic legal system, whereas direct effect is a "separation-of-powers" question as it relates to the issue of whether a norm must be applied by the legislature or the executive and judiciary.

[14] *Van Gend en Loos*, Case 26/62 (supra n. 8).

[15] The provision has been repealed. Strictly speaking, it is therefore not correct to identify Article 30 TEU as the successor provision, for that Article is based on ex-Articles 13 and 16 EEC. The normative content of ex-Article 12 EEC solely concerned the introduction of *new* customs duties; and therefore did not cover the abolition of existing tariff restrictions.

have violated this provision; and believing this to be the case, Van Gend &
Loos – a Dutch import company – brought proceedings in a Dutch court
against the National Inland Revenue. The Dutch court had doubts about the
admissibility and the substance of the case and referred a number of
preliminary questions to the European Court of Justice.

Could a private party enforce an international treaty in a national court?
And if so, was this a question of national or European law? In the course of
the proceedings before the European Court, the Netherlands government
heavily disputed that an individual could enforce an international
Treaty provision against its own government in a national court. Any
alleged infringements had to be submitted to the European Court by the
Commission or a Member State under the "international" infringement
procedures set out in Articles 258 and 259 TFEU.[16] The Belgian government,
having intervened in the case, equally claimed that the question of what
effects an international treaty had within the national legal order "falls
exclusively within the jurisdiction of the Netherlands court".[17] Conversely,
the Commission countered that "the effects of the provisions of the Treaty
on the national law of Member States cannot be determined by the actual
national law of each of them but by the Treaty itself".[18] And since ex-Article
12 EEC was "clear and complete", it was "a rule of law capable of being
effectively applied by the national court".[19] The fact that the European
provision was addressed to the States did "not of itself take away from
individuals who have an interest in it the right to require it to be applied in
the national courts".[20]

Two views thus competed before the European Court. According to the
"international" view, legal rights of private parties could "not derive from
the [Treaties] or the legal measures taken by the institutions, but [solely]
from legal measures enacted by Member States".[21] According to the "constitutional" view, by contrast, European law was capable of directly creating
individual rights. The Court famously favoured the second view. It followed
from the "spirit" of Treaties that European law was no "ordinary" international law. It would thus of itself be directly applicable in the national legal
orders.

---

[16] *Van Gend en Loos*, Case 26/62 (supra n. 8), 6. On enforcement actions by the Commission,
see Chapter 8 – Section 1 below.
[17] *Van Gend en Loos*, Case 26/62 (supra n. 8), 6.   [18] *Ibid.*   [19] *Ibid.*, 7.   [20] *Ibid.*
[21] This was the view of the German government (*ibid.*, 8).

But when would a provision have direct effect, and thus entitle private parties to seek its application by a national court? Having briefly presented the general scheme of the Treaty in relation to customs duties,[22] the Court concentrated on the wording of ex-Article 12 EEC and found as follows:

> The wording of [ex-]Article 12 [EEC] contains a *clear and unconditional prohibition* which is not a positive but a *negative obligation*. This obligation, moreover, is *not qualified by any reservation on the part of the States, which would make its implementation conditional upon a positive legislative measure enacted under national law*. The very nature of this prohibition makes it ideally adapted to produce direct effects in the legal relationship between Member States and their subjects. The implementation of [ex-]Article 12 [EEC] does not require any legislative intervention on the part of the States. The fact that under this Article it is the Member States who are made the subject of the negative obligation does not imply that their nationals cannot benefit from this obligation.[23]

While somewhat repetitive, the test for direct effect is here clearly presented: wherever the Treaties contain a "prohibition" that was "clear" and "unconditional" it will have direct effect. Being an unconditional prohibition thereby required two things. First, the European provision had to be an *automatic* prohibition, that is: it should not depend on subsequent positive legislation by the European Union. And second, the prohibition should ideally be *absolute*, that is: "not qualified by any reservation on the part of the States".

This was a – very – strict test. But ex-Article 12 EEC was indeed "ideally adapted" to satisfy this triple test. It was a clear prohibition and unconditional in the double sense. However, if the Court had insisted on a strict application of all three criteria, very few provisions within the Treaties would have had direct effect. Yet the Court subsequently loosened the test considerably. And as we shall see below, it made it clear that the Treaties could be vertically and horizontally directly effective.

(a) Direct effect: from strict to lenient test

The direct effect test set out in *Van Gend* was informed by three criteria. First, a provision had to be clear. Second, it had to be unconditional in the

---

[22] The Court considered ex-Article 12 EEC as an "essential provision" in the general scheme of the Treaty as it relates to customs duties (*ibid.*, 12).

[23] *Ibid.*, 13 (emphasis added).

sense of being an automatic prohibition. And third, this prohibition would need to be absolute, that is: not allow for reservations. In its subsequent jurisprudence, the Court expanded the concept of direct effect on all three fronts.

First, how clear would a prohibition have to be to be directly effective? Within the Treaties' title on the free movement of goods, we find the following famous prohibition: "Quantitative restrictions on imports and all measures having equivalent effect shall be prohibited between Member States."[24] Was this a clear prohibition? While the notion of "quantitative restrictions" might have been – relatively – clear, what about "measures having equivalent effect"? The Commission had realized the open-ended nature of the concept and offered some early semantic help.[25] And yet, despite all the uncertainty involved, the Court found that the provision had direct effect.[26]

The same lenient interpretation of what "clear" meant was soon applied to even wider provisions. In *Defrenne*,[27] the Court analysed the following prohibition: "[e]ach Member State shall ensure that the principle of equal pay for male and female workers for equal work or work of equal value is applied".[28] Was this a clear prohibition of discrimination? Confusingly, the Court found that the provision may and may not have direct effect. With regard to indirect discrimination, the Court considered the prohibition indeterminate, since it required "the elaboration of criteria whose implementation necessitates the taking of appropriate measures at [European] and national level".[29] Yet in respect of direct discrimination, the prohibition was directly effective.[30]

---

[24] Article 34 TFEU.

[25] Directive 70/50/EEC on the abolition of measures which have an effect equivalent to quantitative restrictions on imports and are not covered by other provisions adopted in pursuance of the EEC Treaty, [1970] OJ English Special Edition 17.

[26] *Iannelli & Volpi SpA* v. *Ditta Paolo Meroni*, Case 74/76, [1977] ECR 557, para. 13: "The prohibition of quantitative restrictions and measures having equivalent effect laid down in Article [34] of the [FEU] Treaty is mandatory and explicit and its implementation does not require any subsequent intervention of the Member States or [Union] institutions. The prohibition therefore has direct effect and creates individual rights which national courts must protect[.]"

[27] *Defrenne* v. *Sabena*, Case 43/75, [1976] ECR 455, para. 19.   [28] Article 157 (1) TFEU.

[29] *Defrenne* v. *Sabena*, Case 43/75 (supra n. 27), para. 19.

[30] *Ibid.*, para. 24. This generous reading was subsequently extended to the yet wider prohibition on "any discrimination on grounds of nationality"; see *Martínez Sala* v. *Freistaat Bayern*, Case C-85/96, [1998] ECR I-2691, para. 63.

What about the second part of the direct effect test? When was a prohibition automatic? Would this be the case, where the Treaties expressly acknowledged the need for positive legislative action by the Union to achieve a Union objective? For example, the Treaty chapter on the right of establishment contains not just a prohibition addressed to the Member States in Article 49 TFEU;[31] the subsequent article states: "In order to attain freedom of establishment as regards a particular activity, the European Parliament and the Council, acting in accordance with the ordinary legislative procedure and after consulting the Economic and Social Committee, shall act by means of directives." Would this not mean that the freedom of establishment was conditional on legislative action? In *Reyners*,[32] the Court rejected this argument. Despite the fact that the general scheme within the chapter on freedom of establishment contained a set of provisions that sought to achieve free movement through positive Union legislation,[33] the Court declared the European right of establishment in Article 49 TFEU to be directly effective. And the Court had no qualms about giving direct effect to the general prohibition on "any discrimination on grounds of nationality" – despite the fact that Article 18 TFEU expressly called on the Union legislator to adopt rules "designed to prohibit such discrimination".[34]

Finally, what about the third requirement? Could relative prohibitions, even if clear, ever be directly effective? The prohibition on quantitative restrictions on imports, discussed above, is subject to a number of legitimate exceptions according to which it "shall not preclude [national] prohibitions or restrictions on imports, exports or goods in transit justified on grounds of public morality, public policy or public security".[35] Was this then a prohibition that was "not qualified by any reservation on the part of the States"? The Court found that this was indeed the case. For although these derogations would "attach particular importance to the interests of Member States, it must be observed that they deal with exceptional cases which are clearly defined and which do not lend themselves to any wide interpretation".[36]

---

[31] Article 49 (1) TFEU states: "Within the framework of the provisions set out below, restrictions on the freedom of establishment of nationals of a Member State in the territory of another Member State shall be prohibited."

[32] *Reyners* v. *Belgian State*, Case 2/74, [1974] ECR 631. For an excellent discussion of this question, see P. Craig, "Once Upon a Time in the West: Direct Effect and the Federalization of EEC Law", 12 (1992) *Oxford Journal of Legal Studies*, 453 at 463–70.

[33] *Reyners*, Case 2/74 (supra n. 32) para. 32.

[34] *Martínez Sala* v. *Freistaat Bayern*, Case C-85/96 (supra n. 30).   [35] Article 36 TFEU.

[36] *Salgoil* v. *Italian Ministry of Foreign Trade*, Case 13/68, [1968] ECR 453 at 463.

And since the application of these exceptions was "subject to judicial control", a Member State's right to invoke them did not prevent the general prohibition "from conferring on individuals rights which are enforceable by them and which the national courts must protect".[37]

What, then, is the test for the direct effect of Treaty provisions in light of these – relaxing – developments? Today, the simple test is this: a provision has direct effect when it is capable of being applied by a national court. Importantly, direct effect does *not* depend on a European norm granting a subjective right;[38] but on the contrary, the subjective right is a result of a directly effective norm.[39] Direct effect simply means that a norm can be "invoked" in and applied by a court. And this is the case, when the Court of Justice says it is! Today, almost all Treaty *prohibitions* have direct effect – even the most general ones. Indeed, in *Mangold*,[40] the Court held that an – unwritten and vague – *general* principle of European law could have direct effect. Should we embrace this development? We should, for the direct effect of a legal rule "must be considered as being the normal condition of any rule of law". The very questioning of the direct effect of European law was an "infant disease" of the young European legal order.[41] And this infant disease has today – largely – been cured but for one area: the Common Foreign and Security Policy.

(b) Vertical and horizontal direct effect

Where a Treaty provision is directly effective, an individual can invoke European law in a national court (or administration). This will normally be as against the State. This situation is called "vertical" effect, since the State is "above" its subjects. But whereas a private party is in a subordinate position vis-à-vis public authorities, it is in a coordinate position vis-à-vis other private parties. The legal effect of a norm between private parties is thus called "horizontal" effect. And while there has never been any doubt

---

[37] *Van Duyn* v. *Home Office*, Case 41/74, [1974] ECR 1337, para. 7.

[38] For the opposite view, see K. Lenaerts and T. Corthaut, "Of Birds and Hedges: the Role of Primacy in Invoking Norms of EU Law", 31 (2006) *European Law Review*, 287.

[39] M. Ruffert, "Rights and Remedies in European Community Law: A Comparative View", 34 (1997) *Common Market Law Review*, 307 at 315.

[40] *Mangold* v. *Helm*, Case C-144/04, [2005] ECR I-9981.

[41] P. Pescatore, "The Doctrine of 'Direct Effect': An Infant Disease of Community Law", 8 (1983) *European Law Review*, 155.

that Treaty provisions can be invoked in a vertical situation, there has been some discussion on their horizontal direct effects.

Should it make a difference whether European law is invoked in proceedings against the Inland Revenue or in a civil dispute between two private parties? Should the Treaties be allowed to impose obligations on individuals? The Court in *Van Gend* had accepted this theoretical possibility.[42] And indeed, the horizontal direct effect of Treaty provisions has never been in doubt for the Court.[43] A good illustration of the horizontal direct effect of Treaty provisions can be found in *Familiapress* v. *Bauer*.[44] The case concerned the interpretation of Article 34 TFEU prohibiting unjustified restriction on the free movement of goods. It arose in a *civil* dispute before the Vienna Commercial Court between Familiapress and a German competitor, Bauer. The latter was accused of violating the Austrian Law on Unfair Competition by publishing prize crossword puzzles – a sales technique that was deemed unfair under Austrian law. Bauer defended itself in the national court by invoking Article 34 TFEU – claiming that the directly effective European right to free movement prevailed over the Austrian law. And the Court of Justice found indeed that a national law that constituted an unjustified restriction of trade would have to be disapplied in the – civil – proceedings.

The question whether a Treaty prohibition has horizontal direct effect must however be distinguished from the question whether it also prohibits private actions. The latter is not simply a question of the *effect* of a provision, but rather of its personal scope. Many Treaty prohibitions are – expressly or impliedly – addressed to the State.[45] However, the Treaties equally contain provisions that are directly addressed to private parties.[46] The question whether a Treaty prohibition covers public as well as private actions is controversial. Should the "equal pay for equal work" principle or the free

---

[42] *Van Gend en Loos*, Case 26/62 (supra n. 8), 12: "[European] law therefore not only imposes obligations on individuals . . . ".

[43] The direct effect of Article 34 TFEU was announced in a "horizontal" case between two private parties; see *Iannelli & Volpi* v. *Meroni*, Case 74/76 (supra n. 26).

[44] *Vereinigte Familiapress Zeitungsverlags- und vertriebs GmbH* v. *Bauer Verlag*, Case C-368/95, [1997] ECR I-3689.

[45] For example, Article 157 TFEU states (emphasis added) that "[e]ach *Member State* shall ensure that the principle of equal pay for male and female workers for equal work or work of equal value is applied"; and Article 34 TFEU prohibits restrictions on the free movement of goods "between Member States".

[46] Article 102 TFEU prohibits "all agreements between undertakings" that restrict competition within the internal market, and is thus addressed to private parties.

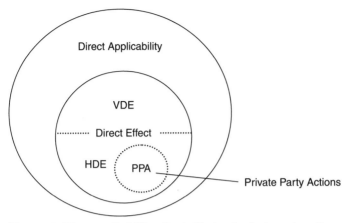

Figure 5.2 Direct applicability, direct effect and private party actions

movement rules – both *expressly* addressed to the Member States – also *impliedly* apply to private associations and their actions? If so, the application of the Treaty will not just impose *indirect* obligations on individuals (when they lose their right to rely on a national law that violates European law); they will be *directly* prohibited from engaging in an activity. The Court has – in principle – confirmed that Treaty provisions, albeit addressed to the Member States, might cover private actions.[47] Thus in *Defrenne*, the Court found that the prohibition on pay discrimination between men and women could equally apply to private employers.[48] And while the exact conditions remain uncertain,[49] the Court has confirmed and reconfirmed the inclusion of private actions within the free movement provisions.[50]

To distinguish the logical relations between the various constitutional concepts of direct applicability, direct effect – both vertical (VDE) and horizontal (HDE), and private party actions, Figure 5.2 may be useful.

---

[47] *Walrave and Koch* v. *Association Union Cycliste Internationale*, Case 36/74, [1974] ECR 1405, para. 19: "to limit the prohibitions in question to acts of a public authority would risk creating inequality in their application".

[48] *Defrenne*, Case 43/75 (supra n. 27), para. 39: "In fact, since Article [157 TFEU] is mandatory in nature, the prohibition on discrimination between men and women applies not only to the action of public authorities, but also extends to all agreements which are intended to regulate paid labour collectively, as well as to contracts between individuals."

[49] The Court generally limits this application to "private" rules that aim to regulate "in a collective manner" (*ibid.*, para. 17). See also *Union royale belge des sociétés de football association ASBL* v. *Jean-Marc Bosman*, Case C-415/93, [1995] ECR I-4921.

[50] On the free movement of persons provisions, see Chapter 10 – footnote 6 below. On the – uncertain and complex – situation governing the free movement of goods, see P. Oliver et al., *Oliver on Free Movement of Goods in the European Union* (Hart, 2010) Chapter 4, esp. 67 et seq.

3. Direct effect of secondary law: directives

When the European Union was born, the Treaties envisaged two instruments that were designed to contain norms that were directly effective: regulations and decisions. By contrast, a third instrument – the directive – appeared to lack this capacity. For according to Article 288 (3) TFEU, "[a] directive shall be binding, as to the result to be achieved, upon each Member State to which it is addressed, but shall leave to the national authorities the choice of form and methods". This formulation suggested that directives were binding *on* States – not *within* States. And on the basis of such a "dualist" reading, directives would have no validity in the national legal orders. They seemed *not* to be directly applicable, and would thus need to be "incorporated" or "implemented" through national legislation. This dualist view was underlined by the fact that Member States were only bound as to the result to be achieved – as obligations of result are common in classic international law.[51]

But could this indirect Union law have direct effects? In a courageous line of jurisprudence, the Court confirmed that directives could – under certain circumstances – have direct effect and thus entitle individuals to have their European rights applied in national courts. However, the Court subjected this finding to two limitations – one temporal, one normative. Direct effect would only arise *after* a Member State had failed properly to "implement" the directive, and then only in relation to the State authorities themselves. The second limitation is known as the "no-horizontal-direct-effect rule". And while this constitutional rule has been confirmed, it has itself been limited and qualified.

(a) Direct effect of directives: conditions and limits

That directives could directly give rise to rights that individuals could claim in national courts was accepted in *Van Duyn* v. *Home Office*.[52] The case concerned a Dutch secretary, whose entry into the United Kingdom had

---

[51] For this view, see L.-J. Constantinesco, *Das Recht der Europäischen Gemeinschaften* (Nomos, 1977), 614.

[52] *Van Duyn* v. *Home Office*, Case 41/74 (supra n. 37).

been denied on the ground that she was a member of the Church of Scientology. Britain had tried to justify this limitation on the free movement of persons by reference to an express derogation that allowed such restrictions on grounds of public policy and public security.[53] However, in an effort to harmonize national derogations from free movement, the Union had adopted a directive according to which "[m]easures taken on grounds of public policy or of public security shall be based exclusively on the personal conduct of the individual concerned".[54] This outlawed national measures that limited free movement for generic reasons, such as membership of a disliked organization. Unfortunately, the United Kingdom had not "implemented" the directive into national law. Could Van Duyn nonetheless directly invoke the directive against the British authorities? The Court of Justice found that this was possible by emphasizing the distinction between direct applicability and direct effect:

[B]y virtue of the provisions of Article [288] regulations are directly applicable and, consequently, may by their very nature have direct effects, it does not follow from this that other categories of acts mentioned in that Article can never have similar effects. It would be incompatible with the binding effect attributed to a directive by Article [288] to exclude, in principle, the possibility that the obligation which it imposes may be invoked by those concerned. In particular, where the [Union] authorities have, by directive, imposed on Member States the obligation to pursue a particular course of conduct, the useful effect of such an act would be weakened if the individuals were prevented from relying on it before their national courts and if the latter were prevented from taking it into consideration as an element of [European] law. Article [267], which empowers national courts to refer to the Court questions concerning the validity and interpretation of all acts of the [Union] institutions, without distinction, implies furthermore that these acts may be invoked by individuals in the national courts.[55]

The Court – rightly – emphasized the distinction between direct applicability and direct effect, yet – wrongly – defined the relationship between these two concepts in order to justify its conclusion. To brush aside the textual argument that regulations are directly applicable while directives are not, it

---

[53] Article 45 (1) and (3) TFEU.

[54] Article 3 (1) Directive 64/221 on the co-ordination of special measures concerning the movement and residence of foreign nationals which are justified on grounds of public policy, public security or public health, OJ (English Special Edition): Chapter 1963–1964/117.

[55] *Van Duyn*, Case 41/74 (supra n. 37), para. 12.

wrongly alluded to the idea that direct effect without direct application was possible.[56] And the direct effect of directives was justified by three different and distinct arguments. First, to exclude direct effect would be incompatible with the "binding effect" of directives. Second, their "useful effect" would be weakened if individuals could not invoke them in national courts. Third, since the preliminary reference procedure did not exclude directives, the latter must be capable of being invoked in national courts.

What was the constitutional value of these arguments? Argument one is a sleight of hand: the fact that a directive is not binding in *national law* is not "incompatible" with its binding effect under *international law*. The second argument is strong, but not of a legal nature: to enhance the useful effect of a rule by making it more binding is a political argument. Finally, the third argument only begs the question: while it is true that the preliminary reference procedure generically refers to all "acts of the institutions", it could be argued that only those acts that are directly effective can be referred. The decision in *Van Duyn* was right, but sadly without reason.

The lack of a convincing *legal* argument to justify the direct effect of directives soon prompted the Court to propose a fourth argument. "A Member State which has not adopted the implementing measures required by the Directive in the prescribed periods may not rely, as against individuals, on its own failure to perform the obligations which the directive entails."[57] This fourth reason has become known as the "estoppel argument" – acknowledging its intellectual debt to English "equity" law. A Member State that fails to implement its European obligations is "estopped" from invoking that failure as a defence, and individuals are consequently – and collaterally – entitled to rely on the directive as against the State. Unlike the three original arguments, this fourth argument is *State*-centric. It locates the rationale for the direct effect of directives not in the nature of the instrument itself, but in the behaviour of the State.

---

[56] In the words of J. Steiner: "How can a law be enforceable by individuals within a Member State if it is not regarded as incorporated in that State?" (J. Steiner, "Direct Applicability in EEC Law – A Chameleon Concept", 98 (1982) *Law Quarterly Review*, 229–48 at 234). The direct effect of a directive presupposes its direct application. And indeed, ever since *Van Gend en Loos* (supra n. 8), all directives must be regarded as directly applicable (see S. Prechal, *Directives in EC Law* (Oxford University Press, 2005), 92 and 229). For the same conclusion, see C. Timmermans, "Community Directives Revisited", 17 (1997) *Yearbook of European Law*, 1–28 at 11–12.

[57] *Ratti*, Case 148/78, [1979] ECR 1629, para. 22.

This (behavioural) rationale would result in two important limitations on the direct effect of directives. Even if provisions within a directive were "unconditional and sufficiently precise" "those provisions may [only] be *relied upon by an individual against the State* where that State fails to implement the Directive in national law *by the end of the period prescribed or where it fails to implement the directive correctly*".[58] This direct effect test for directives differed from that for ordinary Union law, as it added a temporal and a normative limitation. *Temporally*, the direct effect of directives could only arise *after* the failure of the State to implement the directive had occurred. Thus, before the end of the implementation period granted to Member States, no direct effect can take place. And even once this temporal condition has been satisfied, the direct effect would operate only as against the State. This *normative* limitation on the direct effect of directives has become famous as the "no-horizontal-direct-effect rule".

(b) The no-horizontal-direct-effect rule

The Court's jurisprudence of the 1970s had extended the direct effect of Union law to directives. An individual could claim her European rights against a State that had failed to implement a directive into national law. This situation was one of "vertical" direct effect. Could an individual equally invoke a directive against another private party? This "horizontal" direct effect existed for direct Union law; yet should it be extended to directives? The Court's famous answer is a resolute "no": directives could not have horizontal direct effects.

The "no-horizontal-direct-effect rule" was first expressed in *Marshall*.[59] The Court based its negative conclusion on a textual argument:

[A]ccording to Article [288 TFEU] the binding nature of a directive, which constitutes the basis for the possibility of relying on the directive before a national court, exists only in relation to "each Member State to which it is addressed". It follows that a directive may not of itself impose obligations on an individual and that a provision of a directive may not be relied upon as such against such a person.[60]

---

[58] *Kolpinghuis Nijmegen BV*, Case 80/86, [1987] ECR 3969, para. 7 (emphasis added).
[59] *Marshall v. Southampton and South-West Hampshire Area Health Authority*, Case 152/84, [1986] ECR 723.
[60] *Ibid.*, para. 48.

The absence of horizontal direct effect was subsequently confirmed in *Dori*.[61] A private company had approached Ms Dori for an English language correspondence course. The contract had been concluded in Milan's busy central railway station. A few days later, she changed her mind and tried to cancel the contract. A right of cancellation had been provided by the European directive on consumer contracts concluded outside business premises,[62] but Italy had not implemented the directive into national law. Could a private party nonetheless directly rely on the unimplemented directive against another private party? The Court was firm:

[A]s is clear from the judgment in Marshall ... the case-law on the possibility of relying on directives against State entities is based on the fact that under Article [288] a directive is binding only in relation to "each Member State to which it is addressed". That case-law seeks to prevent "the State from taking advantage of its own failure to comply with [European] law" ... The effect of extending that case-law to the sphere of relations between individuals would be to recognize a power in the [Union] to enact obligations for individuals with immediate effect, whereas it has competence to do so only where it is empowered to adopt regulations. It follows that, in the absence of measures transposing the directive within the prescribed time-limit, consumers cannot derive from the directive itself a right of cancellation as against traders with whom they have concluded a contract or enforce such a right in a national court.[63]

This denial of the direct effect of directives in horizontal situations was grounded in three arguments.[64] First, a textual argument: a directive is binding in relation to each Member State to which it is addressed. But had the Court not used this very same argument to establish the direct effect of directives in the first place? Second, the estoppel argument: the direct effect for directives exists to prevent a State from taking advantage of its own failure to comply with European law. And since individuals were not responsible for the non-implementation of a directive, direct effect should not be extended to them. Third, a systematic argument: if horizontal direct effect was given to directives, the distinction between directives and regulations would disappear. This was a weak argument, for a directive's distinct

---

[61] *Faccini Dori* v. *Recreb*, Case C-91/92, [1994] ECR I-3325.

[62] Directive 85/577 concerning protection of the consumer in respect of contracts negotiated away from business premises (OJ 1985 L372/31).

[63] *Dori* (supra n. 61), paras. 22–5.

[64] The Court silently dropped the "useful effect argument" as it would have worked towards the opposite conclusion.

character could be preserved in different ways.[65] In order to bolster its reasoning, the Court added a fourth argument in subsequent jurisprudence: legal certainty.[66] Since directives were not published, they must not impose obligations on those to whom they are not addressed. This argument has lost some of its force,[67] but continues to be very influential today.

All these arguments may be criticized.[68] But the Court of Justice has stuck to its conclusion: directives cannot *directly* impose obligations on individuals. They lack horizontal direct effect. This constitutional rule of European law has nonetheless been qualified by one limitation and one exception.

(c) The limitation to the rule: the wide definition of State (actions)

One way to minimize the no-horizontal-direct-effect rule is to maximize the vertical direct effect of directives. The Court has done this by giving extremely extensive definitions to what constitutes the "State", and what constitute "public actions".

What public authorities count as the "State"? A minimal definition restricts the concept to a State's central organs. Because they failed to implement the directive, the estoppel argument suggested them to be vertically bound by the directive. Yet the Court has never accepted this consequence, and has endorsed a maximal definition of the State. It thus held that directly effective obligations "are binding upon *all authorities of the Member States*"; and this included "all organs of the administration, including decentralised authorities, such as municipalities",[69] even "constitutionally independent" authorities.[70]

---

[65] On this point, see R. Schütze, "The Morphology of Legislative Power in the European Community: Legal Instruments and Federal Division of Powers", 25 (2006) *Yearbook of European Law*, 91.

[66] See *The Queen on the Application of Delena Wells* v. *Secretary of State for Transport, Local Government and the Regions*, C-201/02, [2004] ECR 723, para. 56: "the principle of legal certainty prevents directives from creating obligations for individuals".

[67] The publication of directives is now, in principle, required by Article 297 TFEU.

[68] For an excellent overview of the principal arguments, see P. Craig, "The Legal Effect of Directives: Policy, Rules and Exceptions", 34 (2009) *European Law Review*, 349. But why does Professor Craig concentrate on arguments one and four, instead of paying attention to the strongest of the Court's reasons in the form of argument two?

[69] *Costanzo SpA* v. *Comune di Milano*, Case 103/88, [1989] ECR 1839, para. 31 (emphasis added).

[70] *Johnston* v. *Chief Constable of the Royal Ulster Constabulary*, Case 222/84, [1986] ECR 1651, para. 49.

The best formulation of this maximalist approach was given in *Foster*.[71] Was the "British Gas Corporation" – a statutory corporation for developing and maintaining gas supply – part of the British "State"? The Court held this to be the case. Vertical direct effect would apply to any body "whatever its legal form, which has been made responsible, pursuant to a measure adopted by the State, *for providing a public service under the control of the State and has for that purpose special powers* beyond those which result from the normal rules applicable in relations between individuals".[72] This wide definition of the State consequently covers *private* bodies endowed with *public* functions.

This functional definition of the State, however, suggested that only "public acts", that is: acts adopted in pursuit of a public function, would be covered. Yet there are situations where the State acts horizontally like a private person: it might conclude private contracts and employ private personnel. Would these "private actions" be covered by the doctrine of vertical direct effect? In *Marshall*, the plaintiff argued that the United Kingdom had not properly implemented the Equal Treatment Directive. But could an *employee* of the South-West Hampshire Area Health Authority invoke the direct effect of a directive against this State authority in this horizontal situation? The British government argued that direct effect would only apply "against a Member State *qua* public authority and not against a Member State *qua* employer". "As an employer a State is no different from a private employer"; and "[i]t would not therefore be proper to put persons employed by the State in a better position than those who are employed by a private employer".[73] This was an excellent argument, but the Court would have none of it. According to the Court, an individual could rely on a directive as against the State "regardless of the capacity in which the latter is acting, whether employer or public authority".[74]

Vertical direct effect would thus not only apply to *private* parties exercising public functions, but also to public authorities engaged in *private* activities.[75] This double extension of the doctrine of vertical direct effect can be criticized for treating similar situations dissimilarly. For it creates a discriminatory limitation to the no-horizontal-direct-effect rule.

---

[71] *Foster and others* v. *British Gas*, Case C-188/89, [1990] ECR I-3313.

[72] *Ibid.*, para. 20 (emphasis added). For a more recent confirmation of that test, see *Vassallo* v. *Azienda Ospedaliera Ospedale San Martino di Genova et al.*, Case C-180/04, [2006] ECR I-7251, para. 26.

[73] *Marshall*, Case 152/84 (supra n. 59), para. 43.   [74] *Ibid.*, para. 49.   [75] *Ibid.*, para. 51.

(d) The exception to the rule: incidental horizontal direct effect

In the two previous situations, the Court respected the rule that directives could not have direct horizontal effects, but limited the rule's scope of application. Yet in some cases, the Court has found a directive *directly* to affect the horizontal relations between private parties. This "incidental" horizontal effect of directives must, despite some scholastic effort to the contrary,[76] be seen as an *exception* to the rule. The incidental direct horizontal effect cases violate the rule that directives cannot directly impose obligations on private parties. The two "incidents" chiefly responsible for the doctrine of incidental horizontal direct effects are *CIA Security* and *Unilever Italia*.

In *CIA Security* v. *Signalson and Securitel*,[77] the Court dealt with a dispute between three Belgian competitors whose business was the manufacture and sale of security systems. CIA Security had applied to a commercial court for orders requiring Signalson and Securitel to cease libel. The defendants had alleged that the plaintiff's alarm system did not satisfy Belgian security standards. This was indeed the case, but the Belgian legislation itself violated a European notification requirement established by Directive 83/189. But because the European norm was in a directive, this violation could – theoretically – not be invoked in a horizontal dispute between private parties. Or could it? The Court implicitly rejected the no-horizontal-direct-effect rule by holding the notification requirement to be "unconditional and sufficiently precise" and finding that "[t]he *effectiveness of [Union] control will be that much greater if the directive is interpreted as meaning that breach of the obligation to notify constitutes a substantial procedural defect such as to render the technical regulations in question inapplicable to individuals*".[78] CIA Security could thus rely on

---

[76] This phenomenon has been variously referred to as the "incidental" horizontal effect of directives (see P. Craig and G. de Búrca, *EU Law* (Oxford University Press, 2007), 296 et seq.); the "horizontal side effects of direct effect" (see S. Prechal, *Directives in EC Law* (Oxford University Press, 2005), 261–70); or the "disguised" vertical effect of directives (M. Dougan, "The 'Disguised' Vertical Direct Effect of Directives", 59 (2000) *Cambridge Law Journal*, 586–612). But the argumentative categories that have been developed to justify when a directive can adversely affect a private party and when not, have degenerated into "a form of sophistry which provides no convincing explanation for apparently contradictory lines of case law" (Craig and de Búrca, *ibid.*, at 226).

[77] *CIA Security* v. *Signalson and Securitel*, Case C-194/94, [1996] ECR I-2201.

[78] *Ibid.*, para. 48 (emphasis added).

the directive as against its private competitors. And the national court "must decline to apply a national technical regulation which has not been notified in accordance with the directive".[79] What else was this but horizontal direct effect?

The Court confirmed the decision in *Unilever Italia* v. *Central Food*.[80] In both cases, then, the national courts were indeed required to disapply national legislation in *civil* proceedings between *private* parties. Did CIA Security not "win" a right from the directive to have national legislation disapplied? And did Signalson not "lose" the right to have national law applied? It seems impossible to deny that the directive *did* directly affect the rights and obligations of individuals. It imposed an obligation on the defendants to accept the forfeiting of their national rights. The Court thus *did* create an exception to the principle that a directly effective directive "cannot of itself apply in proceedings exclusively between private parties".[81] However, the exception to the no-horizontal-direct-effect rule has remained an exceptional exception. But even so, there are – strong – arguments for the Court to abandon its constitutional rule altogether.[82]

4. Indirect effects: the doctrine of consistent interpretation

Norms may have direct and indirect effects. A European provision lacking direct effect may still have certain indirect effects in the national legal orders. The lack of direct effect means exactly that: the norm cannot itself – that is *directly* – be invoked. However, European law may still have indirect effects on the interpretation of national law. For the European Court has created a general duty on national courts (and administrations)[83] to interpret national law as far as possible in light of all European law. The doctrine

---

[79] *Ibid.*, para. 55.   [80] *Unilever Italia* v. *Central Food*, Case C-443/98, [2000] ECR I-7535.

[81] *Pfeiffer et al.* v. *Deutsches Rotes Kreuz, Kreisverband Waldshut*, Joined Cases C-397/01 to C-403/01, [2004] ECR I-8835, para. 109.

[82] See Opinion of Advocate General Jacobs in *Vaneetveld* v. *Le Foyer*, Case C-316/93, [1994] ECR I-763, para. 31: "[I]t might well be conducive to greater legal certainty, and to a more coherent system, if the provisions of a directive were held in appropriate circumstances to be directly enforceable against individuals"; as well as Craig, "Legal Effect of Directives" (supra n. 68), 390: "The rationales for the core rule that Directives do not have horizontal direct effect based on the Treaty text, legal certainty and the Regulations/ Directives divide are unconvincing."

[83] *Henkel* v. *Deutsches Patent- und Markenamt*, Case C-218/01, [2004] ECR I-1725.

of consistent interpretation applies as a structural principle to all sources of European law.[84] However, the doctrine has been mainly developed in the context of directives, and many of the cases will thus refer to this particular Union instrument.

The doctrine of consistent interpretation was given an elaborate definition in *Von Colson*:

> [T]he Member States' obligation arising from a Directive to achieve the result envisaged by the Directive and their duty under Article [4(3) TEU] to take all appropriate measures, whether general or particular, to ensure the fulfilment of that obligation, is binding on all the authorities of Member States including, for matters within their jurisdiction, the courts. It follows that, in applying the national law, in particular the provisions of a national law specifically introduced in order to implement [a Directive], national courts are required to interpret their national law in the light of the wording and the purpose of the directive in order to achieve the result referred to in the third paragraph of Article [288].[85]

The duty of consistent interpretation is a duty to achieve the desired result by indirect means. Where a directive is not sufficiently precise to have direct effect, it is – theoretically – addressed to the national legislator. It is the national legislator's prerogative to "concretize" the directive's indeterminate content in line with its own national views. But where the legislator has failed to do so, the task will be partly transferred to the national judiciary. For after the expiry of the implementation period,[86] national courts are

---

[84] In the – brilliant – summary of Advocate General Tizzano in *Mangold*, Case C-144/04 (supra n. 40), para. 117: "It must first be recalled that the duty of consistent interpretation is one of the 'structural' effects of [European] law which, together with the more 'invasive' device of direct effect, enables national law to be brought into line with the substance and aims of [European] law. Because it is structural in nature, the duty applies with respect to all sources of [European] law, whether constituted by primary or secondary legislation, and whether embodied in acts whose legal effects are binding or not. Even in the case of recommendations, the Court has held, 'national courts *are bound* to take [them] into consideration in order to decide disputes submitted to them'."

[85] *Von Colson and Elisabeth Kamann* v. *Land Nordrhein-Westfalen*, Case 14/83, [1984] ECR 1891, para. 26. Because this paragraph was so important in defining the duty of consistent interpretation, it is sometimes referred to as the "Von Colson Principle".

[86] The national authorities are not required to interpret their national law in the light of Union directives *before* the expiry of the implementation deadline. After *Adeneler and Others* v. *Ellinikos Organismos Galaktos (ELOG)*, Case C-212/04, [2006] ECR I-6057, there is no room for speculation on this issue: "[W]here a directive is transposed belatedly, the general obligation owed by national courts to interpret domestic law in conformity with the directive exists only once the period for its transposition has expired" (*ibid.*, para. 115). However, once a directive has been adopted, a Member State will be under the (softer)

under an obligation to "implement" the directive judicially through a "European" interpretation of national law. This duty of consistent interpretation applies regardless of "whether the [national] provisions in question *were adopted before or after the directive*".[87] The duty to interpret national law as far as possible in light of European law will extend to all national law – irrespective of whether the national law was intended to implement the directive. However, where domestic law had been specifically enacted to implement the directive, the national courts must even operate under the presumption "that the Member State, following its exercise of the discretion afforded to it under that provision, had the intention of fulfilling entirely the obligations arising from the directive".[88]

The duty of consistent interpretation may lead to the *indirect* implementation of a directive. For it can *indirectly* impose new obligations – both vertically and horizontally. An illustration of the horizontal *indirect* effect of directives can be seen in *Webb*.[89] The case concerned a claim by Mrs Webb against her employer. The latter had hired the plaintiff to replace a pregnant co-worker during her maternity leave. Two weeks after she had started work, Mrs Webb discovered that she was pregnant herself, and was dismissed for that reason. She brought proceedings before the Industrial Tribunal, pleading sex discrimination. The Industrial Tribunal rejected this on the ground that the reason for her dismissal had not been her sex but her inability to fulfil the primary task for which she had been recruited. The case went on appeal to the House of Lords, which confirmed the interpretation of national law but nonetheless harboured doubts about Britain's European obligations under the Equal Treatment Directive. On a preliminary reference, the European Court indeed found that there was sex discrimination under the directive and that the fact that Mrs Webb had been employed to replace another employee was irrelevant.[90] On receipt of the preliminary ruling, the House of Lords was thus required to change its previous interpretation of national law. Mrs Webb *won* a right, while her employer *lost* the right to dismiss her. The doctrine of indirect effect thus changed the horizontal

---

obligation to "refrain from taking any measures liable seriously to compromise the result prescribed" in the directive: see *Inter-Environnement Wallonie ASBL* v. *Région Wallonne*, C-129/96, [1997] ECR 7411, para. 45. This obligation is, however, independent of the doctrine of indirect effects.

[87] *Marleasing* v. *La Comercial Internacional de Alimentación*, Case C-106/89, [1990] ECR I-4135, para. 8.

[88] *Pfeiffer*, Cases C-397/01 to C-403/01 (supra n. 81), para. 112.

[89] *Webb* v. *EMO Air Cargo*, Case C-32/93, [1994] ECR I-3567.   [90] *Ibid.*, paras. 26–8.

relations between two private parties. The duty of consistent interpretation has consequently been said to amount to "*de facto* (horizontal) direct effect of the directive".[91] This de facto horizontal effect is however an *indirect* effect. For it operates through the medium of national law.

Are there limits to the indirect effect of directives through the doctrine of consistent interpretation? The duty is very demanding: national courts are required to interpret their national law "*as far as possible, in the light of the wording and the purpose of the directive*".[92] But what will "as far as possible" mean? Should national courts be required to behave as if they were the national legislature? This might seriously undermine the (relatively) passive place reserved for judiciaries in many national constitutional orders. And the European legal order has indeed only asked national courts to adjust the interpretation of national law "in so far as it is given discretion to do so *under national law*".[93] The European Court thus accepts that there exist established national judicial methodologies and has permitted national courts to limit themselves to "the application of interpretative methods recognised by national law".[94] National courts are thus not obliged to "invent" or "import" novel interpretative methods.[95] However, within the discretion given to the judiciary under national law, the European doctrine of consistent interpretation requires the referring court "to do whatever lies within its jurisdiction, having regard to the whole body of rules of national law".[96]

But there are also European limits to the duty of consistent interpretation. The Court has clarified that the duty "is limited by the general principles of law which form part of [European] law and in particular the principles of legal certainty and non-retroactivity".[97] This has been taken to imply that the indirect effect of directives cannot aggravate the criminal liability of a private party, as criminal law is subject to particularly strict rules of interpretation.[98] But more importantly, the Court recognizes that the clear

---

[91] See Prechal, *Directives in EC Law* (supra n. 76), 211.

[92] *Marleasing*, Case C-106/89 (supra n. 87), para. 8 (emphasis added).

[93] *Von Colson*, Case 14/83 (supra n. 85), para. 28 (emphasis added).

[94] *Pfeiffer*, Cases C-397/01 to C-403/01 (supra n. 81), para. 116.

[95] See M. Klammert, "Judicial Implementation of Directives and Anticipatory Indirect Effect: Connecting the Dots", 43 (2006) *Common Market Law Review*, 1251 at 1259. For the opposite view, see Prechal, *Directives in EC Law* (supra n. 76), 213.

[96] *Pfeiffer*, Case C-397/01 to C-403/01 (supra n. 81), para. 118.

[97] *Kolpinghuis*, Case 80/86 (supra n. 58), para. 13.

[98] In *Arcaro*, Case C-168/95, [1996] ECR I-4705, the Court claimed that "[the] obligation of the national court to refer to the content of the directive when interpreting the relevant rules

and unambiguous wording of a national provision constitutes an absolute limit to its interpretation.[99] National courts are thus not required to interpret national law *contra legem*.[100] The duty of consistent interpretation would thus find a boundary in the clear wording of a provision. In giving indirect effect to Union law, national courts are therefore not required to stretch the medium of national law beyond breaking point. They are only required to *interpret* the text – and not to *amend* it! The latter continues to be the task of the national legislatures – and not the national judiciaries.

The indirect horizontal effect of European law is consequently *limited* through the medium of national law. The duty of consistent interpretation is therefore a milder incursion on the legislative powers of the Member States than the doctrine of horizontal *direct* effect. For this doctrine may lead to the doctrine of supremacy, which requires national courts to disapply national laws that conflict with directly effective European rules – regardless of their wording.[101]

---

of its own national law reaches a limit where such an interpretation leads to the imposition on an individual of an obligation laid down by a directive which has not been transposed" (*ibid.*, para. 42). This ruling should, however, be interpreted restrictively. The post-*Arcaro* jurisprudence appears to recognize this logical necessity (see S. Drake, "Twenty Years after *Von Colson*: The Impact of 'Indirect Effect' on the Protection of the Individual's Community Rights", 30 (2005) *European Law Review*, 329 at 338).

[99] *Kücükdeveci* v. *Swedex*, Case C-555/07, [2010] ECR I-365, para. 49.

[100] *Adeneler* v. *Ellinikos*, Case C-212/04 (supra n. 86), para. 110: "It is true that the obligation on a national court to refer to the content of a directive when interpreting and applying the relevant rules of domestic law is limited by general principles of law, particularly those of legal certainty and non-retroactivity, and that obligation cannot serve as the basis for an interpretation of national law *contra legem*."

[101] See Schütze, "Morphology" (supra n. 65), 126: "While the doctrine of consistent interpretation is a method to avoid conflicts, the doctrine of supremacy is a method to *solve* – unavoidable – conflicts."

Introduction

Since European law is directly applicable in the Member States, it must be applied alongside national law by national authorities. And since European law may have direct effect, it might come into conflict with national law in a specific situation.

Where two legislative wills come into conflict, each legal order must determine *how* these conflicts are to be resolved. The resolution of legislative conflicts requires a hierarchy of norms. Modern federal States typically resolve conflicts between federal and state legislation in favour of the former: federal law is supreme over State law.[1] This "centralist solution" has become so engrained in our constitutional mentalities that we tend to forget that the "decentralized solution" is also possible: local law may reign supreme over central law.[2] Supremacy and direct effect are thus *not*

---

[1] Article VI (2) of the US Constitution, for example, states: "This Constitution, and the Laws of the United States which shall be made in pursuance thereof; and all treaties made, or which shall be made, under the Authority of the United States, shall be the supreme Law of the Land."

[2] For a long time, the "subsidiarity solution" structured federal relationships during the Middle Ages. Its constitutional spirit is best preserved in the old legal proverb: "Town law breaks county law, county law breaks common law". In the event of a legislative conflict, supremacy was thus given to the rule of the smaller political entity.

different sides of the same coin. While the supremacy of a norm implies its direct effect, the direct effect of a norm will *not* imply its supremacy.[3] Each federal legal order must thus determine which law prevails. The simplest supremacy format is one that is absolute: all law from one legal order is superior to all law from the other. Absolute supremacy may however be given to the legal system of the smaller *or* the bigger political community. Between these two extremes lies a range of possible nuances.

When the Union was born, the European Treaties did not expressly state the supremacy of European law.[4] Did this mean that supremacy was a matter to be determined by the national legal orders; or was there a *Union* doctrine of supremacy? We shall see that there are *two* perspectives on the supremacy question. According to the *European* perspective, all Union law prevails over all national law. This "absolute" view is not shared by the Member States. Indeed, according to the *national* perspective, the supremacy of European law is relative: some national law is considered to be beyond the supremacy of European law. National challenges to the absolute supremacy of European law are traditionally expressed in two contexts. First, some Member States – in particular their Supreme Courts – have fought a battle over human rights within the Union legal order. They claim that European law cannot violate *national* fundamental rights. The most famous battle over the supremacy of European law in this context is the conflict between the European Court of Justice and the German Constitutional Court.[5] A similar contestation occurred in a second context:

---

[3] We can see direct effect without supremacy in the status given to customary international law in the British legal order. The fact that there can be direct effect without supremacy is the reason why there are *two* variants of the monist theory of international law (see H. Kelsen, "Sovereignty" in S. L. Paulson and B. L. Paulson (eds.), *Normativity and Norms: Critical Perspectives on Kelsenian Themes* (Clarendon Press, 1998), 525).

[4] The Constitutional Treaty *would* have added an express provision (Article I-6 CT): "The Constitution and law adopted by the institutions of the Union in exercising competences conferred on it shall have primacy over the law of the Member States." However, the provision was not taken over by the Lisbon Treaty. Yet the Lisbon Treaty has added Declaration 17 which states: "The Conference recalls that, in accordance with well settled case law of the Court of Justice of the European Union, the Treaties and the law adopted by the Union on the basis of the Treaties have primacy over the law of Member States, under the conditions laid down by the said case law."

[5] The following Chapter concentrates on the jurisprudence of the German Constitutional Court. The latter has long been the most pressing and – perhaps – prestigious national court in the Union legal order. For the reaction of the French Supreme Courts, see R. Mehdi, "French Supreme Courts and European Union Law: Between Historical Compromise and Accepted Loyalty", 48 (2011) *Common Market Law Review*, 439. For the views of the Central European

ultra vires control. In denying the Union a *Kompetenz-Kompetenz*,[6] Member States here insist that they have the last word with regard to the competences of the Union.

This Chapter analyses the supremacy doctrine within the Union legal order in four steps. We shall start with the European doctrine of absolute supremacy in Section 1, before looking at the effect of the principle on national law in Section 2. The subsequent sections, by contrast, analyse the national perspective on the supremacy principle in the form of two challenges to the supremacy of European law. Section 3 explores the national claim asserting the relative supremacy of European law in the context of fundamental human rights. Section 4 extends this analysis to the contested question of who is the ultimate arbiter of the scope of the Union's competences.

1. The European perspective: absolute supremacy

The strong dualist traditions within two of the Member States in 1958 posed a serious legal threat to the unity of the Union legal order.[7] Within dualist States, the status of European law is seen as depending on the national act "transposing" the European Treaties. Where this was a parliamentary act, any subsequent parliamentary acts could – expressly or impliedly – repeal the transposition law. Within the British tradition, this follows from the classic doctrine of parliamentary sovereignty: an "old" parliament cannot bind a "new" one. Any "newer" parliamentary act will thus theoretically prevail over the "older" European Union act. But the supremacy of European law could even be threatened in monist States. For even in monist States, the supremacy of European law will find a limit in the State's constitutional structures.

Would the European legal order insist that its law was to prevail over national law, including national constitutions? The Court of Justice did just that in a series of foundational cases. But while the establishment of the

---

Constitutional Courts, see W. Sadurski, "'Solange, Chapter 3': Constitutional Courts in Central Europe – Democracy – European Union", 14 (2008) *European Law Journal*, 1.

[6] On this – strange – (German) notion, see R. Schütze, *European Constitutional Law* (Cambridge University Press, 2012), Chapter 2 – Section 2(a).

[7] C. Sasse, "The Common Market: Between International and Municipal Law", 75 (1965–6) *Yale Law Journal*, 696–753.

supremacy over internal national law was swift, its extension to the international treaties of the Member States was much slower.

(a) Supremacy over internal law of the Member States

Frightened by the decentralized solution to the supremacy issue, the Court centralized the question of supremacy by turning it into a principle of European law. In *Costa* v. *ENEL*,[8] the European judiciary was asked whether national legislation adopted *after* 1958 could prevail over the original Treaties. The litigation involved an unsettled energy bill owed by Costa to the Italian "National Electricity Board". The latter had been created by the 1962 Electricity Nationalization Act, which was challenged by the plaintiff as a violation of the 1957 Treaty. The Italian dualist tradition responded that the European Treaty – like ordinary international law – had been transposed by national legislation that could – following international law logic – be derogated by subsequent national legislation. Could the Member States thus unilaterally determine the status of European law in their national legal order? The Court rejected this reading and distanced itself from the international law thesis:

> By contrast with ordinary international treaties, the E[U] Treaty has created its own legal system which, on the entry into force of the Treaty, became an integral part of the legal systems of the Member States and which their courts are bound to apply ... The integration into the laws of each Member State of provisions which derive from the [Union], and more generally the terms and the spirit of the Treaty, make it impossible for the States, as a corollary, to accord precedence to a unilateral and subsequent measure over a legal system accepted by them on a basis of reciprocity. Such a measure cannot therefore be inconsistent with that legal system. The *executive force* of [European] law cannot vary from one State to another in deference to subsequent domestic laws, without jeopardizing the attainment of the objectives of the Treaty ... It follows from all these observations that the law stemming from the Treaty, an independent source of law, could not, because of its special and original nature, be overridden by domestic legal provisions, however framed, without being deprived of its character as [European] law and without the legal basis of the [Union] itself being called into question.[9]

European law would reign supreme over national law, since its "executive force" must not vary from one State to another. The supremacy of Union

---

[8] *Costa* v. *ENEL*, Case 6/64, [1964] ECR 585.   [9] *Ibid.*, 593–4.

law could not be derived from classic international law;[10] and for that reason the Court had to declare the Union legal order autonomous from ordinary international law. But, how supreme was European law? The fact that the European *Treaties* prevailed over national legislation did not automatically imply that *all* secondary law would prevail over *all* national law. Would the Court accept a "nuanced" solution for certain national norms, such as national constitutional law?

The European Court never accepted the relative scope of the supremacy doctrine. This was clarified in *Internationale Handelsgesellschaft*.[11] A German administrative court had doubted that European legislation could violate fundamental rights as granted by the German Constitution and raised this very question with the European Court of Justice. Were the fundamental structural principles of national constitutions, including human rights, beyond the scope of federal supremacy? The Court disagreed. "Recourse to the legal rules or concepts of national law in order to judge the validity of measures adopted by the institutions of the [Union] would have an adverse effect on the uniformity and efficiency of [European] law. The validity of such measures can only be judged in the light of [European] law."[12] The validity of European laws could thus not be affected – even by the most fundamental norms within the Member States. The Court's vision

---

[10] Some legal scholars refer to the "supremacy" of international law vis-à-vis national law (see F. Morgenstern, "Judicial Practice and the Supremacy of International Law", 27 (1950) *British Yearbook of International Law*, 42). However, the concept of supremacy is here used in an imprecise way. Legal supremacy stands for the priority of one norm over another. For this, two norms must conflict and, therefore, form part of the same legal order. However, classic international law is based on the sovereignty of States and that implies a dualist relation with national law. The dualist veil protected national laws from being overridden by norms adopted by such "supranational" authorities as the Catholic Church or the Holy Roman Empire. When a State opens up to international law, this "monistic" stance is a *national* choice. International law as such has never imposed monism on a State. Reference to the international law doctrine of pacta sunt servanda will here hardly help. The fact that a State cannot invoke its internal law to justify a breach of international obligations is not supremacy. Behind the doctrine of pacta sunt servanda stands the concept of legal responsibility: a State cannot – without legal responsibility – escape its international obligations. The duality of internal and international law is thereby maintained: the former cannot affect the latter (as the latter cannot affect the former).

[11] *Internationale Handelsgesellschaft mbH* v. *Einfuhr- und Vorratsstelle für Getreide und Futtermittel*, Case 11/70, [1970] ECR 1125.

[12] *Ibid.*, para. 3.

of the supremacy of European law over national law was an absolute one: "The whole of [European] law prevails over the whole of national law."[13]

(b) Supremacy over international treaties of the Member States

While the European doctrine of supremacy had quickly emerged with regard to national legislation,[14] its extension to international agreements of the Member States was much slower. From the very beginning, the Treaties here recognized an express exception to the supremacy of European law. According to Article 351 TFEU:

The rights and obligations arising from agreements concluded before 1 January 1958 or, for acceding States, before the date of their accession, between one or more Member States on the one hand, and one or more third countries on the other, shall not be affected by the provisions of the Treaties.[15]

Article 351 codified the "supremacy" of *prior* international agreements of the Member States over conflicting European law. In the event of a conflict between the two, it was European law that could be disapplied *within the national legal orders*. Indeed, Article 351 "would not achieve its purpose if it did not imply a duty on the part of the institutions of the [Union] not to impede the performance of the obligations of Member States which stem from a prior agreement".[16] This was a severe incursion into the integrity of the European legal order, and as such had to be interpreted restrictively.[17]

But would there be internal or external limits to the "supremacy" of prior international treaties of the Member States? The Court indeed clarified that there existed internal limits to the provision. Article 351 (1) would only

---

[13] R. Kovar, "The Relationship between Community Law and National Law", in EC Commission (ed.), *Thirty Years of Community Law* (EC Commission, 1981), 109, at 112–13.

[14] On the establishment of the *social* acceptance of the doctrine, see: K. Alter, *Establishing the Supremacy of European Law: the Making of an International Rule of Law in Europe* (Oxford University Press, 2001).

[15] Paragraph 1. The provision continues (para. 2): "To the extent that such agreements are not compatible with the Treaties, the Member State or States concerned shall take all appropriate steps to eliminate the incompatibilities established. Member States shall, where necessary, assist each other to this end and shall, where appropriate, adopt a common attitude."

[16] *Attorney General* v. *Burgoa*, Case 812/79, [1980] ECR 2787, para. 9. This was confirmed in *Criminal Proceedings against Jean-Claude Levy*, Case C-158/91, [1993] ECR I-4287.

[17] *The Queen* v. *Secretary of State for Home Department, ex parte Evans Medical Ltd and Macfarlan Smith Ltd*, Case C-324/93, [1995] ECR I-563, para. 32.

allow Member States to implement their *obligations* towards *third* states.[18] Member States could thus not rely on Article 351 to enforce their rights; nor could they rely on the provision to fulfil their international obligations between themselves. These internal limitations are complemented by external limitations. The Court clarified their existence in *Kadi*.[19] While admitting that Article 351 TFEU would justify derogations from primary Union law, the Court insisted that the provision "cannot, however, be understood to authorize any derogation from the principles of liberty, democracy and respect for human rights and fundamental freedoms enshrined in Article [2] [T]EU as a foundation of the Union".[20] In the opinion of the Court, "Article [351 TFEU] may in no circumstances permit any challenge to the principles that form part of the very foundations of the [Union] legal order."[21] The Union's constitutional core constituted a limit to the supremacy of prior international treaties concluded by the Member States.

But should the – limited – application of Article 351 TFEU be extended, by analogy, to *subsequent* international agreements?[22] The main constitutional thrust behind the argument is that it protects the effective exercise of the treaty-making powers of the Member States. For "otherwise the Member States could not conclude any international treaty without running the risk of a subsequent conflict with [European] law".[23] This idea has been criticized: there would be no reason why the "normal" constitutional principles characterizing the relationship between European law and unilateral national acts should not also apply to subsequently concluded international agreements.[24] A middle position has proposed limiting the analogous application of Article 351 to situations where the conflict between

---

[18] *Commission* v. *Italy*, Case 10/61, [1962] ECR 1, 10–11: "[T]he terms 'rights and obligations' in Article [351] refer, as regards the 'rights', to the rights of third countries and, as regards the 'obligations', to the obligations of Member States and that, by virtue of the principles of international law, by assuming a new obligation which is incompatible with rights held under a prior treaty, a State ipso facto gives up the exercise of these rights to the extent necessary for the performance of its new obligation ... "

[19] *Kadi and Al Barakaat International Foundation* v. *Council and Commission*, Case C-402/05P, [2008] ECR I-6351. The facts of the case were discussed in Chapter 4 – Section 2 above.

[20] *Ibid.*, para. 303.   [21] *Ibid.*, para. 304.

[22] J. H. F. van Panhuys, "Conflicts between the Law of the European Communities and Other Rules of International Law", 3 (1965–6) *Common Market Law Review*, 420, 434.

[23] E. Pache and J. Bielitz, "Das Verhältnis der EG zu den völkerrechtlichen Verträgen ihrer Mitgliedstaaten", 41 (2006), *Europarecht*, 316 at 327 (my translation).

[24] E. Bülow, "Die Anwendung des Gemeinschaftsrechts im Verhältnis zu Drittländern" in A. Clauder (ed.), *Einführung in die Rechtsfragen der europäischen Integration* (Bonn, Europea Union Verlag, 1972), 52 at 54.

post-accession international treaties of Member States and subsequently adopted European legislation was "objectively unforeseeable" and could therefore not be expected.[25]

None of the proposals to extend Article 351 by analogy has however been mirrored in the jurisprudence of the European Court of Justice.[26] The Court has unconditionally upheld the supremacy of European law over international agreements concluded by the Member States after 1958. In light of the potential international responsibility of the Member States, is this a fair constitutional solution? Should it indeed make a difference whether a rule is adopted by means of a unilateral national measure or by means of an international agreement with a third State? Constitutional solutions still need to be found to solve the Member States' dilemma of choosing between the Scylla of liability under the European Treaties and the Charybdis of international responsibility for breach of contract. Should the Union legal order, therefore, be given an *ex ante* authorization mechanism for Member States' international agreements? Or, should the Union share financial responsibility for breach of contract with the Member State concerned?

These are difficult constitutional questions. They await future constitutional answers.

2. Supremacy's "executive" nature: disapplication, not invalidation

What are the legal consequences of the supremacy of European law over conflicting national law? Must a national court "hold such provisions inapplicable to the extent to which they are incompatible with [European] law", or must it "declare them void"?[27] This question concerns the constitutional effect of the supremacy doctrine in the Member States.

The classic answer to these questions is found in *Simmenthal II*.[28] The issue raised in the national proceedings was this: "What consequences flow

---

[25] E.-U. Petersmann, "Artikel 234" in H. von der Groeben, J. Thiesing and C.-D. Ehlermann (eds.), *Kommentar zum EWG-Vertrag* (Baden-Baden, Normos, 1991), 5725 at 5731 (para. 6).

[26] See *Commission* v. *Belgium & Luxembourg*, Joined Cases C-176 and 177/97, [1998] ECR I-3557.

[27] This very question was raised in *Firma Gebrüder Luck* v. *Hauptzollamt Köln-Rheinau*, Case 34/67, [1968] ECR 245.

[28] *Amministrazione delle Finanze dello Stato* v. *Simmenthal SpA*, Case 106/77, [1978] ECR 629. But also see *Commission* v. *Italy*, Case 48/71, [1978] ECR 629.

from the direct applicability of a provision of [Union] law in the event of incompatibility with a subsequent legislative provision of a Member State?"[29] Within the Italian constitutional order, national legislation could be *repealed* solely by Parliament or the Supreme Court. Would lower national courts thus have to wait until this happened and, in the meantime, apply national laws that violate Union laws? Unsurprisingly, the European Court rejected such a reading. Appealing to the "very foundations of the [Union]", national courts were under a direct obligation to give immediate effect to European law. The supremacy of European law meant that "rules of [European] law must be fully and uniformly applied in all the Member States from the date of their entry into force and for so long as they continue in force".[30] But did this mean that the national court had to *repeal* the national law? According to one view, supremacy indeed meant that national courts must declare conflicting national laws void. European law would "break" national law.[31] Yet the Court preferred a milder – second – view:

[I]n accordance with the *principle of precedence* of [European] law, the relationship between provisions of the Treaty and directly applicable measures of the institutions on the one hand and the national law of the Member States on the other is such that those provisions and measures not only by their entry into force render *automatically inapplicable* any conflicting provision of current national law but – in so far as they are an integral part of, and take precedence in, the legal order applicable in the territory of each of the Member States – also preclude the valid adoption of new legislative measures to the extent to which they would be incompatible with [European] provisions.[32]

Where national measures conflicted with European law, the supremacy of European law would thus not render them void, but only "inapplicable". Not "invalidation" but "disapplication" was required of national courts, where

---

[29] *Simmenthal*, Case 106/77 (supra n. 28), para. 13.   [30] *Ibid.*, para. 14.

[31] This is the very title of a German monograph by E. Grabitz, *Gemeinschaftsrecht bricht nationales Recht* (L. Appel, 1966). This position was shared by Hallstein: "[T]he supremacy of [European] law means essentially two things: its rules take precedence irrespective of the level of the two orders at which the conflict occurs, and further, [European] law *not only invalidates previous national law but also limits subsequent national legislation*" (W. Hallstein quoted in Sasse, "The Common Market" (supra n. 7), 696–753 at 717 (emphasis added)).

[32] *Simmenthal*, Case 106/77 (supra n. 28), para. 17 (emphasis added).

European laws came into conflict with pre-existing national laws. Yet, in the above passage, the effect of the supremacy doctrine appeared stronger in relation to future national legislation. Here, the Court said that the supremacy of European law would "preclude the *valid adoption* of new legislative measures to the extent to which they would be incompatible with [European] provisions".[33] Was this to imply that national legislators were not even *competent* to adopt national laws that would run counter to *existing* European law? Were these national laws void *ab initio*?[34]

In *Ministero delle Finanze* v. *IN.CO.GE.'90*,[35] the Commission picked up this second prong of the *Simmenthal* ruling and argued that "a Member State has *no power whatever to [subsequently] adopt* a fiscal provision that is incompatible with [European] law, with the result that such a provision ... must be treated as *non-existent*".[36] But the European Court of Justice disagreed with this interpretation. Pointing out that *Simmenthal* "did not draw any distinction between pre-existing and subsequently adopted national law",[37] it held that the incompatibility of subsequently adopted rules of national law with European law did not have the effect of rendering these rules non-existent.[38] National courts were thus only under an obligation to disapply a conflicting provision of national law – be it prior *or* subsequent to the Union law.

What will this tell us about the nature of the supremacy doctrine? It tells us that the supremacy doctrine is about the "executive force" of European law. The Union legal order, while integrated with the national legal orders, is not a "unitary" legal order. European law leaves the "validity" of national norms untouched; and will not negate the underlying legislative

---

[33] *Simmenthal*, Case 106/77 (supra n. 28), para. 17 (emphasis added).

[34] A. Barav, "Les Effets du Droit Communautaire Directement Applicable", 14 (1978) *Cahiers de Droit Européen*, 265 at 275–6. See also Grabitz, *Gemeinschaftsrecht*, and Hallstein, quoted in Sasse (both supra n. 31).

[35] *Ministero delle Finanze* v. *IN.CO.GE.'90 Srl and others*, Joined Cases C-10–22/97, [1998] ECR I-6307.

[36] *Ibid.*, para. 18 (emphasis added).

[37] Arguably, the *Simmenthal* Court had indeed not envisaged two different consequences for the supremacy principle. While para. 17 (supra text and n. 33) appears to make a distinction depending on whether national legislation existed or not, the operative part of the judgment referred to both variants. It stated that a national court should refuse of its own motion to "apply any conflicting provision of national legislation" (*Simmenthal*, dictum).

[38] *Ministero delle Finanze*, Cases C-10–22/97 (supra n. 35), paras. 20–1.

competence of the Member States. The supremacy principle is thus not addressed to the State legislatures, but to the national executive and judicial branches. (And while in some situations the national *legislator* will be required to amend or repeal national provisions that give rise to legal uncertainty,[39] this secondary obligation is not a direct result of the supremacy doctrine but derives from Article 4(3) TEU.)[40] The executive force of European law thus generally leaves the normative validity of national law intact. National courts are not obliged to "break" national law. They must only not apply it when in conflict with European law in a specific case. Supremacy may then best be characterized as a "remedy". Indeed, it "is the most general remedy which individuals whose rights have been infringed may institute before a national court of law".[41]

This remedial supremacy doctrine has a number of advantages. First, some national legal orders may not grant their (lower) courts the power to invalidate parliamentary laws. The question of who may invalidate national laws is thus left to the national legal order.[42] Second, comprehensive national laws must only be disapplied to the extent to which they conflict with European law.[43] They will remain operable in purely internal situations. Third, once the Union act is repealed, national legislation may become fully operational again.[44]

---

[39] *Commission* v. *France* Case 167/73, [1974] ECR 359. The Court now appears generally to assume that the presence of a national provision that conflicts with European law will *ipso facto* "give ... rise to an ambiguous state of affairs in so far as it leaves persons concerned in a state of uncertainty as to the possibilities available to them relying on [European] law"; see *Commission* v. *Italy*, Case 104/86, [1988] ECR 1799, para. 12. And see also *Commission* v. *Hellenic Republic*, Case C-185/96, [1998] ECR 6601, esp. para. 32.

[40] See e.g. *Commission* v. *Italy*, Case 104/86 (supra n. 39), para. 13, and *Commission* v. *Germany*, Case 74/86, [1988] ECR 2139, para. 12.

[41] W. van Gerven, "Of Rights, Remedies and Procedures", 37 (2000) *Common Market Law Review*, 501 at 506.

[42] *Filipiak* v. *Dyrektor Izby Skarbowej w Poznaniu*, Case C-314/08, [2009] ECR I-11049, para. 82: "Pursuant to the principle of the primacy of [European] law, a conflict between a provision of national law and a directly applicable provision of the Treaty is to be resolved by a national court applying [European] law, if necessary by refusing to apply the conflicting national provision, and not by a declaration that the national provision is invalid, the powers of authorities, courts and tribunals in that regard being a matter to be determined by each Member State."

[43] B. de Witte, "Direct Effect, Supremacy and the Nature of the Legal Order" in P. Craig and G. de Búrca (eds.), *The Evolution of EU Law* (Oxford University Press, 1999), 177 at 190.

[44] *Ibid.*

3. National challenges I: fundamental rights

The European Union is not a federal State in which the sovereignty question is solved. The European Union is a federal union of States; and each federal union is characterized by a political dualism. Each citizen is indeed a member of *two* political bodies. These *two* political bodies will compete for loyalty and, sometimes, the "national" view on a political question may not correspond with the "European" view on the matter. What happens when the political views of a Member State clash with that of the federal Union?

Controversies over the supremacy of federal law are as old as the (modern) idea of federalism.[45] And while the previous sections espoused the European answer to the supremacy doctrine, this absolute vision is – unsurprisingly – not shared by all the Member States. There exists a competing national view. And this national perspective accepts the supremacy of European law over *some* national law, but *not all* national law. The supremacy of European law is thus seen as relative, since it is granted and limited by national constitutional law.

A first national challenge to the absolute supremacy of European law crystallized around *Internationale Handelsgesellschaft.*[46] For after the European Court of Justice had given its absolute view on the supremacy of European law, the case moved back to the German Constitutional Court.[47] And the German Court here defined its perspective on the question. Could national constitutional law, especially national fundamental rights, affect the application of European law in the domestic legal order? Famously, the German Constitutional Court rejected the European Court's vision and replaced it with its counter-theory of the *relative* supremacy of European law. The reasoning of the German Court was as follows: while the German Constitution expressly allowed for the transfer of sovereign powers to the European Union in its Article 24,[48] such a transfer was itself

---

[45] R. Schütze, "Federalism as Constitutional Pluralism: Letter from America" in J. Kommarek and M. Avbelj (eds.), *Constitutional Pluralism in the European Union and Beyond* (Hart, 2012), Chapter 8.

[46] *Internationale Handelsgesellschaft*, Case 11/70 (supra n. 11).

[47] BVerfGE 37, 271 (*Solange I (Re Internationale Handelsgesellschaft)*). For an English translation, see [1974] 2 CMLR 540.

[48] Article 24 (1) of the German Constitution states: "The Federation may by a law transfer sovereign powers to international organizations." A new article was subsequently inserted into the German Constitution expressly dealing with the European Union (see Article 23 German Constitution).

limited by the "constitutional identity" of the German State. Fundamental constitutional structures were thus beyond the supremacy of European law:

The part of the Constitution dealing with fundamental rights is an *inalienable essential feature of the valid Constitution of the Federal Republic of Germany and one which forms part of the constitutional structure of the Constitution.* Article 24 of the Constitution does not without reservation allow it to be subjected to qualifications. In this, the present state of integration of the [Union] is of crucial importance. The [Union] still lacks ... in particular a codified catalogue of fundamental rights, the substance of which is reliably and unambiguously fixed for the future in the same way as the substance of the Constitution ...

So long as this legal certainty, which is not guaranteed merely by the decisions of the European Court of Justice, favourable though these have been to fundamental rights, is not achieved in the course of the further integration of the [Union], the reservation derived from Article 24 of the Constitution applies ... *Provisionally, therefore, in the hypothetical case of a conflict between [European] law and a part of national constitutional law or, more precisely, of the guarantees of fundamental rights in the Constitution, there arises the question of which system of law takes precedence, that is, ousts the other. In this conflict of norms, the guarantee of fundamental rights in the Constitution prevails* so long as *the competent organs of the [Union] have not removed the conflict of norms in accordance with the Treaty mechanism.*[49]

"So long" as the European legal order had not developed an adequate standard of fundamental rights, the German Constitutional Court would "disapply" European law that conflicted with the fundamental rights guaranteed in the German legal order. There were thus *national* limits to the supremacy of European law. However, these national limits were also *relative*, as they depended on the evolution and nature of European law. This was the very essence of the "so-long" formula. For once the Union legal order had developed equivalent human rights guarantees, the German Constitutional Court would no longer challenge the supremacy of European law.

The Union legal order did indeed subsequently develop extensive human rights bill(s),[50] and the dispute over the supremacy doctrine was significantly softened in the aftermath of a second famous European case with a national coda. In *Wünsche Handelsgesellschaft,*[51] the German

---

[49] *Solange I*, [1974] 2 CMLR 540 at 550–1 (paras. 23–4, emphasis added).
[50] On this point, see Chapter 4 above.
[51] BVerfGE 73, 339 (*Solange II (Re Wünsche Handelsgesellschaft)*). For an English translation, see: [1987] 3 CMLR 225.

Constitutional Court not only recognized the creation of "substantially similar" fundamental right guarantees, it drew a remarkably self-effacing conclusion from this:

In view of those developments it must be held that, *so long as* the European [Union], and in particular in the case law of the European Court, generally ensures an effective protection of fundamental rights as against the sovereign powers of the [Union] which is to be regarded as substantially similar to the protection of funda-mental rights required unconditionally by the Constitution, and in so far as they generally safeguard the essential content of fundamental rights, the Federal Constitutional Court will no longer exercise its jurisdiction to decide on the applic-ability of secondary [Union] legislation cited as the legal basis for any acts of German courts or authorities within the sovereign jurisdiction of the Federal Republic of Germany, and it will no longer review such legislation by the standard of the fundamental rights contained in the Constitution[.][52]

This judgment became known as "So-Long II", for the German Constitutional Court had again recourse to this famous formulation in determining its relationship with European law. But importantly, this time, the "so-long" condition was inverted. The German Court promised not to question the supremacy of European law "so long" as the latter guaranteed substantially similar fundamental rights to those recognized by the German constitution. This was not an absolute promise to respect the absolute supremacy of European law, but a result of the Court's own relative supremacy doctrine having been fulfilled. "So-Long II" thus only refined the national perspective on the limited supremacy of European law in "So-Long I".

4. National challenges II: competences limits

With the constitutional conflict over fundamental rights (temporarily) set-tled, a second concern emerged: the ever-growing competences of the European Union. Who was to control and limit the scope of European law? Was it enough to have the *European* legislator centrally controlled by the *European* Court of Justice? Or should the national constitutional courts be entitled to a decentralized ultra vires review? The European view on this is crystal clear: national courts cannot disapply – let alone

---

[52] *Ibid.*, 265 (para. 48) (emphasis added).

invalidate – European law.[53] Yet unsurprisingly, this absolute view has not been shared by all Member States. And it was again the German Constitutional Court that set the tone and the vocabulary of the academic debate. The ultra vires question was at the heart of its (in)famous *Maastricht Decision* and would be refined in *Honeywell*.

The German Court set out its ultra vires doctrine in *Maastricht*.[54] Starting from the premise that the European Treaties adhere to the principle of conferred powers, the Court found that the Union ought not to be able to extend its own competences. While the Treaties allowed for teleological interpretation, there existed a clear dividing line "between a legal development within the terms of the Treaties and a making of legal rules which breaks through its boundaries and is not covered by valid Treaty law".[55] This led to the following conclusion:

Thus, if European institutions or agencies were to treat or develop the Union Treaty in a way that was no longer covered by the Treaty in the form that is the basis for the Act of Accession, the resultant legislative instruments would not be legally binding within the sphere of German sovereignty. The German state organs would be prevented for constitutional reasons from applying them in Germany. Accordingly the Federal Constitutional Court will review legal instruments of European institutions and agencies to see whether they remain within the limits of the sovereign rights conferred on them or transgress them ...

Whereas a dynamic extension of the existing Treaties has so far been supported on the basis of an open-handed treatment of Article [352] of the [FEU] Treaty as a "competence to round-off the Treaty" as a whole, and on the basis of considerations relating to the "implied powers" of the [Union], and of Treaty interpretation as allowing maximum exploitation of [Union] powers ("effet utile"), in future it will have to be noted as regards interpretation of enabling provisions by [Union] institutions and agencies that the Union Treaty as a matter of principle distinguishes between the exercise of a sovereign power conferred for limited purposes and the amending of the Treaty, so that its interpretation may not have effects that are equivalent to an extension of the Treaty. Such an interpretation of enabling rules would not produce any binding effects for Germany.[56]

The German Constitutional Court thus threatened to disapply European law that it considered to have been adopted ultra vires.

---

[53] On the *Foto-Frost* doctrine, see Chapter 7 – Section 1(a) below.
[54] BVerfGE 89, 155 (*Maastricht Decision*). For an English translation, see [1994] 1 CMLR 57.
[55] *Ibid.*, 105 (para. 98).   [56] *Ibid.*, 105 (para. 99).

This national review power was subsequently confirmed.[57] Yet, the doctrine was limited and refined in *Honeywell*.[58] The case resulted from a constitutional complaint that targeted the European Court's ruling in *Mangold*.[59] The plaintiff argued that the European Court's "discovery" of a European principle that prohibited discrimination on grounds of age was ultra vires as it read something into the Treaties that was not there. In its decision, the German Constitutional Court confirmed its relative supremacy doctrine. It claimed the power to disapply European law that it considered not to be covered by the principle of conferral. The principle of supremacy was thus not unlimited.[60] However, reminiscent of its judicial deference in *So-Long II*, the Court accepted a presumption that the Union would generally act within the scope of its competences:

If each Member State claimed to be able to decide through their own courts on the validity of legal acts by the Union, the primacy of application could be circumvented in practice, and the uniform application of Union law would be placed at risk. If however, on the other hand the Member States were completely to forgo ultra vires review, disposal of the treaty basis would be transferred to the Union bodies alone, even if their understanding of the law led in the practical outcome to an amendment of a Treaty or an expansion of competences. That in the borderline cases of possible transgression of competences on the part of the Union bodies – which is infrequent, as should be expected according to the institutional and procedural precautions of Union law – the [national] constitutional and the Union law perspective do not completely harmonise, is due to the circumstance that the Member States of the European Union also remain the masters of the Treaties ...

Ultra vires review by the Federal Constitutional Court can moreover *only be considered if it is manifest* that acts of the European bodies and institutions have

---

[57] BVerfGE 123, 267 (*Lisbon Decision*). For an English translation, see [2010] 3 CMLR 276. The Court here added a third sequel to its "So-Long" jurisprudence (*ibid.*, 343): "As long as, and insofar as, the principle of conferral is adhered to in an association of sovereign states with clear elements of executive and governmental co-operation, the legitimation provided by national parliaments and governments complemented and sustained by the directly elected European Parliament is sufficient in principle."

[58] 2 BvR 2661/06 (*Re Honeywell*). For an English translation, see [2011] 1 CMLR 1067. For a discussion of the case, see M. Paydandeh, "Constitutional Review of EU Law after *Honeywell*: Contextualizing the Relationship between the German Constitutional Court and the EU Court of Justice", 48 (2011), *Common Market Law Review*, 9.

[59] *Mangold* v. *Helm*, Case C-144/04, [2005] ECR I-9981.

[60] *Honeywell* [2011] 1 CMLR 1067 at 1084: "Unlike the primacy of application of federal law, as provided for by Article 31 of the Basic Law for the German legal system, the primacy of application of Union law cannot be comprehensive." (It is ironic that this is said by the German Federal(!) Constitutional Court.)

taken place outside the transferred competences. A breach of the principle of conferral is only manifest if the European bodies and institutions have transgressed the boundaries of their competences *in a manner specifically violating the principle of conferral*, the breach of competences is in other words sufficiently qualified. This means that the act of the authority of the European Union *must be manifestly in violation of competences* and that the impugned act is highly significant in the structure of competences between the Member States and the Union with regard to the principle of conferral and to the binding nature of the statute under the rule of law.[61]

This limits the national review of European law to "specific" and "manifest" violations of the principle of conferral. There was thus a presumption that the Union institutions would generally act intra vires; and only for clear and exceptional violations would the German Constitutional Court challenge the supremacy of European law. This has – so far – never happened. But even if the German court's behaviour was again "all bark and no bite",[62] the very speech act of articulating national limits to the supremacy of European law was an expression of the continued existence of a dual or plural perspective on the locus of sovereignty in the European Union. It proves the continued existence of two political levels that compete for the loyalty of their citizens. Sovereignty within the Union thus continues to be contested.[63]

---

[61] *Ibid.*, 1085–6 (paras. 42 and 46 (emphasis added)).

[62] C. U. Schmid, "All Bark and No Bite: Notes on the Federal Constitutional Court's 'Banana Decision'", 7 (2001) *European Law Journal*, 95.

[63] In its "*Lisbon Decision*", the German Constitutional Court even added a third constitutional limit to European integration: the "State identity limit". Claiming that European unification could not be achieved in such a way "that not sufficient space is left to the Member States for the political formation of the economic, cultural and social living conditions", the Court identified "[e]ssential areas of democratic formative action". "Particularly sensitive for the ability of a constitutional state to democratically shape itself are decisions on substantive and formal criminal law (1), on the disposition of the monopoly on the use of force by the police within the state and by the military towards the exterior (2), fundamental fiscal decisions on public revenue and public expenditure, the latter being particularly motivated, *inter alia*, by social policy considerations (3), decisions on the shaping of living conditions in a social state (4) and decisions of particular cultural importance, for example on family law, the school and education system and on dealing with religious communities (5)." (See *ibid.*, paras. 249 and 252.)

7 National actions

Introduction

The European Union is based on a system of cooperative federalism: *all* national courts are entitled and obliged to apply European law to disputes before them.[1] This contrasts with the judicial system in the United States in which only federal courts are to have jurisdiction over federal claims. The duty of national courts to apply (directly effective) European law derives from the general duty of sincere cooperation codified in Article 4 (3) TEU.[2] From a

---

[1] In *Amministrazione delle Finanze dello Stato* v. *Simmenthal*, Case 106/77, [1978] ECR 629 the European Court clarified that the duty applies to every national court (*ibid.*, para. 21): "[E]very national court must, in a case within its jurisdiction, apply [European] law in its entirety and protect rights which the latter confers on individuals[.]"

[2] Article 4 (3) TEU states: "Pursuant to the principle of sincere cooperation, the Union and the Member States shall, in full mutual respect, assist each other in carrying out tasks which flow from the Treaties. The Member States shall take any appropriate measure, general or

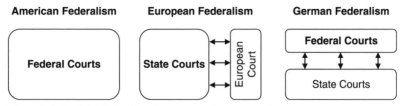

Figure 7.1 Judicial federalism in comparative perspective

functional perspective, the decentralized application of European law –
partly – transforms national courts into "European" courts. But unlike German
judicial federalism, state courts are not hierarchically subordinated under the
appeal jurisdiction of federal courts. The relationship between national courts
and the European Court is based on their *voluntary* cooperation.

In the absence of an "institutional" hierarchy between the European Court
and the national courts, how has the European legal order guaranteed a degree
of uniformity in the judicial application of European law? From the very
beginning, the Treaties contained a mechanism for the interpretative assistance of national courts: the preliminary reference procedure. The general and
specific aspects of the procedure will be discussed in Sections 1 and 2. Suffice
to say here that the European Court is only *indirectly* involved in the judgment
delivered by the national court. It cannot "decide" the case, as this is the
prerogative of the national court.

National courts are the primary enforcers of European law. And the
European legal order has traditionally recognized the procedural autonomy of the national judiciary in the enforcement of European law:
"Where national authorities are responsible for implementing [European
law] it must be recognized that in principle this implementation takes
place with due respect for the forms and procedures of national law."[3] This
formulation has become known as the principle of "national procedural
autonomy".[4] The danger with this decentralized judicial enforcement,

particular, to ensure fulfilment of the obligations arising out of the Treaties or resulting
from the acts of the institutions of the Union. The Member States shall facilitate the achievement of the Union's tasks and refrain from any measure which could jeopardize the attainment of the Union's objectives."

[3] *Norddeutsches Vieh- und Fleischkontor GmbH* v. *Hauptzollamt Hamburg-St. Annen*, Case
39/70, [1971] ECR 49, para. 4.

[4] For a criticism of the notion, see C. N. Kakouris, "Do the Member States Possess Judicial
Procedural 'Autonomy'?", 34 (1997) *Common Market Law Review*, 1389 (arguing that
the Court has never referred to the principle in its case law). However, the Court subsequently
recognized, and now regularly recognizes, the principle in its case law; see *The Queen* v.
Secretary of State for Transport, ex parte Wells, Case C-201/02, [2004] ECR I-723.

however, is that there may be a European *right*, but no national *remedy* to enforce that right. And for that reason, the autonomy of national enforcement powers was never absolute. Indeed, the European Court has imposed two constitutional limitations on the procedural autonomy of the Member States: the principle of equivalence and the principle of effectiveness (Section 3). Both principles still depend on the existence of *national* remedies for the enforcement of European law. And eventually, this came to be seen as insufficient. The European Court thus established a *European* remedy in the national courts: the principle of state liability. Where an individual had not been able to enforce its European rights in a national court, it could – under certain conditions – claim compensatory damages resulting from a breach of European law (Section 4).

1. Preliminary rulings: general aspects

Where national courts encounter problems relating to the interpretation of European law, they can ask "preliminary questions" of the European Court. The questions are "preliminary", since they *precede* the application of European law by the national court. The preliminary rulings procedure indeed constitutes the cornerstone of the Union's judicial federalism. This federalism is *cooperative* in nature: the European Court and the national courts collaborate in the adjudication of a single case. The procedure for preliminary rulings is set out in Article 267 TFEU, which reads:

[1] The Court of Justice of the European Union shall have jurisdiction to give preliminary rulings concerning:

    (a) the interpretation of the Treaties;
    (b) the validity and interpretation of acts of the institutions, bodies, offices or agencies of the Union;

[2] Where such a question is raised before any court or tribunal of a Member State, that court or tribunal may, if it considers that a decision on the question is necessary to enable it to give judgment, request the Court to give a ruling thereon.

[3]   Where any such question is raised in a case pending before a court or tribunal of a Member State against whose decisions there is no judicial remedy under national law, that court or tribunal shall bring the matter before the Court.[5]

The provision establishes a constitutional nexus between the European and the national courts. This section looks at the general aspects of preliminary rulings. We start by analysing the jurisdiction of the European Court under the procedure, and then move to the nature and effect of preliminary rulings in the Union legal order.

(a) The jurisdiction of the European Court

The European Court's jurisdiction, set out in paragraph 1 of Article 267, is limited to *European* law. "The Court is not entitled, within the framework of Article [267 TFEU], to interpret rules pertaining to national law."[6] The Court's competence only extends to questions on the "validity and interpretation" of European law. Preliminary references may thus be made in relation to *two* judicial functions. They can concern the *interpretation* of European law. This includes all types of European law – ranging from the deepest constitutional foundations to the loftiest soft law. But national courts can equally ask about the *validity* of European law. The European legal order however insists on the *exclusive* power of the European Court of Justice to declare European acts invalid.[7] And in exercising its judicial review function, the European Court will be confined to providing a ruling on the validity of acts *below* the Treaties.

The *application* of European law is not within the power of the Court. Article 267 "gives the Court no jurisdiction to apply the Treat[ies] to

---

[5] The (omitted) fourth paragraph states: "If such a question is raised in a case pending before a court or tribunal of a Member State with regard to a person in custody, the Court of Justice of the European Union shall act with the minimum of delay." According to Article 23a of the Court's Statute, there may exist an "urgent preliminary procedure" (in French: "*procédure préjudicielle d'urgence*" or "*PPU*") in the area of freedom, security, and justice. The Court has used this power and defined the procedure in Article 104b of the Court's Rules of Procedure. On the "*PPU*", see C. Barnard, "The PPU: Is it Worth the Candle? An Early Assessment", 34 (2009) *European Law Review*, 281.

[6] *Hoekstra (née Unger)*, Case 75/63, [1964] ECR 177, para. 3.

[7] See *Foto-Frost* v. *Hauptzollamt Lübeck-Ost*, Case 314/85, [1987] ECR 4199. On the constitutional principles governing the indirect review of European law through the preliminary reference procedure, see R. Schütze, *European Constitutional Law* (Cambridge University Press, 2012), Chapter 8 – Section 1(d/ii).

a specific case".[8] However, the distinction between "interpretation" and "application" is sometimes hard to make. The Court has tried to explain it as follows: "When it gives an interpretation of the Treat[ies] in a specific action pending before a national court, the Court limits itself to deducing the meaning of the [European] rules from the wording and spirit of the Treat[ies], it being left to the national court to apply in the particular case the rules which are thus interpreted."[9] Theoretically, this should mean that the Court of Justice cannot decide whether or not a national law, in fact, violates the Treaties. And yet, the Court has often made this very assessment.[10]

A famous illustration of the blurred line between "interpretation" and "application" is provided by the "Sunday trading cases".[11] Would the prohibition on trading on Sundays conflict with the Union's internal market provisions? Preliminary references had been made by a number of English courts to obtain an interpretation on the Treaties' free movement of goods provisions. The Court found that national rules governing opening hours could be justified on public interest grounds, but asked the referring national courts "to ascertain whether the effects of such national rules exceed what is necessary to achieve the aim in view".[12] Yet the decentralized application of this proportionality test led to a judicial fragmentation of the United Kingdom. Simply put, different national courts decided differently. The Court thus ultimately took matters into its own hands and centrally applied the proportionality test.[13] And in holding that the British Sunday trading rules were not disproportionate interferences with the internal market, the Court crossed the line between "interpretation" and "application" of the Treaties.

---

[8] *Costa* v. ENEL, Case 6/64, [1964] ECR 585 at 592.

[9] *Da Costa et al.* v. *Netherlands Inland Revenue Administration*, Joined Cases 28-30/62, [1963] ECR 31 at 38.

[10] For two excellent analyses of this category of cases, see G. Davies, "The Division of Powers between the European Court of Justice and National Courts", *Constitutionalism Web-Papers* 3/2004 (SSRN Network: www.ssrn.com); as well as T. Tridimas, "Constitutional Review of Member State Action: The Virtues and Vices of an Incomplete Jurisdiction", 9 (2011) *International Journal of Constitutional Law*, 737.

[11] See M. Jarvis, "The Sunday Trading Episode: In Defence of the Euro-defence", 44 (1995) *International and Comparative Law Quarterly*, 451.

[12] *Torfaen Borough Council*, Case C-145/88, [1989] ECR I-3851, para. 15.

[13] *Stoke-on-Trent* v. *B & Q*, Case C-169/91, [1992] ECR I-6635.

(b) The legal nature of preliminary rulings

What is the nature of preliminary rulings from the European Court? Preliminary references are not appeals. They are – principally – discretionary acts of a national court asking for interpretative help from the European Court.[14] Once the latter has given a preliminary ruling, this ruling will be binding. But *whom* will it bind – the parties to the national dispute or the national court(s)?

Preliminary rulings cannot bind the parties in the national dispute, since the European Court will not "decide" their case. It is therefore misleading to even speak of a binding effect *inter partes* in the context of preliminary rulings.[15] The Court's rulings are addressed to the national court requesting the reference; and the Court has clarified that "that ruling is binding on the national court as to the interpretation of the [Union] provisions and acts in question".[16] Yet, will the binding effect of a preliminary ruling extend beyond the referring national court? In other words, is a preliminary ruling equivalent to a "decision" addressed to a single court; or will the European Court's interpretation be generally binding on all national courts?

The Court has long clarified that a preliminary ruling is *not* a "decision"; indeed, it is not even seen as an (external) act of a Union institution.[17] What then is the nature of preliminary rulings? The question has been hotly debated in the academic literature. And we may contrast two views competing with each other. According to the common law view, preliminary rulings are – if not *de jure*, at least *de facto* – legal precedents that generally bind all national courts. Judgments of the European Court are binding *erga*

---

[14] *Kempter* v. *Hauptzollamt Hamburg-Jonas*, Case C-2/06, [2008] ECR I-411, para. 41: "the system established by Article [267 TFEU] with a view to ensuring that [European] law is interpreted uniformly in the Member States instituted direct cooperation between the Court of Justice and the national courts by means of a procedure which is completely independent of any initiative by the parties". And *ibid.*, para. 42: "the system of references for a preliminary ruling is based on a dialogue between one court and another, the initiation of which depends entirely on the national court's assessment as to whether a reference is appropriate and necessary".

[15] Contra, see A. Toth, "The Authority of Judgments of the European Court of Justice: Binding Force and Legal Effects", 4 (1984) *Yearbook of European Law*, 1.

[16] *Benedetti* v. *Munari*, Case 52/76, [1977] ECR 163, para. 26.

[17] *Wünsche Handelsgesellschaft* v. *Germany*, Case 69/85 (Order), [1986] ECR 947, para. 16.

omnes.[18] This view typically links the rise of the doctrine of judicial precedent with the evolution of the doctrine of *acte clair*.[19] It is thereby claimed that the Court of Justice transformed its position vis-à-vis national courts from a *horizontal* and *bilateral* relationship to a *vertical* and *multilateral* one.[20]

The problem with this – masterful yet mistaken – theory is that the European Court subscribes to a second constitutional view: the civil law tradition. Accordingly, its judgments do not create "new" legal rules but only clarify "old" ones. In the words of the Court: "The interpretation which, in the exercise of the jurisdiction conferred upon it by Article [267 TFEU], the Court of Justice gives to a rule of [European] law clarifies and defines where necessary the meaning and scope of that rule as it must be or ought to have been understood and applied from the time of its coming into force[.]"[21] The Court of Justice thus adopts the – (in)famous – "declaration theory". And because "the judgments are assumed to be declaring pre-existing law, their binding force applies to all relationships governed by the [positive] legal instrument since it entered into force".[22] The vertical and multilateral effects of preliminary rulings are thus mediated through the positive rule interpreted and not, as the common law view asserts, through a doctrine of precedent.[23]

In light of the "civilian" judicial philosophy of the European Court, its judgments are *not* generally binding.[24] There is no vertical or multilateral

---

[18] See A. Trabucchi, "L'Effet 'erga omnes' des Décision Préjudicielles rendus par la Cour de Justice des Communautés Européennes", 10 (1974) *Revue Trimestrielle de Droit Européen*, 56.

[19] H. Rasmussen, "The European Court's Acte Clair Strategy in C.I.L.F.I.T", 10 (1984) *European Law Review* 242. On the doctrine, see Section 2 (c) below.

[20] This view is popularized in P. Craig and G. de Búrca, *EU Law: Text, Cases and Materials* (Oxford University Press, 2007), 461.

[21] *Amministrazione delle Finanze dello Stato* v. *Denkavit*, Case 61/79, [1980] ECR 1205, para. 16; and more recently *Kühne & Heitz* v. *Productschap voor Pluimvee en Eieren*, Case C-453/00, [2004] ECR I-837, para. 21.

[22] D. Chalmers et al., *European Union Law* (Cambridge University Press, 2010), 171.

[23] Against this civilian background, the argument that the Treaty drafters, by providing for the automatic operation of the obligation to refer, "assumed that the Court's dicta under Article [267] were deprived of authority for any other court than the submitting one" (Rasmussen, "Acte Clair Strategy" supra n. 19, at 249), is flawed. And starting from this false premise, Rasmussen (over)interprets *CILFIT*.

[24] In this sense, see Toth, "The Authority of Judgements" (supra n. 15), 60: "in the cases under discussion the Court itself has never meant to attribute, as is sometimes suggested, a general binding force to interpretative preliminary rulings".

effect of judicial decisions, as "judgments of the European Courts are *not sources* but *authoritative evidences* of [European] law". "[A]n interpretation given by the Court becomes an integral part of the provision interpreted and cannot fail to affect the legal position of all those who may derive rights and obligations from that provision."[25]

Are there constitutional problems with the Union's civil law philosophy? There indeed are "temporal" problems. For the "declaratory" effect of preliminary rulings generally generates "retroactive" effects.[26] For in *Kühne & Heitz*,[27] the Court held that a (new) interpretation of European law must be applied "even to legal relationships which arose or were formed before the Court gave its ruling on the question on interpretation".[28] The Court has nonetheless recognized that its civil law philosophy must – occasionally – be tempered by the principles of legal certainty and financial equity.[29] It has therefore – exceptionally – limited the temporal effects of its preliminary rulings to an effect *ex nunc*, that is: an effect from the time of the ruling. However, the Court has equally clarified that legal certainty will not prevent the retrospective application of a (new) interpretation, where the judgment of a national court of final instance "was, in the light of a decision given by the Court subsequent to it, based on a misinterpretation of [European] law which was adopted without a question being referred to the Court for a preliminary ruling under the third paragraph of Article [267]".[30]

2. Preliminary rulings: special aspects

Article 267 (2) defines the competence of national courts to ask preliminary questions. The provision allows "any court or tribunal of a Member State" to ask a European law question that "is necessary to enable it to give judgment". And while any national courts "may" refer a question to the

---

[25] *Ibid.*, 70 and 74 (emphasis added).

[26] On this point, see G. Bebr, "Preliminary Rulings of the Court of Justice: Their Authority and Temporal Effect", 18 (1981) *Common Market Law Review*, 475, esp. 491: "The retroactive effect of a preliminary interpretative ruling is, according to the Court, the general rule."

[27] *Kühne & Heitz*, Case C-453/00 (supra n. 21).   [28] *Ibid.*, para. 22.

[29] For the former rationale, see *Kempter*, Case C-2/06 (supra n. 14); for the latter rationale, see *Defrenne* v. *Sabena*, Case 43/75, [1976] ECR 455.

[30] *Kempter*, Case C-12/06 (supra, n. 14), para. 39. For a critical analysis of this case, see A. Ward, "Do unto Others as you would have them do unto you: 'Willy Kempter' and the Duty to Raise EC Law in National Litigation", 33 (2008) *European Law Review*, 739.

European Court under paragraph 2, Article 267 (3) imposes an obligation on certain courts. Article 267 (3) defines these as courts "against whose decisions there is no judicial remedy under national law".

Let us look at each of these special aspects of the preliminary reference procedure in turn.

(a) "Who": national courts and tribunals

The formulation "court or tribunal" in Article 267 directly refers to *judicial* authorities, and thus indirectly excludes *administrative* authorities. But what exactly is a "court or tribunal" that can refer questions to the Court of Justice? The Treaties provide no positive definition. Would the concept therefore fall within the competence of the Member States? Unsurprisingly, the European Court has not accepted this idea and has provided a European definition of the phrase. Its definition is extremely wide. In *Dorsch Consult*,[31] the Court stated that it will take account of a variety of factors "such as whether the body is established by law, whether it is permanent, whether its jurisdiction is compulsory, whether its procedure is *inter partes*, whether it applies rules of law and whether it is independent[.]"[32] The last criterion is controlling. Therefore, an authority that is not independent from the State's administrative branch is not a court or tribunal in the meaning of European law.[33]

The enormous breadth of this European definition was illustrated in *Broekmeulen*.[34] The plaintiff had obtained a medical degree from Belgium and tried to register as a "General Practitioner" in the Netherlands. The registration was refused on the ground that Dutch professional qualifications were not satisfied. The plaintiff appealed before the "Appeals Committee for General Medicine" – a professional body set up under private law. This Appeals Committee was not a court or tribunal under Dutch law. Would it nonetheless be a "court or tribunal" under European law, and, as

---

[31] *Dorsch Consult Ingenieurgesellschaft* v. *Bundesbaugesellschaft Berlin*, Case C-54/96, [1997] ECR I-4961.

[32] *Ibid.*, para. 23.

[33] *Syfait et al.* v. *GlaxoSmithKline*, Case C-53/03, [2005] ECR I-4609. On the general question, whether national competition authorities should be considered "courts or tribunals" in the sense of Article 267 TFEU, see A. Komninos, "Article 234 EC and National Competition Authorities in the Era of Decentralisation", 29 (2004) *European Law Review*, 106.

[34] *Broekmeulen* v. *Huisarts Registratie Commissie*, Case 246/80, [1981] ECR 2311.

such, be entitled to make a preliminary reference? The European Court found as follows:

> In order to deal with the question of the applicability in the present case of Article [267 TFEU], it should be noted that it is incumbent upon Member States to take the necessary steps to ensure that within their territory the provisions adopted by the [Union] institutions are implemented in their entirety. If, under the legal system of a Member State, the task of implementing such provisions is assigned to a professional body acting under a degree of governmental supervision, and if that body, in conjunction with the public authorities concerned, creates appeal procedures which may affect the exercise of rights granted by [European] law, it is imperative, in order to ensure the proper functioning of [Union] law, that the Court should have an opportunity of ruling on issues of interpretation and validity arising out of such proceedings. As a result of all the foregoing considerations and in the absence, in practice, of any right of appeal to the ordinary courts, the Appeals Committee, which operates with the consent of the public authorities and with their cooperation, and which, after an adversarial procedure, delivers decisions which are recognized as final, must, in a matter involving the application of [European] law, be considered as a court or tribunal of a Member State within the meaning of Article [267 TFEU].[35]

Can higher national courts limit the power of a lower national court to refer preliminary questions? The European legal order has given short shrift to the attempt to break the cooperative nexus between the European Court and *each level of the national judiciary*. In *Rheinmühlen*,[36] the Court thus held that "a rule of national law whereby a court is bound on points of law by the rulings of a superior court cannot deprive the inferior courts of their power to refer to the Court questions of interpretation of [Union] law involving such rulings".[37] For if inferior courts could not refer to the Court of Justice, "the jurisdiction of the latter to give preliminary rulings and the application of [European] law *at all levels of the judicial systems* of the Member States would be compromised".[38] A national court or tribunal, at any level of the national judicial hierarchy, and at any stage of its judicial procedure, is thus entitled to refer a preliminary question to the European Court of Justice.[39] National rules

---

[35] *Ibid.*, paras. 16–17.   [36] *Rheinmühlen-Düsseldorf,* Case 166/73, [1974] ECR 33.

[37] *Ibid.*, para. 4.

[38] *Ibid.* (emphasis added). For a recent confirmation, see *Elchinov* v. *Natsionalna zdravno-osiguritelna kasa*, Case C-173/09 (nyr), para. 27.

[39] This European entitlement however cannot be transformed into a national obligation; see *Kücükdeveci* v. *Swedex*, Case C-555/07, [2010] ECR I-365, para. 54: "The possibility thus given to the national court by the second paragraph of Article 267 TFEU of asking the Court for a preliminary ruling before disapplying the national provision that is contrary to

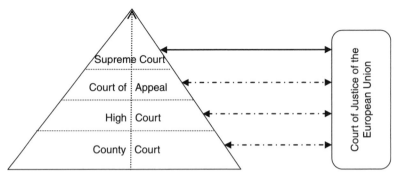

Figure 7.2 Preliminary rulings under Article 267

allowing for an appeal against the decision of a national court to refer a preliminary question to the European Court thus violate "the autonomous jurisdiction which Article [267 TFEU] confers on the referring court".[40] For the English judicial hierarchy, the judicial federalism constructed by the European Court thus looks as Figure 7.2.

(b) "What": necessary questions

National courts are entitled to request a preliminary ruling, where there is a "question" on which they consider it "necessary" for judgment to be given. In the past, the European Court has been eager to encourage national courts to ask preliminary questions. For these questions offered the Court formidable opportunities to say what the European constitution "is".[41] Thus, even where questions were "imperfectly formulated", the Court was willing to extract the "right" ones.[42] Moreover, the Court will generally not "criticize the grounds and purpose of the request for interpretation".[43] Nonetheless,

European Union law cannot, however, be transformed into an obligation because national law does not allow that court to disapply a provision it considers to be contrary to the constitution unless the provision has first been declared unconstitutional by the Constitutional Court. By reason of the principle of the primacy of European Union law, which extends also to the principle of non-discrimination on grounds of age, contrary national legislation which falls within the scope of European Union law must be disapplied."

[40] *Cartesio*, Case C-210/06, [2008] ECR I-9641 para. 95.

[41] In the famous phrase by C. E. Hughes: "We are under a Constitution, but the Constitution is what the judges say it is[.]"

[42] *Costa* v. *ENEL*, Case 6/64, (supra n. 8) 593: "[T]he Court has the power to extract from a question imperfectly formulated by the national court those questions which alone pertain to the interpretation of the Treaty."

[43] *Ibid.*

in – very – exceptional circumstances the Court may reject a request for a preliminary ruling.

This happened in *Foglia* v. *Novello (No. 1)*,[44] where the Court insisted that questions referred to it must be raised in a "genuine" dispute.[45] Where the parties to the national dispute agreed on the desirable outcome, the Court had no jurisdiction.[46] In a sequel to this case, the Court justified this jurisdictional limitation as follows:

[T]he duty assigned to the Court by Article [267] is not that of delivering advisory opinions on general or hypothetical questions but of assisting in the administration of justice in the Member States. It accordingly does not have jurisdiction to reply to questions of interpretation which are submitted to it within the framework of procedural devices arranged by the parties in order to induce the Court to give its views on certain problems of [European] law which do not correspond to an objective requirement inherent in the resolution of a dispute.[47]

The Court of Justice has thus imposed some jurisdictional control on requests for preliminary rulings. To prevent an abuse of the Article 267 procedure, the European Court will be able "to check, as all courts must, whether it has jurisdiction".[48] Yet, it was eager to emphasize that it wished "not in any way [to] trespass upon the prerogatives of the national courts".[49] The Court thus pledged to "place as much reliance as possible upon the assessment by the national court of the extent to which the questions submitted are essential".[50] The Court will therefore decline jurisdiction "only if it is manifest that the interpretation of [European] law or the examination of the validity of a rule of [European] law sought by that court bears no relation to the true facts or the subject-matter of the main proceedings".[51] And even if the question is not strictly speaking necessary, because

---

[44] *Foglia* v. *Novello*, Case 104/79, [1980] ECR 745.

[45] G. Bebr, "The Existence of a Genuine Dispute: an Indispensable Precondition for the Jurisdiction of the Court under Article 177 EEC?", 17 (1980) *Common Market Law Review*, 525.

[46] *Foglia* v. *Novello*, Case 104/79, (supra n. 44) paras. 11–13 (emphasis added): "The duty of the Court of Justice under Article [267] of the [FEU] Treaty is to supply all courts in the [Union] with the information on the interpretation of [European] law which is necessary to enable them to settle *genuine* disputes which are brought before them."

[47] *Foglia* v. *Novello (No. 2)*, Case 244/80 [1981] ECR 3045, para. 18.   [48] *Ibid.*, para. 19.

[49] *Ibid.*, para. 18.   [50] *Ibid.*, para. 19.

[51] *Imperial Chemical Industries (ICI)* v. *Kenneth Hall Colmer (Her Majesty's Inspector of Taxes)*, Case C-264/96, [1998] ECR I-4695, para. 15.

the Court had already answered a very similar one in the past,[52] the Court will accept jurisdiction for questions raised under Article 267, paragraph 2.

(c) The obligation to refer and "*acte clair*"

While any national courts "may" refer a question to the European Court under paragraph 2, Article 267 (3) imposes an obligation: "Where any such question is raised in a case pending before a court or tribunal of a Member State against whose decisions there is no judicial remedy under national law, that court or tribunal shall bring the matter before the Court."

What is the scope of this obligation? Two theoretical options exist. Under the "institutional" theory, the formulation refers to the highest judicial *institution* in the country. This would restrict the obligation to refer preliminary questions to a single court in a Member State – in the United Kingdom: the Supreme Court. By contrast, the "procedural" theory links the definition of the court of last instance to the judicial *procedure* in the particular case. This broadens the obligation to refer to every national court whose decision cannot be appealed in the particular case. And the Court of Justice has – from the very beginning – favoured the second theory.[53] The key concept in Article 267 (3) is thereby the "appeal*ability*" of a judicial decision. What counts is the *ability* of the parties to appeal to a higher court. The fact that the merits of the appeal are subject to a prior declaration of admissibility by the superior court will therefore not deprive the parties of a judicial remedy.[54] Where an appeal is *procedurally* possible, the obligation under Article 267 (3) will not apply.

Apart from the uncertainty concerning what are courts "against whose decisions there is no judicial remedy under national law", the wording of

---

[52] In *Da Costa et al* v. *Netherlands Inland Revenue Administration*, Joined Case 28–30/62, (supra n. 9), the Court was presented with the identical scenario to *Van Gend en Loos* and still held that Article 267 TFEU "always allows a national court, if it considers it desirable, to refer questions of interpretation to the Court again" (*ibid.*, 38).

[53] The procedural theory received support in *Costa* v. *ENEL*, Case 6/64 (supra n. 8), where the ECJ treated an Italian court of *first* instance as a court against whose decision there was no judicial remedy.

[54] *Lyckeskog*, Case C-99/00, [2002] ECR I-4839, paras. 16–17: "Decisions of a national appellate court which can be challenged by the parties before a supreme court are not decisions of a court or tribunal of a Member State against whose decisions there is no judicial remedy under national law within the meaning of Article [267 TFEU]. The fact that examination of the merits of such appeals is subject to a prior declaration of admissibility by the Supreme Court does not have the effect of depriving the parties of a judicial remedy."

Article 267 (3) appears relatively clear. Yet, this picture is – very – deceptive. For the European Court has judicially "amended" the provision in two significant ways. The first "amendment" relates to references on the validity of European law. Despite the restrictive wording of paragraph 3, the European Court has insisted that *all* national courts must refer validity questions to the European Court.[55] This *expansion* of the scope of Article 267 (3) follows from the structure of the Union's judicial federalism, which grants the exclusive power to invalidate European law to the Court of Justice.

By contrast, a second "amendment" has limited the obligation to refer preliminary questions. This *limitation* followed from constitutional common sense. For to ask a question implies uncertainty as to the answer. And where the answer is "clear", there may be no need to raise a question. Yet on its textual face, Article 267 (3) treats national courts "as perpetual children": they are forbidden from interpreting European law – even if the answers are crystal clear.[56] And in order to counter this, the European legal order imported a French legal doctrine under the name of *acte clair*. The doctrine simply means that where it is *clear* how to *act*, a national court need not ask a preliminary question.

The doctrine of *acte clair* began its European career in *Da Costa*.[57] In this case, the Court held that "the authority of an interpretation under Article [267] already given by the Court may deprive the obligation of its purpose and thus empty it of its substance". "Such is the case especially when the question raised is *materially identical* with a question which has already been the subject of a preliminary ruling in a similar case."[58] The Court subsequently clarified that this covered a second situation. Where the European Court had already given a negative answer to a question relating to the *validity* of a Union act, another national court need not raise the same

---

[55] See *The Queen on the Application of International Air Transport Association et al.* v. *Department for Transport*, Case C-344/04, [2006] ECR I-403 para. 30.

[56] J. C. Cohen, "The European Preliminary Reference and U.S. Court Review of State Court Judgments: A Study in Comparative Judicial Federalism", 44 (1996) *American Journal of Comparative Law*, 421 at 438.

[57] *Da Costa et al* v. *Netherlands Inland Revenue Administration*, Joined 28–30/62 (supra n. 9).

[58] *Ibid.*, 38 (emphasis added).

question again.[59] However, general guidelines on the constitutional scope of the *acte clair* doctrine were only offered in *CILFIT*.[60] The Court here widened the doctrine to situations "where previous decisions of the Court have already dealt with the *point of law* in question, irrespective of the nature of the proceedings which led to those decisions, even though the questions at issue are not strictly identical".[61] Yet national courts would only be released from their obligation to refer questions under Article 267 (3) TFEU, where the correct application of European law is "so obvious as to leave no scope for any reasonable doubt as to the matter in which the question raised is to be resolved".[62] This was an extremely high threshold, which the Court linked to the fulfilment of a number of very (!) restrictive conditions.[63]

---

[59] *International Chemical Corporation*, Case 66/80 [1981] ECR 1191, paras. 12–13: "When the Court is moved under Article [267] to declare an act of one of the institutions to be void there are particularly imperative requirements concerning legal certainty in addition to those concerning the uniform application of [European] law. It follows from the very nature of such a declaration that a national court may not apply the act declared to be void without once more creating serious uncertainty as to the [European] law applicable. It follows therefrom that although a judgment of the Court given under Article [267] of the Treaty declaring an act of an institution, in particular a Council or Commission regulation, to be void is directly addressed only to the national court which brought the matter before the Court, it is sufficient reason for any other national court to regard that act as void for the purposes of a judgment which it has to give."

[60] *CILFIT and others* v. *Ministry of Health*, Case 283/81, [1982] ECR 3415.

[61] *Ibid.*, para. 14 (emphasis added).   [62] *Ibid.* para. 16.

[63] *Ibid.*, paras. 16–20: "Before it comes to the conclusion that such is the case, the national court or tribunal must be convinced that the matter is equally obvious to the courts of the other Member States and to the Court of Justice. Only if those conditions are satisfied, may the national court or tribunal refrain from submitting the question to the Court of Justice and take upon itself the responsibility for resolving it. However, the existence of such a possibility must be assessed on the basis of the characteristic features of [European] law and the particular difficulties to which its interpretation gives rise. To begin with, it must be borne in mind that [Union] legislation is drafted in several languages and that the different language versions are all equally authentic. An interpretation of a provision of [European] law thus involves a comparison of the different language versions. It must also be borne in mind, even where the different language versions are entirely in accord with one another, that [European] law uses terminology which is peculiar to it. Furthermore, it must be emphasized that legal concepts do not necessarily have the same meaning in [European] law and in the law of the various Member States. Finally, every provision of [European] law must be placed in its context and interpreted in the light of the provisions of [European] law as a whole, regard being had to the objectives thereof and to its state of evolution at the date on which the provision in question is to be applied."

3. National remedies: equivalence and effectiveness

The general duty governing the decentralized enforcement of European law by national courts is Article 4 (3) TEU.[64] This duty of "sincere cooperation" imposes two limitations on the procedural autonomy of the Member States: the principle of equivalence and the principle of effectiveness. The classic expression of both limitations can be found in *Rewe*:

[I]n the absence of [European] rules on this subject, it is for the domestic legal system of each Member State to designate the courts having jurisdiction and to determine the procedural conditions governing actions at law intended to ensure the protection of the rights which citizens have from the direct effect of [European] law, it being understood that such conditions cannot be less favourable than those relating to similar actions of a domestic nature ... In the absence of such measures of harmonization the right conferred by [European] law must [thus] be exercised before the national courts in accordance with the conditions laid down by national rules. The position would be different only if the [national rules] made it impossible in practice to exercise the rights which the national courts are obliged to protect.[65]

The procedural autonomy of the Member States is thus *relative*. First, national procedural rules cannot make the enforcement of European rights less favourable than the enforcement of similar national rights. This prohibition of procedural discrimination is the principle of equivalence. Second, national procedural rules – even if not discriminatory – ought not to make the enforcement of European rights "impossible in practice". This would become known as the principle of effectiveness. Both principles have led to a *judicial* harmonization of national procedural laws, and this third Section analyses their evolution.

(a) The equivalence principle

The idea behind the principle of equivalence is straightforward: national procedures and remedies for the enforcement of European rights "cannot be less favourable than those relating to similar actions of a domestic

---

[64] For the text of Article 4 (3) TEU, see supra n. 2.

[65] *Rewe*, Case 33/76, [1976] ECR 1989, para. 5. See also *Comet BV* v. *Produktschap voor Siergewassen*, Case 45/76, [1976] ECR 2043. For the modern version, see *Peterbroeck, Van Campenhout & Cie* v. *Belgian State*, Case C-312/93, (1995) ECR I-4599.

nature".[66] When applying European law, national courts must act *as if* they were applying national law. National procedures and remedies must not discriminate between national and European rights. The principle of equivalence will consequently not affect the substance of national remedies. It only requires the formal extension of those remedies to "similar" or "equivalent" actions under European law.

The logic of non-discrimination requires that similar actions be treated similarly. But what are "equivalent" or "similar" actions? The devil always lies in the detail, and much case law on the equivalence principle has concentrated on this devilish question. In *Edis*,[67] a company had been required to pay a registration charge. Believing the charge to be contrary to European law, the plaintiff applied for a refund from the State that was rejected by the Italian courts on the ground that the limitation period for such refunds had expired. However, Italian law recognized various limitation periods – depending on whether the refund was due to be paid by public or private parties. The limitation period for public authorities was shorter than that for private parties. And this posed the following question: was the national court entitled to simply extend the national public refund procedure to charges in breach of European law; or was it required to apply the more generous *private* refund procedure? The Court answered as follows:

Observance of the principle of equivalence implies, for its part, that the procedural rule at issue applies without distinction to actions alleging infringements of [Union] law and to those alleging infringements of national law, with respect to the same kind of charges or dues. *That principle cannot, however, be interpreted as obliging a Member State to extend its most favourable rules governing recovery under national law to all actions for repayment of charges or dues levied in breach of [European] law.* Thus, [European] law does not preclude the legislation of a Member State from laying down, alongside a limitation period applicable under the ordinary law to actions between private individuals for the recovery of sums paid but not due, special detailed rules, which are less favourable, governing claims and legal proceedings to challenge the imposition of charges and other levies. The position would be different only if those detailed rules applied solely to actions based on [European] law for the repayment of such charges or levies.[68]

---

[66] *Rewe*, Case 33/76 (supra n. 65), para. 5.

[67] *Edilizia Industriale Siderurgica Srl (Edis)* v. *Ministero delle Finanze*, Case C-231/96, [1998] ECR I-4951.

[68] *Ibid.*, paras. 36–7 (emphasis added).

In the present case, the "equivalent" action was thus to be based on the national remedies that existed for refunds from *public* bodies. The existence of a more favourable limitation period for refunds from private parties was irrelevant, since the equivalence principle only required treating like actions alike. And the "like" action in this case was the refund procedure applicable to a public body. The national procedural rules thus did not violate the principle of equivalence.

However, matters might not be so straightforward.[69] For the equivalence principle requires national courts to evaluate "whether the actions concerned are similar as regards their purpose, cause of action and essential characteristics".[70] And this teleological comparability test might require them to look beyond the specific procedural regime for a national right.

(b) The effectiveness principle

The power of the effectiveness principle to interfere with the principle of national procedural autonomy was – from the start – much greater. However, the Court's jurisprudence on the principle is disastrously unclear. The best way to analyse the cases is to identify general historical periods and a variety of specific thematic lines.[71] The academic literature on the effectiveness principle thereby typically distinguishes between three periods of evolution. A first period of *restraint* is replaced by a period of *intervention*, which in turn gives way to a period of *balance*.[72] Each of these periods corresponds to a particular effectiveness standard. The European Court began to develop the principle from a minimal standard. National remedies would solely be found ineffective, where they "made it *impossible* in practice to exercise the rights which the national courts are obliged to protect".[73] With time, the Court however increasingly moved to a

---

[69] *Levez* v. *Jennings (Harlow Pools) Ltd*, Case C-326/96, [1998] ECR I-7835.

[70] *Preston et al.* v. *Wolverhampton Healthcare NHS Trust and Others*, Case C-78/98, [2000] ECR I-3201, para. 57.

[71] For illustrations of this – brilliant and necessary – approach, see M. Dougan, *National Remedies before the Court of Justice: Issues of Harmonisation and Differentiation* (Hart, 2004), Chapters 5 and 6; as well as T. Tridimas, *The General Principles of EU Law* (Oxford University Press, 2006), Chapter 9.

[72] A. Arnull, *The European Union and its Court of Justice* (Oxford University Press, 2006), 268; as well as Dougan, *National Remedies* (supra n. 71) 227, and Tridimas, *General Principles* (supra n. 71), 420 et seq.

[73] *Rewe*, Case 33/76 (supra n. 65), para. 5 (emphasis added).

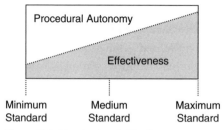

Figure 7.3 Standards of effectiveness

maximum standard insisting on the "full effectiveness" of European law.[74] This maximum standard was eventually replaced by a medium standard in a third period.

Originally, the European Court showed much restraint towards the procedural autonomy of the Member States. The Court indeed pursued a policy of judicial minimalism.[75] The standard for an "effective remedy" was low and simply required that the national procedures must not make the enforcement of European rights (virtually) impossible. This minimalist approach is exemplified by *Rewe*.[76] In that case, the plaintiff had applied for a refund of monies that had been charged in contravention of the European Treaties. The defendant accepted the illegality of the charges, but counter-claimed that the limitation period for a refund had expired. The Court accepted that the existence of a limitation period did not make the enforcement of European rights impossible and found for the defendant.

In subsequent jurisprudence, the Court however developed a more demanding standard of "effectiveness". In *Von Colson*,[77] two female candidates for becoming warden in an all-male prison had been rejected. The State prison had indisputably discriminated against them on the ground that they were women. Their European right to equal treatment had thus been violated, and the question arose how this violation could be remedied. The remedy under German law restricted the claim for damages to the plaintiffs' travel expenses. Was this an effective remedy for the enforcement

---

[74] *The Queen* v. *Secretary of State for Transport, ex parte: Factortame Ltd and others*, Case C-213/89, [1990] ECR I-2433, para. 21.

[75] A. Ward, *Judicial Review and the Rights of Private Parties in EC Law* (Oxford University Press, 2007), 87.

[76] *Rewe*, Case 33/76 (supra n. 65).

[77] *Von Colson and Elisabeth Kamann* v. *Land Nordrhein-Westfalen* Case 14/83, [1984] ECR 1891.

of their European rights? The Court here clarified that the effectiveness principle required that the national remedy "be such as to guarantee real and effective judicial protection".[78] The remedy would need to have "a real deterrent effect on the employer", and in the context of a compensation claim this meant that the latter "must in any event be *adequate* in relation to the damage sustained".[79]

The most famous intervention into the procedural autonomy of a Member State in this second period is however to be found in an English case: *Factortame*.[80] The case concerned a violation of the Union's internal market law through a British nationality requirement imposed on fishing vessels. The case went to the House of Lords, and the Lords found that the substantive conditions for granting interim relief were in place, but held "that the grant of such relief was precluded by the old common-law rule that an interim injunction may not be granted against the Crown, that is to say against the government, in conjunction with the presumption that an Act of Parliament is in conformity with [European] law until such time as a decision on its compatibility with that law has been given".[81] Unsure whether this common law rule itself violated the effectiveness principle under European law, the House of Lords referred the case to Luxembourg. And the European Court answered as follows:

[A]ny provision of a national legal system and any legislative, administrative or judicial practice which might impair the effectiveness of [European] law by with-holding from the national court having jurisdiction to apply such law the power to do everything necessary at the moment of its application to set aside national legislative provisions which might prevent, even temporarily, [European] rules from having full force and effect are incompatible with those requirements, which are the very essence of [European] law. It must be added that the *full effectiveness* of [European] law would be just as much impaired if a rule of national law could prevent a court seised of a dispute governed by [European] law from granting interim relief in order to ensure the full effectiveness of the judgment to be given on the existence of the rights claimed under [European] law. It follows that a court which in those circumstances would grant interim relief, if it were not for a rule of national law, is obliged to set aside that rule.[82]

---

[78] *Ibid.*, para. 23.   [79] *Ibid.* (emphasis added).
[80] *The Queen* v. *Secretary of State for Transport, ex parte Factortame Ltd and others*, Case C-213/89 (supra n. 74).
[81] *Ibid.*, para. 13.   [82] *Ibid.*, paras. 20–1 (emphasis added).

While short of creating a new remedy, this came very close to demanding a maximum standard of effectiveness. Yet the Court soon withdrew from this highly interventionist stance and thereby entered into a third period in the evolution of the effectiveness principle.

In this third period, the Court tried and – still – tries to find a balance between the minimum and the maximum standard of effectiveness.[83] The retreat from the second period of high intervention can be seen in *Steenhorst-Neerings*,[84] where the Court developed a distinction between national procedural rules whose effect was to totally *preclude* individuals from enforcing European rights and those national rules that merely *restrict* their remedies.[85] In *Preston*,[86] the Court had again to deal with the 1970 Equal Pay Act whose section 2 (4) barred any claim that was not brought within a period of six months following cessation of employment. But instead of concentrating on the "full effectiveness" or "adequacy" of the national remedy, the Court stated that "[s]uch a limitation period does not render impossible *or excessively difficult* the exercise of rights conferred by the [European] legal order and is not therefore liable to strike at the very essence of those rights".[87] The Court here had recourse to a – stronger – alternative to the (minimal) impossibility standard: national procedures that would make the exercise of European rights "excessively difficult" would equally fall foul of the principle of effectiveness. This medium standard lies in between the minimum and the maximum standard.[88]

---

[83] F. G. Jacobs, "Enforcing Community Rights and Obligations in National Courts: Striking the Balance" in A. Biondi and J. Lonbay (eds.), *Remedies for Breach of EC Law* (Wiley, 1996). See also Dougan, *National Remedies* (supra n. 71), 29: "There has been a definite retreat back towards the orthodox presumption of national autonomy in the provision of judicial protection. But the contemporary principle of effectiveness surely remains more intrusive than the case law of the 1970s and early 1980s."

[84] *Steenhorst-Neerings* v. *Bestuur van de Bedrijfsvereniging voor Detailhandel, Ambachten en Huisvrouwen*, Case C-338/91, [1993] ECR I-5475.

[85] On the distinction, see Ward, *Judicial Review* (supra n. 75), 131. The distinction was elaborated in *Johnson* v. *Chief Adjudication Officer*, Case C-31/90, [1991] ECR I-3723.

[86] *Preston* v. *Wolverhampton*, Case C-78/98 (supra n. 70).

[87] *Ibid.*, para. 34 (emphasis added).

[88] When would this medium standard of effectiveness be violated? Instead of providing hard and fast rules, the Court has come to prefer a contextual test spelled out for the first time in *Peterbroeck*, Case C-312/93 (supra n. 65). In order to discover whether a national procedural rule makes the enforcement of European rights "excessively difficult", the Court analyses each case "by reference to the role of that provision in the procedure, its progress and its special features, viewed as a whole, before the various national instances" (*ibid.*, para. 14).

4. State liability: the *Francovich* doctrine

Even if the Court had pushed for a degree of uniformity in the decentralized enforcement of European law via the principles of equivalence and effectiveness, it would still be *national* remedies whose scope or substance was extended. But what would happen if no national remedy existed? Would the non-existence of a national remedy not be an absolute barrier to the enforcement of European law? For a long time, the Court appeared to insist that the European Treaties were "not intended to create new remedies in the national courts to ensure the observance of [Union] law other than those already laid down by national law".[89] In what was perceived as a dramatic turn of events, the European Court renounced this position and proclaimed the existence of a *European* remedy for breaches of European law in *Francovich*.[90] The Court here held that in certain situations the State was liable to compensate losses caused by its violation of European law. This final section will look at the birth of the state liability doctrine first, before analysing its conditions.

(a) The birth of the *Francovich* doctrine

For a clairvoyant observer there was "little doubt that one future day the European Court will be asked to say, straightforwardly, whether [European] law requires a remedy in damages to be made available in the national courts".[91] This day came on 8 January 1990. On this day, the Court received a series of preliminary questions in *Francovich and others* v. *Italy*.[92] The facts of the case are memorably sad.[93] Italy had flagrantly flouted its

---

[89] *Rewe Handelsgesellschaft et al.* v.. *Hamptzollamt Kiel (Butter-Cruises)*, Case 158/80, [1981] ECR 1805.

[90] *Francovich and Bonifaci et al* v. *Italy*, Joined Cases C-6/90 and C-9/90, [1991] ECR I-5357.

[91] A. Barav, "Damages in the Domestic Courts for Breach of Community Law by National Public Authorities" in H. G. Schermers et al. (eds.) *Non-Contractual Liability of the European Communities* (Nijhoff, 1988), 149 at 165.

[92] *Francovich and Bonifaci*, Joined Cases C-6/90 and C-9/90 (supra n. 90).

[93] Opinion of Mr Advocate General Mischo (*ibid.*, para. 1): "Rarely has the Court been called upon to decide a case in which the adverse consequences for the individuals concerned of failure to implement a directive were as shocking as in the case now before us."

obligations under the Treaty by failing to implement a European directive designed to protect employees in the event of their employer's insolvency.[94] The Directive had required Member States to pass national legislation guaranteeing the payment of outstanding wages. Francovich had been employed by an Italian company, but had hardly received any wages. He brought proceedings against his employer; yet the employer had gone into insolvency, and for that reason Francovich brought a separate action against the Italian State to cover his losses. In the course of these second proceedings, the national court asked the European Court whether the State itself would be obliged to cover the losses of employees. The European Court found that the Directive had left the Member States a "broad discretion with regard to the organization, operation and financing of the guarantee institutions", and it therefore lacked direct effect.[95] It followed that "the persons concerned cannot enforce those rights against the State before the national courts where no implementing measures are adopted within the prescribed period".[96]

But this was not the end of the story! The Court – unhappy with the negative result flowing from the lack of direct effect – continued:

[T]the principle whereby a State must be liable for loss and damage caused to individuals as a result of breaches of [European] law for which the State can be held responsible is inherent in the system of the Treaty. A further basis for the obligation of Member States to make good such loss and damage is to be found in Article [4(3)] of the Treaty [on European Union], under which the Member States are required to take all appropriate measures, whether general or particular, to ensure fulfilment of their obligations under [European] law. Among these is the obligation to nullify the unlawful consequences of a breach of [European] law. It follows from all the foregoing that it is a principle of [European] law that the Member States are obliged to make good loss and damage caused to individuals by breaches of [European] law for which they can be held responsible.[97]

The European Court here took a qualitative leap in the context of remedies. Up to this point, it could still legitimately be argued that the principle of national procedural autonomy precluded the creation of European remedies

---

[94] The Court had already expressly condemned this failure in *Commission* v. *Italian Republic*, Case 22/87, [1989] ECR 143.

[95] *Francovich and Bonifaci*, Joined Cases C-6/90 and C-9/90 (supra n. 90), para. 25.

[96] *Ibid.*, para. 27.   [97] *Ibid.*, paras. 33–7.

as the principles of equivalence and effectiveness solely required the extension of *national* remedies to violations of European law. With *Francovich*
the Court clarified that the right to reparation for such violations was "a
right founded directly on [European] law".[98] The action for State liability
was thus a *European* remedy that had to be made available in the national
courts.[99] How did the Court justify this "revolutionary" result? It had
recourse to the usual constitutional suspects: the very nature of the
European Treaties and the general duty under Article 4 (3) TEU. A more
sophisticated justification was added by a later judgment. In *Brasserie du
Pecheur*,[100] the Court found:

> Since the Treaty contains no provision expressly and specifically governing the
> consequences of breaches of [European] law by Member States, it is for the Court, in
> pursuance of the task conferred on it by Article [19] of the [EU] Treaty of ensuring
> that in the interpretation and application of the Treaty the law is observed, to rule on
> such a question in accordance with generally accepted methods of interpretation, in
> particular by reference to the fundamental principles of the [Union] legal system
> and, where necessary, general principles common to the legal systems of the Member
> States. Indeed, it is to the general principles common to the laws of the Member
> States that the second paragraph of Article [340] of the [FEU] Treaty refers as the
> basis of the non-contractual liability of the [Union] for damage caused by its
> institutions or by its servants in the performance of their duties. The principle of
> the non-contractual liability of the [Union] expressly laid down in Article [340] of
> the [FEU] Treaty is simply an expression of the general principle familiar to the legal
> systems of the Member States that an unlawful act or omission gives rise to an
> obligation to make good the damage caused. That provision also reflects the obli-
> gation on public authorities to make good damage caused in the performance of
> their duties.[101]

The principle of State liability was thus rooted in the constitutional traditions
common to the Member States and was equally recognized in the principle of
Union liability for breaches of European law.[102] There was consequently a
parallel between *State* liability and *Union* liability for tortious acts of public

---

[98] *Ibid.*, para. 41.

[99] On the application of this principle in the United Kingdom, see J. Convery, "State Liability
in the United Kingdom after *Brasserie du Pêcheur*", 34 (1997) *Common Market Law Review*,
603.

[100] *Brasserie du Pêcheur SA* v. *Bundesrepublik Deutschland* and *The Queen* v. *Secretary of
State for Transport, ex parte Factortame Ltd and others*, Joined Cases C-46/93 and C-48/93,
[1996] ECR I-1029.

[101] *Ibid.*, paras. 27–9.   [102] On this point, see Chapter 8 – Section 4 below.

authorities. And this parallelism would have a decisive effect on the conditions for State liability for breaches of European law.

(b) The three conditions for State liability

Having created the liability principle for State actions, the *Francovich* Court nonetheless made the principle dependent on the fulfilment of three conditions:

The first of those conditions is that the result prescribed by the directive should entail the grant of rights to individuals. The second condition is that it should be possible to identify the content of those rights on the basis of the provisions of the directive. Finally, the third condition is the existence of a causal link between the breach of the State's obligation and the loss and damage suffered by the injured parties. Those conditions are sufficient to give rise to a right on the part of individuals to obtain reparation, a right founded directly on [European] law.[103]

The original liability test was thus as follows: the European act must have been intended to grant individual rights, and these rights would – despite their lack of direct effect – have to be identifiable.[104] If this was the case, and if European law was breached by a Member State not guaranteeing these rights, any loss that was caused by that breach could be claimed by the individual.[105] On its face, this test appeared to be complete and was thus one of *strict* liability: any breach of an identifiable European right would give rise to State liability. But the Court subsequently clarified that this was *not* the case, for the *Francovich* test was to be confined to the specific context of a flagrant non-implementation of a European Directive.

Drawing on its jurisprudence on *Union* liability, the Court subsequently introduced a more restrictive principle of State liability in *Brasserie du Pêcheur*.[106] The Court here clarified that State liability was to be confined

---

[103] *Francovich and Bonifaci*, Joined Cases C-6/90 and C-9/90 (supra n. 90) paras. 40–1.

[104] For an analysis of this criterion, see Dougan, *National Remedies* (supra n. 71), 238 et seq. For a case in which the European Court found that a Directive did not grant rights, see *Paul et al.* v. *Germany*, Case C-222/02, [2004] ECR I-9425.

[105] For an analysis of this criterion, see Tridimas, *General Principles* (supra n. 71), 529–33. See particularly *Brinkmann Tabakfabriken GmbH* v. *Skatteministeriet*, Case C-319/96, [1998] ECR I-5255.

[106] *Brasserie du Pêcheur*, Joined Cases C-46/93 and C-48/93 (supra n. 100), para. 42: "The protection of the rights which individuals derive from [European] law cannot vary depending on whether a national authority or a [Union] authority is responsible for the damage." On the constitutional principles governing Union liability, see Chapter 8 – Section 4.

to "sufficiently serious" breaches. To cover up the fact that it had implicitly added a "fourth" condition to its *Francovich* test, the Court replaced the new condition with the second criterion of its "old" test. The new liability test could thus continue to insist on three – necessary and sufficient – conditions, but now read as follows:

> [European] law confers a right to reparation where three conditions are met: the rule of law infringed must be intended to confer rights on individuals; the breach must be sufficiently serious; and there must be a direct causal link between the breach of the obligation resting on the State and the damage sustained by the injured parties.[107]

The Court justified its limitation of State liability to "sufficiently serious" breaches by reference to the wide discretion that Member States might enjoy, especially when exercising legislative powers. The "limited liability" of the legislature is indeed a common constitutional tradition of the Member States and equally applies to the Union legislature. Where legislative functions are concerned, Member States "must not be hindered by the prospect of actions for damages".[108] The special democratic legitimacy attached to parliamentary legislation provided thus an argument against public liability for breaches of private rights, "unless the institution concerned has manifestly and gravely disregarded the limits on the exercise of its powers".[109] And in analysing whether a breach was sufficiently serious in the sense of a "manifest[ ] and grave[ ] disregard[ ]", the Court would balance a number of diverse factors,[110] such as the degree of discretion enjoyed by the Member States as well as the clarity of the Union norm breached.

Unfortunately, there are very few hard and fast rules to determine when a breach is sufficiently serious. Indeed, the second criterion of the *Brasserie*

---

[107] *Ibid.*, para. 51.   [108] *Ibid.*, para. 45.

[109] *Ibid.* See also *The Queen* v. *H. M. Treasury, ex parte British Telecommunications*, Case C-392/93, (1996) ECR I-10631, para. 42.

[110] *Brasserie du Pêcheur*, Joined Cases C-46/93 and C-48/93 (supra n. 100), para. 56: "The factors which the competent court may take into consideration include the clarity and precision of the rule breached, the measure of discretion left by that rule to the national or [Union] authorities, whether the infringement and the damage caused was intentional or involuntary, whether any error of law was excusable or inexcusable, the fact that the position taken by a [Union] institution may have contributed towards the omission, and the adoption or retention of national measures or practices contrary to [European] law."

test has been subject to much uncertainty. Would the manifest and grave disregard test only apply to the legislative function? The Court appears to have answered this question in *Hedley Lomas*,[111] when dealing with the failure of the national *executive* to correctly apply European law. The Court found: "where, at the time when it committed the infringement, the Member State in question was not called upon to make any legislative choices and had only considerably reduced, or even no, discretion, the mere infringement of [European] law may be sufficient to establish the existence of a sufficiently serious breach".[112]

While thus affirming that all breaches must be sufficiently serious to trigger State liability, the less discretion, the less limited would the liability of a State be.[113] The Court here seemed to acknowledge two alternatives within the second *Brasserie* condition – depending on whether the State violated European law via its legislative or executive branch. The existence of these two alternatives would find expression in *Larsy*,[114] where the Court found:

[A] breach of [European] law is sufficiently serious where a Member State, in the exercise of its legislative powers, has manifestly and gravely disregarded the limits on its powers and, secondly, that where, at the time when it committed the infringement, the Member State in question had only considerably reduced, or even no, discretion, the mere infringement of [European] law may be sufficient to establish the existence of a sufficiently serious breach.[115]

For an executive failure, the threshold for establishing State liability is thus much lower than the liability threshold for legislative actions. While the incorrect *application* of a clear European norm by the national executive will incur automatic liability, the incorrect implementation of a directive by the national legislature may not.[116] Nonetheless, the European

---

[111] *The Queen* v. *Ministry of Agriculture, Fisheries and Food, ex parte Hedley Lomas*, Case C-5/94, [1996] ECR I-2553.

[112] *Ibid.*, para. 28.

[113] *Haim* v. *Kassenzahnärztliche Vereinigung Nordrhein*, Case C-424/97, [2000] ECR I-5123, para. 38. See also *A.G.M.-COS.MET et al.* v. *Suomen valtio et al*, Case C-470/03, [2007] ECR I-2749.

[114] *Larsy* v. *Institut national d'assurances sociales pour travailleurs indépendants*, Case C-118/00, [2001] ECR I-5063.

[115] *Ibid.*, para. 38.

[116] *Denkavit et al.* v. *Bundesamt für Finanzen*, Cases C-283 and 291–2/94, [1996] ECR I-4845.

Court distinguishes the *incorrect* implementation of a directive from its *non*-implementation. The use of a stricter liability regime for legislative *non*-action makes much sense, for the failure of the State cannot be excused by reference to the exercise of legislative discretion. The Court has consequently held that the non-implementation of a directive could *per se* constitute a sufficiently serious breach.[117]

---

[117] *Dillenkofer* v. *Germany*, Case C-178/94, [1996] ECR I-4845, para. 29: "[F]ailure to take any measure to transpose a directive in order to achieve the result it prescribes within the period laid down for that purpose constitutes per se a serious breach of [European] law and consequently gives rise to a right of reparation for individuals suffering injury if the result prescribed by the directive entails the grant to individuals of rights whose content is identifiable and a causal link exists between the breach of the State's obligation and the loss and damage suffered."

8 European actions

Introduction

The European Treaties establish a dual enforcement mechanism for European law. Apart from the decentralized enforcement by national courts, the Union legal order equally envisages the centralized enforcement of European Law in the European Courts. The judicial competences of the European Courts are enumerated in the section of the Treaty on the Functioning of the European Union dealing with the Court of Justice of the European Union.

Four classes of judicial actions will be discussed in this Chapter. The first class is typically labelled an "enforcement action" in the strict sense of the term. This action is set out in Articles 258 and 259 TFEU and concerns the failure of a Member State to act in accordance with European law (Section 1). The three remaining actions "enforce" the European Treaties against the Union

Table 8 Judicial competences and procedures

Judicial Competences and Procedures (Articles 258–281 TFEU)			
Article 258	Enforcement Action brought by the Commission	Article 269	Jurisdiction for Article 7 TEU
Article 259	Enforcement Action brought by another Member State	Article 270	Jurisdiction in Staff Cases
Article 260	Action for a Failure to Comply with a Court judgment	Article 271	Jurisdiction for Cases involving the European Investment Bank and the European Central Bank
Article 261	Jurisdiction for Penalties in Regulations	Article 272	Jurisdiction granted by Arbitration Clauses
Article 262	(Potential) Jurisdiction for disputes relating to European intellectual property rights	Article 273	Jurisdiction granted by special agreement between the Member States
Article 263	Action for Judicial Review	Article 274	Jurisdiction of national courts involving the Union
Article 265	(Enforcement) Action for the Union's Failure to Act	Article 275	Non-Jurisdiction for the Union's Common Foreign and Security Policy
Article 267	Preliminary Rulings	Article 276	Jurisdictional Limits within the Area of Freedom, Security and Justice
Article 268	Jurisdiction in Damages Actions under Article 340	Article 277	Collateral (Judicial) Review for acts of general application

itself. These actions can be brought for a failure to act (Section 2), for judicial review (Section 3), and for damages (Section 4).

Importantly, the Treaties acknowledge two general limitations on the jurisdiction of the European Court: Articles 275 and 276 TFEU. The former declares that the European Court "shall *not* have jurisdiction with respect to the provisions relating to the common foreign and security policy nor with respect to acts adopted on the basis of those provisions".[1] And Article 276

---

[1] Article 275 (1) TFEU (emphasis added). Yet, there are two exceptions within that exception. First, the Court is allowed to review acts adopted under the Union's CFSP, where it is claimed that they should have been adopted within one of the Union's special external policies (Article 275 (2) TFEU). Second, a CFSP act is reviewable, where it is claimed to restrict the rights of a natural or legal person (*ibid.*).

TFEU decrees that the European Court "shall have *no* jurisdiction to review the validity or proportionality of operations carried out by the police or other law-enforcement services of a Member State or the exercise of the responsibilities incumbent upon Member States with regard to the maintenance of law and order and the safeguarding of internal security".[2]

1. Enforcement actions against Member States

Where a Member State breaches European law, the central way to "enforce" the Treaties is to bring that State before the European Court.[3] The European legal order envisages two potential applicants for enforcement actions against a failing Member State: the Commission and another Member State. The procedure governing the former scenario is set out in Article 258; and the – almost – identical procedure governing the second scenario is set out in Article 259. Both procedures are inspired by international law logic. For not only are individuals excluded from enforcing their rights under that procedure, but the European Court cannot repeal national laws that violate European law. Its judgment will simply "declare" that a violation of European law has taken place. However, as we shall see below, this declaration may now be backed up by financial sanctions.

(a) The procedural conditions under Article 258

Enforcement actions against a Member State are "the *ultima ratio* enabling the [Union] interests enshrined in the Treat[ies] to prevail over the inertia and resistance of Member States".[4] They are typically brought by the Commission.[5] For it is the Commission, acting in the general interest of the Union, that is charged to ensure that the Member States give effect to European law.[6] The

---

[2] Article 276 TFEU (emphasis added).

[3] Exceptionally, it is not the Court but the "political forum" of the European Council that is to "determine the existence of a serious and persistent breach by a Member State"; see Article 7 (2) TEU. This determination may even lead to a suspension of membership rights: Article 7(3) TEU. According to Article 269 TFEU, the Member State concerned can however challenge this determination before the Court, but the Court's jurisdiction is confined to procedural aspects.

[4] *Italy* v. *High Authority*, Case 20/59, [1960] ECR 325 at 339.

[5] The following section therefore concentrates on proceedings brought by the Commission. Member States do very rarely bring actions against another Member State; but see *Spain* v. *United Kingdom*, Case C-145/04, [2006] ECR I-7917.

[6] See *Commission* v. *Germany*, [1995] ECR I-2189. On the Commission's powers in this context, see Chapter 1 – Section 3(c).

procedural regime for enforcement actions brought by the Commission is set out in Article 258 TFEU, which states:

If the Commission considers that a Member State has failed to fulfil an obligation under the Treaties, it shall deliver a reasoned opinion on the matter after giving the State concerned the opportunity to submit its observations. If the State concerned does not comply with the opinion within the period laid down by the Commission, the latter may bring the matter before the Court of Justice of the European Union.

The provision clarifies that before the Commission can bring the matter to the Court, it must pass through an administrative stage. The purpose of this pre-litigation stage is "to give the Member State concerned an opportunity, on the one hand, to comply with its obligations under [European] law and, on the other, to avail itself of its right to defend itself against the complaints made by the Commission".[7] This administrative stage expressly requires a "reasoned opinion", and before that – even if not expressly mentioned in Article 258 – a "letter of formal notice".[8] In the "letter of formal notice" the Commission will notify the State that it believes it to violate European law, and ask it to submit its observations. Where the Commission is not convinced by the explanations offered by a Member State, it will issue a "reasoned opinion"; and after that second administrative stage,[9] it will go to court.

What violations of European law may be litigated under the enforcement procedure? With the general exceptions mentioned above,[10] the Commission can raise any violation of European law, including breaches of the Union's international agreements.[11] However, the breach must be committed by the "State". This includes its legislature, its executive and – in theory – its judiciary.[12] The Member State might also be responsible for violations of the

---

[7] *Commission* v. *Belgium*, Case 293/85, [1988] ECR 305, para. 13.

[8] There are exceptions to this rule. Practically the most important exception can be found in the shortened procedure within the Union's state aid provisions; see Article 108 (2) TFEU.

[9] The Court has insisted that the Member State must – again – be given a reasonable period to correct its behaviour; see *Commission* v. *Belgium*, Case 293/85 (supra n. 7).

[10] See Articles 275 and 276 TFEU.

[11] *Commission* v. *Germany (IDA)*, Case C-61/94, [1996] ECR I-3989.

[12] The Court of Justice has been fairly shy in finding that a national court has violated the Treaty. In the past, it has preferred to attribute the fact that a national judiciary persistently interpreted national law in a manner that violated European law to the *legislature's* failure to adopt clearer national laws; see *Commission* v. *Italy*, Case C-129/00, [2003] ECR I-14637. On this point, see C. Timmermans, "Use of the Infringement Procedure in Cases of Judicial Errors" in J. de Zwaan et al. (eds.), *The European Union – An Ongoing Process of Integration* (Asser Press, 2004), 155.

Treaties by territorially autonomous regions.[13] And even the behaviour of its nationals may – exceptionally – be attributed to the Member State.[14]

Are there any defences that a State may raise to justify its breach of European law? Early on, the Court clarified that breaches of European law by one Member State cannot justify breaches by another. In *Commission* v. *Luxembourg and Belgium*,[15] the defendants had argued that "since international law allows a party, injured by the failure of another party to perform its obligations, to withhold performance of its own, the Commission has lost the right to plead infringement of the Treaty".[16] The Court did not accept this "international law" reading of the European Treaties. The latter were "not limited to creating reciprocal obligations between the different natural and legal persons to whom it is applicable, but establish[] a new legal order, which governs the powers, rights and obligations of the said persons, as well as the necessary procedures for taking cognizance of and penalizing any breach of it".[17] The binding effect of European law was thus comparable to the effect of "national" or "institutional" law.[18] The Court has also denied the availability of "internal" constitutional problems,[19] or budgetary restraints, as justifications.[20] However, one of the arguments that the Court has accepted in the past is the idea of *force majeure* in an emergency situation.[21]

(b) Judicial enforcement through financial sanctions

The European Court is not entitled to void national laws that violate European law. It may only declare national laws or practices incompatible with European law.[22] Where the Court has found that a Member State has failed to fulfil an obligation under the Treaties, "the State shall be required to take the necessary measures to comply with the judgment of the Court".[23]

---

[13] See *Commission* v. *Germany*, Case C-383/00, [2002] ECR I-4219.

[14] *Commission* v. *Ireland (Buy Irish)*, Case 249/81, [1982] ECR 4005.

[15] *Commission* v. *Luxembourg and Belgium*, Case 90–91/63, [1964] ECR 625.

[16] *Ibid.*, 631.   [17] *Ibid.*

[18] P. Pescatore, *The Law of Integration: Emergence of a New Phenomenon in International Relations Based on the Experience of the European Communities* (Sijthoff, 1974), 67 and 69.

[19] See *Commission* v. *Ireland*, Case C-39/88, [1990] ECR I-4271, para. 11: "a Member State may not plead internal circumstances in order to justify a failure to comply with obligations and time-limits resulting from [European] law".

[20] See *Commission* v. *Italy*, Case 30/72, [1973] ECR 161.

[21] For an excellent discussion of the case law, see L. Prete and B. Smulders, "The Coming of Age of Infringement Proceedings", 47 (2010) *Common Market Law Review*, 9 at 44.

[22] *France* v. *Commission*, Cases 15 & 16/76, [1979] ECR 32.   [23] Article 260 (1) TFEU.

Inspired by international law logic, the European legal order here builds on the normative distinctiveness of European and national law. It remains within the competence of the Member States to remove national laws or practices that are incompatible with European law.

Nonetheless, the Union legal order may "punish" violations by imposing financial sanctions on a recalcitrant State. The sanction regime for breaches by a Member State is set out in Article 260 (2) and (3) TFEU. Importantly, financial sanctions will not automatically follow from every breach of European law. According to Article 260 (2), the Commission may only apply for a "lump sum or penalty payment",[24] where a Member State has failed to comply with a *judgment of the Court*. And even in this limited situation, the Commission must bring a second (!) case before the Court.[25] There is only one exception to the requirement of a second judgment. This "exceptional" treatment corresponds to a not too exceptional situation: the failure of a Member State properly to transpose a "directive".[26] Where a Member State fails to fulfil its obligation "to notify measures transposing a directive adopted under a legislative procedure",[27] the Commission can apply for a financial sanction in the first enforcement action. The payment must take effect on the date set by the Court in its judgment, and is thus directed at the specific breach of European law.

2. Actions against the Union: failure to act

Enforcement actions primarily target a Member State's failure to act (properly). However, infringement proceedings may also be brought against Union institutions. Actions for failure to act are thereby governed by Article 265 TFEU, which states:

---

[24] The Court has held that Article 265 TFEU allows it to impose a "lump sum" *and* a "penalty payment" at the same time (see *Commission* v. *France (French Fisheries II)*, Case C-304/02, [2005] ECR I-6262).

[25] The Court has softened this procedural requirement somewhat by specifically punishing "general and persistent" infringements; see *Commission* v. *Ireland (Irish Waste)*, Case C-494/01 [2005] ECR I-3331. For an extensive discussion of this type of infringement, see P. Wennerås, "A New Dawn for Commission Enforcement under Articles 226 and 228 EC: General and Persistent (GAP) Infringements, Lump Sums and Penalty Payments", 43 (2006) *Common Market Law Review*, 31 at 33–50.

[26] On the legal instrument "Directive", see Chapter 5 – Section 3 above.

[27] Article 260 (3) TFEU.

Should the European Parliament, the European Council, the Council, the Commission or the European Central Bank, in infringement of the Treaties, fail to act, the Member States and the other institutions of the Union may bring an action before the Court of Justice of the European Union to have the infringement established. This Article shall apply, under the same conditions, to bodies, offices and agencies of the Union which fail to act.

The action shall be admissible only if the institution, body, office or agency concerned has first been called upon to act. If, within two months of being so called upon, the institution, body, office or agency concerned has not defined its position, the action may be brought within a further period of two months.

Any natural or legal person may, under the conditions laid down in the preceding paragraphs, complain to the Court that an institution, body, office or agency of the Union has failed to address to that person any act other than a recommendation or an opinion.

An action for failure to act may thus be brought against any Union institution or body – with the exception of the Court of Auditors and the European Court. It can be brought by another Union institution or body, a Member State, and even a private party.[28] What are the procedural stages of this action? As with enforcement actions against a Member State, the procedure is divided into an administrative and a judicial stage. The judicial stage will only commence once the relevant institution has been "called upon to act", and has not "defined its position" within two months.[29]

What types of "inactions" can be challenged? In its early jurisprudence, the Court appeared to interpret the scope of Article 265 in parallel with the scope of Article 263.[30] This suggested that only those inactions with (external) legal effects might be challenged. However, the wording of the provision points the other way – at least for non-private applicants. And this wider reading was indeed confirmed in *Parliament* v. *Council*

---

[28] However, with regard to private parties, the Court appears to read a "direct and individual concern" criterion into Article 265 TFEU; see *T. Port GmbH & Co.* v. *Bundesanstalt für Landwirtschaft und Ernährung*, Case C-68/95, [1996] ECR I-6065.

[29] On what may count as a "defined" position, see *Parliament* v. *Council*, Case 377/87, [1988] ECR 4017, and *Pesqueras Echebastar* v. *Commission*, Case C-25/91, [1993] ECR I-1719.

[30] *Chevallery* v. *Commission*, Case 15/70, [1970] ECR 975, para. 6: "[T]he concept of a measure capable of giving rise to an action is identical in Articles [263] and [265], as both provisions merely prescribe one and the same method of recourse."

(Comitology),[31] where the Court found that "[t]here is no necessary link between the action for annulment and the action for failure to act".[32] Actions for failure to act can thus also be brought in relation to "preparatory acts".[33] The material scope of Article 265 is, in this respect, wider than that of Article 263.

However, in one important respect the scope of Article 265 is much smaller than that of Article 263. For the European Court has added an "unwritten" limitation that cannot be found in the text of Article 265. It insists that a finding of a failure to act requires the existence of an *obligation to act*. Where an institution has "the right, but not the duty" to act, no failure to act can be established.[34] This is, for example, the case with regard to the Commission's competence to bring enforcement actions under Article 258. Under this article "the Commission is not bound to commence the proceedings provided for in that provision but in this regard has a discretion which excludes the right for individuals to require that institution to adopt a specific position".[35] The existence of institutional discretion thus excludes an obligation to act.

In *Parliament* v. *Council (Common Transport Policy)*,[36] the Court offered further commentary on what the existence of an obligation to act requires. Parliament had brought proceedings against the Council claiming that it had failed to lay down a framework for the common transport policy. The Council responded by arguing that a failure to act under Article 265 "was designed for cases where the institution in question has a legal obligation to adopt a *specific* measure and that it is an inappropriate instrument for resolving cases involving the introduction of a whole system of measures within the framework of a complex legislative process".[37] The Court joined the Council and rejected the idea that enforcement proceedings could be brought for the failure to fulfil the *general* obligation to develop a Union policy. The failure to act would have to be "sufficiently defined"; and this would only be the case, where the missing Union act could be "identified individually".[38]

---

[31] *Parliament* v. *Council*, Case 302/87, [1988] ECR 5615.   [32] *Ibid.*, para. 1.

[33] *Parliament* v. *Council*, Case 377/87 (supra n. 29).

[34] *Star Fruit Co* v. *Commission*, Case 247/87, [1989] ECR 291, esp. para. 12.

[35] *Ibid.*, para. 11.   [36] *Parliament* v. *Council*, Case 13/83, [1985] ECR 1513.

[37] *Ibid.*, para. 29 (emphasis added).

[38] *Ibid.*, para. 37. The Court thus held in para. 53 that "the absence of a common policy which the Treaty requires to be brought into being does not in itself necessarily constitute a failure to act sufficiently specific in nature to form the subject of an action under Article [265]".

What are the consequences of an established failure to act on the part of the Union? According to Article 266, the institution "whose failure to act has been declared contrary to the Treaties shall be required to take the necessary measures to comply with the judgment of the Court of Justice of the European Union". And in the absence of an express time-limit for such compliance, the Court acknowledges that the institution "has a reasonable period for that purpose".[39]

3. Annulment actions: judicial review

The action for judicial review in the European Union legal order is set out in Article 263 TFEU. The provision reads:

[1] The Court of Justice of the European Union shall review the legality of legislative acts, of acts of the Council, of the Commission and of the European Central Bank, other than recommendations and opinions, and of acts of the European Parliament and of the European Council intended to produce legal effects vis-à-vis third parties. It shall also review the legality of acts of bodies, offices or agencies of the Union intended to produce legal effects vis-à-vis third parties.

[2] It shall for this purpose have jurisdiction in actions brought by a Member State, the European Parliament, the Council or the Commission on grounds of lack of competence, infringement of an essential procedural requirement, infringement of the Treaties or of any rule of law relating to their application, or misuse of powers.

[3] The Court shall have jurisdiction under the same conditions in actions brought by the Court of Auditors, by the European Central Bank and by the Committee of the Regions for the purpose of protecting their prerogatives.

[4] Any natural or legal person may, under the conditions laid down in the first and second paragraphs, institute proceedings against an act addressed to that person or which is of direct and individual concern to them, and against a regulatory act which is of direct concern to them and does not entail implementing measures. (. . .)

[6] The proceedings provided for in this Article shall be instituted within two months of the publication of the measure, or of its notification to the plaintiff, or, in the absence thereof, of the day on which it came to the knowledge of the latter, as the case may be.[40]

---

[39] *Ibid.*, para. 69.

[40] The omitted paragraph 5 lays down special rules for Union agencies and bodies. It states: "Acts setting up bodies, offices and agencies of the Union may lay down specific conditions and arrangements concerning actions brought by natural or legal persons against acts of

Where an action for judicial review is well founded, the Court of Justice "shall declare the acts concerned to be void".[41] The Union will henceforth "be required to take the necessary measures to comply with the judgment of the Court of Justice of the European Union";[42] and may even be subject to paying compensation for damage caused by the illegal act.[43] But what are the procedural requirements for a judicial review action? Article 263 follows a complex structure; and the easiest way to understand its logic is to break it down into four constituent components. Paragraph 1 concerns the question *whether* the Court has the power to review particular types of Union acts. Paragraph 2 tells us *why* there can be judicial review, that is: on what grounds one can challenge the legality of a European act. Paragraphs 2–4 concern the question of *who* may ask for judicial review and thereby distinguish between three classes of applicants. Finally, paragraph 6 tells us *when* an application for review must be made, namely: within two months.

(a) "Whether": the existence of a "reviewable" act

Paragraph 1 determines whether there can be judicial review. This question has two dimensions. The first dimension relates to *whose* acts may be challenged; the second dimension clarifies *which* acts might be reviewed.

Whose acts can be challenged in judicial review proceedings? According to Article 263 (1), the Court is entitled to review "legislative acts"; that is: acts whose joint authors are the European Parliament and the Council. It can also review unilateral acts of all Union institutions and bodies, except for the Court of Auditors. By contrast, the Court cannot judicially review acts of the Member States. And this prohibition includes unilateral national acts, as well as international agreements of the Member States. The European Treaties thus cannot – despite their being the foundation of European law – be reviewed by the Court. For as collective acts of the

---

these bodies, offices or agencies intended to produce legal effects in relation to them." The following Section will not deal with this special aspect of judicial review. For an overview, see J. Saurer, "Individualrechtsschutz gegen das Handeln der Europäischen Agenturen", 45 (2010) *Europarecht*, 51.

[41] Article 264 (1) TFEU. However, according to Article 264 (2) TFEU, the Court can – exceptionally – "if it considers this necessary, state which of the effects of the act which it has declared void shall be considered as definitive".

[42] Article 266 TFEU.   [43] Articles 268 and 340 TFEU. On this point, see Section 4 below.

Member States, they cannot be attributed to the Union institutions, and as such are beyond the review powers of the European Court.

Which acts of the Union institutions can be reviewed? Instead of a positive definition, Article 263 (1) only negatively tells us which acts cannot be reviewed. Accordingly, there will be no judicial review for "recommendations" or "opinions". The reason for this exclusion is that both instruments "have no binding force",[44] and there is thus no need to challenge their *legality*.[45] The provision equally excludes judicial review for acts of the European Parliament, the European Council, and of other Union bodies not "intended to produce legal effects vis-à-vis third parties". The rationale behind this limitation is that it excludes acts that are "internal" to an institution. And despite being textually limited to *some* Union institutions, the requirement of an "external" effect has been extended to all Union acts. The Court has thus clarified that purely preparatory acts of the Commission or the Council cannot be challenged. "[A]n act is open to review only if it is a measure definitely laying down the position of the Commission or the Council."[46] In a legislative or executive procedure involving several stages, all preparatory acts are consequently considered "internal" acts; and as such cannot be reviewed. But apart from this insistence on a legal effect outside the Union institution(s), the Court has embraced a wide definition of which acts may be reviewed. The nature of the act would thereby be irrelevant. In *ERTA*,[47] the Court thus found:

Since the only matters excluded from the scope of the action for annulment open to the Member States and the institutions are "recommendations or opinions" – which by the final paragraph of Article [288 TFEU] are declared to have no binding force – Article [263 TFEU] treats as acts open to review by the Court all measures adopted by the institutions which are intended to have legal force. The objective of this review is to ensure, as required by Article [19 TEU], observance of the law in the interpretation and application of the Treaty. It would be inconsistent with this objective to interpret the conditions under which the action is admissible so restrictively as to limit the availability of this procedure merely to the categories of measures referred to by Article [288 TFEU]. *An action for annulment must therefore be available in the case*

---

[44] Article 288 (5) TFEU.
[45] Strangely, sometimes such "soft law" may however have "legal" effects. On this point see L. Senden, *Soft Law in European Community Law* (Hart, 2004).
[46] *International Business Machines (IBM)* v. *Commission*, Case 60/81, [1981] ECR 2639, para. 10.
[47] *Commission* v. *Council (ERTA)*, Case 22/70, [1971] ECR 263.

of all measures adopted by the institutions, whatever their nature or form, which are intended to have legal effects.[48]

The Court's wide review jurisdiction is however externally limited by Articles 275 and 276 TFEU – as discussed above in the *Introduction*.

(b) "Why": legitimate grounds for review

Not every reason is a sufficient reason to request judicial review. While the existence of judicial review is an essential element of all political orders subject to the "rule of law", the extent of judicial review will differ depending on whether a procedural or a substantive version is chosen. The British legal order has traditionally followed a *procedural* definition of the rule of law. Accordingly, courts are (chiefly) entitled to review whether in the adoption of an act the respective legislative or executive procedures have been followed.[49] The "merit" or "substance" of a legislative act is here beyond the review powers of the courts. By contrast, the American constitutional order has traditionally followed a substantive definition of the rule of law. Courts are here obliged to review the content of a legislative act, in particular: whether it violates fundamental human rights as guaranteed in the Constitution. A substantive rule of law entails the danger of a "government of judges"; that is: the government of philosophical guardians whose views might not reflect the democratic will of the political majority. Yet, many modern States recognize the need for non-majoritarian institutions to protect individual rights against the "tyranny of the multitude".[50]

For the European legal order, Article 263 (2) TFEU limits judicial review to four legitimate grounds: "lack of competence", "infringement of an essential procedural requirement", "infringement of the Treaties or any rule of law relating to their application", and "misuse of powers". Do these reasons indicate whether the Union subscribes to a formal or substantive rule of law?

Let us look at this general question first, before analysing the principle of proportionality as a specific ground of review.

---

[48] *Ibid.*, paras. 39–42 (emphasis added).

[49] A. W. Bradley and K. D. Ewing, *Constitutional and Administrative Law* (Pearson, 2003), Chapters 30 and 31.

[50] The phrase is attributed to E. Burke. For an overview of Burke's thought, see L. Gottschalk, "Reflections on Burke's Reflections on the French Revolution", 100 (1956) *Proceedings of the American Philosophical Society*, 417.

(i) "Formal" and "substantive" grounds

The Union legal order recognizes three "formal" grounds of review.

First, a European act can be challenged on the ground that the Union lacked the competence to adopt it. The ultra vires review of European law thereby extends to primary and secondary legislation. The review of the former originates in the principle of conferral.[51] Since the Union may only exercise those powers conferred on it by the Treaties, any action beyond these powers is ultra vires and thus voidable. With regard to secondary legislation, this follows not from the (vertical) principal of conferral, but from the (horizontal) principle protecting the institutional balance within the Union.[52]

Second, a Union act can be challenged if it infringes an essential procedural requirement. According to this second ground of review, not all procedural irregularities may invalidate a Union act but only those that are "essential". When are "essential" procedural requirements breached? The constitutional principles developed under this jurisdictional head are the result of an extensive "legal basis litigation".[53] An essential procedural step is breached when the Union adopts an act under a procedure that leaves out an institution that was entitled to be involved.[54] Alternatively, the Union may have adopted an act on the basis of a wrong voting arrangement *within* one institution. Thus, where the Council voted by unanimity instead of a qualified majority, an essential procedural requirement is breached.[55] By contrast, no essential procedural requirement is infringed when the Union acts under a "wrong" competence, which nonetheless envisages an identical legislative procedure.[56]

---

[51] On the principle of conferral, see Chapter 3 – Introduction above.

[52] On the delegation doctrine in the Union legal order, see R. Schütze, *European Constitutional Law* (Cambridge University Press, 2012), Chapter 7 – Section 2(a).

[53] On the phenomenon of "legal basis litigation" in the Union legal order, see H. Cullen and A. Worth, "Diplomacy by Other Means: the Use of Legal Basis Litigation as a Political Strategy by the European Parliament and Member States", 36 (1999) *Common Market Law Review*, 1243.

[54] See *Commission* v. *Council (ERTA)*, Case 22/70, (supra n. 47), as well as *Parliament* v. *Council (Chernobyl)*, Case C-70/88, [1990] ECR I-2041.

[55] See *United Kingdom* v. *Council*, Case 68/86, [1988] ECR 855, as well as *Commission* v. *Council*, Case C-300/89, [1991] ECR I-2867.

[56] *Commission* v. *Council*, Case 165/87, [1988] ECR 5545, para. 19: "only a purely formal defect which cannot make the measure void".

The third formal ground of review is "misuse of powers", which has remained relatively obscure.[57] The subjective rationale behind it is the prohibition on pursuing a different objective from the one underpinning the legal competence.[58]

Finally, a Union act can be challenged on the ground that it represents an "infringement of the Treaties or any other rule of law relating to their application". This constitutes a "residual" ground of review. And the European Court has used it as a constitutional gate to import a range of "unwritten" general principles into the Union legal order.[59] These principles include, inter alia, the principles of legal certainty and legitimate expectations.[60] And the introduction of these principles has added a *substantive* dimension to the rule of law in the European Union.[61] For it has been used to review the content of Union legislation against fundamental rights.[62] One expression of the Union's choice in favour of the substantive dimension of the rule of law is the principle of proportionality.

(ii) Proportionality: a substantive ground

The constitutional function of the proportionality principle is to protect liberal values.[63] It constitutes one of the "oldest" general principles of the Union legal order.[64] Beginning its career as an unwritten principle, the proportionality principle is now codified in Article 5(4) TEU: "Under the principle of proportionality, the content and form of Union action shall not exceed what is necessary to achieve the objectives of the

---

[57] For a more extensive discussion of this ground of review, see H. Schermers and D. Waelbroeck, *Judicial Protection in the European Union* (Kluwer, 2001), 402 et seq.

[58] See *Gutmann* v. *Commission*, Joined Cases 18 and 35/65, [1965] ECR 103.

[59] On the general principles in the Union legal order see T. Tridimas, *General Principles* (Oxford University Press, 2007).

[60] For both principles, see *ibid.*, Chapter 6.

[61] For an express confirmation that the Union legal order subscribes to the substantive rule of law version, see *Commission* v. *Sytraval and Brink's*, Case C-367/95 P, [1998] ECR I-1719, para. 67, as well as *Commission* v. *Parliament and Council*, Case C-378/00, [2003] ECR I-937, para. 34.

[62] On the emergence of fundamental rights as general principles of Union law, see Chapter 4 – Section 1 above.

[63] On the origins of the proportionality principle, see J. Schwarze, *European Administrative Law* (Sweet & Marwell, 2006), 678–9.

[64] An implicit acknowledgement of the principle may be found in *Fédération Charbonnière de Belgique* v. *High Authority of the ECSC*, Case 8/55, [1954–56] ECR 245 at 306: "not exceed the limits of what is strictly necessary".

Treaties."[65] The proportionality principle has been characterized as "the most far-reaching ground for review", and "the most potent weapon in the arsenal of the public law judge".[66] But, as we saw in the *Introduction* above, the Treaties expressly limit its pervasive power in Article 276 TFEU with regard to police operations in the area of freedom, security and justice.

How will the Court assess the proportionality of a Union act? The Court has developed a proportionality test. In its most elaborate form, the test follows a tripartite structure.[67] It analyses the *suitability, necessity*, and *proportionality* (in the strict sense) of a Union act. (However, the Court does not always distinguish between the second and third prong.) Within its suitability review, the Court will check whether the European measure was suitable to achieve a given objective. This might be extremely straightforward.[68] The necessity test is, on the other hand, more demanding. The Union will have to show that the act adopted represents the *least restrictive means* to achieve a given objective. Finally, even the *least* restrictive means to achieve a public policy objective might disproportionately interfere with individual rights. Proportionality in a strict sense thus weighs whether the burden imposed on an individual is excessive it not.

While this tripartite test may – in theory – be hard to satisfy, the Court has granted the Union a wide margin of appreciation wherever it enjoys a sphere of discretion. The legality of a discretionary Union act will only be affected "if the measure is manifestly inappropriate".[69] This relaxed standard of review has meant that the European Court rarely finds a Union measure to be disproportionately interfering with fundamental rights.

---

[65] The provision continues: "The institutions of the Union shall apply the principle of proportionality as laid down in the Protocol on the application of the principles of subsidiarity and proportionality."

[66] Tridimas, *General Principles* (supra n. 59), 140.

[67] See *The Queen* v. *Minister of Agriculture, Fisheries and Food and Secretary of State for Health, ex parte Fedesa and others*, Case C-331/88, [1990] ECR I-4023, para. 13: "[T]he principle of proportionality is one of the general principles of [Union] law . By virtue of that principle, the lawfulness of the prohibition of an economic activity is subject to the condition that the prohibitory measures are appropriate and necessary in order to achieve the objectives legitimately pursued by the legislation in question; when there is a choice between several appropriate measures recourse must be had to the least onerous, and the disadvantages caused must not be disproportionate to the aims pursued."

[68] For a – rare – example where the test was not satisfied, see *Crispoltoni* v. *Fattoria autonoma tabacchi di Città di Castello*, Case C-368/89, [1991] ECR I-3695, esp. para. 20.

[69] *Fedesa*, Case C-331/88 (supra n. 67), para. 14. See also *Germany* v. *Council (Bananas)*, Case C-122/95, [1998] ECR I-973, para. 79.

However, we find a good illustration of a disproportionate Union act in *Kadi*.[70] In its fight against international terrorism, the Union had adopted a Regulation freezing the assets of people suspected to be associated with Al-Qaeda. The applicant alleged, inter alia, that the Union act disproportionately restricted his right to property. The Court held that the right to property was not absolute and "the exercise of the right to property may be restricted, provided that those restrictions in fact correspond to objectives of public interest pursued by the [Union] and do not constitute, in relation to the aim pursued, a disproportionate and intolerable interference, impairing the very substance of the right so guaranteed".[71] And this required that "a fair balance has been struck between the demands of the public interest and the interest of the individuals concerned".[72] This fair balance had not been struck for the applicant;[73] and the Union act would, so far as it concerned the applicant,[74] have to be annulled.

(c) "Who": legal standing before the European Courts

The Treaties distinguish between three types of applicants in three distinct paragraphs of Article 263 TFEU.

Paragraph 2 mentions the applicants that can always bring an action for judicial review. These "privileged" applicants are: the Member States, the European Parliament,[75] the Council, and the Commission. The reason for their privileged status is that they are *ex officio* deemed to be affected by the adoption of a Union act.

Paragraph 3 lists applicants that are "semi-privileged". These are the Court of Auditors, the European Central Bank, and the Committee of the

---

[70] *Kadi and Al Barakaat International Foundation* v. *Council and Commission* Case C-402P, [2008] ECR I-6351.

[71] *Ibid.*, para. 355.   [72] *Ibid.*, para. 360.   [73] *Ibid.*, para. 371.

[74] *Ibid.*, para. 372. However, the Court found that the Union act as such could, in principle, be justified (*ibid.*, para. 366).

[75] Under the original Rome Treaty, the European Parliament was not a privileged applicant. The reason for this lay in its mere "consultative" role in the adoption of Union law. With the rise of parliamentary involvement after the Single European Act, this position became constitutionally problematic. How could Parliament cooperate or even co-decide in the legislative process, yet not be able to challenge an act that infringed its procedural prerogatives? To close this constitutional gap, the Court judicially "amended" ex-Article 173 EEC by giving the Parliament the status of a "semi-privileged" applicant (see *Parliament* v. *Council (Chernobyl)*, Case 70/88 (supra n. 54)). This status was codified in the Maastricht Treaty; and the Nice Treaty finally recognized Parliament's status as a fully privileged applicant under ex-Article 230 (2) EC.

regions. They are "partly privileged", as they may solely bring review proceedings "for the purpose of protecting their prerogatives".[76]

Paragraph 4 – finally – addresses the standing of natural or legal persons. These applicants are "non-privileged" applicants, as they must demonstrate that the Union act affects them specifically. This fourth paragraph has been highly contested in the past fifty years. And in order to make sense of the Court's jurisprudence, we must start with a historical analysis of its "Rome formulation", before moving to the current "Lisbon formulation" of that paragraph.

(i) The Rome formulation and its judicial interpretation

The Rome Treaty granted individual applicants the right to apply for judicial review in ex-Article 230 (4) EC. Paragraph 4 of that provision allowed any natural or legal person to "institute proceedings against a *decision* addressed to that person or against a *decision* which, although in the form of a regulation or *decision* addressed to another person, is of *direct and individual concern* to the former".[77]

This "Roman" formulation must be understood against the background of two constitutional choices. *First*, the drafters of the Rome Treaty had wished to confine the standing of private parties to challenges of individual "decisions", that is: administrative acts. The Rome Treaty thereby distinguished between three types of decisions: decisions addressed to the applicant, decisions addressed to another person, and decisions "in the form of a regulation". This third decision was a decision "in substance", which had been put into the wrong legal form.[78] Judicial review was here desirable to

---

[76] For a definition of this phrase in the context of Parliament's struggle to protect its prerogatives before the Nice Treaty, see *Parliament* v. *Council*, Case C-316/91, [1994] ECR I-625, as well as *Parliament* v. *Council*, Case C-187/93, [1994] ECR I-2857.

[77] Ex-Article 230 (4) EC (emphasis added).

[78] On the various instruments in the European legal order, see Chapter 5 – Introduction above. On the material distinction between "decisions" and "regulations", see *Confédération nationale des producteurs de fruits et légumes and others* v. *Council*, Case 16–17/62, [1962] ECR 471, where the Court found that the Treaty "makes a clear distinction between the concept of a 'decision' and that of a 'regulation'" (*ibid.*, 478). Regulations were originally considered the sole "generally applicable" instrument of the European Union, and their general character distinguished them from individual decisions. The crucial characteristic of a regulation was the "openness" of the group of persons to whom it applied. Where the group of persons was "fixed in time", the Court regarded the European act as a bundle of individual decisions addressed to each member of the group (see *International Fruit Company and others* v. *Commission*, Case 41–44/70, [1971] ECR 411, esp. para. 17).

avert an abuse of powers. *Second,* not every challenge of a decision by private parties was permitted. Only those decisions that were of "direct and individual concern" to a private party could be challenged. And while this concern was presumed for decisions addressed to the applicant, it had to be proven for all other decisions. Private applicants were thus "non-privileged" applicants in a dual sense. Not only could they *not* challenge all legal acts, they were – with the exception of decisions addressed to them – not presumed to have a legitimate interest in challenging the act.

Both constitutional choices severely restricted the standing of private parties and were heavily disputed. In the Union legal order prior to Lisbon, they were subject to an extensive judicial and academic commentary.[79] In a first line of jurisprudence, the Court succeeded significantly in "re-writing" ex-Article 230 (4) EC by deserting the text's insistence on a "decision". While it had originally paid homage to that text in denying private party review of generally applicable acts,[80] the Court famously abandoned its classic test and clarified that the general nature of a Union act was irrele-vant. In *Codorniu,*[81] the Court thus found that "[a]lthough it is true that according to the criteria in the [fourth] paragraph of [ex-]Article [230] of the [EC] Treaty the contested provision is, by nature and by virtue of its sphere of application, of a legislative nature in that it applies to the traders concerned in general, that does not prevent it from being of individual concern to some of them."[82] This judicial "amendment" cut the Gordian

---

[79] For the academic controversy (in chronological order), see A. Barav, "Direct and Individual Concern: an Almost Insurmountable Barrier to the Admissibility of Individual Appeal to the EEC Court", 11(1974), *Common Market Law Review*, 191; H. Rasmussen, "Why is Article 173 Interpreted Against Private Plaintiffs?", 5 (1980) *European Law Review,* 112; N. Neuwahl, "Article 173 Paragraph 4 EC: Past, Present and Possible Future", 21 (1996) *European Law,* 17; A. Arnull, "Private Applicants and the Action for Annulment since *Codorniu*", 38 (2001), *Common Market Law,* 8; and A. Ward, *Judicial Review and the Rights of Private Parties in EU Law* (Oxford University Press, 2007).

[80] The Court's classic test concentrated on whether – from a material point of view – the challenged act was a "real" regulation. The "test" is spelled out in *Calpak* v. *Commission,* Case 790/79, [1980] ECR 1949, paras. 8–9: "By virtue of the second paragraph of Article [288] of the Treaty [on the Functioning of the European Union] the criterion for distinguish-ing between a regulation and a decision is whether the measure at issue is of general application or not."

[81] *Codorniu* v. *Council,* Case C-309/89, [1994] ECR I-1853.

[82] *Ibid.,* para. 19. See also *Eurocoton et al* v. *Council,* Case 76/01P, [2003] ECR I-10091, para. 73: "Although regulations imposing anti-dumping duties are legislative in nature and scope, in that they apply to all economic operators, they may nevertheless be of individual concern[.]"

knot between the "executive" nature of an act and ex-Article 230 (4) EC. Private parties could henceforth challenge single provisions within *any* legal act – even generally applicable acts like regulations or directives – as long as they could demonstrate "direct and individual concern".

This brings us to the second famous battleground under ex-Article 230 (4) EC. What was the meaning of the "direct and individual concern" formula? The criterion of direct concern was taken to mean that the contested measure *as such* would have to affect the position of the applicant.[83] Sadly, the criterion of "individual concern" was less straightforward. It was given an authoritative interpretation in *the* seminal case on the standing of private parties under ex-Article 230 (4) EC: the *Plaumann* case. Plaumann, an importer of clementines, had challenged a Commission decision refusing to lower European customs duties on that fruit. But since the decision was not addressed to him – it was addressed to his Member State: Germany – he had to demonstrate that the decision was of "individual concern" to him. The European Court defined the criterion as follows:

> Persons other than those to whom a decision is addressed may only claim to be individually concerned if that decision affects them by reason of certain attributes which are peculiar to them or by reason of circumstances in which they are differentiated from all other persons and by virtue of these factors distinguishes them individually just as in the case of the person addressed.[84]

This formulation became famous as the "*Plaumann* test". If private applicants wish to challenge an act not addressed to them, it is not sufficient to rely on the adverse – absolute – effects that the act has on them. Instead, they must show that – relative to everybody else – the effects of the act are "peculiar to them". This *relational* standard insists that they must be "differentiated from all other persons". The applicants must be *singled* out as if they were specifically addressed. In the present case, the Court denied this *individual* concern, as Plaumann was seen to be only *generally* concerned "as an importer of clementines, that is to say, by reason of a commercial activity which may at any time be practised by any person".[85] The

---

[83] See *Parti écologiste "Les Verts"* v. *European Parliament*, Case 294/83, [1986] ECR 1339 para. 31: "The contested measures are of direct concern to the applicant association. They constitute a complete set of rules which are sufficient in themselves and which require no implementing provisions."

[84] *Plaumann* v. *Commission*, Case 25/62, [1963] ECR 95 at 107.   [85] *Ibid.*

Plaumann test is therefore *very* strict: whenever a private party is a member of an "open group" of persons – anybody could decide to become an importers of clementines tomorrow – legal standing under ex-Article 230 (4) EC will be denied.[86]

Unsurprisingly, this restrictive reading of private party standing was heavily criticized as an unjustified limitation of an individual's fundamental right to judicial review.[87] And the Court would partly soften its stance in specific areas of European law.[88] However, it generally refused to introduce a more liberal approach to the standing of private applicants until the Lisbon Treaty. In *Unión de Pequeños Agricultores (UPA)*,[89] the Court indeed expressly rejected overruling its own jurisprudence on the – disingenuous[90] – ground that "[w]hile it is, admittedly, possible to envisage a system of judicial review of the legality of [Union] measures of general application different from that established by the founding Treaty and never amended as to its principles, it is for the Member States, if necessary, in accordance with Article 48 TEU, to reform the system currently in force".[91]

Has this – requested – constitutional reform taken place? Let us look at the Lisbon formulation dealing with the standing of private parties.

(ii) The Lisbon formulation and its interpretative problems

The Lisbon Treaty has substantially amended the Rome formulation. The standing of private parties is now enshrined in Article 263 (4) TFEU, which allows any natural or legal person to "institute proceedings against an *act*

---

[86] Even assuming that Plaumann was the only clementine importer in Germany at the time of the decision, the category of "clementine importers" was open: future German importers could wish to get involved in the clementine trade. Will there ever be "closed groups" in light of this definition? For the Court's approach in this respect, see *CAM* v. *Commission*, Case 100/74, [1975] ECR 1393, as well as *Piraiki-Patraiki and others* v. *Commission*, Case 11/82, [1985] ECR 207.

[87] See Article 6 of the European Convention on Human Rights: "In the determination of his civil rights and obligations or of any criminal charge against him, everyone is entitled to a fair and public hearing within a reasonable time by an independent and impartial tribunal established by law."

[88] This had happened – for example – in the area of European competition law; see *Metro-SB-Großmärkte* v. *Commission*, Case 26/76, [1977] ECR 1875.

[89] *Unión de Pequeños Agricultores, (UPA)* v. *Council*, Case C-50/00, [2002] ECR I-6677.

[90] The *Plaumann* test is a result of the Court's own interpretation of what "individual concern" means, and the Court could have therefore – theoretically – "overruled" itself. This has indeed happened in other areas of European law; see *Criminal Proceedings against Keck and Mithouard*, Joined Cases C-267/91 and C-268/91, [1993] ECR I-6097.

[91] *Unión de Pequeños Agricultores (UPA)* v. *Council*, Case C-50/00 (supra n. 89), para. 45.

addressed to that person or which is of *direct and individual concern* to them, and against a *regulatory act* which is of direct concern to them and does not entail implementing measures".[92]

The new formulation of paragraph 4 textually recognizes the judicial decoupling of private party standing from the nature of the Union act challenged. In codifying *Codorniu*, an individual can thus potentially challenge any Union "act" with legal effects. However, depending on the nature of the act, Article 263 (4) TFEU still distinguishes three scenarios. Decisions addressed to the applicant can automatically be challenged. For "regulatory" acts, the private party must prove "direct concern".[93] For all other acts, the applicant must continue to show "direct *and* individual concern". The Lisbon amendments thus abandon the requirement of an "individual concern" only for the second but not the third category of acts. The dividing line between the second and third category is thus poised to become *the* post-Lisbon interpretative battlefield within Article 263 (4) TFEU.

What are "regulatory acts"? The term is not defined in the Treaties. Two interpretative options exist. According to a first view, the concept of "regulatory acts" is positively defined as all "generally applicable acts".[94] This reading liberalizes the standing of private applicants significantly, as the second category would materially cover legislative as well as executive acts of a general nature. According to a second view, the concept must however be negatively defined in contradistinction to "legislative acts". Regulatory acts are understood as non-legislative acts.[95] This view would

---

[92] Article 263 (4) TFEU (emphasis added).

[93] This should theoretically mean that no implementing act is needed. Why then does Article 263 (4) TFEU repeat this expressly? The answer might lie in the prior jurisprudence of the Court (see *Regione Siciliana* v. *Commission*, Case C-417/04 P, [2006] ECR I-3881). The Court was here not concerned whether there was a formal need for implementing measures. It was only interested in whether the act materially determined the situation of the applicant as such. Thus, even a Directive could be potentially of direct concern; see *Union Européenne de l'artisanat et des petites et moyennes entreprises (UEAPME)* v. *Council*, Case T-135/96, [1998] ECR II-02335. From this perspective, the new Article 263 (4) TFEU, and its insistence on the absence of an implementing act, might signal the wish of the Lisbon Treaty-makers for a return to a more restrictive – formal – position.

[94] See M. Dougan, "The Treaty of Lisbon 2007: Winning Minds, not Hearts", 45 (2008) *Common Market Law Review*, 617; and J. Bast, "Legal Instruments and Judicial Protection", in A. von Bogdandy and J. Bast (eds.), *Principles of European Constitutional Law* (Hart, 2009), 345 at 396.

[95] A. Ward, "The Draft EU Constitution and Private Party Access to Judicial Review of EU Measures", in T. Tridimas and P. Nebbia (eds.), *European Union Law for the Twenty-First Century* (Hart, 2005), 201 at 221; as well as A. Dashwood and A. Johnston, "The Institutions

place acts adopted under the – ordinary or special – legislative procedure outside the second category. The judicial review of formal legislation would consequently require "direct *and* individual concern", and would thus remain relatively immune from private party challenges. Which of the two options should be chosen by the Court? Legally, the drafting history of Article 263 (4) TFEU is inconclusive.[96] Nor do textual arguments clearly favour one view over the other.[97] And teleological arguments point in both directions – depending which *telos* one prefers. Those favouring individual rights will thus prefer the – wider – first view, whereas those wishing to protect democratic values will prefer the second view.

Regardless of how the Court eventually settles the meaning of "regulatory acts", the third category of acts still requires a "direct and individual concern". Reports of the death of *Plaumann* may thus turn out to be greatly exaggerated.[98] If the Court were to continue its past jurisprudence, what substantive arguments could be marshalled against it? The strongest critique of the *Plaumann* test has come from the pen of Advocate General Jacobs. In *Unión de Pequeños Agricultores (UPA)*,[99] his learned opinion pointed to the test's anomalous logic. It is indeed absurd that "the greater the number of persons affected the less likely it is that effective judicial review is available".[100] What alternative test might then be suitable? "The only satisfactory solution is therefore to recognise that an applicant is individually concerned by a [Union] measure where the measure has, or is liable to have, a *substantial adverse effect* on his interests."[101] As we saw in

of the Enlarged EU under the Regime of the Constitutional Treaty", 41 (2004) *Common Market Law Review*, 1481 at 1509.

[96] *Final Report of the Discussion Circle on the Court of Justice* (CONV 636/03). And see also M. Varju, "The Debate on the Future of Standing under Article 230 (4) TEC in the European Convention", 10 (2004) *European Public Law*, 43.

[97] A comparison of the different language versions of Article 263 (4) TFEU is not conclusive. Systematic and textual arguments are equally inconclusive. For Article 277 TFEU (on collateral review) uses the term "act of general application" – a fact that could be taken to mean that the phrase "regulatory" act is different. However, Article 290 TFEU expressly uses the concept of "non-legislative acts of general application" – which could, in turn, be taken to mean that "regulatory act" in Article 263 (4) TFEU must mean something different here too.

[98] On the "end" of *Plaumann*, see S. Balthasar, "Locus Standi Rules for Challenges to Regulatory Acts by Private Applicants: the New Article 263(4) TFEU", 35 (2010) *European Law Review*, 542 at 548; as well as M. Kottmann, "*Plaumanns* Ende: ein Vorschlag zu Article 263 Abs. 4 AEUV", 70 (2010) *Zeitschrift für ausländisches öffentliches Recht und Völkerrecht*, 547.

[99] *Unión de Pequeños Agricultores*, Case C-50/00 (supra n. 89).

[100] Opinion of Advocate General Jacobs, in *ibid*, para. 59.

[101] *Ibid.*, para. 102 (emphasis added).

the previous subsection, the Court rejected this reinterpretation on the formal ground that abandoning *Plaumann* would require Treaty amendment. However, the Court also provided a substantive ground to justify its restrictive stance towards private parties:

> By Article [263] and Article [277], on the one hand, and by Article [267], on the other, the Treaty has established a complete system of legal remedies and procedures designed to ensure judicial review of the legality of acts of the institutions, and has entrusted such review to the [Union] Courts. Under that system, where natural or legal persons cannot, by reason of the conditions for admissibility laid down in the fourth paragraph of Article [263] of the Treaty, directly challenge [Union] measures of general application, they are able, depending on the case, either indirectly to plead the invalidity of such acts before the [European] Courts under Article [277] of the Treaty or to do so before the national courts and ask them, since they have no jurisdiction themselves to declare those measures invalid, to make a reference to the Court of Justice for a preliminary ruling on validity.[102]

The Court here justified its restrictive stance on the *direct* review of European law by pointing to its expansive stance on the *indirect* review of European law via the preliminary reference procedure.[103]

4. Damages actions: Union liability

Where the Union has acted illegally, may the Court grant damages for losses incurred? The European Treaties do acknowledge an action for damages in Article 268 TFEU;[104] yet, for a strange reason the article refers to another provision: Article 340 TFEU. This provision reads:

> The contractual liability of the Union shall be governed by the law applicable to the contract in question.
>
> In the case of non-contractual liability, the Union shall, in accordance with the general principles common to the laws of the Member States, make good any damage caused by its institutions or by its servants in the performance of their duties.[105]

---

[102] *Ibid.*, para. 40.

[103] *Ibid.*, paras. 41-2. On this procedure, see Chapter 7 – Sections 1 & 2 above.

[104] Article 268 TFEU: "The Court of Justice of the European Union shall have jurisdiction in disputes relating to compensation for damage provided for in the second and third paragraphs of Article 340."

[105] Article 340 (1) and (2) TFEU.

The provision distinguishes between contractual liability in paragraph 1, and non-contractual liability in paragraph 2. While the former is governed by national law, the latter is governed by European law. Paragraph 2 recognizes that the Union can do "wrong" either as an institution or through its servants,[106] and that it will be under an obligation to make good damage incurred. What are the European constitutional principles underpinning an action for the non-contractual liability of the Union? Article 340 (2) has had a colourful and complex constitutional history. It has not only been transformed from a dependent action to an independent action; its substantial conditions have changed significantly. This final section will briefly analyse the procedural and substantive conditions of Union liability actions.

(a) Procedural conditions: from dependent to independent action

The action for damages under Article 340 (2) started its life as a dependent action, that is: an action that hinged on the prior success of another action. In *Plaumann* – a case discussed in the previous section – a clementine importer had brought an annulment action against a Union decision, while at the same time asking for compensation equivalent to the customs duties that had been paid as a consequence of the European decision. However, as we saw above, the action for annulment failed due to the restrictive standing requirements under Article 263 (4). And the Court found that this would equally end the liability action for damages:

In the present case, the contested decision has not been annulled. An administrative measure which has not been annulled cannot of itself constitute a wrongful act on the part of the administration inflicting damage upon those whom it affects. The latter cannot therefore claim damages by reason of that measure. The Court cannot by way of an action for compensation take steps which would nullify the legal effects of a decision which, as stated, has not been annulled.[107]

A liability action thus had to be preceded by a (successful) annulment action. The *Plaumann* Court insisted on a "certificate of illegality" before

---

[106] As regards the Union's civil servants, only their "official acts" will be attributed to the Union. With regard to their personal liability, Article 340 (4) TFEU states: "The personal liability of its servants towards the Union shall be governed by the provisions laid down in their Staff Regulations or in the Conditions of Employment applicable to them."

[107] *Plaumann*, Case 25/62 (supra n. 84), 108.

even considering the substantive merits of Union liability. This dramatically changed in *Lütticke*.[108] The case constitutes the "declaration of independence" for liability actions. "Article [340] was established by the Treaty as an independent form of action with a particular purpose to fulfil within the system of actions and subject to conditions for its use, conceived with a view to its specific purpose."[109] And according to the Court, it would be contrary to "the independent nature" of this action as well as to "the efficacy of the general system of forms of action created by the Treaty" to deny admissibility of the damages action on the ground that it might lead to a similar result as an annulment action.[110]

What are the procedural requirements for liability actions? The proceedings may be brought against any Union action or inaction that is claimed to have caused damage. The act (or omission) must however be an "official act", that is: it must be attributable to the Union.[111] Unlike Article 263 TFEU, there are no limitations on the potential applicants: anyone who feels "wronged" by a Union (in)action may bring proceedings under Article 340 (2).[112] And against whom? With the exception of the European Central Bank,[113] the provision only generically identifies the Union as the potential defendant. However, the Court has clarified that "in the interests of a good administration of justice", the Union "should be represented before the Court by the institution or institutions against which the matter giving rise to liability is alleged".[114] When will the action have to be brought? Unlike the strict two-months limitation period for annulment actions,

---

[108] *Lütticke et al.* v. *Commission*, Joined Cases 31/62 and 33/62, [1962] ECR 501.

[109] *Ibid.*, para. 6.

[110] *Ibid.* In the present case, the Court dealt with an infringement action for failure to act under Article 265 TFEU (see Section 2 above), but the same result applies to annulment actions; see *Schöppenstedt* v. *Council*, Case 5/71, [1971] ECR 975.

[111] The Union must be the author of the act, and this means that the Treaties themselves – as collective acts of the Member States – cannot be the basis of a liability action (see *Compagnie Continentale France* v. *Council*, Case 169/73, [1975] ECR 117, para. 16).

[112] See *CMC Cooperativa muratori e cementisti and others* v. *Commission*, Case 118/83, [1985] ECR 2325, para. 31: "Any person who claims to have been injured by such acts or conduct must therefore have the possibility of bringing an action, if he is able to establish liability, that is, the existence of damage caused by an illegal act or by illegal conduct on the part of the [Union]." This also included the Member States (see A. Biondi and M. Farley, *The Right to Damages in European Law* (Kluwer, 2009), 88).

[113] Article 340 (3) TFEU.

[114] *Werhahn Hansamühle and others* v. *Council*, Case 63-69/72, [1973] ECR 1229, para. 7.

liability actions can be brought within a five-year period.[115] The procedural requirements for liability actions are thus much more liberal than the procedural regime governing annulment actions.

(b) Substantive conditions: from *Schöppenstedt* to *Bergaderm*

The constitutional regime governing the substantive conditions for liability actions may be divided into two historical phases. In a first phase, the European Court distinguished between "administrative" and "legislative" Union acts.[116] The former were subject to a relatively low liability threshold. The Union would be liable for (almost) any illegal action that had caused damage.[117] By contrast, legislative acts were subject to the so-called "*Schöppenstedt* formula".[118] The latter stated that "where *legislative* action involving measures of economic policy is concerned, the [Union] does not incur non-contractual liability for damage suffered by individuals as a consequence of that action, by virtue of the provisions contained in Article [340], second paragraph, of the Treaty, *unless a sufficiently flagrant violation of a superior rule of law for the protection of the individual has occurred*".[119] This formula made Union liability for legislative acts dependent on the breach of a "superior rule" of Union law – whatever that meant[120] – which aimed to grant rights to individuals.[121] And the breach of that rule would have to be sufficiently serious.[122]

This test was significantly "reformed" in *Bergaderm*.[123] The reason for this reform was the Court's wish to align the liability regime for breaches of

---

[115] Article 46 Statute of the Court.

[116] Tridimas, *General Principles* (supra n. 59), 478 et seq.

[117] See *Adams* v. *Commission*, Case 145/83, [1985] ECR 3539, para. 44: "[B]y failing to make all reasonable efforts ... the Commission has incurred liability towards the applicant in respect of that damage." On the liability regime for administrative acts in this historical phase, see M. van der Woude, "Liability for Administrative Acts under Article 215 (2) EC" in T. Heukels and A. McDonnell (eds.), *The Action for Damages in Community Law* (Kluwer, 1997), 109–28.

[118] *Schöppenstedt* v. *Council*, Case 5/71 (supra n. 110).

[119] *Ibid.*, para. 11 (emphasis added).

[120] On the concept of a "superior rule", see Tridimas, *General Principles* (supra n. 59), 480–2.

[121] *Vreugdenhil BV* v *Commission*, Case C-282/90, [1992] ECR I-1937.

[122] See *Bayerische HNL Vermehrungsbetriebe and others* v. *Council and Commission*, Joined Cases 83 and 94/76, 4, 15 and 40/77, [1978] ECR 1209.

[123] *Bergaderm et al.* v. *Commission*, Case C-352/98P, [2000] ECR I-5291.

European law by the Union with the liability regime governing the Member States.[124] Today, European law confers a right to reparation

where three conditions are met: the rule of law infringed must be intended to confer rights on individuals; the breach must be sufficiently serious; and there must be a direct causal link between the breach of the obligation resting on the State and the damage sustained by the injured parties.[125]

Two important changes were reflected in the "*Bergaderm* formula".[126] First, the Court abandoned the distinction between "administrative" and "legislative" acts. The new test would apply to all Union acts regardless of their nature.[127] Second, the Court dropped the idea that a "superior rule" had to be infringed. Henceforth, it was only necessary to show that the Union had breached a rule intended to confer individual rights, and that the breach was sufficiently serious. And the decisive test for finding that a breach of European law was sufficiently serious was whether the Union "manifestly and gravely disregarded the limits on its discretion".[128]

---

[124] *Ibid.*, para. 41. This inspiration was "mutual". For as we saw in Chapter 7 – Section 4, the Court used Article 340 (2) TFEU as a rationale for the creation of a liability regime for the Member States.

[125] *Ibid.*, para. 42.

[126] See C. Hilson, "The Role of Discretion in EC Law on Non-contractual Liability", 42 (2005) *Common Market Law Review*, 676 at 682.

[127] *Bergaderm*, Case C-352/98P (supra n. 123), para. 46. See also *Holcim* v. *Commission*, Case C-282/05P, [2007] ECR I-2941.

[128] *Bergaderm*, Case C-352/98P (supra n. 123), para. 43. However, where there was no discretion, "the mere infringement of [Union] law may be sufficient to establish the existence of a sufficiently serious breach" (*ibid.* para. 44).

Part III

European Law: Substance

This final Part analyses the substantive heart of European law, that is: the law governing the internal market and European competition law. From the very beginning, *the* central economic task of the European Union was the creation of a "common market". The Rome Treaty had not solely provided for a common market in goods. It equally required the abolition of obstacles to the free movement of persons, services and capital. Europe's "internal market" was thus to comprise four fundamental freedoms. Two of these freedoms will be discussed in turn: Chapter 9 looks at the free movement of goods, while Chapter 10 examines the free movement of persons. The two subsequent chapters analyse two pillars of European competition law: Articles 101 and 102 TFEU. The former deals with anti-competitive agreements, the latter concerns the abuse of a dominant position by an undertaking. European competition law is thereby traditionally seen as a functional complement to the internal market. It would – primarily – protect the internal market from *private* power.

Chapter 9   Internal market: goods

Chapter 10 Internal market: persons

Chapter 11 Competition law: cartels

Chapter 12 Competition law: abuse

Introduction

The traditional heart within common markets is the free movement of goods.[1] And in order to create a European "common market" in goods, the Union legal order has established a constitutional regime in which illegal barriers to intra-Union trade must be removed. This constitutional regime is however split over two sites within Part III of the Treaty on the Functioning of the European Union. It finds its principal place in Title II governing the free movement of goods. But the latter is complemented by a chapter on "Tax Provisions" within Title VII.

This Chapter analyses the free movement of goods provisions in four steps. Section 1 examines the prohibition on customs duties. These are fiscal

---

[1] On the notion of "goods", see *Commission* v. *Italy*, Case 7/68, [1968] ECR 423, at 428: "products which can be valued in money and which are capable, as such, of forming the subject of commercial transactions".

Table 9 Treaty provisions on the free movement of goods

Title II: Free Movement of Goods	Title VII: Competition, Taxation, Approximation
Chapter 1 Customs Union	Chapter 1 Rules on Competition
Article 30 Prohibition on CD and CEE	Chapter 2 Tax Provisions
Article 31 Common Customs Tariff	Article 110 Prohibition of Discriminatory Taxes
Article 32 Commission Duties	Article 111 Repayment of Internal Taxes
Chapter 2 Customs Cooperation	Article 112 Countervailing Charges
Chapter 3 Quantitative Restrictions	Article 113 Harmonization of Indirect Taxes
Article 34 Prohibition of QR and MEE on Imports	Chapter 3 Approximation of Laws
Article 35 Prohibition of QR and MEE on Exports	Article 114 Internal Market Competence I
Article 36 Justifications	Article 115 Internal Market Competence II
Article 37 State Monopolies of a Commercial Character	

duties charged when goods cross (national) borders.[2] Section 2 moves to the second type of fiscal charge: discriminatory taxes imposed on foreign goods. Section 3 then investigates the legality of regulatory restrictions to the free movement of goods. Regulatory restrictions are not, unlike fiscal duties, pecuniary charges. They simply "regulate" access to the national market by – for example – establishing product or labelling requirements. Finally, Section 4 will look at possible justifications for regulatory restrictions to trade in goods.

1. Fiscal barriers I: customs duties

Customs duties are the classic commercial weapon of the protectionist state. They are traditionally employed to "protect" domestic goods against

---

[2] The reference to borders should theoretically mean "national" borders as Article 30 prohibits charges "between Member States". However, the Court has extended the scope of the prohibition to include some charges imposed on goods crossing *regional* frontiers; see *Administration des Douanes et Droits Indirects* v. *Léopold Legros and others*, Case C-163/90, [1992] ECR I-4625.

cheaper imports. Customs duties operate like a "countervailing" charge, which is typically demanded at the national border. Within a customs union, these pecuniary charges are prohibited. Within the European Union, they are outlawed by Article 30 TFEU. The provision states:

> Customs duties on imports and exports and charges having equivalent effect shall be prohibited between Member States. The prohibition shall also apply to customs duties of a fiscal nature.

Textually, the prohibition applies to charges on imports and exports; and no exceptions are made. But these textual commands were however only partly followed. For while the European Court would indeed develop a single constitutional regime for imports and exports, it has allowed for objective justifications within Article 30.

(a) Article 30: an absolute prohibition

What is a customs duty? With no definition in the European Treaties, the Court has defined the concept in a general way. It is "any pecuniary charge" that is "imposed on goods by reason of the fact that they cross a frontier".[3] Yet the Treaty not only outlaws customs duties in this strict sense. For Article 30 extends the prohibition to "charges having equivalent effect" (CEE). This wording betrayed "a general intention to prohibit not only measures which obviously take the form of the classic customs duty".[4] Article 30 was also to cover all those charges with an equivalent result. And in *Commission* v. *Italy*,[5] the Court thus defined a CEE as "any charge which, by altering the price of an article exported, has the same restrictive effect on the free circulation of that article as a customs duty".[6] The purpose of the charge would thereby be irrelevant, as Article 30 "ma[de] no distinction based on the purpose of the duties and charges the abolition of which it requires".[7] All that mattered was the effect of a charge, and even the smallest of effects would matter.[8]

   Would Article 30 nonetheless require a *protectionist* effect, that is: an effect that protected domestic goods? Despite a brief flirtation with a

---

[3] *Commission* v. *Italy (Statistical Lery)*, Case 24/68, [1969] ECR 193, para. 7.
[4] *Commission* v. *Luxembourg and Belgium*, Case 2 and 3/62, [1962] ECR 425, 432.
[5] *Commission* v. *Italy*, Case 7/68 (supra n. 1) 423.   [6] *Ibid.*, 429.   [7] *Ibid.*
[8] *Commission* v. *Italy (Statistical Levy)*, Case 24/68 (supra n. 3) para. 14: "The very low rate of the charge cannot change its character with regard to the principles of the Treaty[.]"

protectionist rationale,[9] the Court has chosen a different standard. The mere presence of a *restricting* effect on the free movement of goods will trigger Article 30. This constitutional choice was made in *Statistical Levy*.[10] Italy had imposed a levy on goods leaving (or entering) Italy for the purpose of collecting statistical data. Since the levy applied universally to all goods crossing the national border, it argued that the measure could not constitute a CEE "since any protection of domestic production or discrimination is eliminated".[11] The Court disagreed:

> [T]he purpose of the abolition of customs barriers is not merely to eliminate their protective nature, as the Treaty sought on the contrary to give general scope and effect to the rule on the elimination of customs duties and charges having equivalent effect, in order to ensure the free movement of goods. It follows from the system as a whole and from the general and absolute nature of the prohibition of any customs duty applicable to goods moving between Member States that customs duties are prohibited independently of any consideration of the purpose for which they were introduced and the destination of the revenue obtained therefrom.[12]

Statistical Levy clarified that Article 30 outlawed *all* restrictions – including non-discriminatory restrictions devoid of a protectionist effect.[13] The "general and absolute nature of the prohibition of any customs duties" was confirmed in subsequent jurisprudence.[14] "[A]ny pecuniary charge – however small – imposed on goods by reason of the fact that they cross a frontier constitutes an obstacle to the movement of such goods."[15] And such an obstacle remained an obstacle "even if it is not imposed for the benefit of the State, is not discriminatory or protective in effect or if the product on which the charge is imposed is not in competition with any domestic product".[16]

The restriction rationale underlying Article 30 thereby stems from the material scope of Article 30. For the prohibition only outlaws national

---

[9] *Commission* v. *Luxembourg and Belgium*, Case 2 and 3/62 (supra n. 4), 432.

[10] *Commission* v. *Italy (Statistical Levy)*, Case 24/68 (supra n. 3).   [11] *Ibid.*, para. 12.

[12] *Ibid.*, paras. 6–7.   [13] *Ibid.*, para. 9.

[14] *Sociaal Fonds voor de Diamantarbeiders* v. *S.A. Ch. Brachfeld & Sons and Chougol Diamond Co*, Case 2/69, [1969] ECR 211, para. 11/14.

[15] *Ibid.*

[16] *Ibid.*, paras. 15/18. And see also *Carbonati Apuani Srl* v. *Comune di Carrara*, Case C-72/03, [2004] ECR I-8027.

measures that impose a charge on the frontier-crossing of goods. These measures are – by definition – not applicable to goods never leaving the domestic market.[17] A discrimination rationale would here simply not work. This explains an important conceptual limit to the scope of Article 30. For if it only applies to *frontier* measures it cannot cover measures qualifying as *internal* taxation. The question thus arises as to when a fiscal charge constitutes a measure having an effect equivalent to a customs duty, and when it constitutes an internal tax.[18] In its past jurisprudence, the Court demarcated the respective spheres of Articles 30 and 110 by treating the latter as a *lex specialis*. It has thus found that "financial charges within a general system of internal taxation *applying systematically to domestic and imported products according to the same criteria* are not to be considered as charges having equivalent effect".[19] Equally applicable fiscal charges that apply the "same criteria" to domestic and imported goods will thus not fall under Article 30.[20]

(b) Objective "justifications"

May a State exceptionally impose customs duties in certain situations? There are no express justifications for fiscal barriers to trade in goods. This absence contrasts with the presence of such express justifications for regulatory barriers under Article 36.[21] Could the latter provision nonetheless apply by analogy to fiscal barriers? In *Commission* v. *Italy*,[22] the defendant tried to justify a charge on the export of goods with artistic or historical value by pointing to Article 36. Yet the Court rejected this reasoning. Exceptions to the free movement of goods had to be interpreted restrictively. And with regard to Article 36 this meant that it "is not possible to apply the exception laid down in the latter provision to measures which

---

[17] For the exception to this rule with regard to "regional" charges, see supra n. 2.

[18] And since the Treaty only outlaws *discriminatory* internal taxes, the answer to this question will conclusively determine the legality of *non*-discriminatory fiscal charges. On this point, see Section 2 below.

[19] *Capolongo* v. *Azienda Agricole*, Case 77/72, [1973] ECR 611, para. 12 (emphasis added).

[20] The Court has interpreted the requirement of an application of the "same criteria" strictly. In *Denkavit Loire* v. *France*, Case 132/78, [1979] ECR 1923, the Court had to deal with a French health measure that generally imposed a financial charge on meat. However, the calculation base of the charge differed depending on whether the meat had been slaughtered on French territory or whether it had been imported. The Court held that such a differential system would not apply the "same criteria" to domestic and imported products (*ibid.*, para. 8).

[21] See Table 9 above. For the text of Article 36 and its interpretation, see Section 4 below.

[22] *Commission* v. *Italy* (*Art Treasures*), Case 7/68 (supra n. 1).

fall outside the scope of the prohibitions referred to in the chapter relating to the elimination of quantitative restrictions between Member States".[23] Article 36 was thus confined to *regulatory* restrictions and could not be extended to *fiscal* charges. And since there were no specific justifications for measures falling into Article 30, the Court concluded that the provision "does not permit of any exceptions".[24]

The Court however subsequently recognized two *implied* exceptions. The first exception relates to the situation where a fiscal charge constitutes consideration for a service rendered. In *Statistical Levy*,[25] the Italian government thus argued that its wish to create statistical data for imports and exports benefited individual traders, and that this commercial advantage "justifies their paying for this public service" as a *quid pro quo*.[26] The Court indeed accepted the abstract idea;[27] yet it nonetheless found against Italy, since the charge was not consideration for a specific service benefiting *individual traders*. The statistical information was only "beneficial to the economy as a whole", and the advantage was thus "so general" that the charge could not be regarded "as the consideration for a *specific* benefit".[28]

The second (implied) exception from the absolute prohibition of fiscal charges are charges that a Member State levies as compensation for frontier checks that are required under European law.[29] The rationale behind this

---

[23] *Ibid.*, 430.

[24] *Commission* v. *Italy (Statistical Levy)*, Case 24/68 (supra n. 3), para. 10; and see also *Sociaal Fonds voor de Diamantarbeiders* v. *S.A. Ch. Brachfeld*, Case 2/69 (supra n. 14), paras. 19/21.

[25] *Commission* v. *Italy (Statistical Levy)*, Case 24/68 (supra n. 3).   [26] *Ibid.*, para. 15.

[27] *Ibid.*, para. 11: "Although it is not impossible that in certain circumstances a specific service actually rendered may form consideration for a possible proportional payment for the service in question, this may only apply in specific cases which cannot lead to the circumvention of the provisions of [Article 30] of the Treaty."

[28] *Ibid.*, para. 16 (emphasis added). See also *Rewe-Zentralfinanz eGmbH* v. *Direktor der Landwirtschaftskammer Westfalen-Lippe*, Case 39/73, [1973] ECR 1039, esp. para. 4.

[29] In *Bauhuis* v. *The Netherlands*, Case 46/76, [1977] ECR 5, the Court had been asked to deal with a Union law that required veterinary and public health inspections by the exporting Member State so as to make multiple frontier inspections unnecessary. The health inspections were thus not unilaterally imposed by a Member State but reflected "the general interest of the [Union]" (*ibid.*, para. 29); and as such, they would not hinder trade in goods (*ibid.*, para. 30). National charges for these "Union" inspections were thus legal (*ibid.*, para. 31). For a subsequent codification of the *Bauhuis* test, see *Commission* v. *Germany*, Case 18/87, [1988] ECR 5427, para. 8: "[S]uch fees may not be classified as charges having an effect equivalent to a customs duty if the following conditions are satisfied: (a) they do not exceed the actual costs of the inspections in connection with which they are charged; (b) the inspections in question are obligatory and uniform for all the products concerned in the

exception is that the Member States here act on behalf of the Union, and in a way that facilitates the free movement of goods.

2. Fiscal barriers II: discriminatory internal taxation

The prohibition of customs duties and the prohibition of protectionist taxation are two sides of the same coin. The prohibition established in Article 110 TFEU indeed complements Article 30 TFEU: "Article [110] supplements the provision[] on the abolition of customs duties and charges having equivalent effect. Its aim is to ensure free movement of goods between the Member States in normal conditions of competition by the elimination of all forms of protection which may result from the application of internal taxation."[30] Despite their complementary aims, the material scopes of Articles 30 and 110 are nonetheless fundamentally different. The former catches national measures that impose a charge on goods when crossing a frontier. By contrast, Article 110 applies where foreign goods are subject – with domestic goods – to internal taxation. The scopes of Articles 30 and 110 are thus mutually exclusive.[31]

Article 110 deals with measures that apply to foreign *and* domestic goods. The provision is therefore – unlike Article 30 – not formulated as an absolute prohibition. Instead it states:

[1] No Member State shall impose, directly or indirectly, on the products of other Member States any internal taxation of any kind *in excess of* that imposed directly or indirectly on similar domestic products.

[2] Furthermore, no Member State shall impose on the products of other Member States any internal taxation of such a nature to afford *indirect protection* to other products.

The aim behind Article 110 is to outlaw domestic tax systems that protect national goods. It thereby distinguishes between two types of protectionist

[Union]; (c) they are prescribed by [European] law in the general interest of the [Union]; (d) they promote the free movement of goods, in particular by neutralizing obstacles which could arise from unilateral measures of inspection adopted in accordance with Article 36 of the Treaty".

[30] *Bergandi* v. *Directeur général des impôts*, Case 252/86, [1988] ECR 1342, para. 17.

[31] *Compagnie Commerciale de l'Ouest and others* v. *Receveur Principal des Douanes de La Pallice Port*, Case C-78/90, [1992] ECR I-1847, para. 22: "The provisions on charges having equivalent effect and those on discriminatory internal taxation cannot be applied together. The scope of each of those provisions must therefore be defined."

taxes. Paragraph 1 declares illegal all national tax laws that *discriminate* between foreign and domestic goods. Discrimination here means that "similar" foreign goods are treated dissimilarly. This might occur through direct or indirect means. Direct discrimination takes place where national tax legislation *legally* disadvantages foreign goods by – for example – imposing a higher tax rate than that for domestic goods.[32] Indirect discrimination occurs where the same national tax formally applies to both foreign and domestic goods, but materially imposes a *heavier* fiscal burden on the former.[33]

Paragraph 2 covers a second variant of fiscal protectionism. Strictly speaking, it is not based on a discrimination rationale. For its scope is wider than outlawing the dissimilar treatment of "similar" goods.[34] Yet by insisting on proof of a protectionist effect it is stricter than paragraph 1,[35] since the latter will not require evidence of such an effect.

Let us look at both protectionist variants in turn.

(a) Paragraph 1: discrimination against "similar" foreign goods

Article 110 (1) prohibits foreign goods to be taxed "in excess of" similar domestic goods. The key to this prohibition lies in the concept of "similarity". When are domestic and foreign goods *similar?* Early on, the Court clarified that similarity is wider than identity;[36] and that similarity relates to comparability.[37] Comparability thereby means that two goods "have similar characteristics and meet the same needs from the point of view of consumers".[38] But are "whisky" and "cognac" comparable drinks?[39] Or should it make a difference that the former is seen as an *apéritif*, while the latter constitutes a *digestif*?[40]

---

[32] See *Lütticke GmbH* v. *Hauptzollamt Sarrelouis*, Case 57/65, [1966] ECR 205; as well as *Hansen & Balle* v. *Hauptzollamt de Flensburg*, Case 148/77, [1978] ECR 1787.

[33] On this point, see my discussion of *Humblot* v. *Directeur des services fiscaux*, Case 112/84 in Section 2(a) below.

[34] On the two distinct tests for Article 110(1) and 110(2) TFEU, see *Fink-Frucht GmbH* v. *Hauptzollamt München-Landsbergerstrasse*, Case 27/67, [1967] ECR 223.

[35] See *Commission* v. *Sweden*, C-167/05, [2008] ECR I-2127.

[36] See *Hansen & Balle*, Case 148/77 (supra n. 32), para. 19: "The application of that provision is based not on a strict requirement that the products should be identical but on their 'similarity'."

[37] See *Commission* v. *France (Whisky v Cognac)*, Case 168/78, [1980] ECR 347, para. 5.

[38] *Rewe-Zentrale des Lebensmittel-Großhandels GmbH* v. *Hauptzollamt Landau/Pfalz*, Case 45/75, [1976] ECR 181.

[39] *Commission* v. *France (Whisky v Cognac)*, Case 168/78 (supra n. 37).   [40] *Ibid.*, para. 33.

The Court has endorsed a "broad interpretation of the concept of similarity",[41] which however takes account of "objective" differences between two seemingly similar products. An excellent illustration of this approach is *Humblot*.[42] Monsieur Humblot had acquired a (German) Mercedes car in France. The car possessed 36 CV (fiscal horsepower) and he had to pay a special tax imposed by the French Revenue Code, which distinguished between a progressive annual tax for cars up to 16 CV and a single special tax for cars above this rate. The special tax was nearly five times higher than the highest rate of the general progressive tax. And as France did not produce any cars above 16 CV, the question arose whether the special tax was "in excess of" the national tax on domestic goods. But are small (French) cars comparable to big (German) cars? The French government defended its internal tax regime by arguing that "the special tax is charged solely on luxury vehicles, which are *not similar*, within the meaning of the first paragraph of Article [110] to cars liable to the differential tax".[43] The Court disagreed. For while it acknowledged the power of the Member States to "subject products such as cars to a system of road tax which increases progressively in amount depending on an *objective criterion*, such as the power rating",[44] the French tax system did not do so and thus indirectly discriminated against foreign cars.[45]

What "objective" criteria may however be used fiscally to distinguish between seemingly similar products?[46] This question is – misleadingly – called the question of "objective justification".[47] What stands behind this misnomer is the idea that while a national tax system must be neutral towards foreign goods, it can discriminate between goods "on the basis of objective criteria".[48] Thus, where a Member State discriminates on the basis of a regional policy objective, such a public policy objective will not amount to protectionist discrimination. The discrimination is here "justified" by

---

[41] *John Walker* v. *Ministeriet for Skatter og Afgifter*, Case 243/84, [1986] ECR 875, para. 11.
[42] *Humblot* v. *Directeur des services fiscaux*, Case 112/84, [1985] ECR 1367.
[43] *Ibid.*, para. 9.   [44] *Ibid.*, para. 12.
[45] While the Court was coy with regard to the exact violation, the case appears to acknowledge a partial violation of Article 110 (1) in para. 14. For a subsequent case on the – reformed – French car tax system, see *Feldain* v. *Directeur des services fiscaux du département du Haut-Rhin*, Case 433/85, [1987] ECR 3521.
[46] *Commission* v. *Italy (Regenerated Oil)*, Case 21/79, [1980] ECR 1.
[47] The term is used in *ibid*, para. 16: "objectively justified".
[48] *John Walker* v. *Ministeriet for Skatter og Afgifter*, Case 243/84 (supra n. 41), para. 23.

"objective" criteria that distinguish two products. This can be seen in *Commission* v. *France (Natural Sweet Wines)*.[49] The Commission had brought proceedings against a French tax scheme that exempted naturally sweet wines from the higher consumption duty on liqueur wines. The French Government defended this differential treatment by pointing to the fact that "natural sweet wines are made in regions characterized by low rainfall and relatively poor soil, in which the difficulty of growing other crops means that the local economy depends heavily on their production".[50] This regional policy objective gave preferential treatment to a "traditional and customary production" over similar goods resulting from industrial production. And this "objective" criterion was not discriminating against foreign goods.[51]

(b) Paragraph 2: protection against "competing" foreign goods

Strictly speaking, the rationale behind Article 110 (2) is not a prohibition on discriminatory taxation. For the idea of discrimination implies treating similar products dissimilarly. And where there are no similar domestic products, there cannot be discrimination.[52] The scope of Article 110 (2) is thus wider. It outlaws all internal taxes that grant "indirect protection" to domestic goods. Unlike national taxes that are discriminatory, the provision targets national taxes that generally disadvantage foreign goods. However, the Court has held that such indirect protection only occurs where domestic goods are *in competition* with imported goods.[53] Article 110 (2) consequently requires two elements to be fulfilled before a national tax is found to hinder the free movement of goods. First, the national law will tax *competing* goods differently. And second, this differentiation indirectly protects *national* goods.

When will two goods be in competition? Within Article 110 (2), the Court has generally adopted a flexible approach. This can be seen in *Commission* v. *United Kingdom (Beer & Wine)*.[54] The Commission had brought

---

[49] *Commission* v. *France (Natural Sweet Wines)*, Case 196/85, [1987] ECR 1597.

[50] *Ibid.*, para. 9.   [51] *Ibid.*, para. 10.

[52] *Commission* v. *Italy (Bananas)*, Case 184/85, [1987] ECR 2013.

[53] Where this is not the case, Article 110 (2) will indeed not apply; see *Commission* v. *Denmark*, Case 47/88, [1990] ECRI 4509; as well as *De Danske Bilimportører* v *Skatteministeriet, Told-og Skattestyrelsen*, Case C-383/01, [2003] ECR I-6065.

[54] *Commission* v. *United Kingdom (Beer & Wine, Interim Judgment)*, Case 170/78, [1980] ECR 417.

infringement proceedings against Great Britain in the belief that its tax regime for wine granted indirect protection to British beer. The excise tax on wine was indeed significantly higher than that on beer, and as Britain produced very little wine but a lot of beer, the suspicion of indirect protectionism arose. Britain counterclaimed that there was no competitive relationship between beer and wine, and that there could thus be no such protectionist effect. Not only were the two products "entirely different" with regard to their production and price structure,[55] the goods would hardly ever be substituted by consumers.[56] The Court was not impressed with this line of argument, and espoused its dynamic understanding of product substitution:

> In order to determine the existence of a competitive relationship under the second paragraph of Article [110], it is necessary to consider not only the present state of the market but also the possibilities for development within the context of the free movement of goods at the [Union] level and the further potential for the substitution of products for one another which may be revealed by intensification of trade, so as fully to develop the complementary features of the economies of the Member States in accordance with the objectives laid down by Article [3] of the [EU] Treaty . . . For the purpose of measuring the degree of substitution, it is impossible to restrict oneself to consumer habits in a Member State or in a given region. In fact, those habits, which are essentially variable in time and space, cannot be considered to be a fixed rule; the tax policy of a Member State must not therefore crystallize given consumer habits so as to consolidate an advantage acquired by national industries concerned to comply with them.[57]

The Court here brilliantly attacked the chicken-and-egg-problem within Article 110(2). For two goods might not presently be in competition *because* of the artificial price differences created by internal taxation. The British argument that its tax policy only reflected a social habit in which beer was mass-consumed, while wine was an "elitist" drink, disregarded the fact that the social habit might itself – at least partly – be the product of its fiscal policy. And once this fiscal policy disappeared, beer and wine *could* be in

---

[55] *Ibid.*, para. 13.
[56] *Ibid.*: "As regards consumer habits, the Government of the United Kingdom states that in accordance with long-established tradition in the United Kingdom, beer is a popular drink consumed preferably in public-houses or in connexion with work; domestic consumption and consumption with meals is negligible. In contrast, the consumption of wine is more unusual and special from the point of view of social custom."
[57] *Ibid.*, paras. 6 and 14.

competition. This *dynamic* understanding of product substitutability acknowledges the ability of fiscal regimes to *dynamically* shape consumer preferences.

Once a foreign product has been found to be in competition with a domestic product, the Court will investigate whether the national tax regime generates a protectionist effect. In the above case, the Court indeed found that the higher tax burden on wine would afford protection to domestic beer production.[58] And in another case involving "drinks in Luxembourg",[59] the Court considered a clear protectionist effect to exist where "an essential part of domestic production" came within the most favourable tax category whereas competing products – "almost all of which [were] imported from other Member States" – were subject to higher taxation.[60]

3. Regulatory barriers: quantitative restrictions

Regulatory barriers are legal obstacles to trade which cannot be overcome by the payment of money.[61] They potentially range from a complete ban on (foreign) products to the partial restriction of a product's use.

What types of legal barriers to the free movement of goods do the Treaties outlaw? The Treaty regime for regulatory barriers is set out in Chapter 3 of Title II. The chapter outlaws quantitative restrictions on imports (Article 34) and exports (Article 35); yet it also contains a provision according to which restrictions on imports or exports can be justified (Article 36). Two systemic features of this constitutional arrangement strike the attentive eye. First, unlike the legal regime governing customs duties, the Treaties expressly distinguish between *two* prohibitions: one for imports, and one for exports. And second, the constitutional regime for regulatory barriers expressly

---

[58] *Commission* v. *United Kingdom (Beer & Wine, Final Judgment)*, Case 170/78, [1983] ECR 2265, para. 27.

[59] G. Rodrigues Iglesias, "Drinks in Luxembourg: Alcoholic Beverages and the Case Law of the European Court of Justice", in D. O'Keeffe (ed.), *Judicial Review in European Union Law: Liber Amicorum in Honour of Lord Slynn of Hadley* (Kluwer, 2000), 523.

[60] *Commission* v. *France (Whisky v Cognac)*, Case 168/78 (supra n. 37), para. 41.

[61] This general rule was expressed in *Iannelli & Volpi* v. *Meroni*, Case 74/76, [1977] ECR 557, para. 9: "[O]bstacles which are of a fiscal nature or have equivalent effect and are covered by Articles [30 and 110] of the Treaty do not fall within the prohibition in Article [34]."

allows for exceptions. This section deals with the first feature and analyses the – respective – prohibitions for quantitative restrictions on imports and exports. Section 4 will then examine the express (and implied) justifications for regulatory restrictions on the free movement of goods.

(a) Quantitative restrictions on imports: Article 34

The central provision governing regulatory barriers to imports is Article 34 TFEU. It states: "Quantitative restrictions on imports and all measures having equivalent effect shall be prohibited between Member States." The core of this prohibition consists of the concept of "quantitative restrictions". These are restrictions that legally limit the quantity of imported goods to a fixed amount.[62] Quantitative restrictions are quotas, which – in their most extreme form – amount to a total ban.[63] Import quotas operate as absolute frontier barriers: once a quota for a product is exhausted, foreign imports cannot enter the domestic market. However, the text of Article 34 covers – like that of Article 30 on customs duties – a second category of measures, namely "Measures having an Equivalent Effect to Quantitative Restrictions" (MEEQR). And it is this category that has been at the centre of judicial and academic attention in the past half-century.

What are these mysterious MEEQR? We find a first (legislative) definition of these measures in Directive 70/50.[64] The Directive distinguishes between two types of MEEQR. National measures that are *not* "applicable equally" to domestic and foreign products and "which hinder imports which could otherwise take place" are dealt with in its Article 2. They are seen as MEEQR. By contrast, measures that are "applicable equally" are not generally seen as equivalent to those of quantitative restrictions.[65] Yet Article 3 of the Directive nonetheless extends the concept of MEEQR to certain equally applicable measures (emphasis added):

---

[62] See *Geddo* v. *Ente Nazionale Risi*, Case 2/73, [1973] ECR 865, para. 7: "The prohibition on quantitative restrictions covers measures which amount to a total or a partial restraint of, according to the circumstances, imports, exports, or goods in transit."

[63] *Regina* v. *Henn and Darby*, Case 34/79, [1979] ECR 3795, para. 12: "[P]rohibition on imports ... is the most extreme form of restriction."

[64] Commission Directive 70/50 on the abolition of measures which have an effect equivalent to quantitative restrictions on imports and are not covered by other provisions adopted in pursuance of the EEC Treaty, [1970] OJ L13/29.

[65] *Ibid.*, recital 8.

This Directive also covers measures governing the marketing of products which deal, in particular, with shape, size, weight, composition, presentation, identification or putting up and which are equally applicable to domestic and imported products, *where the restrictive effect of such measures on the free movement of goods exceeds the effects intrinsic to trade rules.*

This is the case, in particular, where:

– the restrictive effects on the free movement of goods are out of proportion to their purpose;
– the same objective can be attained by other means which are less of a hindrance to trade.

This provision was informed by a fundamental constitutional choice. Product requirements that were equally applicable to domestic and imported goods were – in principle – considered outside the scope of Article 34. For their restrictive effects on the free movement of goods were seen as "*inherent in the disparities* between rules applied by Member States".[66] And these legislative disparities would need to be removed through the Union's harmonization powers.[67] Equally applicable marketing measures could only *exceptionally* fall within the scope of Article 34, where they had "a restrictive effect on the free movement of goods over and above that which is intrinsic to such rules".[68]

Despite the Directive's strong impact on the early case law,[69] the Court eventually developed a second definition in *Dassonville*.[70] The case involved the legality of Belgian rules that made the sale of Scotch whisky dependent on having a "certificate of origin" from the British customs authorities. Was this certification requirement a MEEQR? The Court thought so, and famously declared that "[a]ll trading rules enacted by Member States which are capable of hindering, directly or indirectly, actually or potentially, intra-[Union] trade are to be considered as measures having an effect equivalent to quantitative restrictions".[71] This formulation became known as the "*Dassonville* formula". On its surface, the formula did not distinguish between equally and non-equally applicable

---

[66] *Ibid.* (emphasis added).
[67] On the scope of Article 114 TFEU, see Chapter 3 – Section 2 (a) above.
[68] Directive 70/50 (supra n. 64), recital 9.
[69] See *Commission* v. *Germany*, Case 12/74, [1975] ECR 181.
[70] *Procureur du Roi* v. *Dassonville*, Case 8/74, [1974] ECR 837.   [71] *Ibid.*, para. 5.

rules; yet like Directive 70/50, it seemed to focus on unreasonable restrictions to the free movement of goods.[72]

But what were unreasonable restrictions? Whatever the original intentions behind *Dassonville*, a lasting answer to this question was given in *Cassis de Dijon*.[73] The case concerned a German marketing rule that fixed the minimum alcohol strength of liqueurs at 25 per cent. This national rule prohibited the sale of Cassis de Dijon as a liqueur in Germany, for the distinguished French drink only had an alcohol content below 20 per cent. Formally, the national measure applied equally to foreign and domestic goods. Would the Court thus search for a disproportionate restrictive effect? The Court gave the following famous answer:

Obstacles to movement within the [Union] resulting from disparities between national laws relating to the marketing of the products in question must be accepted in so far as those provisions may be recognized as being necessary in order to satisfy mandatory requirements relating in particular to the effectiveness of fiscal supervision, the protection of public health, the fairness of commercial transactions and the defence of the consumer ...

[T]he requirements relating to the minimum alcohol content of alcoholic beverages do not serve a purpose which is in the general interest and such as to take precedence over the requirements of the free movement of goods, which constitutes one of the fundamental rules of the [Union] ... There is therefore no valid reason why, provided that they have been lawfully produced and marketed in one of the Member States, alcoholic beverages should not be introduced into any other Member State; the sale of such products may not be subject to a legal prohibition on the marketing of beverages with an alcohol content lower than the limit set by the national rules.[74]

While the judgment can superficially be aligned with the formal logic behind Directive 70/50, it implicitly overruled its substantive presumption that trade restrictions flowing from disparities between equally applicable product requirements will only *exceptionally* qualify as MEEQR. *Cassis* inverts this presumption of legality, and transforms it into a presumption

---

[72] *Ibid.*, para. 6: "In the absence of a [Union] system guaranteeing for consumers the authenticity of a product's designation of origin, if a Member State takes measures to prevent unfair practices in this connexion, it is however subject to the condition that these measures should be reasonable and that the means of proof required should not act as a hindrance to trade between Member States[.]"

[73] *Rewe-Zentral AG* v. *Bundesmonopolverwaltung für Branntwein*, Case 120/78, [1979] ECR 649.

[74] *Ibid.*, paras. 8 and 14.

of illegality. Thus, *unless* there are mandatory requirements in the general interest, Member States are *not* entitled to impose their domestic product standards on imported goods. This presumption of illegality would become known as the "principle of mutual recognition". Member States must – in principle – mutually recognize each other's product standards.[75]

With *Cassis*, the idea of a discrimination rationale behind Article 34 appeared to be side-lined.[76] And in a subsequent period, the Court indeed cultivated an absolute prohibition for all regulatory restrictions to trade in goods. A striking illustration of this anti-regulatory philosophy is *Torfaen*.[77] The case formed part of the *Sunday Trading* cases.[78] It had been brought by Torfaen Borough Council, which alleged that B & Q had infringed the 1950 (British) Shops Act by trading on Sunday. The defendant counterclaimed that the British restriction on opening times of shops was a MEEQR. The national law reduced the absolute amount of total sales; and since a percentage of these sales were foreign goods, the Sunday trading ban constituted a restriction on imports. The European Court, drawing on its jurisprudential line on sales restrictions,[79] indeed held that the Shops Act

---

[75] This constitutional principle would, in turn, influence the scope of positive integration under the harmonization competences of the Union. On this point, see R. Schütze, *From Dual to Cooperative Federalism: The Changing Structure of European Law* (Oxford University Press, 2009), 205 et seq.

[76] The requirement to comply with the product standards of the importing state can, admittedly, be constructed as discriminatory. However, discrimination is here judged from a "European" perspective and not from a national perspective. Under the "European" perspective, the imposition of domestic product requirements on foreign goods can be seen as imposing a "double burden". From the "national" perspective of a single State, however, many equally applicable product requirements are non-discriminatory. And this was the perspective originally chosen by the European Court (see *Criminal Proceedings against Gilli and Andres*, Case 788/79, [1980] ECR 2071). On the distinction between discriminatory and non-discriminatory measures in the context of Article 36 and mandatory requirements, see Section 4 below.

[77] *Torfaen Borough Council* v. *B & Q*, Case 145/88, [1989] ECR 3851.

[78] For an analysis of these cases, see C. Barnard, "Sunday Trading: A Drama in Five Acts", 57 (1994) *Modern Law Review*, 449.

[79] The two judicial precedents in this respect were *Oebel*, Case 155/80, [1981] ECR 1993, and *Cinéthèque and others* v. *Fédération nationale des cinémas français*, Case 60 and 61/84, [1985] ECR 2605. The former case concerned a German law on working hours in bakeries; the latter case involved a French law on audio-visual communication that restricted the sale of video cassettes to a time period after the film had been shown in cinemas. In *Cinéthèque*, the Court had indeed held that the time limitation on the sale of goods could constitute a MEEQR (*ibid.*, paras. 21–22).

would constitute a MEEQR if "the effects of such national rules exceed what is necessary to achieve the aim in view".[80]

This judicial signal was fatally effective. For it encouraged commercial traders to challenge virtually all national laws that somehow restricted the marketing of goods on the basis of the *Dassonville* formula.[81] It soon dawned on the Court that its jurisprudence had gone too far. And it therefore announced a judicial retreat in *Keck*.[82] In this case criminal proceedings had been brought against a supermarket manager who had allowed products to be sold at a loss. This form of sales promotion was prohibited in France, but Keck argued that the prohibition constituted a MEEQR because it restricted intra-Union trade in goods.[83] The Court disagreed. While confirming the *Dassonville* formula, it held that certain measures would only fall foul of Article 34 if they were discriminatory:

National legislation imposing a general prohibition on resale at a loss is not designed to regulate trade in goods between Member States. Such legislation may, admittedly, restrict the volume of sales, and hence the volume of sales of products from other Member States, in so far as it deprives traders of a method of sales promotion. But the question remains whether such a possibility is sufficient to characterize the legislation in question as a measure having equivalent effect to a quantitative restriction on imports . . .

It is established by the case-law beginning with "Cassis de Dijon" that, in the absence of harmonization of legislation, obstacles to free movement of goods which are the consequence of applying, to goods coming from other Member States where they are lawfully manufactured and marketed, rules that lay down requirements to be met by such goods (such as those relating to designation, form, size, weight, composition, presentation, labelling, packaging) constitute measures of equivalent effect prohibited by Article [34]. This is so even if those rules apply without distinction to all products unless their application can be justified by a public-interest objective taking precedence over the free movement of goods. *By contrast, contrary to what has previously been decided, the application to products from other Member States of national provisions restricting or*

---

[80] *Torfaen*, Case 145/88 (supra n. 77), para. 15. The Court expressly referred to Article 3 of Directive 70/50 (supra n. 64) as inspiration for this test.

[81] See D. Chalmers, "Free Movement of Goods within the European Community: An Unhealthy Addiction to Scotch Whisky", 42 (1993) *International and Comparative Law Quarterly*, 269.

[82] *Criminal Proceedings against Keck and Mithouard*, Joined Cases C-267 and C-268/91, [1993] ECR I-6097.

[83] *Ibid.*, para. 3.

prohibiting certain selling arrangements is not such as to hinder directly or indirectly, actually or potentially, trade between Member States within the meaning of the Dassonville *judgment, so long as those provisions apply to all relevant traders operating within the national territory and so long as they affect in the same manner, in law and in fact, the marketing of domestic products and of those from other Member States.*[84]

The case constitutes a symbolic watershed. Drawing a distinction between product requirements and "selling arrangements",[85] *Keck* clarified that the latter would only constitute MEEQR where they *discriminated* against the marketing of foreign goods.[86] Only discriminatory selling arrangements would violate the free movement of goods provisions.[87] Product requirements, by contrast, would not need to be discriminatory to fall within the scope of Article 34. And in light of the two distinct constitutional tests, the distinction between product requirements and selling arrangements has become *the* classificatory battle in the post-*Keck* jurisprudence.[88] One must however bear in mind that "product requirements" and "selling arrangements" are only two specific categories of measures that potentially constitute MEEQR. Other categories, such as national laws restricting the use of a product,[89] may equally fall foul of Article 34.

(b) Quantitative restrictions on exports: Article 35

The wording in Article 35 mirrors that of Article 34: "Quantitative restrictions on exports, and all measures having equivalent effect, shall be prohibited between Member States."

---

[84] *Ibid.*, paras. 12–16 (emphasis added).

[85] The distinction had been – academically – suggested by E. White, "In Search of the Limits of Article 30 of the EEC Treaty", 26 (1989) *Common Market Law Review*, 235.

[86] For an important first evaluation of *Keck*, see S. Weatherill, "After Keck: Some Thoughts on How to Clarify the Clarification", 33 (1996), *Common Market Law Review*, 885.

[87] See *Konsumentombudsmannen (KO)* v. *Gourmet*, Case C-405/98, [2001] ECR I-1795, esp. para. 25.

[88] See *Familiapress* v. *Bauer Verlag*, Case C-368/95, [1997] ECR I-3689. On the general classification of advertising restrictions as selling arrangements, see *Hünermund and others* v. *Landesapothekerkammer Baden-Württemberg*, Case C-292/92, [1993] ECR 6787.

[89] See *Commission* v. *Italy*, Case C-110/05, [2009] ECR I-519; and *Åklagaren* v. *Mickelsson and Roos*, Case C-142/05, [2009] ECR I-4274. For an analysis of these cases, see E. Spaventa, "Leaving *Keck* behind? The Free Movement of Goods after the Rulings in *Commission* v. *Italy and Mickelsson and Roos*", 34 (2009) *European Law Review*, 914.

Would it not be "logical" if the legal principles governing quantitative restrictions on exports mirrored those on imports? This argument will work for some measures;[90] yet – importantly – not for others, as the scope of Article 35 is indirectly limited by the scope of Article 34. For if the *Cassis* principle of mutual recognition is to work, the product standards of the exporting state must be presumed legitimate. With regard to product requirements, the Court has consequently interpreted Article 35 to include only those national laws that specifically discriminate against exports. This logical extension of *Cassis* was made in *Groenveld.*[91] A wholesaler of horsemeat had challenged the legality of a Dutch law prohibiting the (industrial) production of horsemeat sausages. The law had been adopted in order to protect Dutch meat exports in light of the fact that the consumption of horsemeat was not allowed in the national markets of some important trading partners. The Court held that the prohibition on the (industrial) production of horsemeat sausages did not constitute a MEEQR on exports:

[Article 35] concerns national measures which have as their specific object or effect the restriction of patterns of exports and thereby the establishment of a difference in treatment between the domestic trade of a Member State and its export trade in such a way as to provide a particular advantage for national production or for the domestic market of the State in question at the expense of the production or of the trade of other Member States. This is not so in the case of a prohibition like that in question which is applied objectively to the production of goods of a certain kind without drawing a distinction depending on whether such goods are intended for the national market or for export.[92]

Equally applicable product requirements would thus *not* constitute MEEQR on exports. But did this mean that Article 35 would never apply to equally applicable national laws? It took almost thirty years before the Court gave a decisive answer to this question in *Gysbrechts.*[93] The case involved a Belgian law that prohibited distant selling contracts from requiring the

---

[90] See *Procureur de la République de Besançon* v. *Les Sieurs Bouhelier and others*, Case 53/76, [1977] ECR 197.

[91] *Groenveld* v. *Produktschap voor Vee en Vlees*, Case 15/79, [1979] ECR 3409.

[92] *Ibid.*, para. 7.

[93] *Gysbrechts and Santurel Inter*, Case C-205/07, [2008] ECR I-9947. For an analysis of this case, see M. Szydlo, "Export Restrictions within the Structure of Free Movement of Goods. Reconsideration of an Old Paradigm", 47 (2010) *Common Market Law Review*, 753.

consumer to provide his or her credit card number before a period of seven working days (within which withdrawal from the contract was possible).[94] Was this a MEEQR on exports? The Court found that the national measure indeed "deprive[d] the traders concerned of an efficient tool with which to guard against the risk of non-payment", and thus restricted trade. But in light of the equally applicable nature of the measure, did it fulfil the *Groenveld* formula?[95] The Court found that this was indeed the case, since "its actual effect is none the less greater on goods leaving the market of the exporting Member State than on the marketing of goods in the domestic market of that Member State".[96] Equally applicable measures may thus constitute MEEQR on exports, where they indirectly discriminate. And the discriminatory selling arrangement in the present case would thus need to be justified.

4. Justifying regulatory barriers: Article 36 and mandatory requirements

From the very beginning, the Treaty acknowledged that some quantitative restrictions or measures having equivalent effect could be justified on certain grounds. This express acknowledgement reflected the fact that regulatory barriers to trade often pursue a legitimate regulatory interest. These legitimate interests are set out in Article 36, which states:

The provisions of Articles 34 and 35 shall not preclude prohibitions or restrictions on imports, exports or goods in transit justified on grounds of public morality, public policy or public security; the protection of health and life of humans, animals or plants; the protection of national treasures possessing artistic, historic or archaeo-logical value; or the protection of industrial and commercial property. Such prohib-itions or restrictions shall not, however, constitute a means of arbitrary discrimination or a disguised restriction on trade between Member States.

---

[94] *Gysbrechts*, Case C-205/07 (supra n. 93), para. 13.

[95] The Court expressly confirmed *Groenveld*, Case 15/79 (supra n. 91) in *Gysbrechts*, Case C-205/07 (supra n. 93), para. 40.

[96] *Ibid.*, para. 43. This point was explained in para. 42: "As is clear from the order for reference, the consequences of such a prohibition are generally more significant in cross-border sales made directly to consumers, in particular, in sales made by means of the internet, by reason, inter alia, of the obstacles to bringing any legal proceedings in another Member State against consumers who default, especially when the sales involve relatively small sums."

The provision exempts restrictions on the free movement of goods, where they are justified on grounds of public morality,[97] public policy,[98] public security,[99] public health,[100] national treasures,[101] and the protection of intellectual property.[102] The Court has found this list to be exhaustive: the exceptions listed in Article 36 "cannot be extended to cases other than those specifically laid down".[103] The Court has further found that since Article 36 "constitutes a derogation from the basic rule that all obstacles to the free movement of goods between Member States shall be eliminated", it "must be interpreted strictly".[104] And yet, despite limiting the scope of the Treaty's express derogations, the Court has allowed for implied derogations. These implied justifications for restrictions to the free movement of goods are called "mandatory requirements".

(a) Implied justifications: mandatory requirements

Despite having found the *express* exceptions in Article 36 to be exhaustive, the Court has recognized the existence of *implied* justifications. In *Cassis de Dijon*,[105] the Court thus exempted obstacles to the free movement of goods that were "necessary in order to satisfy *mandatory requirements* relating in particular to the effectiveness of fiscal supervision, the protection of public health, the fairness of commercial transactions and the defence of the consumer".[106] The best explanation for the acceptance of implied justifications may be the dramatically expanded scope of Article 34, which – after *Cassis* – henceforth outlawed all non-discriminatory obstacles to trade that resulted from national disparities in product requirements. Subsequently, the Court indeed clarified that these mandatory requirements solely justified

---

[97] See *Regina* v. *Henn and Darby*, Case 34/79 (supra n. 63).

[98] See *R.* v. *Thompson, Johnson & Woodiwiss*, Case 7/78, [1978] ECR 2247.

[99] See *Campus Oil and others* v. *Minister for Industry and Energy and others*, Case 72/83, [1984] ECR 2727.

[100] See *Commission* v. *United Kingdom*, Case 40/82, [1982] ECR 2793.

[101] According to P. Oliver et al., *Free Movement of Goods in the European Union* (Hart, 2010), 281 there is no case law on the direct application of this ground.

[102] See *Van Zuylen frères* v. *Hag AG*, Case 192/73, [1974] ECR 731.

[103] *Commission* v. *Ireland (Irish Souvenirs)*, Case 113/80, [1981] ECR 1625, para. 7.

[104] *Bauhuis*, Case 46/76 (supra n. 29), para. 12.

[105] *Rewe-Zentral AG* v. *Bundesmonopolverwaltung für Branntwein*, Case 120/78 (supra n. 73)

[106] *Ibid*, para. 8 (emphasis added).

national laws "which apply without discrimination to both domestic and imported products".[107]

The nature of a national restriction – whether discriminatory or not – thus determines which justifications are available to a Member State. Discriminatory national measures can only be justified by reference to the express – and exhaustive – list of public interest grounds in Article 36.[108] By contrast, national measures that do not discriminate will benefit from an open-ended list of implied "mandatory requirements".[109] This distinction has been criticized;[110] and the Court has sometimes tried to evade it by sharp scholastic means,[111] or by bluntly fudging the issue of the (non-)discriminatory character of a national measure.[112] One of the interesting questions in this context is whether selling arrangements that fall within the scope of Article 34 may ever be justified by mandatory requirements. Theoretically, this should not be the case if constitutional logic is followed.[113] However, the Court has given reason to believe that a softer rule might apply in practice.[114]

---

[107] *Criminal Proceedings against Gilli and Andres*, Case 788/79, (supra n. 76), para. 6.

[108] *Commission* v. *Ireland (Irish Souvenirs)*, Case 113/80 (supra n. 103), esp. para.11.

[109] This list is very long and includes, inter alia: consumer protection (see *Commission* v. *Germany*, Case 178/84, [1987] ECR 1227); the prevention of unfair competition (*Cassis de Dijon*, Case 120/78 (supra n. 73)); the protection of the environment (see *Commission* v. *Denmark*, Case 302/86, [1988] ECR 4607); the improvement of working conditions (see *Oebel*, Case 155/80 (supra n. 79); the diversity of the press (see *Familiapress* v. *Bauer*, Case C-368/95 (supra n. 88) and many others.

[110] See Advocate General F. Jacobs in *PreussenElektra* v. *Schleswag*, Case C-379/98, [2001] ECR I-2099, paras. 227 et seq.

[111] See *Commission* v. *Belgium (Walloon Waste)*, Case C-2/90, [1992] ECR I-4431.

[112] *PreussenElektra* v. *Schleswag*, Case C-379/98 (supra n. 110).

[113] We saw above that solely discriminatory selling arrangements can constitute MEEQR, and therefore these national measures could, in theory, solely be justified on the grounds mentioned in Article 36 (see *Konsumentombudsmannen* v. *Gourmet*, Case C-405/98 (supra n. 87)).

[114] See *Konsumentombudsmannen* v. *De Agostini*, Case C-34/95, [1997] ECR I-3843, paras. 39-45 (emphasis added): "[T]he Court held that legislation which prohibits television advertising in a particular sector concerns selling arrangements for products belonging to that sector in that it prohibits a particular form of promotion of a particular method of marketing products . . . Consequently, an outright ban on advertising aimed at children less than 12 years of age and of misleading advertising, as provided for by the Swedish legislation, is not covered by Article [34] of the Treaty, unless it is shown that the ban does not affect in the same way, in fact and in law, the marketing of national products and of products from other Member States. In the latter case, it is for the national court to determine whether the ban is necessary to satisfy *overriding requirements of general public importance* or one of the aims listed in Article 36 of the [FEU] Treaty if it is proportionate

(b) The proportionality principle and national standards

Even if a legitimate public interest can be found to justify a national measure, restrictions on the free movement of goods will be subject to a proportionality test. The Court has insisted that national laws authorized by Article 36 "only comply with the Treaty in so far as they are justified, that is to say, *necessary* for the attainment of the objectives referred to by this provision".[115] And this proportionality test has been extended to mandatory requirements.[116]

What will proportionality in this context mean? Proportionality generally means "that national legislation which restricts or is liable to restrict intra-[Union] trade must be proportionate to the objectives pursued and that those objectives must not be attainable by measures which are less restrictive of such trade".[117] This least-restrictive-means test constitutes the cornerstone of the proportionality inquiry. But behind this test stands an important question: what standard of protection will it be based on? If the British legislature favours a high level of public morality and bans all imports of pornography, should it matter that other Member States do not prefer to stand on such high moral ground? Or, should Germany be allowed to insist on "beer purity" as the highest standard of consumer protection, while other Member States allow their beer to be brewed with artificial ingredients? The question of proportionality is thus intrinsically linked to the desirable standard of protection. And unfortunately, this is a question to which the Court has not given consistent answers.[118]

We find acceptance of a State's (high) national standard in *Henn & Darby*.[119] The case concerned the importation of pornographic films and magazines from Denmark, which violated the British import ban for such

---

to that purpose and if those aims or requirements could not have been attained or fulfilled by measures less restrictive of intra-[Union] trade."

[115] *Simmenthal* v. *Ministero delle Finanze italiano*, Case 35/76, [1976] ECR 1871, para. 10 (emphasis added).

[116] *Rewe-Zentral* v. *Bundesmonopolverwaltung für Branntwein*, Case 120/78 (supra n. 73); as well as *Rau Lebensmittelwerke* v. *De Smedt*, Case 261/81, [1982] ECR 3961, para. 12: "It is also necessary for such rules to be proportionate to the aim in view."

[117] See *Aher-Waggon GmbH* v. *Germany*, Case C-389/96, [1998] ECR I-4473, para. 20.

[118] On this point, see G. De Búrca, "The Principle of Proportionality and its Application in EC Law", 13 (1993) *Yearbook of European Law*, 105.

[119] *Regina* v. *Henn and Darby*, Case 34/79 (supra n. 63).

goods. Could this national law be justified on grounds of public morality, or would the "lower" Danish standard provide an argument that public morality can survive in a society that is more permissive of pornography? The Court chose the higher British standard as its baseline. It held that it was, as a rule, "for each Member State to determine in accordance with its own scale of values and in the form selected by it the requirements of public morality in its territory".[120] However, the Court subsequently clarified that "a Member State may not rely on grounds of public morality in order to prohibit the importation of goods from other Member States when its legislation contains no prohibition on the manufacture or marketing of the same goods on its territory".[121] Yet this qualification did not "preclude the authorities of the Member State concerned from applying to those goods, once imported, the same restrictions on marketing which are applied to similar products manufactured and marketed within the country".[122] It indeed did not undermine the legality of a (high) national standard, but only eliminated "arbitrary discriminations" that led to a "disguised restriction on trade between Member States".[123]

In other areas, by contrast, the Court has not deferred to a high national standard. In *Commission* v. *Germany (Beer Purity)*,[124] the Court thus rejected the claim that a German law confining the designation "beer" to beverages brewed without artificial additives was a proportionate means to protect consumers.[125] Pointing to its dynamic consumer perception – developed in another context[126] – it found that German consumers could be sufficiently protected by suitable labelling requirements.[127] In the Court's view, a high national standard must thus not "crystallize given consumer habits so as to consolidate an advantage acquired by national

---

[120] *Ibid.*, para. 15.
[121] *Conegate* v. *HM Customs & Excise*, Case 121/85, [1986] ECR 1007, para. 16. In this respect *Conegate* overruled *Henn & Darby*.
[122] *Conegate* v. *HM Customs & Excise*, Case 121/85 (supra n. 121), para. 21.
[123] Article 36 TFEU – second sentence.
[124] *Commission* v. *Germany*, Case 178/84, [1987] ECR 1227.
[125] *Ibid.*, para. 53: "[I]n so far as the German rules on additives in beer entail a general ban on additives, their application to beers imported from other Member States is contrary to the requirements of [Union] law as laid down in the case-law of the Court, since that prohibition is contrary to the principle of proportionality."
[126] On this point, see Section 2(b) above.
[127] *Commission* v. *Germany*, Case 178/84 (supra n. 124), para. 35.

industries concerned to comply with them".[128] The Court consequently did not allow Germany to choose its own "scale of values" and insisted on the European standard of the "reasonably circumspect consumer".[129] And it is against this Court-chosen standard that the necessity of a national restriction on the free movement of goods is often judged.

---

[128] *Ibid.*, para. 32. The Court expressly referred to *Commission* v. *United Kingdom*, Case 170/78 (supra n. 58).

[129] See *Verband Sozialer Wettbewerb eV* v. *Clinique Laboratoires and Estée Lauder Cosmetics*, Case C-315/92, [1994] ECR I-317, para. 24; and *Verein gegen Unwesen in Handel und Gewerbe Köln eV.* v. *Mars*, Case C-470/93, [1995] ECR I-1923, para. 24.

10 Internal market: persons

Introduction

From the very beginning, the European Treaties tried to ensure the free movement of certain categories of persons. However, the constitutional choice for an internal market in persons was informed by an economic rationale. The market-building philosophy behind the European Treaties originally limited the right to move across national borders to economically active persons. The Treaties thereby distinguished between two classes of economic migrants, namely: "employed" and "self-employed" persons. The Treaty title dealing with the movement of persons consequently addresses "Workers" in Chapter 1 and the "Right of Establishment" in Chapter 2.

Each of the two chapters contains a central prohibition, whose wording outlaws restriction on the "import" of persons by the (host) State. Yet the Court has found that both provisions can equally apply to restrictions on the free

Table 10 Treaty provisions on the free movement of persons

Free Movement of Persons	
Free Movement of Workers	Freedom of Establishment
Article 45 Prohibition on (unjustified) restrictions	Article 49 Prohibition on national restrictions
Article 46 Union competence to attain the free movement of workers	Article 50 Union competence to attain the freedom of establishment
Article 47 Duty to encourage the exchange of young workers	Article 51 Official Authority Exception for self-employed persons
Article 48 Union competence in the field of social security	Article 52 Legitimate justifications for national restrictions
	Article 53 Union competence on mutual recognition
	Article 54 Extension to legal persons (companies)
	Article 55 Establishment through participation in a company's capital

movement of persons by the "exporting" (home) State.[1] Both chapters also contain a number of legislative competences for the Union. These competences have been widely exercised in the past; and for this reason, European law

---

[1] The Court expresses this constitutional choice by referring to the expanded personal scope of both provisions. With regard to workers, the Court has thus held in *Scholz* v. *Opera Universitaria di Cagliari and Cinzia Porcedda*, Case C-419/92, [1994] ECR I-505, para. 9 that "[a]ny [Union] national who, irrespective of his place of residence and his nationality, has exercised the right to freedom of movement for workers and who has been employed in another Member State, falls within the scope of the aforesaid provisions". By contrast, the inclusion of restrictions for self-employed persons by the home State was much harder. For Article 49 TFEU expressly referes to "restrictions on the freedom of establishment of nationals of a Member State in the territory of another Member State". Nonetheless, the Court clarified in *Knoors* v. *Staatssecretaris van Economische Zaken*, Case 115/78, [1979] ECR 399, para. 24 that "the reference in Article [49] to 'nationals of a Member State' who wish to establish themselves 'in the territory of another Member State' cannot be interpreted in such a way as to exclude from the benefit of [Union] law a given Member State's own nationals when the latter, owing to the fact that they have lawfully resided on the territory of another Member State and have there acquired a trade qualification which is recognized by the provisions of [Union] law, are, with regard to their state of origin, in a situation which may be assimilated to that of any other person enjoying the rights and liberties guaranteed by the Treaty".

on the free movement of persons is a rich mixture of primary and secondary law. But the complexity within this area is also due to a second factor: the existence of European citizenship rights.[2] Article 20 TFEU grants every European citizen the "right to move and reside freely within the territory of the Member States".[3] This general movement right is however a residual right. It must "be exercised in accordance with the conditions and limits defined by the Treaties and by the measures adopted thereunder".[4] Yet the general provisions on European citizenship have themselves had an effect on the specific movement rights for economically active citizens. This symbiotic relationship is embodied in the "Citizenship Directive".[5]

This Chapter looks into the complex constitutional arrangements governing the free movement of persons in four sections. Sections 1 and 2 analyse the special free movement rights for economically active persons, that is, workers and the self-employed. Section 3 explores the various possible justifications to restrictions on the free movement of persons. Section 4 investigates the general rights to free movement granted to all European citizens.

1. Free movement of workers

The Treaty contains a single provision that governs national restrictions and possible justifications to the free movement of workers. The text of Article 45 TFEU reads as follows:

1. Freedom of movement for workers shall be secured within the Union.
2. Such freedom of movement shall entail the abolition of any discrimination based on nationality between workers of the Member States as regards employment, remuneration and other conditions of work and employment.
3. It shall entail the right, subject to limitations justified on grounds of public policy, public security or public health:

    (a) to accept offers of employment actually made;
    (b) to move freely within the territory of Member States for this purpose;

---

[2] Part Two of the TFEU.

[3] Article 20 (2) (a) TFEU, which is elaborated in Article 21 TFEU. A similar right is enshrined in Article 45 EU Charter of Fundamental Rights.

[4] Article 20 (2) TFEU – last indent.

[5] Directive 2004/38 on the right of citizens of the Union and their family members to move and reside freely within the territory of the Member States, [2004] OJ L158/77.

(c) to stay in a Member State for the purpose of employment in accordance with the provisions governing the employment of nationals of that State laid down by law, regulation or administrative action;

(d) to remain in the territory of a Member State after having been employed in that State, subject to conditions which shall be embodied in regulations to be drawn up by the Commission.

4. The provisions of this Article shall not apply to employment in the public service.

The article has been given direct effect.[6] It thus grants European rights that individuals can invoke in national courts. Yet many of the rights workers will enjoy under Article 45 are also codified in Union legislation. The two pertinent pieces of legislation in this context are Regulation 492/2011 "on freedom of movement of workers within the Union",[7] and Directive 2004/38 "on the right of citizens and their family members to move and reside freely within the territory of the Member States".[8] What is the personal and material scope of the rights granted by Article 45 and the relevant Union legislation? Who is considered to be a "worker"? And what types of national restrictions are prohibited? Let us look at both aspects in turn.

(a) Personal scope: workers and "quasi-workers"

When is a person a "worker"? Will part-time work be sufficient? And are persons searching for work already "workers"? These questions concern the

---

[6] See *Commission* v. *France*, Case 167/73, [1974] ECR 359, but see also more famously *Van Duyn* v. *Home Office*, Case 41/74, [1947] ECR 1337, esp. paras. 6–7: "These provisions impose on Member States a precise obligation which does not require the adoption of any further measure on the part of the [Union] institutions or of the Member States and which leaves them, in relation to its implementation, no discretionary power. Paragraph 3, which defines the rights implied by the principle of freedom of movement for workers, subjects them to limitations justified on grounds of public policy, public security or public health. The application of these limitations is, however, subject to judicial control, so that a Member State's right to invoke the limitations does not prevent the provisions of Article [45], which enshrine the principle of freedom of movement for workers, from conferring on individuals rights which are enforceable by them and which the national courts must protect." Article 45 TFEU has also been held to apply to private party actions: see *Walrave and Koch* v. *Association Union Cycliste Internationale*, Case 36/74, [1974] ECR 1405, as well as *Union royale belge des sociétés de football association ASBL* v. *Jean-Marc Bosman*, Case C-415/93, [1995] ECR I-4921. On the doctrine of direct effect generally see Chapter 5 – Section 2.

[7] Regulation 492/2011 on freedom of movement for workers within the Union, [2011] OJ L141/1.

[8] Directive 2004/38 on the right of citizens of the Union and their family members to move and reside freely within the territory of the Member States (supra n. 5).

personal scope of Article 45, which defines the categories of persons falling within the scope of the provision.[9] The Court of Justice has thereby insisted that it alone enjoys the "hermeneutic monopoly" to determine the scope of the term "worker".[10] For "[i]f the definition of this term were a matter within the competence of national law, it would therefore be possible for each Member State to modify the meaning of the concept of 'migrant worker' and to eliminate at will the protection afforded by the Treaty to certain categories of persons."[11] The concept of "worker" had to be a European legal concept, as "the Treaty would be frustrated if the meaning of such a term could be unilaterally fixed and modified by national law".[12]

What then is the European scope of the concept of "worker"? The Court has given an extremely broad definition in *Lawrie-Blum*.[13] The term was to be defined "in accordance with objective criteria which distinguish the employment relationship by reference to the rights and duties of the persons concerned". The essential feature was "that for a certain period of *time* a person performs services for and *under the direction of another person* in return for which he receives *remuneration*".[14] This definition contained three criteria. First, a person would have to be "settled".[15] Second, the person would have to be under the direction of someone else; and consideration for this subordination was – third – the payment of remuneration.[16]

But what form of remuneration would be required to trigger the scope of Article 45? In *Levin*,[17] a British national was refused a residence permit in

---

[9] The section concentrates on the "worker" as the primary beneficiary of Article 45 TFEU. However, the provision, and in particular European legislation on the matter, equally entitles additional classes of persons and especially a worker's family. The case law on these secondary beneficiaries is extensive (see C. Barnard, *The Substantive Law of the EU* (Oxford University Press, 2010), 425 et seq.).

[10] F. Mancini, "The Free Movement of Workers in the Case-Law of the European Court of Justice" in D. Curtin and D. O'Keeffe (eds.), *Constitutional Adjudication in the European Community and National Law* (Butterworths, 1992), 67.

[11] *Hoekstra (née Unger)* v. *Bestuur der Bedrijfsvereniging voor Detailhandel en Ambachten*, Case 75/63, [1964] ECR 177, 184.

[12] *Ibid.*   [13] *Lawrie-Blum* v. *Land Baden-Württemberg*, Case 66/85, [1986] ECR 2121.

[14] *Ibid.*, para. 17 (emphasis added).

[15] This requirement of "permanency" distinguishes "workers" under Article 45 TFEU from "posted workers" who fall within the scope of the free movement of services. On "posted workers" as a distinct category, see P. Davies, "Posted Workers: Single Market or Protection of National Labour Law Systems?", 34 (1977) *Common Market Law Review*, 571.

[16] In this sense, see *Trojani* v. *Centre public d'aide sociale de Bruxelles*, Case C-456/02, [2004] ECR I-7573, para. 22: "the constituent elements of any paid employment relationship, namely subordination and the payment of remuneration".

[17] *Levin* v. *Staatssecretaris van Justitie*, Case 53/81, [1982] ECR 1035.

the Netherlands on the ground that she was not engaged in work that provided her with remuneration "commensurate with the means of subsistence considered as necessary by the legislation of the Member State".[18] Would the rights under Article 45 thus depend on receiving a minimum salary within the host Member State? The Court, anxious to avoid a definition that differed depending on the Member State involved, held otherwise:

Since part-time employment, although it may provide an income lower than what is considered to be the minimum required for subsistence, constitutes for a large number of persons an effective means of improving their living conditions, the effectiveness of [Union] law would be impaired and the achievement of the objectives of the Treaty would be jeopardized if the enjoyment of rights conferred by the principle of freedom of movement for workers were reserved solely to persons engaged in full-time employment and earning, as a result, a wage at least equivalent to the guaranteed minimum wage in the sector under consideration . . .

In this regard no distinction may be made between those who wish to make do with their income from such an activity and those who supplement that income with other income, whether the latter is derived from property or from the employment of a member of their family who accompanies them. *It should however be stated that whilst part-time employment is not excluded from the field of application of the rules on freedom of movement for workers, those rules cover only the pursuit of effective and genuine activities, to the exclusion of activities on such a small scale as to be regarded as purely marginal and ancillary.*[19]

The Court here defined a "worker" as a person remunerated for an "effective and genuine" activity. Under this minimalist definition, the number of working hours and the level of remuneration was irrelevant, except where the activity was so small that it was "purely marginal and ancillary". Subsequent jurisprudence has consolidated this minimalist standard.[20] It thus held that benefits in kind could be considered "remuneration" as long as the work done was "capable of being regarded as forming part of the normal labour market".[21] But what about people who could not support themselves in the host state? The Court here insisted that even where a person needs financial assistance *from the State* to supplement his income,

---

[18] *Ibid.*, para. 10.   [19] *Ibid.*, paras. 15–17 (emphasis added).

[20] See *Kempf* v. *Staatssecretaris van Justitie*, Case 139/85, [1986] ECR 1741; *Bettray* v. *Staatssecretaris van Justitie*, Case 344/87, [1989] ECR 1621; as well as *Trojani*, Case C-456/02 (supra n. 16).

[21] *Trojani*, Case C-456/02 (supra n. 16), para. 24.

this would still be irrelevant for his status as a "worker" as long as he was engaged in an effective and genuine activity.[22]

The Court's minimalist definition of "worker" had given an extremely broad personal scope to Article 45. Yet it still hinged on the *presence* of a genuine employment relationship. But would Article 45 also cover people searching for *future* employment, or persons who had engaged in *past* employment? The Court has indeed found that these "quasi-workers" form part of the personal scope of Article 45. For former employees this solution is suggested by the provision itself;[23] and the Court emphatically confirmed this in *Lair*.[24] A French national had brought proceedings against a German University for refusing to award her a maintenance grant. This was a social advantage which a worker would have been entitled to claim under Article 45.[25] But could Mrs Lair claim this right *after* having ceased work in the host State? Three Member States intervened in the case and argued that "a person loses the status of worker, on which the social advantages depend, when, in the host State, [s]he gives up either [her] previous occupational activity or, if unemployed, [her] search for employment in order to pursue full-time studies".[26] The Court disagreed, and found that "the rights guaranteed to migrant workers *do not necessarily depend on the actual or continuing existence of an employment relationship*".[27] Non-employed persons would thus continue to enjoy "certain rights linked to the status of worker even when they are no longer in an employment relationship".[28] However, these rights required "some continuity between the

---

[22] *Kempf* v. *Staatssecretaris van Justitie*, Case 139/85 (supra n. 20), para. 14: "It follows that the rules on this topic must be interpreted as meaning that a person in effective and genuine part-time employment cannot be excluded from their sphere of application merely because the remuneration he derives from it is below the level of the minimum means of subsistence and he seeks to supplement it by other lawful means of subsistence. In that regard it is irrelevant whether those supplementary means of subsistence are derived from property or from the employment of a member of his family, as was the case in *Levin*, or whether, as in this instance, they are obtained from financial assistance drawn from the public funds of the Member State in which he resides, provided that the effective and genuine nature of his work is established."

[23] Article 45 (3) (d) TFEU expressly refers to the right "to remain in the territory of a Member State after having been employed in that State, subject to conditions which shall be embodied in regulations to be drawn up by the Commission".

[24] *Lair* v. *Universität Hannover*, Case 39/86, [1988] ECR 3161.

[25] *Ibid.*, para. 28. On the material scope of Article 45 TFEU and the notion of social advantage under Article 7(2) of Regulation 492/2011, see Section 1(b) below.

[26] *Ibid.*, para. 29.   [27] *Ibid.*, para. 31 (emphasis added).   [28] *Ibid.*, para. 36.

previous occupational activity and the course of study".[29] This qualification was to prevent abuses of the host state's social welfare system.[30]

What about persons seeking future employment? The Court expressly expanded the personal scope of Article 45 to job-seekers in *Antonissen*.[31] The case arose from a preliminary question by an English High Court on the compatibility of a British law permitting the deportation of foreigners after six months of unemployment. Was such a temporal limitation on the status of (potential) workers possible? While the Court confirmed that the personal scope of Article 45 included job-seekers, it accepted that the mobility of workers would not be undermined by national measures offering "a reasonable time" to find work.[32] And in the absence of Union harmonization on the matter, a period of six months was considered reasonable.[33] The Court was nonetheless eager to add that "if after the expiry of that period the person concerned provides evidence that he is continuing to seek employment and that he has genuine chances of being engaged", the job-seeker could not be forced to leave the territory of the host Member State.[34]

(b) Material scope: discrimination and beyond

Which rights will workers enjoy on the basis of Article 45 TFEU and Union legislation? Article 45 (2) expressly refers to "the abolition of any discrimination based on nationality between workers of the Member States as regards employment, remuneration and other conditions of work and employment"; and Article 45 (3) clarifies that this "shall entail the right" to accept offers, to move freely and to stay within the territory of a Member State for that purpose. These textual bones are given substantive flesh by

---

[29] *Ibid.* para. 37. The Court however qualified this qualification as follows: "Such continuity may not, however, be required where a migrant has involuntarily become unemployed and is obliged by conditions on the job market to undertake occupational retraining in another field of activity." For a broad definition of "involuntary", see *Ninni-Orasche* v. *Bundesminister für Wissenschaft, Verkehr und Kunst*, Case C-413/01, [2003] ECR I-13187.

[30] *Lair* v. *Universität Hannover*, Case 39/86 (supra n. 24), para. 43. In *Brown* v. *The Secretary of State for Scotland*, Case 197/86, [1988] ECR 3205, the Court thus imposed strict requirements when a former worker was entitled to educational rights, such as a grant for university studies.

[31] *The Queen* v. *Immigration Appeal Tribunal, ex parte Antonissen*, Case C-292/89, [1991] ECR I-745.

[32] *Ibid.*, para. 16.   [33] *Ibid.*, para. 21.   [34] *Ibid.*

Directive 2004/38 and Regulation 492/2011.[35] The latter sets out the specific rights for workers and their families.[36] In addition to outlawing access restrictions to the labour market of the host State,[37] the Regulation confirms the principle of equal treatment during an employment relationship. The central provision here is Article 7:

1. A worker who is a national of a Member State may not, in the territory of another Member State, be *treated differently from national workers by reason of his nationality* in respect of any conditions of employment and work, in particular as regards remuneration, dismissal, and, should he become unemployed, reinstatement or re-employment.
2. He shall enjoy the *same social and tax advantages* as national workers.[38]

Despite the direct effect of Article 45 TFEU, Article 7 of the Regulation – or, better, its predecessor – has had a profound impact on the material scope of the free movement of workers. It provides a negative expression of the equal treatment principle in paragraph 1, and a positive expression of that principle in paragraph 2.

Was Article 7(1) inspired by a discrimination rationale; and if so, which one? In *Sotgiu*,[39] the Court clarified that the formulation "by reason of his nationality" was not confined to direct discrimination. "The rules regarding equality of treatment, both in the Treaty and in Article 7 of Regulation [492/2011], forbid not only overt discrimination by reason of nationality but also *all covert forms of discrimination* which, by the application of other criteria

---

[35] Regulation 492/2011 on freedom of movement for workers within the Union, [2011] OJ L141/1. The Regulation replaced "in the interests of clarity and rationality" (*ibid.*, recital 1) Regulation 1612/68 on freedom of movement for workers within the Community, [1968] OJ L257/2. The Regulation has three Chapters. Chapter 1 deals with "Equality, Equal Treatment and Workers' Families". Chapter 2 concerns "Clearance of Vacancies and Applications for Employment". Finally, Chapter 3 sets up a "Committee for ensuring close cooperation between the Member States in matters concerning the freedom of movement of workers and their employment".

[36] These rights are set out in Chapter 1 of the Regulation. Chapter 1 is divided into three Sections: Section 1 is on "Eligibility for Employment" (Articles 1-6). Section 2 deals with "Employment and Equality of Treatment" (Articles 7-9), while Section 3 concerns "Workers' Families" (Article 10).

[37] See Article 4 (1) of the Regulation: "Provisions laid down by law, regulation or administrative action of the Member States which restrict by number or percentage the employment of foreign nationals in any undertaking, branch of activity or region, or at a national level, shall not apply to nationals of the other Member States."

[38] Emphasis added.   [39] *Sotgiu* v. *Deutsche Bundespost*, Case 152/73, [1974] ECR 153.

of differentiation, lead in fact to the same result."[40] Article 7 (1) of the Regulation thus covers forms of direct and indirect discrimination. Where national legislation treated workers differently on grounds of their origin or residence, this *could* be "tantamount, as regards their practical effect, to discrimination on the grounds of nationality".[41] Subsequent jurisprudence thereby crystallized two situations in which national laws would appear to be *indirectly* discriminatory.[42] The first situation concerns national laws that "although applicable irrespective of nationality" nonetheless "affect essentially migrant workers or the great majority of those affected are migrant workers".[43] The second situation arises where national laws "are indistinctly applicable but can more easily be satisfied by national workers than by migrant workers or where there is a risk that they may operate to the particular detriment of migrant workers".[44] Unless the differential treatment can here be objectively justified, both types of national laws would violate Article 7 (1) of the Regulation.

A positive expression of equal treatment rights for migrant workers is set out in Article 7 (2) of the Regulation. Foreign workers are here granted "the same social and tax advantages as national workers".[45] The notion of "social advantage" has received a wide teleological meaning. In *Cristini*,[46] the Court found the phrase to refer to "all social and tax advantages, whether or not attached to the contract of employment";[47] and this included travel reductions in fares for large families offered by the State. This definition was confirmed in *Lair*,[48] where the Court further broadened the concept of social advantage to all advantages which entailed "the possibility of improving [a worker's] living and working conditions and promoting his social advancement".[49] This included all advantages that "whether or not linked to a contract of employment, are generally granted to national

---

[40] *Ibid.*, para. 11 (emphasis added).   [41] *Ibid.*

[42] See *O'Flynn* v. *Adjudication Officer*, Case C-237/94, [1996] ECR I-2617.

[43] *Ibid.*, para. 18 (with extensive references to the case law).

[44] *Ibid.* (with extensive references to the case law).

[45] Originally, the Court excluded job-seekers from the scope of Article 7(2) of Regulation 1612/68. In *Centre public d'aide sociale de Courcelles* v. *Lebon*, Case 316/85, [1987] ECR 2811, the Court held (*ibid.* para. 26): "[T]he right to equal treatment with regard to social and tax advantages applies only to workers. Those who move in search of employment qualify for equal treatment only as regards access to employment in accordance with Article [45] of the [FEU] Treaty and Articles 2 and 5 of Regulation 1612/68." This judgment was overruled in *Collins* v. *Secretary of State for Work and Pensions*, Case C-138/02, [2004] ECR I-2703.

[46] *Cristini* v. *SNCF*, Case 32/75, [1975] ECR 1085.   [47] *Ibid.*, para. 13.

[48] *Lair* v. *Universität Hannover*, Case 39/86, (supra n. 24).   [49] *Ibid.*, para. 20.

workers primarily because of their status as workers or by virtue of the mere fact of their residence on the national territory and whose extension to workers who are nationals of other Member States therefore seems likely to facilitate the mobility of such workers within the [Union]".[50] However, as under Article 7(1) of the Regulation, Member States are entitled to justify differential treatment "if it is based on objective considerations that are independent of the nationality of the persons concerned and proportionate to the legitimate aim of the national provisions".[51] A residence requirement might thus be legitimate, where a Member States wishes "to ensure that there is a genuine link between an applicant for an allowance in the nature of a social advantage within the meaning of Article 7(2) of Regulation".[52]

Finally, what about *non*-discriminatory restrictions to the free movement of workers? While much of the case law on workers focuses on discriminatory national laws, the Court accepts that non-discriminatory measures might also fall within the scope of Article 45 TFEU. The famous confirmation of that possibility is *Bosman*.[53] The case concerned a professional football rule according to which a footballer could not be employed by another club unless the latter paid a transfer or training fee. This was a non-discriminatory rule that applied to nationals and non-nationals alike.[54] Nonetheless, the Court found that "those rules are likely to restrict the freedom of movement of players who wish to pursue their activity in another Member State by preventing or deterring them from leaving the clubs to which they belong even after the expiry of their contracts of employment with those clubs".[55] The said rules would thus "constitute an obstacle to freedom of movement for workers",[56] since they "*directly affect players' access to the employment market in other Member States*".[57]

---

[50] *Ibid.*, para. 21. The Court has thus refused to consider a World War service invalidity pension as a social advantage (see *Even and ONPTS*, Case 207/78, [1979] ECR 2019, para. 24: "Such a benefit, which is based on a scheme of national recognition, cannot therefore be considered as an advantage granted to a national worker by reason primarily of his status of worker or resident on the national territory and for that reason does not fulfil the essential characteristics of the 'social advantages' referred to in Article 7(2) of Regulation [492/211]").

[51] *Collins* v. *Secretary of State for Work and Pensions*, Case C-138/02 (supra n. 45), para. 66.

[52] *Ibid.*, para. 67.

[53] *Union royale belge des sociétés de football association ASBL* v. *Jean-Marc Bosman*, Case C-415/93 (supra n. 6).

[54] *Ibid.*, para. 98.   [55] *Ibid.*, para. 99.   [56] *Ibid.*, para. 100.

[57] *Ibid.*, para. 103 (emphasis added). On this point, see also *Lehtonen et al.* v. *Fédération royale belge des sociétés de basket-ball*, Case C-176/96, [2000] ECR I-2681, paras. 49-50.

Formulated as a general principle, this suggests that "[n]ational provisions which *preclude or deter a national of a Member State from leaving his country of origin* in order to exercise his right to freedom of movement therefore constitute restrictions on that freedom even if they apply without regard to the nationality of the workers concerned".[58] Non-discriminatory restrictions are thus covered by Article 45 TFEU.

2. Freedom of establishment

Freedom of establishment constitutes the second side of the European coin on the free movement of persons. It guarantees the free movement of self-employed persons. To achieve this aim, the relevant Treaty chapter contains a prohibition on illegal national barriers, and grants the Union two legis-lative competences.[59] This Section will concentrate on the prohibition in the form of Article 49,[60] which states:

Within the framework of the provisions set out below, restrictions on the freedom of establishment of nationals of a Member State in the territory of another Member State shall be prohibited. Such prohibition shall also apply to restrictions on the setting-up of agencies, branches or subsidiaries by nationals of any Member State established in the territory of any Member State.

Freedom of establishment shall include the right to take up and pursue activities as self-employed persons and to set up and manage undertakings, in particular companies or firms within the meaning of the second paragraph of Article 54, under the conditions laid down for its own nationals by the law of the country where such establishment is effected, subject to the provisions of the Chapter relating to capital.

---

[58] *Olympique Lyonnais* v. *Bernard and Newcastle UFC*, Case C-325/08, [2010] ECR I-2177, para. 34 (emphasis added). See also *Commission* v. *Denmark*, Case 464/02, [2005] ECR I-7929, para. 45: "It is settled case-law that Article [45 TFEU] prohibits not only all discrim-ination, direct or indirect, based on nationality, but also national rules which are applicable irrespective of the nationality of the workers concerned but impede their freedom of movement."

[59] See Articles 50 and 53 TFEU. This section will not deal with the various legislative instru-ments in this context. The most important instrument adopted under Article 53 TFEU is Directive 2005/36 on the recognition of professional qualifications, [2005] OJ L255/22. For a detailed analysis of the Directive, see C. Barnard, *The Substantive Law of the EU* (Oxford University Press, 2010), 309 et seq.

[60] The provision was given direct effect in *Reyners* v. *Belgium*, Case 2/74, [1974] ECR 631. On this controversial constitutional choice, see Chapter 5 – Section 2 above.

(a) Personal scope: self-employed persons (and companies)

The personal scope of Article 49 captures "self-employed" persons. Like workers, self-employed persons will need to be engaged in a genuine economic activity. However, unlike workers, self-employed persons do not work under the direction of an employer and will not receive a "salary" compensating for their subordination. The personal scopes of Articles 45 and 49 are thus "mutually exclusive".[61] The definition of "worker" thereby negatively determines the personal scope of the freedom of establishment. Importantly, self-employed persons might be natural *or* legal persons. For Article 54 TFEU expressly provides that the freedom of establishment covers companies and firms.[62]

Self-employed persons (and companies) will typically produce goods or perform services. And while there are no delineation problems with regard to goods, the Union legal order had to delimit the personal scope of Article 49 from the perspective of the free movement of services. For this third freedom protects, among other things, persons offering a service in another State.[63] What then is the characteristic feature underlying the personal scope of the freedom of establishment? The Court has identified it as follows:

The right of establishment, provided for in Articles [49] to [54] of the Treaty, is granted both to legal persons within the meaning of Article [54] and to natural persons who are nationals of a Member State of the [Union]. Subject to the exceptions and conditions laid down, it allows all types of self-employed activity to be taken up and pursued on the territory of any other Member State, undertakings to be formed and operated, and agencies, branches or subsidiaries to be set up . . .

---

[61] *Gebhard* v. *Consiglio dell'Ordine degli Avvocati e Procuratori di Milano*, Case 55/94, [1995] ECR I-4165, para. 20.

[62] Article 54 TFEU states: "Companies or firms formed in accordance with the law of a Member State and having their registered office, central administration or principal place of business within the Union shall, for the purposes of this Chapter, be treated in the same way as natural persons who are nationals of Member States. 'Companies or firms' means companies or firms constituted under civil or commercial law, including cooperative societies, and other legal persons governed by public or private law, save for those which are non-profit-making."

[63] According to Article 56 TFEU, "restrictions on freedom to provide services within the Union shall be prohibited in respect of nationals of Member States who are established in a Member State other than that of the person for whom the services are intended".

The concept of establishment within the meaning of the Treaty is therefore a very broad one, allowing a [Union] national to participate, *on a stable and continuous basis, in the economic life of a Member State* other than his State of origin and to profit therefrom, so contributing to economic and social interpenetration within the [Union] in the sphere of activities as self-employed persons. In contrast, where the provider of services moves to another Member State, the provisions of the chapter on services, in particular the third paragraph of Article [57], envisage that he is to pursue his activity there on a temporary basis.[64]

The decisive criterion distinguishing "established" service providers from "temporary" service providers is thus the "stable and continuous basis" on which the former participate in the economy of the host Member State. A "stable and continuous" presence will trigger the personal scope of the freedom of establishment. However, the concept of establishment will not require exclusive presence in the host State (as this would rule out secondary establishment). The applicability of Article 49 however is determined by the "duration", "regularity, periodicity or continuity" of the services provided.[65] A continuous presence will not need to take the form of a "branch" or "agency" but may consist of an "office".[66] Yet the existence of some infrastructure – like an office – is not conclusive evidence in favour of establishment.[67]

(b) Material scope: discrimination and beyond

Article 49 prohibits "restrictions on the freedom of establishment". The prohibition thereby expressly covers primary and secondary establishment. Primary establishment occurs where a natural or legal person establishes itself for the first time. The right to establishment is, however, "not confined to the right to create a single establishment within the [Union]", but includes "freedom to set up and maintain, subject to observance of the professional rules of conduct, more than one place of work within the [Union]".[68]

---

[64] *Gebhard*, Case 55/94 (supra n. 61), paras. 23–6 (emphasis added). The third paragraph of Article 57 TFEU states that "[w]ithout prejudice to the provisions of the Chapter relating to the right of establishment, the person providing a service may, in order to do so, temporarily pursue his activity in the Member State where the service is provided, under the same conditions as are imposed by that State on its own nationals".

[65] *Gebhard*, Case 55/94 (supra n. 61) para. 27.

[66] See *Commission* v. *Germany*, Case 205/84, [1986] ECR 3755, para. 21.

[67] *Gebhard*, Case 55/94 (supra n. 61), para. 27.

[68] *Ordre des avocats au Barreau de Paris* v. *Klopp*, Case 107/83, [1984] ECR 2971, para. 19.

Secondary establishment indeed covers "the setting-up of agencies, branches or subsidiaries by nationals of any Member State [already] established in the territory of any Member State".[69] This right of secondary establishment is thereby given to every company lawfully established in a Member State of the Union, even if it has no business in the State of primary establishment.[70] This constitutional choice allows a company to freely choose its Member State of incorporation within the Union. (However, where a company moves to another Member State, it may lose its legal personality in its original home state.[71] This principle – which partly restricts the right of secondary establishment – follows from the right of each Member State to decide when a company is "primarily" established.)[72]

Which types of restrictions will Article 49 prohibit? The wording of the provision clearly covers discriminatory measures. This includes *directly* discriminatory national laws,[73] and equally prohibits *indirect* discrimination on grounds of nationality.[74] Whether the scope of Article 49 also covered non-discriminatory measures remained uncertain for some time.[75] This uncertainty was ultimately removed in *Gebhard.*[76] The case involved a German lawyer who had practised in Italy under the title "avvocato" without being formally admitted to the Italian Bar. This violated the relevant national rules on the organization of the legal profession. Yet despite their "non-discriminatory" character, the Court unambiguously found them to violate Article 49 because they were "liable to hinder or

---

[69] Article 49 TFEU – first indent.

[70] *Segers* v. *Bestuur van de Bedrijfsvereniging voor Bank- en Verzekeringswezen, Groothandel en Vrije Beroepen*, Case 79/85, [1986] ECR 2375. The *Segers* principle was confirmed in *Centros* v. *Erhvervs- og Selskabsstyrelsen*, Case C-212/97, [1999] ECR I-1459.

[71] *The Queen* v. *HM Treasury and Commissioners of Inland Revenue, ex parte Daily Mail*, Case 81/87, [1988] ECR 5483. This distinguishes legal persons from natural persons, as the latter will not lose their nationality when moving their primary establishment to another Member State.

[72] This is recognized in Article 54 TFEU, which defers to the laws of the Member States with regard to the formation of companies. National laws typically follow one of two theories. According to the "incorporation theory", a company is "established" through the simple act of formal registration. This contrasts with the "seat theory", which makes formal registration dependent on the company having its managerial and business centre within the State of registration.

[73] See *Reyners* v. *Belgium*, Case 2/74 (supra n. 60); as well as *The Queen* v. *Secretary of State for Transport, ex parte Factortame (Factortame II)*, Case C-221/89, [1991] ECR I-3905.

[74] *Thieffry* v. *Conseil de l'ordre des avocats à la cour de Paris*, Case 71/76, [1977] ECR 765; as well as *Engelmann*, Case C-64/08, [2010] ECR I-8219.

[75] See *Commission* v. *Belgium*, Case 221/85, [1987] ECR 719.

[76] *Gebhard*, Case 55/94 (supra n. 61).

make less attractive" the freedom of establishment.[77] This *Dassonville*-like formula potentially included all types of regulatory barriers. However, the Court appears to limit its negative ambit to national measures that hinder "[a]ccess to the market" of foreign establishments.[78]

3. Justifying restrictions on (self-)employed persons

Restrictions on the free movement of persons might be justified on the basis of legitimate public interests. For workers, Article 45 (3) expressly allows for "limitations justified on grounds of public policy, public security or public health". And for the freedom of establishment, Article 52 permits the "special treatment for foreign nationals on grounds of public policy, public security or public health". Many problems encountered in the context of goods will thus apply, mutatis mutandis, to justified restrictions on the free movement of persons.[79] However, unlike the provisions on goods, the Treaties recognize an additional justification for national restrictions: the public service exception.

(a) Express justifications and (implied) imperative requirements

The express justifications for restrictions on persons mentioned in the Treaties are substantially identical to those on goods. However, unlike the casuistic approach governing goods, Directive 2004/38 has partly codified the case law.[80] Article 27 of the Directive thereby confirms the power of the Member States to "restrict the freedom of movement and residence of Union citizens and their family members, irrespective of nationality, on grounds of public policy, public security or public health". With regard to the first two

---

[77] *Ibid.*, para. 37.

[78] *CaixaBank France* v. *Ministère de l'Économie, des Finances et de l'Industrie*, Case C-442/02, [2004] ECR I-8961, para. 14; as well as *Commission* v. *Spain*, Case C-400/08 (nyr), para. 64: "In that context, it should be borne in mind that the concept of 'restriction' for the purposes of Article [49 TFEU] covers measures taken by a Member State which, although applicable without distinction, affect access to the market for undertakings from other Member States and thereby hinder intra-[Union] trade." For an analysis of the case law on persons in light of the market access test, see E. Spaventa, *Free Movement of Persons in the European Union: Barriers to Movement in Their Constitutional Context* (Kluwer, 2007), Chapter 5.

[79] On justified restrictions to the free movement of goods, see Chapter 9 – Section 4.

[80] Directive 2004/38 (supra n. 5), Chapter VI (Articles 27–33).

public interest grounds, the Directive further clarifies that national restrictions must "be based exclusively on the personal conduct of the individual concerned",[81] and that this personal conduct "must represent a genuine, present and sufficiently serious threat affecting one of the fundamental interests of society".[82] With regard to public health, Article 29 of the Directive subsequently determines that only "diseases with epidemic potential" and the like will justify measures restricting free movement.[83]

Is the list of public interest justifications exhaustive? The Court has indeed held that discriminatory measures – whether direct or indirect – can solely be justified by reference to the express justifications recognized by the Treaty (and secondary law).[84] Yet as soon as the Court had acknowledged that non-discriminatory measures could potentially violate the free movement provisions, it simultaneously recognized the existence of additional – implied – justifications. Unfortunately, these implied justifications were not called "mandatory requirements", but rather "imperative requirements" or "overriding requirements" relating to the public interest.[85] The Court indeed accepts a whole range of such imperative requirements.[86] The constitutional principles governing these imperative requirements are set out in *Gebhard*,[87] where the Court held:

[N]ational measures liable to hinder or make less attractive the exercise of fundamental freedoms guaranteed by the Treaty must fulfil four conditions: they must be applied in a non-discriminatory manner; they must be justified by imperative requirements in the general interest; they must be suitable for securing the

---

[81] Article 27 (2) of Directive 2004/38 – first indent. For an early judicial definition of what constitutes personal conduct, see *Van Duyn* v. *Home Office*, Case 41/74 (supra n. 6).

[82] Article 27 (2) of Directive 2004/38 – second indent. For an early judicial definition of what constitutes a "present" threat, see *Régina* v. *Pierre Bouchereau*, Case 30/77, [1977] ECR 1999.

[83] Article 29 (1) of Directive 2004/38.

[84] See *Engelmann*, Case C-64/08 (supra n. 74), para. 34.

[85] The terminology of the Court is – sadly – not uniform; see *Centros*, Case C-212/97 (supra n. 70), para. 32 ("imperative requirements"); *CaixaBank France*, Case C-442/02 (supra n. 78) para. 17 ("overriding requirements"). Sometimes, the Court even replaces "requirements" with "reasons"; see *Marks & Spencer plc* v. *David Halsey (Her Majesty's Inspector of Taxes)*, Case C-446/03, [2005] ECR I-10837, para. 35 ("imperative reasons").

[86] Such imperative requirements include consumer protection (see *Commission* v. *France*, 220/83, [1986] ECR 3663), environmental protection (see *De Coster*, Case C-17/00, [2001] ECR I-9445), and many, many more. For an excellent overview, see Barnard, *Substantial Law* (supra n. 59), 512–16.

[87] *Gebhard*, Case 55/94, (supra n. 61).

attainment of the objective which they pursue; and they must not go beyond what is necessary in order to attain it.[88]

Imperative requirements offered by the Member States as potential justifications will thus only apply to non-discriminatory measures and will be subject to the principle of proportionality.[89]

(b) The public service exception

Many States prefer to reserve "State jobs" for their nationals. And the Treaties concede a public service exception for restrictions on the free movement of persons. For workers, we find this special justification in Article 45 (4) TFEU, which states that "[t]he provisions of this Article shall not apply to *employment in the public service*".[90] For the freedom of establishment this special limitation can be found in Article 51 excluding activities "connected, even occasionally, with the *exercise of official authority*". On their surface, both provisions appear to exclude different activities from their respective scopes. For workers, the wording suggests employment by a State institution, that is: an *institutional* definition. By contrast, the provision on establishment seems to adopt a *functional* definition, as it links the exception to the exercise of official authority by a private party.[91]

Yet despite these textual disparities, the Court has developed a uniform definition for both freedoms. Early on, the Court clarified that it was of "no interest whether a worker is engaged as a workman (*ouvrier*), a clerk (*employé*) or an official (*fonctionnaire*) or even whether the terms on which he is employed come under public or private law".[92] Since these designations could "be varied at the whim of national legislatures", they

---

[88] *Ibid.*, para. 37.

[89] On the principle of proportionality in the context of the free movement of goods, see Chapter 9 – Section 4 (b) above.

[90] Emphasis added.

[91] This functional definition was confirmed by the Court in *Reyners*, Case 2/74 (supra n. 60), paras. 44–5 (emphasis added): "The first paragraph of Article [51] must enable Member States to exclude non-nationals from taking up *functions* involving the exercise of official authority, which are connected with one of the activities of self-employed persons provided for in Article [49]. This need is fully satisfied when the exclusion of nationals is limited to those activities which, taken on their own, constitute a direct and specific connection with the exercise of official authority."

[92] *Sotgiu* v. *Deutsche Bundespost*, Case 152/73 (supra n. 39), para. 5.

could not provide a criterion for the interpretation of European law.[93] In *Commission* v. *Belgium*,[94] the Court explained this choice in favour of a single functional definition of "public service" as follows:

[D]etermining the sphere of application of Article [45 (4)] raises special difficulties since in the various Member States authorities acting under powers conferred by public law have assumed responsibilities of an economic and social nature or are involved in activities which are not identifiable with the functions which are typical of the public service yet which by their nature still come under the sphere of application of the Treaty. In these circumstances the effect of extending the exception contained in Article [45 (4)] to posts which, whilst coming under the State or other organizations governed by public law, still do not involve any association with tasks belonging to the public service properly so called, would be to remove a considerable number of posts from the ambit of the principles set out in the Treaty and to create inequalities between Member States according to the different ways in which the state and certain sectors of economic life are organized.[95]

Because the meaning of the concept "public service" required a "uniform interpretation",[96] the Court here rejected an institutional definition and favoured a functional definition in Article 45 (4). This functional classification thereby "depends on whether or not the posts in question are typical of the specific activities of the public service in so far as the exercise of powers conferred by public law and responsibility for safeguarding the general interest of the State are vested in it".[97] This definition of public service potentially includes employees of a private company, where the latter performs public functions.[98] The Court has however subjected its functional test to "very strict conditions".[99] The work must involve "a *special relationship of allegiance* to the State and reciprocity of rights and duties which form the foundation of the bond of nationality".[100] The simple transfer of some public powers to employees is not enough. It is necessary that these public powers are exercised "on a regular basis by those holders and do not represent a very minor part of their activities".[101]

---

[93] *Ibid.*   [94] *Commission* v. *Belgium*, Case 149/79, [1980] ECR 3881.

[95] *Ibid.*, para. 11.   [96] *Ibid.*, para. 12.   [97] *Ibid.*

[98] *Anker et al.* v. *Germany*, Case C-47/02, [2003] ECR I-10447.

[99] *Lawrie-Blum*, Case 66/85 (supra n. 13), para. 28.

[100] *Commission* v. *Belgium*, Case 149/79 (supra n. 94), para. 10 (emphasis added).

[101] *Anker et al.* v. *Germany*, Case C-47/02 (supra n. 98), para. 63. And despite the express reference to the lower threshold of "occasional" exercise of public powers in Article 51 TFEU, the case law on that provision appears to run in parallel to that on Article 45 (4); see Barnard, *Substantial Law* (supra n. 59), 503–4.

In a separate jurisprudential line, the Court has moreover clarified that the public service exception only permits restrictions on the *access to* but not *discriminations inside a position* involving public power. Thus, where foreigners have been admitted to a public service post, they will benefit from the equal treatment principle. In the words of the Court: Article 45 (4) "cannot justify discriminatory measures", since "[t]he interests which this derogation allows Member States to protect are satisfied by the opportunity of restricting admission of foreign nationals to certain activities in the public service". "The very fact that they have been admitted shows indeed that those interests which justify the exceptions to the principle of non-discrimination permitted by Article [45(4)] are not at issue."[102] The reasoning under Article 45 (4) applies, mutatis mutandis, to Article 51 and restrictions to professions involving public power.

4. European citizenship: a general right to move and stay?

With the formal introduction of the provisions on European citizenship,[103] the European Treaties recognize a range of rights that pertain to all "Europeans" by virtue of being Union citizens.[104] These rights are generally set out in Article 20 TFEU, and specified in subsequent articles. With regard to free movement, Article 21 TFEU states:

1. Every citizen of the Union shall have the right to move and reside freely within the territory of the Member States, subject to the limitations and conditions laid down in the Treaties and by the measures adopted to give them effect.
2. If action by the Union should prove necessary to attain this objective and the Treaties have not provided the necessary powers, the European Parliament and the Council, acting in accordance with the ordinary legislative procedure, may

---

[102] *Sotgiu* v. *Deutsche Bundespost*, Case 152/73 (supra n. 39) para. 4. And see also *Commission* v. *Belgium*, Case 149/79 (supra n. 94), esp. paras. 20–2.

[103] The citizenship provisions were introduced by the (old) Treaty on European Union concluded in Maastricht. For an early analysis of these provisions, see C. Closa, "The Concept of Citizenship in the Treaty on European Union", 29 (1992) *Common Market Law Review*, 1137. And for an excellent re-evaluation, see D. Kochenov, "Ius Tractum of Many Faces: European Citizenship and the Difficult Relationship between Status and Rights", 15 (2009) *Columbia Journal of European Law*, 169.

[104] This European citizenship is "additional" to their national citizenship (see Article 20 (1) TFEU).

adopt provisions with a view to facilitating the exercise of the rights referred to in paragraph 1.[105]

Does paragraph 1 establish a general right for all Union citizens to move and reside within the Union? Was this a clear and unconditional provision? Paragraph 2 grants the Union a legislative competence to facilitate the exercise of the free movement rights in paragraph 1. The competence has been used – together with special movement competences – for the adoption of Directive 2004/38 "on the right of citizens of the Union and their family members to move and reside freely within the territory of the Member States".[106] What movement rights have been granted by the "Citizens Directive"?

(a) Article 21 (1): a direct source of movement rights

Would Article 21 (1) TFEU be directly effective, and thus directly grant movement rights to European citizens? Having approached the matter from various directions,[107] the Court finally gave a straightforward answer in *Baumbast*.[108] The question put before the European Court was this: would a Union citizen, who no longer enjoyed a right of residence as a migrant worker, nonetheless enjoy a right of residence on the basis of Article 21 (1)? The Court's positive response was as follows:

[T]he Treaty on European Union does not require that citizens of the Union pursue a professional or trade activity, whether as an employed or self-employed person, in order to enjoy the rights provided in Part Two of the [FEU] Treaty, on citizenship of the Union. Furthermore, there is nothing in the text of that Treaty to permit the conclusion that citizens of the Union who have established themselves in another Member State in order to carry on an activity as an employed person there are deprived, where that activity comes to an end, of the rights which are conferred on them by the [FEU] Treaty by virtue of that citizenship. *As regards, in particular, the*

---

[105] Article 21 (3) TFEU provides a special Union competence for measures concerning social security or social protection.

[106] [2004] OJ L 158/77. The Directive was adopted on the legal bases of Article 18 (non-discrimination), Article 46 (workers), Article 50 (establishment), and Article 59 (services) TFEU.

[107] See *Martínez Sala* v. *Freistaat Bayern*, Case C-85/96, [1998] ECR I-2691; and *Grzelczyk* v. *Centre public d'aide sociale d'Ottignies-Louvain-la-Neuve*, Case C-184/99, [2001] ECR I-6193. In the latter case the Court famously held (*ibid.*, para. 31) that "Union citizenship is destined to be the fundamental status of nationals of the Member States".

[108] *Baumbast and R* v. *Secretary of State for the Home Department*, Case C-413/99, [2002] ECR I-7091.

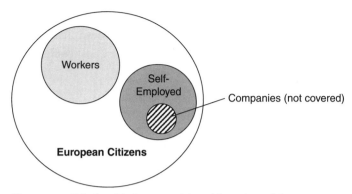

Figure 10.1 Relationship between citizenship and special competences

right to reside within the territory of the Member States under Article [21 (1)] that right is conferred directly on every citizen of the Union by a clear and precise provision of [that] Treaty.

Purely as a national of a Member State, and consequently a citizen of the Union, Mr Baumbast therefore has the right to rely on Article [21(1)]. Admittedly, that right for citizens of the Union to reside within the territory of another Member State is conferred subject to the limitations and conditions laid down by the [Treaties] and by the measures adopted to give it effect. However, the application of the limitations and conditions acknowledged in Article [21(1)] in respect of the exercise of that right of residence is subject to judicial review. Consequently, any limitations and conditions imposed on that right do not prevent the provisions of Article [21(1)] from conferring on individuals rights which are enforceable by them and which the national courts must protect.[109]

The Court here clarified four things. First, Article 21 (1) was directly effective and would thus grant general movement rights that can be invoked against national law. The fact that these rights were subject to limitations and conditions was thereby no barrier to their direct effect. Second, the personal scope of the citizenship provisions did not depend on the economic status of a person. Europeans enjoyed free movement rights as *citizenship* rights; and citizenship was a "fundamental status" independent of someone's economic position.[110] Third, with regard to their material scope, the citizenship provisions would be residual provisions. They would not apply whenever one of the specialized movement regimes

---

[109] *Ibid.*, paras. 83–6 (emphasis added) (with express reference to the reasoning in *Van Duyn* v. *Home Office*, Case 41/74 (supra n. 6)).

[110] *Ibid.*, para. 82 (with reference to Grzelczyk, Case C-184/99 (supra n. 107)).

was applicable. Fourth, any limitation on citizenship rights through European legislation would be subject to judicial review. And where these legislative limitations were disproportionate, the Court could strike them down on the basis of Article 21 (1).[111]

(b) Directive 2004/38: rights and limitations

The Directive on the right of citizens to move and reside freely within the Union was adopted to codify in "a single legislative act" the various secondary sources governing the free movement of persons.[112] It lays down "the conditions governing the *exercise* of the right of free movement and residence within the territory of the Member States by Union citizens" (and their family members).[113] The Directive contains five substantive chapters. Chapter II concerns the rights of exit and entry (Articles 4–5). Chapter III details the rights of residence (Articles 6–15). Chapter IV lays down rules for the right of permanent residence (Articles 16–21). Chapter V assembles provisons that are common to the right of (temporary) residence and permanent residence (Articles 22–6). Finally, Chapter VI provides detailed rules on legitimate restrictions to the right of entry and residence on grounds of public policy, public security or public health (Articles 27–33).

What are the most important rights recognized in the Directive? Having spelled out the right to exit and enter a Member State on condition of a valid identity card or passport, the Directive distinguishes three classes of residency rights. According to Article 6, all Union citizens will have the short-term right to reside in the territory of another Member State for a period of

---

[111] *Ibid.,* paras. 91–3. In *Vatsouras and Koupatantze,* Joined Cases C-22 and C-23/08, [2009] ECR I-4585 the Court was asked to review the legality of Article 24 (2) of Directive 2004/38 in light of Article 18 TFEU, read in conjunction with Article 45 TFEU. Yet instead of finding a conflict, the Court interpreted the derogation provided for in the Directive in light of Article 45 (2) TFEU.

[112] Directive 2004/38, Preamble 4. Prior to the Citizenship Directive, and in addition to various specific legislative measures for economically active citizens, the Union had adopted three residency directives for non-economically active persons; see Directive 90/364 (general residence right, [1990] OJ L180/26), Directive 90/365 (retired persons' residence, [1990] OJ L180/28), and Directive 90/366 (student residence, [1990] OJ L180/30). The Student Directive was subsequently declared void (see *Parliament* v. *Council,* Case C-295/90, [1992] ECR I-4193), and replaced by Directive 93/96 on the right of residence for students ([1993] OJ L317/59).

[113] Directive 2004/38, Article 1(a). Article 3 however restricts the personal scope to "Union citizens who move to or reside in a Member State *other than that of which they are a national*" (emphasis added).

up to three months "as long as they do not become an unreasonable burden on the social assistance system of the host Member State".[114] A second class of residency rights is established by Article 7, whose first paragraph states:

All Union citizens shall have the right of residence on the territory of another Member State for a period of longer than three months if they:

(a) are workers or self-employed persons in the host Member State; or

(b) have sufficient resources for themselves and their family members not to become a burden on the social assistance system of the host Member State during their period of residence and have comprehensive sickness insurance cover in the host Member State; or

(c) – are enrolled at a private or public establishment, accredited or financed by the host Member State on the basis of its legislation or administrative practice, for the principal purpose of following a course of study, including vocational training; and

– have comprehensive sickness insurance cover in the host Member State and assure the relevant national authority, by means of a declaration or by such equivalent means as they may choose, that they have sufficient resources for themselves and their family members not to become a burden on the social assistance system of the host Member State during their period of residence; or

(d) are family members accompanying or joining a Union citizen who satisfies the conditions referred to in points (a), (b) or (c).

The provision acknowledges four categories of persons who will benefit from mid-term residency rights. Subparagraph a refers to the economically active migrant expressly recognized by the Treaties. (Article 7(3) of the Directive subsequently confirms that Union citizens who are no longer working or self-employed "shall retain the status of worker or self-employed" in certain circumstances.) This is extended to all persons with "sufficient resources" and with "comprehensive sickness insurance" (subparagraph b),[115] with students benefiting from a slightly more generous

---

[114] *Ibid.*, Article 14(1).

[115] Article 8(4) of the Directive thereby partly defines "sufficient resources" by stating: "Member States may not lay down a fixed amount which they regard as 'sufficient resources', but they must take into account the personal situation of the person concerned. In all cases this amount shall not be higher than the threshold below which nationals of the host Member State become eligible for social assistance, or, where this criterion is not applicable, higher than the minimum social security pension paid by the host Member State."

treatment (subparagraph c). Family members will be entitled to accompany or join (subparagraph d).

Finally, the Directive grants a third class of right: the "right of permanent residence" in certain situations. The general rules for this are laid down in Article 16, which confers such a right after lawful presence in the host State "for a continuous period of five years".[116] Importantly, this right of long-term residency is independent of the economic status and the financial means of the person concerned.

Once a person is legally resident in another Member State, the Directive expressly grants this person a right to equal treatment in Article 24. The connection between lawful residence and equal treatment has been firmly established in the jurisprudence of the European Court.[117] In principle, a Member State must thus treat all legally resident Union citizens within its territory like its own nationals.[118] This general principle is however subject to such "specific provisions as are expressly provided for in the Treaty and secondary law".[119] Controversially, the equality principle has specifically been derogated by Article 24 (2) with regard to social assistance and main-tenance aid for studies. Moreover, the general derogations to the right of residence and equal treatment, found in Chapter VI of the Directive, may also apply here. Article 27 (1) thus confirms that the "Member States may restrict the freedom of movement and residence of Union citizens and their family members, irrespective of nationality, on grounds of public policy, public security or public health". The norm has already been discussed above.

---

[116] Article 17 thereby establishes a more preferable regime for former workers or self-employed persons, and Article 18 deals with the acquisition of the right of permanent residence by certain family members.

[117] See *Martínez Sala*, Case C-85/96 and *Grzelczyk*, Case C-184/99 (both supra n. 107), as well as *Bidar*, Case C-209/03, [2005] ECR I-2119.

[118] See Trojani (supra n.16), para. 40.   [119] Article 24 (1) of Directive 2004/38.

Competition law: cartels

Introduction

The inclusion of a Treaty chapter on competition stemmed from the "general agreement that the elimination of tariff barriers would not achieve its objectives if private agreements of economically powerful firms were permitted to be used to manipulate the flow of trade".[1] Originally, European competition law was thus primarily conceived as a functional complement of the European law governing the internal market.[2] While the free movement provisions were to protect the internal market from *public*

---

[1] D. Gerber, *Law and Competition in Twentieth-Century Europe: Protecting Prometheus* (Oxford University Press, 2001), 343.

[2] B. E. Hawk, "The American (Anti-trust) Revolution: Lessons for the EEC?", 9 (1988) *European Competition Law Review*, 53.

interferences, the rules on competition were designed to protect it from *private* power. This link between the internal market and European competition law continues to be textually anchored in the Treaties.[3] For the principal provisions on European competition law are found in Chapter 1 of Title VII on "Common Rules on Competition, Taxation and Approximation of Laws". The Chapter is thereby divided into two Sections – one dealing with classic competition law, that is: "[r]ules applying to undertakings"; the other with public interferences in the market through "[a]ids granted by States" to private undertakings. Chapters 11 and 12 of this book will deal with the Treaty's section on undertakings.

The English word "undertaking" has traditionally not meant what the European Treaties want it to mean.[4] The word is a translation from the German and French equivalents, and was deliberately chosen to avoid pre-existing meanings in British company law.[5] According to the European Court, an undertaking is "every entity engaged in an economic activity, regardless of the legal status of the entity and the way in which it is financed".[6] This definition ties the notion of undertaking to an *activity* instead of the institutional form of the actor. This *functional* definition broadens the personal scope of the competition rules to include entities that may – formally – not be regarded as companies.[7] However, by concentrating on *economic* activities, the Court has excluded activities of a public

---

[3] See Article 3(3) TEU (emphasis added): "The Union shall establish an internal market. It shall work for the sustainable development of Europe based on balanced economic growth and price stability, [and] a highly *competitive* social market economy, aiming at full employment and social progress." The meaning of the provision is clarified in Protocol (No. 27) "On the Internal Market and Competition", according to which the internal market as set out in Article 3 of the Treaty on European Union "*includes a system ensuring that competition is not distorted*" (emphasis added). And within the Treaty on the Functioning of the European Union, Article 3 (1) (b) grants the Union an exclusive competence for "the establishing of the competition rules necessary for the functioning of the *internal market*" (emphasis added).

[4] In its sinister and saddest form, the word refers to the preparations for a funeral service.

[5] R. Lane, *EC Competition Law* (Longman, 2001), 33.

[6] *Höfner and Elser* v. *Macrotron*, Case C-41/90, [1991] ECR I-1979, para. 21.

[7] The provision thus catches, inter alia, natural persons (see *Hydrotherm* v. *Compact*, Case 170/83, [1984] ECR 2999, para. 11), including "professionals", like barristers (*Wouters et al.* v. *Algemene Raad van de Nederlandse Orde van Advocaten*, Case C-309/99, [2002] ECR I-1577, para. 49). Even the "State", and its public bodies, may sometimes be regarded as an undertaking; see *Commission* v. *Italy*, Case 118/85, [1987] ECR 2599.

nature.[8] The advantage of a functional definition is its flexibility; its disadvantage however is its uncertainty. For depending on its actions, an entity may or may not be an "undertaking" within the meaning of EU competition law.[9]

The first pillar of European competition law is Article 101. It outlaws anti-competitive collusions between undertakings, that is: "cartels". Historically, this form of illegal behaviour has been the most dangerous anti-competitive practice. Unlike the abusive behaviour of a monopolist, it requires the combined – evil – effort of a number of undertakings.[10] The prohibition on any collusion between undertakings to restrict competition is set out in Article 101 as follows:

1. The following shall be prohibited as incompatible with the internal market: all agreements between undertakings, decisions by associations of undertakings and concerted practices which may affect trade between Member States and which have as their object or effect the prevention, restriction or distortion of competition within the internal market . . .
2. Any agreements or decisions prohibited pursuant to this Article shall be automatically void.
3. The provisions of paragraph 1 may, however, be declared inapplicable in the case of:

   - any agreement or category of agreements between undertakings,
   - any decision or category of decisions by associations of undertakings,
   - any concerted practice or category of concerted practices,

---

[8] Where a private body regulates in the public interest, the activity is thus not seen to be of an "economic" nature; see *Calì & Figli Srl* v. *Servizi ecologici porto di Genova*, Case C-343/95, [1997] ECR I-1547.

[9] "[T]he notion of undertaking is a relative concept in the sense that a given entity might be regarded as an undertaking for one part of its activities while the rest falls outside the competition rules." (See Advocate General F. Jacobs, *Firma Ambulanz Glöckner* v. *Landkreis Südwestpfalz*, Case C-475/99, [2001] ECR I-8089, para. 72.)

[10] The collusion must be "between" undertakings; and for that reason, Article 101 will not apply to actions "within" one undertaking. The question as to what constitutes one single undertaking can be complex. It is examined by the "single economic unit" doctrine. According to the doctrine, undertakings that are not independent economic actors form part of a single economic unit. On this point, see *Centrafarm BV and Adriaan de Peijper* v. *Sterling Drug Inc*, *Centrafarm*, Case 15/74, [1974] ECR 1147; *Béguelin Import Co.* v. *S.A.G.L. Import Export*, Case 22/71, [1971] ECR 949; and *Akzo Nobel NV and Others* v. *Commission*, Case C-C97/08P, [2009] ECR I-8237.

which contributes to improving the production or distribution of goods or to promoting technical or economic progress, while allowing consumers a fair share of the resulting benefit, and which does not:

(a) impose on the undertakings concerned restrictions which are not indispensable to the attainment of these objectives;

(b) afford such undertakings the possibility of eliminating competition in respect of a substantial part of the products in question.

Article 101 follows a tripartite structure. Paragraph 1 prohibits as incompatible with the internal market collusions between undertakings that are anti-competitive by object or effect if they affect trade between Member States. Paragraph 3 exonerates certain collusions that are justified by their overall pro-competitive effects for the Union economy. In between this dual structure of prohibition and justification – oddly – lies paragraph 2, which determines that illegal collusive practices are automatically void and thus cannot be enforced in court.[11]

This Chapter analyses paragraphs 1 and 3 of Article 101. We start by considering the types of collusive behaviour caught by Article 101 (1) in Section 1, and look at the "effect on trade between Member States" requirement in Section 2. Both criteria are "jurisdictional" criteria.[12] For they do not define an illegal behaviour as such, but merely trigger the applicability of Article 101. The two "substantive" criteria within Article 101 are found in the requirement of an *anti*-competitive collusion in Article 101 (1), and its potential *pro*-competitive justifications in Article 101 (3). Each of these two substantive requirements, and their relationship to each other, will be discussed in Sections 3 and 4.

1. Forms of collusion between undertakings

Article 101 covers anti-competitive collusions *between* undertakings. The prohibited action must thus be *multilateral*. But what types of multilateral

---

[11] This is not the sole consequence of a violation of Article 101 TFEU. The Union has typically used its powers to impose significant fines on undertakings violating the provision. On the enforcement of European competition law generally, see W. Wils, *Principles of European Antitrust Enforcement* (Hart, 2005).

[12] In this sense: O. Odudu, *The Boundaries of EC Competition Law* (Oxford University Press, 2006), 58.

collusions are covered by the prohibition? Article 101 refers to three types of collusions: "agreements between undertakings, decisions by associations of undertakings and concerted practices". Agreements appear to be a straightforward category. In addition to agreements, the provision also catches "concerted practices". This category of collusion is the most mysterious one, and has been subject to much uncertainty and intense debate. Finally, Article 101 covers "decisions of associations of undertakings".

Let us look at each collusive form in turn.

(a) Agreements I: horizontal and vertical agreements

The European concept of "agreement" has been given an extremely wide conceptual scope.[13] The Union legal order is indeed not interested whether the agreement formally constitutes a "contract" under national law.[14] What counts is "a concurrence of wills" between economic operators.[15] "Gentlemen's agreements" have thus been classified as agreements under Article 101, as long as the parties consider them binding.[16]

One of the central concerns within the early Union legal order was the question whether Article 101 covers "horizontal" as well as "vertical" agreements. Horizontal agreements are agreements between undertakings that are competing with each other, that is: horizontally placed at the same commercial level. Vertical agreements, by contrast, are agreements between undertakings at different levels of the commercial chain. Since Article 101 prohibits anti-competitive agreements, would it not follow that only "horizontal" agreements between *competitors* are covered? This logic is not without its problems. For while vertical agreements between a producer (P) and a distributor (D) may increase efficiency through a

---

[13] For an analysis of the concept of "agreement", see J. Shaw, "The Concept of Agreement in Article 85 EEC", 16 (1991) *European Law Review*, 262.

[14] On the notion of contract under English law, see G. Treitel et al., *The Law of Contract* (Sweet & Maxwell, 2007).

[15] See *Bayer AG* v. *Commission*, Case T-41/96, [2000] ECR II-3383, para. 69; and *Bundesverband der Arzneimittel-Importeure and Commission* v. *Bayer*, Case C-2 and 3/01 P, [2004] ECR I-23, para. 97.

[16] See *ACF Chemiefarma* v. *Commission*, Case 41/69, [1979] ECR 661, paras. 106 et seq.

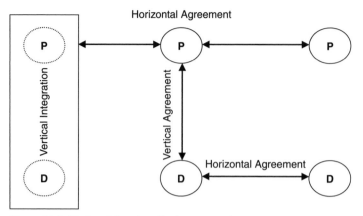

Figure 11.1 Horizontal and vertical agreements

specialized division of labour,[17] they may also significantly harm the consumer through a restriction of price competition.[18]

Would vertical agreements fall within the jurisdictional scope of Article 101? The European Court has – famously – answered this question in *Consten & Grundig* v. *Commission*.[19] The German producer Grundig had concluded a distribution agreement for the French market with Consten. This agreement was said to breach European competition law. The applicants argued that the Union lacked jurisdiction under Article 101 as "distributorship contracts do not constitute 'agreements between undertakings' within the meaning of that provision, since the parties are not on a footing of equality".[20] The Court disagreed:

Article [101] refers in a general way to all agreements which distort competition within the common market and does not lay down any distinction between those agreements based on whether they are made between competitors operating at the same level in the economic process or between non-competing persons operating at different levels. In principle, no distinction can be made where the Treaty does not make any distinction.

---

[17] Lane, *EC Competition Law* (supra n. 5), 92: "Their prime advantage is that they allow for net economic efficiency: they enable the producer to concentrate upon production and relieve it of the obligation of shifting the goods on the market, for that will be the concern of the (specialist) distributor who is better suited to the task."

[18] *Ibid.*, 97: "Looking at the economics, it is not surprising: the factory gate value of goods is sometimes a fraction of their shop value[.]"

[19] *Consten and Grundig* v. *Commission*, Case 56 and 58/64, [1964] ECR 299.   [20] *Ibid.*, 339.

Furthermore, the possible application of Article [101] to a sole distributorship contract cannot be excluded merely because the grantor and the concessionaire are not competitors inter se and not on a footing of equality. Competition may be distorted within the meaning of Article [101(1)] not only by agreements which limit it as between the parties, but also by agreements which prevent or restrict competition which might take place between one of them and third parties. For this purpose, it is irrelevant whether the parties to the agreement are or are not on a footing of equality as regards their position and function in the economy. This applies all the more, since, by such an agreement, the parties might seek, by preventing or limiting the competition of third parties in respect of the products, to create or guarantee for their benefit an unjustified advantage at the expense of the consumer or user, contrary to the general aims of Article [101].[21]

The arguments in favour of including vertical agreements were thus textual and teleological. Within its text, Article 101 did not make a distinction between horizontal and vertical agreements, and thus seemed to generically cover both types. Teleologically, Article 101 was said not solely to protect against restrictions of competition imposed on the distributor, but it would equally protect third parties, namely: consumers and competitors. And since vertical agreements could create unjustified disadvantages for these third parties, they would have to be within the jurisdiction of European competition law.[22]

(b) Agreements II: "tacit acquiescence" versus "unilateral conduct"

Every agreement – whether horizontal or vertical – must be concluded on the basis of common consent between the parties. It must be formed by a concurrence of *two* wills. The idea of an "agreement" will thus find a conceptual boundary where one party *unilaterally* imposes its will on the other. Yet there may sometimes be a fine line between tacit acceptance and unilateral imposition. And the European Courts have struggled to demarcate this line for the Union legal order.[23] The reason for this conceptual

---

[21] *Ibid.*

[22] This second argument was an important one: vertical agreements would need to be within the scope of Article 101 TFEU because they could have an anti-competitive effect both with regard to intra-brand competition, that is: price competition between distributors, but also inter-brand competition between different producers. On the distinction between inter-brand and intra-brand competition, see Section 3(a) below.

[23] See *AEG* v. *Commission*, Case 107/82, [1983] ECR 3151; *Ford–Werke AG and Ford of Europe Inc.* v. *Commission*, Joined Cases 25 and 26/84, [1985] ECR 2725; and *BMW* v. *ALD Auto-Leasing*, Case C-70/93, [1995] ECR I-3439.

fuzziness lies in what the Courts call "apparently unilateral" behaviour in continuous contractual relations between two parties.

A good illustration of such "apparently unilateral behaviour" can be found in *Ford* v. *Commission.*[24] The American car manufacturer had established a selective distribution system in Europe, and in particular in Britain and Germany, on the basis of a "main dealer agreement". That agreement appeared not to violate Article 101, and originally allowed German distributors to order right-hand as well as left-hand drive cars. However, as the prices for Ford cars on the British market suddenly increased significantly, British customers began buying from German dealers. Afraid that its British distributor would suffer the consequences, Ford notified its German dealers that it would no longer accept their orders for right-hand drive cars. (These would now be exclusively reserved for the British market.) Was the decision to discontinue supplies to the German dealers an agreement? Ford claimed that the discontinuance decision was of a unilateral nature; and "a unilateral act cannot be included among agreements".[25] The Court however held otherwise: "Such a decision on the part of the manufacturer does not constitute, on the part of the undertaking, a unilateral act which, as the applicants claim, would be exempt from the prohibition contained in Article [101 (1)] of the Treaty. On the contrary, *it forms part of the contractual relations between the undertaking and its dealers.*"[26]

This extremely generous interpretation of "consent" has however found some limits. In *Bayer* v. *Commission,*[27] the German pharmaceutical company used its distribution system to market "Adalat" – a medical product designed to treat cardiovascular disease. The price of the product differed significantly as it was indirectly fixed by the respective national health authorities. The prices fixed by the Spanish and French health services were thereby on average 40 per cent lower than prices in the United Kingdom; and following commercial logic, Spanish and French wholesalers began exporting to the British market. With its British dealer registering an enormous loss of turnover, Bayer decided to stop delivering large orders to Spanish and French wholesalers. Instead, it provided them with the quantities that it thought would only saturate their national markets. Was this indirect export restriction a consensual agreement? The General Court rejected this view. While accepting that

---

[24] *Ford-Werke AG and Ford of Europe Inc.* v. *Commission*, Joined Cases 25 and 26/84 (supra n. 23).

[25] *Ibid.*, para. 15.   [26] *Ibid.*, para. 21 (emphasis added).

[27] *Bayer AG* v. *Commission*, Case T-41/96 (supra n. 15).

"apparently unilateral conduct" can qualify as an agreement, the latter required – as a conceptual minimum – the "existence of an acquiescence by the other partners, express or implied, in the attitude adopted by the manufacturer".[28] And in the present case, even tacit acquiescence was missing.[29] For the mere continuation of the business relationship could not as such be tacit acquiescence.[30]

The judgment was confirmed on appeal,[31] where the European Court concisely clarified the situation as follows: "The mere concomitant existence of an agreement which is in itself neutral and a measure restricting competition that has been imposed unilaterally does not amount to an agreement prohibited by that provision."[32] Put the other way around: for an "apparently unilateral" measure to become part of a continuous contractual relationship, the other party must – at the very least – tacitly acquiesce. And this tacit acquiescence must be shown through actual compliance with the "apparently unilateral" measure.

(c) Concerted practices and parallel conduct

The conclusion of an agreement is but one form of collusion between undertakings. Another form mentioned in Article 101 (1) is "concerted practices". The concept was designed as a safety net to catch all forms of collusive behaviour falling short of an agreement.[33] This has been confirmed by the European Court, which identifies the aim behind the concept of concerted practice as "to bring within the prohibition of that Article a form of

---

[28] *Ibid.*, para. 72.

[29] *Ibid.*, paras. 151 et seq: "Examination of the attitude and actual conduct of the wholesalers shows that the Commission has no foundation for claiming that they aligned themselves on the applicant's policy designed to reduce parallel imports. ... [T]he wholesalers continued to try to obtain packets of Adalat for export and persisted in that line of activity, even if, for that purpose, they considered it more productive to use different systems to obtain supplies, namely the system of distributing orders intended for export among the various agencies on the one hand, and that of placing orders indirectly through small wholesalers on the other."

[30] For this point, see I. Lianos, "Collusion in Vertical Relations under Article 81 EC", 45 (2008) *Common Market Law Review*, 1027 at 1044.

[31] *Bundesverband der Arzneimittel-Importeure and Commission* v. *Bayer*, Case C-2 & 3/01 P (supra n. 15).

[32] *Ibid.*, para. 141.

[33] For that reason, there may be no need for a categorical dividing line between an agreement and a concerted practice; see *Commission* v. *Anic Partecipazioni*, Case C-49/92P, [1999] ECR I-4125, para. 132: "[W]hilst the concepts of an agreement and of a concerted practice have particularly different elements, they are not mutually incompatible."

coordination between undertakings which, without having reached the stage where an agreement properly so-called has been concluded, knowingly substitutes practical cooperation between them for the risk of competition".[34]

The heart of a concerted practice is seen in a "coordination" between undertakings "which becomes apparent from the behaviour of the participants".[35] Yet the Court was quick to point out that not all "parallel behaviour" between undertakings – such as the parallel raising of prices – can be identified with a concerted practice.[36] Article 101 would "not deprive economic operators of the right to adapt themselves intelligently to the existing and anticipated conduct of their competitors".[37] Parallel behaviour that follows from market forces would be beyond reproach. In the absence of any form of "practical cooperation" through "direct or indirect contact",[38] undertakings will thus be allowed to align their commercial behaviour to the "logic" of the market.[39]

(d) Cartel decisions through associations of undertakings

This third category of collusion is designed to catch institutionalized cartels; and this may include professional bodies, such as the Bar Council.[40] The inclusion of this form of collusion into Article 101 clarified that undertakings could not escape the scope of Article 101 by substituting *multilateral* collusion between them by establishing an association that would adopt *unilateral* decisions on their behalf. A cartel decision – even in the soft form of a "recommendation" – will thus be caught as collusive behaviour under Article 101 (1).[41]

---

[34] *Imperial Chemical Industries* v. *Commission*, Case 48/69, [1972] ECR 619, para. 64; as well as *Commission* v. *Anic Partecipazioni*, Case C-49/92 P (supra n. 33), para.115.

[35] *Imperial Chemical Industries* v. *Commission*, Case 48/69 (supra n. 34), para. 65.

[36] *Ibid.*, para. 66.

[37] *Coöperatieve Vereniging "Suiker Unie" UA and others* v. *Commission*, Joined Cases 40 to 48, 50, 54 to 56, 111, 113 and 114/73, [1975] ECR 1663, para. 174; as well as *Commission* v. *Anic Partecipazioni*, Case C-49/92 P (supra n. 33), para. 117.

[38] *"Suiker Unie"* v. *Commission*, para. 27 and para. 174; as well as *Commission* v. *Anic Partecipazioni*, Case C-49/92 P (supra n. 33), para. 117.

[39] The evidentiary burden on the Commission is very high; see *Ahlström Osakeyhtiö and others* v. *Commission*, Joined Cases C-89/85, C-104/85, C-114/85, C-116/85, C-117/85 and C-125/85 to C-129/85, [1993] ECR I-1307, para. 71: "[P]arallel conduct cannot be regarded as furnishing proof of concertation unless concertation is the only plausible explanation for such conduct."

[40] See *Wouters et al.* v. *Algemene Raad van de Nederlandse Orde van Advocaten*, Case C-309/99 (supra n. 7).

[41] See *Van Landewyck and others* v. *Commission*, Joined Cases 209 to 215 and 218/78, [1980] ECR 3125, para. 89.

2. (Potential) effect on trade between Member States

Not all agreements – not even anti-competitive ones – will fall within the jurisdictional scope of Article 101.[42] Article 101 only catches agreements "which may affect trade between Member States". What is the point behind this jurisdictional limitation around Article 101? The answer lies – partly – in the principle of subsidiarity.[43] The *European* Union will only concern itself with agreements that have a *European* dimension. And this European dimension shows itself through a (potential) effect on trade *between* Member States. In the words of the European Court:

The concept of an agreement "which may affect trade between Member States" is intended to define, in the law governing cartels, the boundary between the areas respectively covered by [European] law and national law. It is only to the extent to which the agreement may affect trade between Member States that the deterioration in competition caused by the agreement falls under the prohibition of [European] law contained in Article [101]; otherwise it escapes that prohibition.[44]

Agreements must thus have an *inter-state* dimension; otherwise they will be outside the sphere of European competition law. But what is the "European" sphere of competition law? The jurisdictional scope of Article 101 has been – very – expansively interpreted.[45] And the Court has developed a number of constitutional tests as to when inter-state trade has been affected. An agreement would need to be "capable of constituting a threat, either direct or indirect, actual or potential, to freedom of trade between Member States in a manner which might harm the attainment of the objectives of a single market between States".[46] This formula was amended in *Société Technique Minière*, where the Court held Article 101 to apply to any agreement that "may have an influence, direct or indirect, actual or potential, on the *pattern of trade*

---

[42] Sections 3 and 4 below refer to "agreements", but the analysis applies, mutatis mutandis, to decisions of associations of undertakings, and concerted practices.

[43] On the various notions of "subsidiarity" in the Union legal order, see R. Schütze, *From Dual to Cooperative Federalism: The Changing Structure of European Law* (Oxford University Press, 2009), 243 et seq.

[44] *Consten and Grundig* v. *Commission*, Case 56 and 58/64 (supra n. 19), 341.

[45] Article 101 TFEU. For a general analysis of this criterion, see J. Faull, "Effect on Trade Between Member States", 26 (1999), *Fordham Corporate Law Institute*, 481.

[46] *Consten and Grundig* v. *Commission*, Case 56 and 58/64 (supra n. 19), 341.

between Member States".[47] This "pattern-of-trade" test is extremely broad as it captures both quantitative as well as qualitative changes to trade.[48] The fact that an agreement relates to a single Member State will not necessarily mean that Article 101 is not applicable.[49] What counts are the (potential) *effects* of the national agreement on the European markets.[50]

Not all effects on inter-state trade will however lead to the applicability of Article 101. For the effects "must not be insignificant".[51] The Commission will only police agreements that *appreciably* affect intra-Union trade.[52] According to its "non-appreciably-affecting-trade" (NAAT) rule,[53] agreements will not fall within the jurisdictional scope of Article 101 if two cumulative conditions are met. First, "[t]he aggregate market share of the parties on any relevant market within the [Union] affected by the agreement does not exceed 5 %". And second, "the aggregate annual [Union] turnover of the undertakings concerned in the products covered by the agreement does not exceed 40 million euro".[54] However, it is important to note that agreements will thereby "be considered in the economic and legal context in which they occur", and that it will thus "be necessary to have regard to any *cumulative* effects of parallel networks of similar agreements".[55]

---

[47] *Société Technique Minière* v. *Maschinenbau Ulm*, Case 56/65, [1965] ECR 235 at 249 (emphasis added).

[48] On the substantive "neutrality" of the "pattern-of-trade" test, see also Commission, "Guidelines on the effect on trade concept contained in Articles 81 and 82 of the Treaty", [2004] OJ C101/81, paras. 34–5: "The term 'pattern-of-trade' is neutral. It is not a condition that trade be restricted or reduced. Patterns of trade can also be affected when an agreement or practice causes an increase in trade."

[49] See *Erste Group Bank* v. *Commission*, C-125/07P, [2009] ECR 8681, para. 38. as well as *Belasco and others* v. *Commission*, Case 246/86, [1989] ECR 2117, para.38: "Accordingly, although the contested agreement relates only to the marketing of products in a single Member State, it must be held to be capable of influencing intra-[Union] trade."

[50] See *Brasserie de Haecht* v. *Wilkin-Janssen*, Case 48/72, [1973] ECR 77, paras. 26 et seq.

[51] *Javico International and Javico AG* v. *Yves Saint Laurent Parfums SA (YSLP)*, Case C-306/96, [1998] ECR I-1983, para. 16 (with reference to *Völk* v. *Vervaecke*, Case 5/69, [1969] ECR 295).

[52] The Commission makes a clear distinction between an appreciable effect on inter-state *trade* on the one hand, and appreciable restrictions on *competition* on the other. The former will be discussed here, while the latter will be discussed in Section 3(d) below.

[53] "Guidelines on the effect on trade concept contained in Articles 81 and 82 of the Treaty" (supra n. 48), para. 50.

[54] *Ibid.*, para. 52.

[55] *Ibid.*, para. 49 (emphasis added). This reflects the jurisprudence of the European Courts; see *Delimitis* v. *Henninger Bräu*, Case C-234/89, [1991] ECR I-935.

3. Restriction of competition: anti-competitive object or effect

In order for an agreement to violate the prohibition of Article 101 (1), it must be anti-competitive; that is: it must be a "prevention, restriction or distortion of competition".[56]

The meaning of "restriction of competition" in this context has been very controversial. If it simply referred to a restriction of the *individual* freedom to trade, then all binding agreements would be anti-competitive. For "[t]o bind, to restrain, is of their very essence".[57] This individualist definition of restriction has never been dominant in the Union legal order.[58] A second view has therefore argued that Article 101, while not protecting the individual freedom of a specific competitor, nonetheless protects the *structural* freedom offered by the market to – actual or potential – competitors. This view emphasizes the exclusionary effects of restrictions of competition and corresponds to the "Harvard School".[59] A third view has finally imported the "Chicago School" into the debate on the scope of Article 101 (1). It argues that the prohibition should exclusively outlaw "exploitative effects" in the form of allocative inefficiencies to consumer welfare.[60] The case law of the European Courts has been closest to the second view – even if the European administration has recently tried hard to move towards the third view.[61]

This Section analyses four aspects of what constitutes a restriction of competition in the Union legal order. We start by looking at the various dimensions of competition, before examining the two modes of violating

---

[56] This formulation covers hypothetical, quantitative and qualitative limitations of competition. In this Section, "restriction" of competition will be employed as a generic term.

[57] See *Chicago Board of Trade* v. *United States*, 246 US 231 (1918) 238.

[58] The early case law may however be read as unduly concentrating on the freedom of individuals; see E. Rousseva, *Rethinking Exclusionary Abuses in EU Competition Law* (Hart, 2010), 83 et seq.

[59] The "European" equivalent of the "Harvard School" is the "Freiberg School", which has become famous for its "ordoliberalism". For a concise overview of the philosophical positions of that school, see D. Gerber, "Constitutionalizing the Economy: German Neo-Liberalism, Competition Law and the 'New Europe'", 42 (1994) *American Journal of Comparative Law*, 25.

[60] Odudu, *The Boundaries* (supra n. 12), 102.

[61] See Commission, "Guidelines on the application of Article 81(3) of the Treaty", [2004] OJ C101/97. However, see also *GlaxoSmithKline and others* v. *Commission*, Joined Cases C-501/06 P, C-513/06 P, C-515/06 P and C-519/06 P, [2009] ECR I-9291, where the Court rejected the "Chicagoization" of European competition law.

Article 101 (1) – that is: restrictions by "object or effect". This includes an analysis of whether the "ancillary restraints" doctrine represents a "rule of reason" in disguise. A final subsection offers a brief encounter with the de minimis limitation on restrictions of competition.

(a) Two dimensions: inter-brand and intra-brand competition

A restriction of competition is primarily a restriction between competitors. Early on, the European Court had however confirmed that competition could be restricted by horizontal as well as vertical agreements.[62] But was this solely an admission that vertical agreements could restrict *inter*-brand competition, that is: competition between producers of different brands? Or did the inclusion of vertical agreements into the scope of Article 101 (1) signal that *intra*-brand competition – that is: competition between distributors of the same brand – was independently prohibited? The European Court has preferred the second reading. The Union legal order consequently recognizes two independent dimensions of competition: inter-brand and intra-brand competition. In *Consten & Grundig*,[63] the Court thus rejected the plaintiffs' argument that there could be no restriction of competition through vertical agreements:

> The principle of freedom of competition concerns the various stages and manifestations of competition. Although competition between producers is generally more noticeable than that between distributors of products of the same make, it does not thereby follow that an agreement tending to restrict the latter kind of competition should escape the prohibition of Article [101 (1)] merely because it might increase the former.[64]

Would every restriction of competition through vertical agreements violate Article 101(1)? In a later decision, the Court recognized that a pro-competitive effect in inter-brand competition might come at the price of a restriction of intra-brand competition. This holistic approach can be

---

[62] For a discussion of this point, see Section 1(a) above.

[63] *Consten and Grundig* v. *Commission*, Case 56 and 58/64 (supra n. 19).

[64] *Ibid.*, 342. And at a later part of the judgment (*ibid*, 343), the Court provided the rationale for this choice: "Because of the considerable impact of distribution costs on the aggregate cost price, it seems important that competition between dealers should also be stimulated. The efforts of the dealer are stimulated by competition between distributors of products of the same make."

seen in *Société Technique Minière*,[65] where the Court found an exclusive distribution agreement *not* to violate Article 101 on the following ground:

> The competition in question must be understood within the actual context in which it would occur in the absence of the agreement in dispute. In particular it may be doubted whether there is an interference with competition if the said agreement seems really necessary for the penetration of a new area by an undertaking. Therefore, in order to decide whether an agreement containing a clause "granting an exclusive right of sale" is to be considered as prohibited by reason of its object or of its effect, it is appropriate to take into account in particular the nature and quantity, limited or otherwise, of the products covered by the agreement, [and] *the position and importance of the grantor and the concessionaire on the market for the products concerned*[.][66]

The existence of a restriction of competition will thus have to be evaluated alongside both "brand" dimensions, and by balancing both dimensions. The Commission appears to share this holistic approach.[67]

(b) Restrictions by object: European "per se rules"

An agreement may fall within Article 101 (1) if it is anti-competitive by "object or effect". These are alternative conditions.[68] The fulfilment of one will fulfil Article 101 (1).

The possibility of violating European competition law "by object" will not mean that purely imaginary restrictions intended by the parties are covered. The reference to the purpose of an agreement must not be misunderstood as referring to the subjective intentions of the parties. On the contrary, it refers to the objective content of the agreement. It is designed to identify certain "hardcore restrictions" within an agreement, which need not be subjected to a detailed effects analysis.[69] These hardcore restrictions can simply be presumed to be "sufficiently deleterious" to competition.[70] In this sense,

---

[65] *Société Technique Minière* v. *Maschinenbau Ulm*, Case 56/65 (supra n. 47).
[66] *Ibid.*, 250 (emphasis added).
[67] Commission, "Guidelines on Article 81 (3)" (supra n. 61), para. 17 et seq.
[68] *Société Technique Minière* v. *Maschinenbau Ulm*, Case 56/65 (supra n. 47), 249.
[69] *Consten and Grundig* v. *Commission*, Case 56 and 58/64 (supra n. 19), 342: "Besides, for the purpose of applying Article [101 (1)], there is no need to take account of the concrete effects of an agreement once it appears that it has as its object the prevention, restriction or distortion of competition."
[70] *Société Technique Minière* v. *Maschinenbau Ulm*, Case 56/65 (supra n. 47), 249. And see also *T-Mobile Netherlands and others* v. *Raad van bestuur van de Nederlandse*

restrictions by object operate as "per se rules", that is: rules whose breach "as such" constitutes a violation of competition law. (However, European competition law allows even hardcore restrictions to be potentially justified under Article 101(3); and for that reason they are not as absolute as American "per se" rules.)

What are the hardcore restrictions that the Union legal order considers restrictions by object? Various contractual clauses have been given this status – in both horizontal and vertical agreements. With regard to horizontal agreements, they have been said to include price-fixing clauses,[71] output-limiting clauses,[72] and market-sharing clauses.[73] With regard to vertical agreements, restrictions by object will be presumed to exist if the agreement contains a clause that imposed a fixed (minimum) resale price,[74] grants absolute territorial protection,[75] or is a "restriction of active or passive sales to end users by members of a selective distribution system operating at the retail level of trade".[76]

The most contentious type of hardcore restriction has however been clauses that restrict parallel trade. And the classic case here is – once more – *Consten and Grundig*.[77] Grundig had appointed Consten its exclusive distributor in France. Consten had thereby promised to market and service the German products in France – a potentially costly commitment. In exchange, Grundig agreed not to deliver its goods to other traders on the French market, and also agreed to contractually prohibit its German wholesalers from exporting goods into France. This level of territorial protection was still *relative*, since it solely applied to Grundig's own distribution system. Yet in order to prevent "parallel traders" – that is: third parties trading in parallel to the official distribution channel – from selling its

---

Mededingingsautoriteit, Case C-8/08, [2009] ECR I-4529, para. 29: "by their very nature, as being injurious to the proper functioning of normal competition".

[71] See Article 101 (1) (a): "directly or indirectly fix purchase or selling prices or any other trading conditions"; and see in particular *Imperial Chemical Industries* v. *Commission*, Case 48/69 (supra n. 34).

[72] See Article 101 (1) (b): "limit or control production, markets, technical development, or investment", and see in particular *Chemiefarma* v. *Commission*, Case 41/69 (supra n. 16).

[73] See Article 101 (1) (c): "share markets or sources of supply"; and see in particular *Coöperatieve Vereniging "Suiker Unie" UA and others* v. *Commission*, Joined Cases 40 to 48, 50, 54 to 56, 111, 113 and 1141–73 (supra n. 37).

[74] Article 4(a) of (Commission) Regulation 330/2010 on the application of Article 101(3) of the Treaty on the Functioning of the European Union to categories of vertical agreements and concerted practices, [2010] OJ L102, 1.

[75] *Ibid.*, Article 4 (b).   [76] *Ibid.*, Article 4 (c).

[77] *Consten and Grundig* v. *Commission*, Case 56 and 58/64 (supra n. 19).

products in France, Grundig granted an intellectual property right to Consten. This intellectual property right established *absolute* territorial protection for Consten. For not a single trader within France could sell Grundig products without the official distributor's consent. In the eyes of the European Court, such an agreement establishing absolute territorial protection betrayed a clear wish of the parties "to eliminate any possibility of competition at the wholesale level",[78] and thus constituted an agreement that had as its *object* the restriction of competition.[79]

(c) Restrictions by effect: a European "rule of reason"?

Where agreements do not contain clauses that are automatically deemed restrictions of competition, Article 101 (1) requires proof of the agreement's anti-competitive *effect*.[80] The central question here is: will the prohibition be triggered as soon as an agreement contains clauses that have *some* anti-competitive effects; or will it only apply to agreements that are *overall* anti-competitive? Put differently: should Article 101(1) catch agreements that limit – in absolute terms – production, yet enhance – in relative terms – competition through the development of a new product?

The wording of Article 101 (1) suggests an absolute test, but the argument has been made that an absolute test is over-inclusive and should be replaced by a relative test that weighs the anti-competitive effects of an agreement against its pro-competitive effects. The debate on whether Article 101 (1) follows an absolute or a relative test has been associated with the American doctrine of a "rule of reason". According to the latter, the absolute prohibition of anti-competitive agreements in American competition law will not apply to reasonable restrictions of trade. Should such an implied limitation

---

[78] *Ibid.*, 343.

[79] For a confirmation of this "tough" view on restrictions of parallel trade as a restriction by object, see *GlaxoSmithKline and others* v. *Commission*, Joined Cases C-501/06 P, C-513/06 P, C-515/06 P and C-519/06 P (supra n. 61) – which overruled the General Court's attempt to soften that principle of European competition law in *GlaxoSmithKline Services* v. *Commission*, Case T-168/01, [2006] ECR II-2969.

[80] In order to assess the effect of an individual agreement *on* the market, the Court will analyse the agreement's position *within* the market. It thereby applies a contextual approach that places an individual agreement within its economic context. Where an agreement forms part of a network of agreements, the Courts may thus look at the "cumulative" effects within the market. On this "economic" contextualism, see in particular *Delimitis* v. *Henninger Bräu*, Case C-234/89 (supra n. 55).

also apply to Article 101 (1) – even though the article already recognizes an express justification in Article 101 (3)? The existence of a rule of reason doctrine has been hotly debated in European circles.[81] And the debate is not just theoretical: the constitutional choice concerning whether there exists an implicit rule of reason in Article 101(1) may have significant practical consequences.[82]

What have the European Courts said? They have given ambivalent signals. For while the Courts – in theory – deny the existence of a rule of reason under Article 101 (1),[83] there are a number of jurisprudential lines that come very close to a practical application of the doctrine. Did the European Court not insist that a restriction of competition was not anti-competitive if "*necessary* for the penetration of a new area by an undertaking"?[84] Was this balancing of anti-competitive effects against pro-competitive effects not a rule of reason in disguise? The European Courts have denied this, and have instead developed alternative doctrines to explain their reasoning. The most famous doctrine in this respect is the doctrine of ancillary restraints.

Is the doctrine of ancillary restraints a rule of reason doctrine in disguise? Three cases may assist us in answering this question. In *Remia & Nutricia*,[85] the Court had to deal with the legality of a "non-compete clause". These clauses prevent the seller of a business from competing with the buyer within a period of time after the sale. This is undoubtedly a restriction of competition on the part of the seller; yet very few undertakings would be willing to purchase a business without a guarantee that its previous owner will temporarily stay out of the market. Finding that transfer agreements generally "contribute to the promotion of competition because they lead to an increase in the number of undertakings in the market", the Court nonetheless recognized that without the non-compete clause, "the agreement for

---

[81] See Odudu, *The Boundaries of EC Competition law* (supra n. 12); as well as R. Nazzini, "Article 81 EC between Time Present and Time Past: A Normative Critique of 'Restrictions of Competition' in EU Law", 43 (2006) *Common Market Law Review*, 497.

[82] It will be seen below that Article 101(3) is not a "neutral" exemption for pro-competitive agreements, since it makes the exemption dependent on the fulfilment of four conditions.

[83] See *Métropole Télévision (M6) and others* v. *Commission*, Case T-112/99, [2001] ECR II-2459; as well as *O2 (Germany)* v. *Commission*, T-328/03, [2006] ECR II-1231. For an extended discussion of the second case, see M. Marquis, "O2 (Germany) v Commission and the exotic mysteries of Article 81(1) EC", 32 (2007) *European Law Review*, 29.

[84] See *Société Technique Minière* v. *Maschinenbau Ulm*, Case 56/65 (supra n. 47), 250.

[85] *Remia and others* v. *Commission*, Case 42/84, [1985] ECR 2545.

the transfer of the undertaking could not be given effect".[86] However, such ancillary restrictions within an overall pro-competitive agreement would fall outside the scope of Article 101(1). This ancillary restraints doctrine was confirmed in *Pronuptia* in the context of a franchise agreement,[87] and received its most elaborate form in *Métropole Télévision*.[88] The General Court here held as follows:

> In [European] competition law the concept of an "ancillary restriction" covers any restriction which is directly related and necessary to the implementation of a main operation ... The condition that a restriction be necessary implies a two-fold examination. It is necessary to establish, first, whether the restriction is objectively necessary for the implementation of the main operation and, second, whether it is proportionate to it. As regards the objective necessity of a restriction, it must be observed that inasmuch as ... the existence of a rule of reason in [European] competition law cannot be upheld, it would be wrong, when classifying ancillary restrictions, to interpret the requirement for objective necessity as implying a need to weigh the pro- and anti-competitive effects of an agreement. Such an analysis can take place only in the specific framework of Article [101(3)] of the [FEU] Treaty.[89]

The doctrine of ancillary restraints thus differs from a rule of reason in that it will not involve a concrete balancing of the pro-competitive and anti-competitive effects of the agreement. The operation of the doctrine is, according to the Court, "relatively abstract".[90] It only tolerates contractual clauses restricting competition without which the "the main agreement is difficult or even impossible to implement".[91] Only *objectively necessary restrictions* of competition within an overall pro-competitive agreement will thus be accepted. And these objectively necessary restrictions must be "ancillary", that is: "subordinate" to the object of the main agreement.[92]

---

[86] *Ibid.*, para. 19.
[87] *Pronuptia de Paris* v. *Pronuptia de Paris Irmgard Schillgallis*, Case 161/84, [1986] ECR 353, paras. 16 et seq. and especially paras. 17 and 18: "[T]he franchisor must be able to take the measures necessary for maintaining the identity and reputation of the network bearing his business name or symbol. It follows that provisions which establish the means of control necessary for that purpose do not constitute restrictions on competition for the purposes of Article [101 (1)]. The same is true of the franchisee's obligation to apply the business methods developed by the franchisor and to use the know-how provided."
[88] *Métropole Télévision (M6)* v. *Commission*, Case T-112/99 (supra n. 83).
[89] *Ibid.*, paras. 104 (references omitted).   [90] *Ibid.*, para. 109.   [91] *Ibid.*
[92] See Commission, "Guidelines on Article 81 (3)" (supra n. 61), paras. 29 and 30.

(d) Non-appreciable restrictions: the de minimis rule

According to the common law principle "de minimis non curat lex", the law will not concern itself with trifles. Translated into the present context, the European Court has declared that it will not use Article 101 to establish "perfect competition" but only "workable competition" within the internal market.[93] Minor market imperfections will thus be tolerated. Restrictions of competition will only fall within Article 101 (1), where they do so "to an appreciable extent".[94] This is called the de minimis rule.

According to the Court, de minimis is measured not in quantitative or qualitative trade terms, but depends on the relevant market share. This view is shared by the Commission, which has offered guidance in its "De Minimis Notice".[95] The Notice is designed to "quantif[y], with the help of market share thresholds, what is not an appreciable restriction of competition under Article [101] of the [FEU] Treaty".[96] With the exception of "hardcore" restrictions,[97] the Commission considers that a 10 per cent aggregate market share for the parties to horizontal agreements and a 15 per cent aggregate market share for parties to vertical agreements will not appreciably restrict competition within the meaning of Article 101 (1).[98] Importantly, the Commission and the Courts thereby investigate an individual agreement's economic context.[99]

---

[93] *Metro SB-Großmärkte GmbH & Co. KG* v. *Commission*, Case 26/76, [1977] ECR 1875, para. 20; and confirmed in *Metro SB-Großmärkte GmbH & Co. KG* v. *Commission*, Case 75/84, [1986] ECR 3021, para. 65.

[94] *Société Technique Minière* v. *Maschinenbau Ulm*, Case 56/65 (supra n. 47), 249.

[95] The exact title of the Notice is: "Commission Notice on agreements of minor importance which do not appreciably restrict competition under Article 81(1) of the Treaty establishing the European Community (de minimis)", [2001] OJ C 368/13.

[96] *Ibid.*, para. 2.

[97] *Ibid.*, para. 11. However, the exclusion of the hardcore restrictions from the Commission's de minimis test will not automatically mean that they are always appreciable restrictions. The better view holds that the market thresholds for these types of restrictions must here simply be significantly lower to compensate for the gravity of their restrictive character. This is in line with *Völk* v. *Vervaecke*, Case 5/69 (supra n. 51)

[98] "Commission Notice on Minor Agreements" (supra n. 95), para. 7.

[99] On this contextual examination of a single agreement, see supra n. 55.

4. Article 101 (3): exemptions through pro-competitive effects

Where an agreement has been found to be anti-competitive under Article 101 (1), it will be void – unless it is justified and exempted under Article 101 (3). The provision theoretically applies to all agreements that violate Article 101 (1) – and thus even restrictions per object. It is directly effective and can thus be invoked as a protective shield by any undertaking facing legal proceedings.[100] In an effort to enhance legal certainty, the Union has however adopted a variety of exemption regulations which provide detailed criteria when certain categories of agreements are exempted under Article 101 (3).

(a) Direct exemptions under Article 101 (3)

Article 101 (3) potentially covers any agreement – even agreements that have been found to restrict competition by object. However, it makes the exemption conditional on four cumulative criteria. The first two criteria are positive, the other two criteria negative in nature.[101]

Positively, Article 101(3) stipulates that the agreement must "contribute[] to improving the production or distribution of goods or to promoting technical or economic progress, while allowing consumers a fair share of the resulting benefit".[102] Where the agreement thus generates *productive* or

---

[100] The direct effect of Article 101 (3) had not always been the case. Indeed it was one of the "revolutionary" changes brought by Regulation 1/2003 on the implementation of the rules on competition laid down in Articles 81 and 82 of the Treaty, [2003] OJ L1/1. On this point, see K. Lenaerts and D. Gerard, "Decentralisation of EC Competition Law Enforcement: Judges in the Frontline", 27 (2004) *World Competition*, 313.

[101] There has been a spirited debate on whether these criteria – all of which are "economic" in nature – are exhaustive or not. The Commission considers them exhaustive (see Commission, "Guidelines on Article 81(3)" (supra n. 61), para. 42): "The four conditions of Article [101(3)] are also exhaustive. When they are met the exception is applicable and may not be made dependent on any other condition. Goals pursued by other Treaty provisions can be taken into account to the extent that they can be subsumed under the four conditions of Article [101(3)]." Nonetheless, it is important to note that the Treaties' competition rules cannot be completely isolated from other policies; and this is particularly true for those policies – like environmental policy – that contain an express horizontal clause (see Article 11 TFEU (emphasis added): "Environmental protection requirements must be integrated *into the definition and implementation of the Union's policies and activities*, in particular with a view to promoting sustainable development").

[102] Article 101 (3) TFEU.

dynamic efficiencies,[103] these efficiency gains might outweigh the economic inefficiencies identified in Article 101 (1) but only under the condition that consumers get a fair share in the resulting overall benefit. What is a "fair share"? According to the Commission, "[t]he concept of '*fair share*' implies that the pass-on of benefits must at least compensate consumers for any actual or likely negative impact caused to them by the restriction of competition found under Article [101 (1)]". "If such consumers are worse off following the agreement, the second condition of Article [101 (3)] is not fulfilled."[104]

But even if that is the case, Article 101 (3) will not allow anti-competitive restrictions that are "not indispensable" for the pro-competitive effects of the agreement; or agreements which "eliminat[e] competition in respect of a substantial part of the products in question".[105] A violation of either one of these negative conditions will mean that an agreement cannot benefit from an exemption. With regard to the indispensability of a restriction, the Commission has developed a two-fold test. "First, the restrictive agreement as such must be reasonably necessary in order to achieve the efficiencies. Secondly, the individual restrictions of competition that flow from the agreement must also be reasonably necessary for the attainment of the efficiencies."[106] The first test thereby requires "that the efficiencies be specific to the agreement in question in the sense that there are no other economically practicable and less restrictive means of achieving the efficiencies".[107] Once this global test has been passed, the Commission will then analyse the indispensability of each individual restriction of competition. Here, it will assess "whether individual restrictions are reasonably necessary in order to produce the efficiencies".[108]

Finally, a specific restriction – even if indispensable for the pro-competitive effects of the agreement – must not substantially eliminate competition. This absolute limit on the exemptability of an agreement will be a function of the structure of the market.[109]

---

[103] For an elaboration of this, see Commission, "Guidelines on Article 81 (3)" (supra n. 61), paras. 48 et seq. The typical example for an agreement enhancing "productive efficiency" is a "specialization agreement". A "Research and Development" agreement is an example for an agreement that may enhance dynamic efficiency.

[104] *Ibid.*, para. 85.   [105] Article 101(3) TFEU.

[106] Commission, "Guidelines on Article 81 (3)" (supra n. 61), para. 73.   [107] *Ibid.*, para. 75.

[108] *Ibid.*, para. 78.

[109] *Ibid.*, para. 107: "Whether competition is being eliminated within the meaning of the last condition of Article [101 (3)] depends on the degree of competition existing prior to the

(b) Exemptions by category: block exemption regulations

In order to enhance legal certainty, Article 101 (3) envisaged from the very beginning that an entire "category of agreements" might be exempted.[110] Article 103 thereby allowed the Council to "lay down detailed rules for the application of Article 101 (3)".[111] This legal base was used early on;[112] and in a way that delegated the power to exempt agreements "en bloc" by means of regulations to the Commission. The Commission has adopted a variety of so-called "block exemption regulations".[113] It however retains the power to withdraw the benefit of a block exemption from an individual agreement.[114]

Many block exemption regulations originally followed a formal "category" approach. They would contain a "white list" of desirable clauses, and a "black list" of hardcore restrictions for a type of agreement.[115] This sector-specific approach towards block exemptions has been overtaken by a more flexible and economic approach. The flagship illustration of the new structure of block exemption regulations is the Regulation for vertical

---

agreement and on the impact of the restrictive agreement on competition, i.e. the reduction in competition that the agreement brings about. The more competition is already weakened in the market concerned, the slighter the further reduction required for competition to be eliminated within the meaning of Article [101(3)]."

[110] For this excellent textual point, see Lane, *EC Competition Law* (supra n. 5), 125.

[111] Article 103 (2) (b) TFEU.

[112] Council Regulation 19/65 on application of Article 85 (3) of the Treaty to certain categories of agreements and concerted practices, [1965] OJ L36/533; and Council Regulation 2821/71 on application of Article 85 (3) of the Treaty to categories of agreements, decisions and concerted practices, [1971] OJ L285/46.

[113] See Commission Regulation 330/2010 on the application of Article 101(3) of the Treaty on the Functioning of the European Union to categories of vertical agreements and concerted practices, [2010] OJ L102/1; Commission Regulation 461/2010 on the application of Article 101(3) of the Treaty on the Functioning of the European Union to categories of vertical agreements and concerted practices in the motor vehicle sector, [2010] OJ L129/52; Commission Regulation 1217/2010 on the application of Article 101(3) of the Treaty on the Functioning of the European Union to categories of research and development agreements, [2010] OJ L335/36; Commission Regulation 1218/2010 on the application of Article 101(3) of the Treaty to categories of specialization agreements, [2010] OJ L335/43; Commission Regulation 772/2004 of 27 April 2004 on the application of Article 81(3) of the Treaty to categories of technology transfer agreements, [2004] OJ L123/11. For the numerous "sectoral" block exemption regulations, see: http://ec.europa.eu/competition/antitrust/legislation/legislation.html.

[114] See Article 29 of Regulation 1/2003 (Withdrawal in individual cases), [2003] OJ L1/1.

[115] For a criticism of this "formalist" approach in the context of vertical agreements, see B. Hawk, "System Failure: Vertical Restraints and EC Competition Law", 32 (1995) *Common Market Law Review*, 973.

agreements.[116] The Regulation exempts all vertical agreements,[117] provided that "the market share held by the supplier does not exceed 30% of the relevant market on which it sells the contract goods or services and the market share held by the buyer does not exceed 30% of the relevant market on which it purchases the contract goods or services".[118] The Regulation still contains a "black list" of hardcore restrictions.[119] Yet there no longer exists a white list of permissible contractual clauses and the Regulation thus concentrates essentially on the economic effect of an agreement in following the liberal principle that all is allowed that is not prohibited.

---

[116] See Commission Regulation 330/2010 (supra n. 113). For a discussion of this Regulation, see R. Wish and D. Bailey, "Regulation 330/2010: The Commission's New Block Exemption for Vertical Agreements", 47 (2010) *Common Market Law Review*, 1757.

[117] Commission Regulation 330/2010 (supra n. 113), Article 2.   [118] *Ibid.*, Article 3(1).

[119] *Ibid.*, Article 4.

Introduction

The second pillar of European competition law focuses – in principle – on the behaviour of a single undertaking. Article 102 does not require the collusive behaviour of two or more economic actors. It can sanction the *unilateral* behaviour of a dominant undertaking where this behaviour amounts to a "market abuse". The provision states:

Any abuse by one or more undertakings of a dominant position within the internal market or in a substantial part of it shall be prohibited as incompatible with the internal market in so far as it may affect trade between Member States.
   Such abuse may, in particular, consist in:

(a) directly or indirectly imposing unfair purchase or selling prices or other unfair trading conditions;
(b) limiting production, markets or technical development to the prejudice of consumers;
(c) applying dissimilar conditions to equivalent transactions with other trading parties, thereby placing them at a competitive disadvantage;

(d) making the conclusion of contracts subject to acceptance by the other parties of supplementary obligations which, by their nature or according to commercial usage, have no connection with the subject of such contracts.

The provision encapsulates a number of fundamental choices with regard to the European *economic* constitution. For by concentrating on a "dominant position within the internal market," Article 102 goes beyond penalizing pure monopolies. In that respect it is wider than its American counterpart.[1] But by insisting on market *abuse*, it is narrower than the American prohibition. For unlike the latter, Article 102 will not directly outlaw distorted market *structures*. Dominance is not itself prohibited – only the *abuse* of a dominant position.[2] Once this abuse is however established it appears to be prohibited as such. For Article 102 has – unlike Article 101 – no "third paragraph" exempting abusive behaviour on the ground of its pro-competitive effects. However, like Article 101, the prohibition of market abuse will only apply where the abusive behaviour "may affect trade between Member States". This jurisdictional condition indeed defines the scope of all European competition law.[3]

The finding of an abuse of a dominant position within the European market therefore implies the satisfaction of three criteria. First, we must establish what the "market" is in which the undertaking operates. Second, the undertaking must be "dominant" within that market. And third, the undertaking must have "abused" its dominance.[4] All three aspects will be discussed below. Finally, we will analyse whether the Union legal order has – despite the absence of an express exemption – allowed for "objective justifications" of abusive conduct.

---

[1] Section 2 of the US American Sherman Act states: "Every person who shall monopolize, or attempt to monopolize, or combine or conspire with any other person or persons, to monopolize any part of the trade or commerce among the several States, or with foreign nations, shall be deemed guilty of a felony[.]"

[2] *Europemballage and Continental Can* v. *Commission*, Case 6/72, [1973] ECR 215, para. 26.

[3] On this point, see Chapter 11 – Section 2 above.

[4] Article 102 TFEU does not mention a "restriction of competition" as part of this provision. However, the Court has found that this element is an implied requirement; see *Michelin* v. *Commission (Michelin II)*, Case T-203/01, [2003] ECR II-4071, para. 237: "Unlike Article [101 (1) TFEU], Article [102 TFEU] contains no reference to the anti-competitive aim or anti-competitive effect of the practice referred to. However, in the light of the context of Article [102 TFEU], conduct will be regarded as abusive only if it restricts competition."

1. The "market": product and geographic dimensions

Dominance is relational: it is the power to master something; and under Article 102 this "something" is the "market". However, there is not one market in which all undertakings compete. Undertakings compete in different products and in different areas. The market concept is thus a concept with two dimensions: a *product* dimension and a *geographic* dimension. The first dimension concerns the question as to what goods or services compete with each other. Where two products do not compete, they are not in the same market. According to this functional concept of the market, there is thus not one market but many separate "product" markets. But two competing goods must also "physically" meet in the same area. This aspect of the market concept is called its geographic dimension.

How has the Union legal order defined both dimensions? In relation to the product market, it concentrates on the "interchangeability" of two products. In the words of the European Court: "The concept of the relevant market in fact implies that there can be effective competition between the products which form part of it and this presupposes that there is a *sufficient degree of interchangeability between all the products* forming part of the same market in so far as a specific use of such products is concerned."[5] The interchangeability or "substitutability" of a product typically expresses itself in *demand* substitution. Demand substitution analyses whether the consumer regards two products as interchangeable "by reason of the products' characteristics, their prices and their intended use".[6] The principal test here is that of cross-price elasticity. Cross-price elasticity measures whether a "small but significant non-transitory increase in price" (SSNIP) in one product incentivizes consumers to switch to another

---

[5] *Hoffmann-La Roche & Co. AG* v. *Commission*, Case 85/76, [1979] ECR 461, para. 28 (emphasis added). And see also *Europemballage and Continental Can* v. *Commission*, Case 6/72 (supra n. 2), para. 32: "The definition of the relevant market is of essential significance, for the possibilities of competition can only be judged in relation to those characteristics of the products in question by virtue of which those products are particularly apt to satisfy an inelastic need and are only to a limited extent interchangeable with other products."

[6] Commission, "Notice on the Definition of relevant market for the purposes of Community competition law", [1997] OJ C372/5, para. 7: "A relevant product market comprises all those products and/or services which are regarded as interchangeable or substitutable by the consumer, by reason of the products' characteristics, their prices and their intended use."

product.[7] Where this is the case, two goods are – from an econometric point of view – in the same product market. But apart from purely quantitative criteria, the European Courts may use additional *qualitative* criteria.[8] Moreover, they may even analyse the degree of potential competition by future market entrants. This aspect is called *supply substitution*; that is: the extent to which an undertaking could switch from a non-competing to a competing product.[9]

If two products are (theoretically) found to be competing, they must still be offered in the same geographic market. "The opportunities for competition under Article [102] of the Treaty must be considered having regard to the particular features of the product in question *and with reference to a clearly defined geographic area in which it is marketed and where the conditions of competition are sufficiently homogeneous*[.]"[10] Two competing products might not be offered in the same (national) market for legal reasons;[11] or, if they are, foreign products might be disadvantaged.[12] And

---

[7] *Ibid.*, para. 15: "The assessment of demand substitution entails a determination of the range of products which are viewed as substitutes by the consumer. One way of making this determination can be viewed as a speculative experiment, postulating a hypothetical small, lasting change in relative prices and evaluating the likely reactions of customers to that increase. The exercise of market definition focuses on prices for operational and practical purposes, and more precisely on demand substitution arising from small, permanent changes in relative prices. This concept can provide clear indications as to the evidence that is relevant in defining markets." The problem with this – relational – test is that it cannot measure whether the price of the examined product is – in absolute terms – already inflated. This fallacy of the SSNIP test has become known as the "Cellophane Fallacy" after the American Supreme Court's decision in *US* v. *Du Pont*, 351 US 377 (1956).

[8] See *United Brands Company and United Brands Continentaal BV* v. *Commission*, Case 27/76, [1978] ECR 207, where the Court found that in light of its distinct qualities, the "banana market is a market which is sufficiently distinct from other fresh fruit markets" (*ibid.*, para. 35).

[9] See *Michelin* v. *Commission (Michelin I)*, Case 322/81, [1983] ECR 3461.

[10] *United Brands* v. *Commission*, Case 27/76 (supra n. 8), para. 11 (emphasis added). And see also *Deutsche Bahn* v. *Commission*, Case T-229/94, [1997] ECR II-1689, para. 92: "Inasmuch as the applicant submits that the Commission's definition of the geographical market is undermined by the difference in the competitive situation, it is sufficient to state that the definition of the geographical market does not require the objective conditions of competition between traders to be perfectly homogeneous. It is sufficient if they are 'similar' or 'sufficiently homogeneous' and, accordingly, only areas in which the objective conditions of competition are 'heterogeneous' may not be considered to constitute a uniform market."

[11] The primary "culprit" here is often (national) intellectual property rights. On the nature and effects of these rights, see L. Bently and B. Sherman, *Intellectual Property Law* (Oxford University Press, 2008), Chapter 1.

[12] We saw in Chapter 9 above that the free movement of goods provisions allow for the discriminatory treatments of foreign goods *if* justified on grounds of public policy.

even if two products are competing in a similar legal context, transportation costs might limit the geographic market considerably.[13] The question thus is this: when are competitive conditions "sufficiently homogeneous" so as to "be distinguished from neighbouring areas because the conditions of competition are appreciably different in those areas"?[14] That is a question of fact that the Courts will have to answer;[15] and if they have answered it positively, the geographic market for a product so identified must represent a "substantial part" of the internal market. What is a "substantial part" of the European market? The European Courts have established a presumption that the territory of a Member State constitutes a substantial part of the internal market.[16] However, they have equally found this requirement to be satisfied for a part of a Member State,[17] and even a port within a city.[18]

2. Market dominance

(a) General considerations

There exists an inverse relationship between the identified "market" and the potential "dominance" of an undertaking within that market. The greater the market the smaller will be the likelihood of dominance; and, alternatively, the smaller the market the greater will be the likelihood of dominance. Put colloquially: a big fish in a big pond is different from a big fish in a small pond. And sometimes the pond might be so small that there is only room for one fish.[19]

---

[13] See Commission Decision 88/518 relating to a proceeding under Article 86 of the EEC Treaty (Case No. IV/30.178 Napier Brown – British Sugar), [1988] OJ L284/41.

[14] "Commission Notice on the Definition of relevant market" (supra n. 6), para. 8.

[15] In the absence of any special legal or factual elements, the geographic market is the entire internal market of the Union; see *Hilti AG* v. *Commission*, Case T-30/89, [1991] ECR II-1439.

[16] See *Belgische Radio en Televisie (BRT) and others* v. *SABAM and others*, Case 127/73, [1974] ECR 313; *Michelin I*, Case 322/81 (supra n. 9); and *Radio Telefis Eireann (RTE) and Independent Television Publications Ltd (ITP)* v. *Commission*, Case 241/91P, [1995] ECR I-743.

[17] See *Coöperatieve Vereniging "Suiker Unie" UA and others* v. *Commission*, Case 40/73, [1975] ECR 1663.

[18] See *Merci convenzionali porto di Genova* v. *Siderurgica Gabrielli*, Case C-179/90, [1991] ECR I-5889.

[19] In *Hugin* v. *Commission*, Case 22/78, [1979] ECR 1869, the Court defined the relevant market in such narrow terms that only one undertaking – the plaintiff – was found to inhabit the "pond" of spare parts for Hugin's cash registers.

What then is market dominance? Dominance is wider than monopoly. Whereas monopoly technically refers to a situation in which *one* single undertaking dominates the market, Article 102 is not confined to that situation. But as to when an undertaking is dominant the provision does not tell. The European Courts have therefore tried to define dominance by distinguishing it from related phenomena such as monopoly. In *Hoffmann-La Roche*,[20] the European Court thus held:

> The dominant position thus referred to relates to a position of economic strength enjoyed by an undertaking which enables it to prevent the effective competition being maintained on the relevant market by affording it the power to behave to an appreciable extent independently of its competitors, its customers and ultimately of the consumers. *Such a position does not preclude some competition, which it does where there is a monopoly or a quasi-monopoly*, but enables the undertaking which profits by it, if not to determine, at least to have an appreciable influence on the conditions under which that competition will develop, and in any case to act largely in disregard of it so long as such conduct does not operate to its detriment. *A dominant position must also be distinguished from parallel courses of conduct which are peculiar to oligopolies* in that in an oligopoly the courses of conduct interact, while in the case of an undertaking occupying a dominant position the conduct of the undertaking which derives profits from that position is to a great extent determined unilaterally.[21]

A dominant position is thus distinct from a monopolistic position as well as from an oligopolistic position. While the former excludes all competition, oligopolies are market structures in which a "few" undertakings dominate the market.[22] But what characterizes market dominance specifically? The Court admitted that the answer to that question was determined by several factors, yet nonetheless found that "among these factors a highly important one is the existence of very large market shares".[23] Thus, the higher the market share, the higher the probability of dominance. The Court has indeed held that a market share above 50 per cent was a clear indication of market dominance.[24] But even below 50 per cent, the Court may find market dominance. However, a finding of dominance here involves a number of

---

[20] *Hoffmann-La Roche & Co. AG v. Commission*, Case 85/76 (supra n. 5).

[21] *Ibid.*, paras. 38–9.   [22] "Oligo" means "few" in Greek.   [23] *Ibid.*, para. 39.

[24] *AKZO Chemie BV v. Commission*, Case C-62/86, [1991] ECR I-3359, para. 60: "With regard to market shares the Court has held that very large shares are in themselves, and save in exceptional circumstances, evidence of the existence of a dominant position. That is the situation where there is a market share of 50% such as that found to exist in this case."

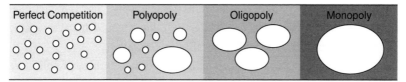

Figure 12.1 Market structures

determinants,[25] in particular: the structure of the relevant market.[26] This second factor compares the market share of the accused undertaking with those of its biggest competitors.[27] For while an undertaking may not have "absolute" dominance over the market, it might still enjoy a "relative" dominance over its competitors.[28] The Court has nonetheless found that if an undertaking has a market share below 40 per cent of the relevant market, a finding of dominance is unlikely.[29]

(b) Collective dominance

A dominant position appears to be fundamentally different from an oligopoly. For the latter involves a situation in which a small number of undertakings are – more or less – equally strong within the market, and it would seem that none of them could *individually* dominate the market. But could Article 102 capture these oligopolistic undertakings *collectively*? The concept of collective dominance is suggested by the very wording of the provision. Article 102 refers to an "abuse of one *or more undertakings of a dominant position*".[30] And, teleologically, it would be logical to capture

[25] See Commission, "Guidance on the Commission's enforcement priorities in applying Article 82 of the EC Treaty to abusive exclusionary conduct by dominant undertakings", [2009] OJ C45/7, para. 20.

[26] *Hoffmann-La Roche & Co. AG* v. *Commission*, Case 85/76 (supra n. 5), para. 40: "A substantial market share as evidence of the existence of a dominant position is not a constant factor and its importance varies from market to market according to the structure of these markets, especially as far as production, supply and demand are concerned."

[27] See *United Brands*, Case 27/76 (supra n. 8), esp. paras. 110 et seq. The Court is likely to infer dominance where the market share of an undertaking is twice as big as those of all of its competitors combined (see *British Airways* v. *Commission*, Case T-219/99, [2003] ECR II-5917).

[28] Another factor that may influence a finding of dominance are entry barriers through the existence of a service network (see *Michelin* v. *Commission*, Case 322/81 (supra n. 9)).

[29] Commission, "Guidance on the Commission's enforcement priorities in applying Article 82" (supra n. 25), para. 14.

[30] Article 102 TFEU (emphasis added).

situations in which oligopolistic undertakings went beyond "parallel courses of conduct".[31] Indeed: a collective *abuse* would have the same consequences as that of a single dominant undertaking.[32]

The European Courts have – belatedly – accepted the idea of collective dominance.[33] In *Vetro et al* v. *Commission*,[34] three Italian producers of flat-glass challenged a Commission decision that had found them guilty of violating Article 102. Their joint market shares were 95 per cent, and the Commission claimed that the undertakings would "present themselves on the market as a single entity and not as individuals".[35] To cement this argument the Commission pointed to the existence of collusive behaviour under Article 101. Intervening in the proceedings, the United Kingdom objected that it was "only in very special circumstances that two or more undertakings may jointly hold a dominant position within the meaning of Article [102], namely, when the undertakings concerned fall to be treated as a single economic unit in which the individual undertakings do not enjoy a genuine autonomy in determining their conduct on the market and are not to be treated as economically independent of one another".[36] The General Court – rightly – rejected that argument, since it implied that the notion of "undertaking" in Article 102 was different from that in Article 101.[37] And moving from text to teleology, the Court continued:

There is nothing, in principle, to prevent two or more independent economic entities from being, on a specific market, *united by such economic links* that, by virtue of

---

[31] *Hoffmann-La Roche & Co. AG* v. *Commission*, Case 85/76, (supra n. 5) para. 39.

[32] Suffice to say here that once the Union has found collective dominance to exist, the abuse of this dominant position may be collective or individual; see *Irish Sugar plc* v. *Commission*, Case T-228/97, [1999] ECR II-2969, para. 66: "Whilst the existence of a joint dominant position may be deduced from the position which the economic entities concerned together hold on the market in question, the abuse does not necessarily have to be the action of all the undertakings in question. It only has to be capable of being identified as one of the manifestations of such a joint dominant position being held. Therefore, undertakings occupying a joint dominant position may engage in joint or individual abusive conduct. It is enough for that abusive conduct to relate to the exploitation of the joint dominant position which the undertakings hold in the market."

[33] For an overview of the case law, see R. Wish, "Collective Dominance" in D. O'Keeffe et al. (eds.), *Judicial Review in European Union Law: Liber Amicorum in Honour of Lord Slynn of Hadley* (Kluwer, 2000), 581.

[34] *Vetro, Pisana and Vernante Pennitalia* v. *Commission*, Joined Cases T-68/89, T-77/89 and T-78/89, [1992] ECR II-1403. The Commission claimed that this was the first case on collective dominance and for that reason suggested not imposing any fines (*ibid.*, para. 33).

[35] *Ibid.*, para. 31.   [36] *Ibid.*, para. 342.

[37] *Ibid.*, para. 358. On the notion of "undertaking", see Chapter 11 – Introduction (supra).

that fact, together they hold a dominant position vis-à-vis the other operators on the same market ... However, it should be pointed out that for the purposes of establishing an infringement of Article [102] of the Treaty, it is not sufficient ... to "recycle" the facts constituting an infringement of Article [101], deducing from them the finding that the parties to an agreement or to an unlawful practice jointly hold a substantial share of the market, that by virtue of that fact alone they hold a collective dominant position, and that their unlawful behaviour constitutes an abuse of that collective dominant position.[38]

The simple existence of contractual or collusive relations between the three undertakings was thus not sufficient to establish collective dominance. But what did the requirement that the firms be united by "economic links" then mean?

Some clarification was given in *CEWAL*,[39] where the European Court confirmed the General Court's finding that "a dominant position may be held by several undertakings".[40] Collective dominance thereby required that legally independent undertakings "present themselves or act together on a particular market as a collective entity".[41] And "[i]n order to establish the existence of a collective entity as defined above, it is necessary to examine the economic links or factors which give rise to a connection between the undertakings concerned".[42] The mere existence of collusion within the meaning of Article 101 was inconclusive; yet, such collusion could "undoubtedly, where it is implemented, result in the undertakings concerned being so linked as to their conduct on a particular market that they present themselves on that market as a collective entity vis-à-vis their competitors, their trading partners and consumers".[43] All depends on the "nature and terms of an agreement, from the way in which it is implemented and, consequently, from the links or factors which give rise to a connection between undertakings".[44]

While an agreement between undertakings may thus indicate collective dominance, the European Courts have found that this is not the only way. And in *Piau*,[45] the General Court provided the following abstract criteria for a finding of collective dominance:

---

[38] *Ibid.*, paras. 358 and 360 (emphasis added).
[39] *Compagnie maritime belge transports SA, Compagnie maritime belge and Dafra-Lines* v. *Commission*, Joined Cases C-395/96 P and C-396/96 P, [2000] ECR I-1365.
[40] *Ibid.*, para. 35.   [41] *Ibid.*, para. 36.   [42] *Ibid.*, para. 41.   [43] *Ibid.*, para. 44.
[44] *Ibid.*, para. 45.   [45] *Piau* v. *Commission*, Case T-193/02, [2005] ECR II-209.

Three cumulative conditions must be met for a finding of collective dominance: first, each member of the dominant oligopoly must have the ability to know how the other members are behaving in order to monitor whether or not they are adopting the common policy; second, the situation of tacit coordination must be sustainable over time, that is to say, there must be an incentive not to depart from the common policy on the market; thirdly, the foreseeable reaction of current and future competitors, as well as of consumers, must not jeopardise the results expected from the common policy.[46]

3. Abuse of market dominance

If dominance is a relational concept, abuse is a situational concept. Situational concepts are like semantic chameleons: their meaning depends on the context in which they are used. What counts as "abuse" in Article 102 indeed depends not so much on the type of behaviour as such as on the "context"; namely, that this is the behaviour of a *dominant* undertaking. Thus, where a non-dominant undertaking refuses to supply a distributor, this behaviour is a perfectly legitimate offspring of the freedom of contract. However, were a dominant undertaking to do the same, this might constitute an illegitimate abuse. The abusive character of the behaviour is here added from "outside" the undertaking. It is the market structure that "colours" the behaviour. And since that market structure is – like physical space around big stellar masses – distorted by the very presence of a dominant firm, the latter's action may have an anti-competitive effect, even if the same action of a non-dominant undertaking would not.[47]

---

[46] *Ibid.*, paras. 110–11.

[47] The European Court has tried to express this conceptual link between the concept of "abuse" and market dominance in *Hoffmann-La Roche & Co. AG* v. *Commission*, Case 85/76 (supra n. 5), para. 91: "The concept of abuse is an objective concept relating to the behaviour of an undertaking in a dominant position which is such as to influence the structure of a market where, as a result of the very presence of the undertaking in question, the degree of competition is weakened and which, through recourse to methods different from those which condition normal competition in products or services on the basis of the transactions of commercial operators, has the effect of hindering the maintenance of the degree of competition still existing in the market or the growth of that competition." For an even more explicit judicial statement, see *France Télécom* v. *Commission*, Case T-340/03, [2007] ECR II-107, para. 186: "[I]t follows from the nature of the obligations imposed by Article [102 TFEU] that, in specific circumstances, undertakings in a dominant position may be deprived of the right to adopt a course of

What we see as examples of abusive behaviour in Article 102 must be understood in this light. These forms of action are not illegal as such, but they become illegal because of the standing of the actor within the market. For within that market the dominant undertaking has "a special responsibility".[48] And because of that special responsibility, there are special duties imposed on a dominant undertaking. However, these special duties will find a limit in its right to self-defence. "[T]he fact that an undertaking is in a dominant position cannot disentitle it from protecting its own commercial interests if they are attacked[.]"[49] What types of abusive behaviour are covered by Article 102? The provision covers both exploitative as well as exclusionary abuses. "[T]he provision is not only aimed at practices which may cause damage to consumers directly, but also at those which are detrimental to them through their impact on an effective competition structure[.]"[50]

The "maintenance of effective competition on the relevant market" is indeed the central aim behind Article 102.[51] What will "relevant" market here mean? A restrictive reading would insist that the special duties imposed on a dominant undertaking are confined to the market that it dominates. But the Union legal order has preferred a - slightly - wider reading. It has extended the prohibition of abuse to "downstream" or "adjacent" markets in which the undertaking is *not* dominant.[52] The application of Article 102 in "distinct, but associated" markets is thus possible. However in *Tetra Pak*,[53] the European Court insisted on "a link between the dominant position and the alleged abusive conduct, which is normally not present where conduct on a market distinct from the dominated market produces effects on that distinct market".[54] Article 102 would thus only apply in "special circumstances" to conduct found in the associated market, in which the undertaking was not dominant.[55]

---

conduct or take measures which are not in themselves abuses and which would even be unobjectionable if adopted or taken by non-dominant undertakings."

[48] *Michelin* v. *Commission*, Case 322/81 (supra n. 9), para. 57.

[49] *United Brands* v. *Commission*, Case 27/76 (supra n. 8), para. 189.

[50] *Europemballage Corporation and Continental Can Company* v. *Commission*, Case 6/72 (supra n. 2), para. 26.

[51] *Michelin* v. *Commission*, Case 322/81 (supra n. 9), para. 30.

[52] See *Istituto Chemioterapico Italiano and Commercial Solvents Corporation* v. *Commission*, Cases 6 and 7/73, [1974] ECR 223.

[53] *Tetra Pak International* v. *Commission*, Case C-333/94 P, [1996] ECR I-5961.

[54] *Ibid.*, para. 27.   [55] *Ibid.*

The following subsections look at common forms of abusive behaviour within each of the forms exemplified in the (non-exhaustive) list in Article 102.

(a) Article 102 [2] (a) and "predatory pricing"

The first illustration of abusive behaviour given by Article 102 consists of "directly or indirectly imposing unfair purchase or selling prices or other unfair trading conditions".[56] This wide category includes "excessive pricing", as well as "predatory pricing". The former exploits the consumer, while the latter is designed to exclude a competitor. Excessive pricing is hard to establish.[57] For predatory pricing, on the other hand, the European Courts have developed a detector test that indicates when abusive conduct is, or is likely to be, present.

In *AKZO*,[58] the European Court had to deal with two undertakings producing organic peroxides. Peroxides are used in the plastics industry, but can equally be used as bleaching agents for flour. AKZO had traditionally been active with regard to both applications, whereas a second company – ECS – had only recently extended its activities from the flour to the plastics application. In order to secure ECS's withdrawal from the plastics application, AKZO attacked its competitor on the flour application by systematically offering "unreasonably low prices designed to damage ECS's business viability, compelling ECS either to abandon the customer to AKZO or to match a loss-making price in order to retain the customer".[59] This was a commercially clever strategy, since AKZO used price reductions in a sector which was vital for its competitor but of limited importance to itself.[60] But was this a commercially legitimate strategy? The Court found that AKZO held a dominant position and that therefore "not all competition by means of price can be regarded as legitimate".[61] What then was the distinction between legitimate and illegitimate price competition? In the opinion of the Court it was this:

---

[56] Article 102 [2] (a) TFEU.

[57] See *United Brands* v. *Commission*, Case 27/76 (supra n. 8), paras. 235 et seq. However, see also *General Motors Continental NV* v. *Commission*, Case 26/75, [1975] ECR 1367.

[58] *AKZO Chemie BV* v. *Commission*, Case C-62/86 (supra n. 24).   [59] *Ibid.*, para. 9.

[60] *Ibid.*, para. 42.   [61] *Ibid.*, para. 70.

Prices below average variable costs (that is to say, those which vary depending on the quantities produced) by means of which a dominant undertaking seeks to eliminate a competitor must be regarded as abusive. A dominant undertaking has no interest in applying such prices except that of eliminating competitors so as to enable it subsequently to raise its prices by taking advantage of its monopolistic position, since each sale generates a loss, namely the total amount of the fixed costs (that is to say, those which remain constant regardless of the quantities produced) and, at least, part of the variable costs relating to the unit produced. Moreover, prices below average total costs, that is to say, fixed costs plus variable costs, but above average variable costs, must be regarded as abusive if they are determined as part of a plan for eliminating a competitor. Such prices can drive from the market undertakings which are perhaps as efficient as the dominant undertaking but which, because of their smaller financial resources, are incapable of withstanding the competition waged against them.[62]

The Court here established a rule and a presumption for illegitimate predatory pricing.[63] Where the price of the product was below average variable costs the pricing policy of an undertaking was abusive per se. It thereby would not matter whether there existed a possibility of recuperating the losses in the long term.[64] By contrast, where the price was between average variable costs and average total costs, there was still a possibility that this could be an abuse of dominance. However, an abusive behaviour would here only be established where the pricing policy could be shown to be part of a strategic plan to eliminate a competitor. This "subjective" element within the definition of predatory pricing undermines, to some extent, the Court's idea that the concept of abuse is an "objective" concept.[65] The General Court has tried

---

[62] Ibid., para. 71–2.

[63] The ruling was confirmed in *Tetra Pak International SA* v. *Commission*, Case C-333/94P (supra n. 53), esp. paras. 39 et seq. According to the Commission's "Article 82 Guidance" (supra n. 25), the Commission will apply a slightly different test (*ibid.*, para. 26): "The cost benchmarks that the Commission is likely to use are average avoidable cost (AAC) and long-run average incremental cost (LRAIC). Failure to cover AAC indicates that the dominant undertaking is sacrificing profits in the short term and that an equally efficient competitor cannot serve the targeted customers without incurring a loss. LRAIC is usually above AAC because, in contrast to AAC (which only includes fixed costs if incurred during the period under examination), LRAIC includes product specific fixed costs made before the period in which allegedly abusive conduct took place. Failure to cover LRAIC indicates that the dominant undertaking is not recovering all the (attributable) fixed costs of producing the good or service in question and that an equally efficient competitor could be foreclosed from the market."

[64] See *France Télécom* v. *Commission*, C-202/07P, [2009] ECR I-2369, esp. para. 110.

[65] See *Hoffmann-La Roche* v. *Commission*, Case 85/76 (supra n. 5), para. 91.

to gloss over this development by asserting that an anti-competitive intent and an anti-competitive effect may – occasionally – "be one and the same thing".[66]

(b) Article 102 [2] (b) and "refusal to supply"

The Treaties define a second form of abusive conduct as "limiting production, markets or technical development to the prejudice of consumers".[67] One can consider the "refusal to supply" as a generic expression of that category. This potentially abusive type of conduct best illustrates the "special responsibilities" of a dominant undertaking. For the general principle of freedom of contract would normally allow any contracting party to reject an offer for a contract. But this freedom cannot be granted where the market structure is such that there is no alternative supply.

In *Commercial Solvents*,[68] the Court had to deal with the refusal by the dominant producer of the raw material aminobutanol to Zoja – a manufacturer of ethambutol. The producer had decided to expand its production to the manufacture of the finished product; and in pursuit of this vertical integration strategy, it had decided to cut off the supply of raw materials "to certain parties in order to facilitate its own access to the market for the derivatives".[69] In unequivocal terms, the Court found that this was not a legitimate commercial strategy for a dominant undertaking:

[A]n undertaking being in a dominant position as regards the production of raw material and therefore able to control the supply to manufacturers of derivatives, cannot, just because it decides to start manufacturing these derivatives (in competition with its former customers) act in such a way as to eliminate their competition which in the case in question, would amount to eliminating one of the principal manufacturers of ethambutol in the common market.[70]

The Court consequently considered the refusal to supply an abuse of a dominant position that violated Article 102. This reasoning was confirmed in *Magill*.[71] In the absence of a comprehensive weekly television guide in

---

[66] *France Télécom* v. *Commission*, Case T-340/03, [2007] ECR II-107, para. 195.
[67] Article 102[2] (b) TFEU.
[68] See *Istituto Chemioterapico Italiano* v. *Commission*, Cases 6 and 7/73 (supra n. 52).
[69] *Ibid.*, para. 24.   [70] *Ibid.*, para. 25.
[71] *Radio Telefis Eireann (RTE) and Independent Television Publications Ltd (ITP)* v. *Commission*, Joined Cases C-241/91P and C-242/91P (supra n. 16).

Ireland, each television station here published its own guide, while licensing daily newspapers to produce daily listings free of charge. Magill saw a commercial gap and tried to fill it. Yet it was prevented from publishing a comprehensive weekly guide by the Irish television stations (as well as the BBC). Was this an abuse of a dominant position? The European Courts thought this was a clear violation of Article 102 [2] (b), as the refusal to supply the information "prevented the appearance of a new product" that the dominant undertakings "did not offer and for which there was a potential consumer demand".[72]

Did *Magill* endorse a European "essential facilities" doctrine?[73] The question was raised in *Bronner*.[74] The applicant here was a producer of a small Austrian newspaper, who wished to use the – integrated – home-delivery distribution network of a dominant competitor "against payment of reasonable remuneration".[75] Bronner argued that the normal postal delivery service would not constitute an alternative delivery option, as it would not take place until the late morning; and the establishment of its own home-delivery service was "entirely unprofitable".[76] Could it therefore demand to use its competitor's distributional infrastructure? The Court disagreed, and gave an extremely restrictive reading of its prior jurisprudence. Only when the service was "indispensable" for carrying on the business in question, because it was "impossible" to develop a new product without the service, would the Union – in "exceptional circumstances" – require a competitor to make available its facilities.[77] And this was not the case here. For even if the Court admitted that there was only one nationwide home-delivery scheme in the Member State,[78] other methods of distribution were available and it was furthermore not impossible for any publisher of daily newspapers to establish – alone or in cooperation with other publishers – a second home-delivery scheme.[79] This restrictive stance has been confirmed in later jurisprudence.[80]

---

[72] *Ibid.*, paras. 54 et seq.

[73] For critical overviews of the American doctrine, see B. Doherty, "Just What are Essential Facilities?", 38 (2001) *Common Market Law Review*, 397; as well as A. Rodenhausen, "The Rise and Fall of the Essential Facilities Doctrine", 29 (2008) *European Competition Law Review*, 310.

[74] *Bronner* v. *Mediaprint Zeitungs- und Zeitschriftenverlag and others*, Case C-7/97, [1998] ECR I-7791.

[75] *Ibid.*, para. 8.   [76] *Ibid.*   [77] *Ibid.*, paras. 38–41.   [78] *Ibid.*, para. 42.

[79] *Ibid.* para. 44.

[80] See *IMS Health* v. *NDC Health*, Case C-418/01, [2004] ECR I-5039; and *Microsoft* v. *Commission*, Case T-201/04, [2007] ECR II-3601.

(c) Article 102 [2] (c) and "discretionary pricing"

A third category of abusive behaviour is defined as "applying dissimilar conditions to equivalent transactions with other trading parties, thereby placing them at a competitive disadvantage".[81] The emblematic expression of this is discriminatory pricing. Price discrimination may thereby take place directly or indirectly. Direct discrimination might be found where an undertaking charges different prices depending on the nationality or location of its customers.[82] The best-known commercial techniques of indirect price discrimination are discounts or rebates. They have been subject to an extensive European jurisprudence.[83]

In *Hoffmann-La Roche*,[84] the Court was asked to analyse the commercial lure of a loyalty rebate offered by a dominant undertaking. Fidelity rebates are discounts that are conditional – regardless of the quantity bought – on the customer's promise to buy exclusively from one undertaking. According to the Commission, this had a discriminatory effect since Roche "offer[ed] two purchasers two different prices for an identical quantity of the same product depending on whether these two buyers agree or not to forego obtaining their supplies from Roche's competitors".[85] The Court agreed:

> The *fidelity* rebate, unlike *quantity* rebates exclusively linked with the volume of purchases from the producer concerned, is designed through the grant of a financial advantage to prevent customers from obtaining their supplies from competing producers. Furthermore the effect of fidelity rebates is to apply dissimilar conditions to equivalent transactions with other trading parties in that two purchasers pay a different price for the same quantity of the same product depending on whether they obtain their supplies exclusively from the undertaking in a dominant position or have several sources of supply.[86]

The Court here distinguished between legitimate "quantity rebates" and illegitimate "fidelity rebates". However, the dividing line between the two has never been easy to draw. This is illustrated by *Michelin I*.[87] Was a "target discount", that is: a discount that was given once the seller had

---

[81] Article 102[2] (c) TFEU.

[82] *United Brands* v. *Commission*, Case 27/76 (supra n. 8), paras. 204 et seq.

[83] For an overview, see A. Jones and B. Sufrin, *EU Competition Law: Text, Cases and Materials* (Oxford University Press, 2011), 425 et seq.

[84] *Hoffmann-La Roche* v. *Commission*, Case 85/76 (supra n. 5).   [85] *Ibid.*, para. 80.

[86] *Ibid.*, para. 90.   [87] *Michelin* v. *Commission*, Case 322/81 (supra n. 9).

achieved a given sales target, a quantitative or a loyalty discount? The Court found that the discount system operated by Michelin did "not amount to a mere quantity discount linked solely to the volume of goods purchased", as it "depended primarily on the dealer's turnover in Michelin tyres without distinction of category and not on the number".[88] However, neither was the rebate a clear fidelity rebate, as the Commission had not succeeded in demonstrating that the discount system was discriminatory.[89] In *Michelin II*,[90] the General Court appears to have followed this logic to its end by suggesting that while there is a presumption of legality for quantity discounts, they must nonetheless be subjected to a detailed analysis as to their potentially abusive character.[91]

The evolution of the case law thus shows a blurring of the traditional dichotomy between (per se legal) quantity discounts and (per se illegal) loyalty discounts.[92] The modern effects-based test has thereby introduced a more economic approach into the analysis of Article 102.

(d) Article 102 [2] (d) and "tying or bundling"

The fourth expressly mentioned illustration of an abusive behaviour outlaws the commercial practice of "making the conclusion of contracts subject to acceptance by the other parties of *supplementary obligations which, by their nature or according to commercial usage, have no connection with the subject of such contracts*".[93] This mouthful is often simply referred to as "tying" and "bundling". While there is a subtle distinction between both

---

[88] *Ibid.*, paras. 72 and 89.   [89] *Ibid.*, para. 91.

[90] *Michelin* v. *Commission*, Case T-203/01 (supra n. 4).

[91] *Ibid.*, paras. 58–9: "Quantity rebate systems linked solely to the volume of purchases made from an undertaking occupying a dominant position are generally considered not to have the foreclosure effect prohibited by Article [102 TFEU]. If increasing the quantity supplied results in lower costs for the supplier, the latter is entitled to pass on that reduction to the customer in the form of a more favourable tariff. Quantity rebates are therefore deemed to reflect gains in efficiency and economies of scale made by the undertaking in a dominant position. It follows that a rebate system in which the rate of the discount increases according to the volume purchased will not infringe Article [102 TFEU] unless the criteria and rules for granting the rebate reveal that the system is not based on an economically justified countervailing advantage but tends, following the example of a loyalty and target rebate, to prevent customers from obtaining their supplies from competitors."

[92] See *British Airways* v. *Commission*, Case C-95/04P, [2007] ECR I-2331, paras. 67–8.

[93] Article 102[2] (d) TFEU (emphasis added).

commercial techniques,[94] both express themselves in "connecting" the sale of one product to the sale of another.[95]

We find a good illustration of this sales technique in *Tetra Pak II*,[96] involving a dominant manufacturer of cartons and carton-filling machines. Tetra Pak had tied the sale of the former to the sale of the latter – claiming that the machinery for packaging was indivisible from the cartons. The General Court rejected that claim. Finding that there were independent manufacturers specializing in cartons for machines from different manufacturers,[97] and that Tetra's own cartons could be used on different machines,[98] carton and carton-filling machines were considered products that could be separately sold. And since their tying was not in line with commercial usage,[99] the dominant undertaking had abused its market power.[100]

This form of analysis was refined in *Microsoft* – one of the longer judgments of European law.[101] The case examined the choice of the software giant to tie a media player to its operating system. The General Court here had recourse to four analytical elements in showing an abuse of dominance. In addition to the existence of two separate products,[102] the Union competition authorities would need to demonstrate that

[94] E. Rousseva, *Rethinking Exclusionary Abuses in EU Competition Law* (Hart, 2010), 219: "The distinction between bundling and tying is technical. In the case of tying, one of the products, that is the tied product, can be purchased independently. In the case of bundling, no distinction is made between the purchases of the products involved. Either none of the products can be purchased independently of the other (pure bundling) or both products can be purchased independently but their joint sale gives customers a discount (mixed bundling)."

[95] The European Courts appear to use both terms interchangeably; see *Microsoft* v. *Commission*, Case T-201/04 (supra n. 80), para. 935.

[96] *Tetra Pak* v. *Commission*, Case T-83/91, [1994] ECR II-755. But see also *Hilti* v. *Commission*, Case T-30/89 (supra n. 15).

[97] *Tetra Pak* v. *Commission*, Case T-83/91 (supra n. 96), para. 82. Much of the argument concentrated on non-aseptic cartons.

[98] *Ibid.*, para. 132.   [99] *Ibid.*, para. 137.

[100] *Ibid.*, para. 140. The judgment was confirmed on appeal; see *Tetra Pak* v. *Commission*, Case C-333/94 P (supra n. 53), where the Court even pointed out that (*ibid.*, para. 37) "[i]t must, moreover, be stressed that the list of abusive practices set out in the second paragraph of Article [102] of the Treaty is not exhaustive". "Consequently, even where tied sales of two products are in accordance with commercial usage or there is a natural link between the two products in question, such sales may still constitute abuse within the meaning of Article [102] unless they are objectively justified."

[101] *Microsoft* v. *Commission*, Case T-201/04 (supra n. 80). The judgment contains 1,373 paragraphs of factual and legal arguments.

[102] *Ibid.*, paras. 872 et seq.

the dominant undertaking "coerced" customers to buy the tied product by not giving them a choice (not) to obtain the product.[103] And even though the Windows Media Player was a media functionality that did not require consumers to pay extra, the Court found that "in consequence of the impugned conduct, consumers are unable to acquire the Windows client PC operating system without simultaneously acquiring Windows Media Player, which means that the condition that the conclusion of contracts is made subject to acceptance of supplementary obligations must be considered to be satisfied".[104] The third element of the test then examined whether this technique foreclosed competition for the bundled product,[105] while the fourth element analysed the absence of an objective justification for the seemingly abusive conduct.

This last element theoretically applies to all types of abuse and will be considered in the final section.

4. Objective justification: apparently abusive behaviour?

Article 102 contains – unlike Article 101 – no separate paragraph dealing with possible justifications for abuses of a dominant position.[106] Article 102 thus appears to be an "absolute" prohibition. However, the European Courts do examine whether there exists an "objective justification" of the apparently abusive behaviour of a market leader.[107] The existence of unwritten grounds of justification is not uncommon and can be seen in other areas of European law.[108] And yet, the idea of objective justifications

---

[103] *Ibid.*, paras. 945 et seq.

[104] *Ibid.*, para. 961. For a criticism of the application of this second criterion in the *Microsoft* decision itself, see Rousseva, *Rethinking Exclusionary Abuses* (supra n. 94), 252: "the mere fact that consumers did not have to pay an extra price for [the Windows Media Player] and could also freely download an alternative media player meant that consumers had a choice".

[105] *Microsoft* v. *Commission*, Case T-201/04 (supra n. 80), paras. 976 et seq.

[106] Cf. *Atlantic Container Line and Others* v. *Commission*, Joined Cases T-191/98, T-212/98 to T-214/98, [2003] ECR II-3275, para. 1109: "Before considering those grounds for justification, it must be noted at the outset that there is no exception to the principle in [European] competition law prohibiting abuse of a dominant position. Unlike Article [101] of the Treaty, Article [102] of the Treaty does not allow undertakings in a dominant position to seek to obtain exemption for their abusive practices."

[107] For an analysis of the case law, see Rousseva, *Rethinking Exclusionary Abuses* (supra n. 94), Chapter 7.

[108] On the emergence of implied justifications within the free movement of goods provisions, see Chapter 9 – Sections 1(b) and 4(a) above.

has remained "one of the most vague concepts associated with the application of Article [102]".[109]

In order to explain the European jurisprudence on the concept of objective justification, two jurisprudential lines are traditionally distinguished. According to a first line, the behaviour of a dominant firm is not considered abusive due to a special context. Thus: where a crisis within an industry leads to general supply shortages, the refusal to supply non-traditional customers has not been seen as abusive behaviour.[110] However, the European Courts insist that the special context must be "beyond the control of the dominant undertaking and which it cannot overcome by any means other than by adopting the conduct which is prima facie abusive".[111] Moreover, the special context justification has generally not been extended to public policy considerations. Thus: the fact that an undertaking may deal with products that are potentially dangerous for the health of consumers was not deemed an objective justification for the abusive conduct towards a competitor. For the undertaking will here need to explain why the special context was not addressed by the relevant public authorities.[112]

A second jurisprudential line concerns the "efficiency defence". In *British Airways*,[113] the European Court indeed appeared to use a relative concept of abuse when examining the legality of a system of discounts and bonuses established by a dominant undertaking. For according to the Court, "the exclusionary effect arising from such a system, which is disadvantageous

---

[109] Rousseva, *Rethinking Exclusionary Abuses* (supra n. 94), 259.
[110] *Benzine en Petroleum Handelsmaatschappij and others* v. *Commission*, Case 77/77, [1978] ECR 1513, esp. paras. 33 and 34.
[111] Rousseva, *Rethinking Exclusionary Abuses* (supra n. 94), 265.
[112] See *Tetra Pak* v. *Commission*, Case T-83/91 (supra n. 96), para. 84: "Moreover, even on the assumption, shared by the applicant, that machinery and cartons from various sources cannot be used together without the characteristics of the system being affected thereby, the remedy must lie in appropriate legislation or regulations, and not in rules adopted unilaterally by manufacturers, which would amount to prohibiting independent manufacturers from conducting the essential part of their business." See now Commission, "Guidance on Article 82" (supra n. 25), para. 29: "Exclusionary conduct may, for example, be considered objectively necessary for health or safety reasons related to the nature of the product in question. However, proof of whether conduct of this kind is objectively necessary must take into account that it is normally the task of public authorities to set and enforce public health and safety standards. It is not the task of a dominant undertaking to take steps on its own initiative to exclude products which it regards, rightly or wrongly, as dangerous or inferior to its own product."
[113] *British Airways* v. *Commission*, Case C-95/04P (supra n. 92).

for competition, may be counterbalanced, or outweighed, by advantages in terms of efficiency which also benefit the consumer".[114] However, other judgments have expressly pointed in the opposite direction.[115] The most elaborate discussion of the efficiency defence has taken place in *Microsoft*.[116] Here, the General Court appeared to accept the theoretical existence of an objective justification on the ground of productive or dynamic efficiencies. However, with regard to the practical application of the defence in this case it held that Microsoft had not shown "that the integration of Windows Media Player in Windows creates technical efficiencies or, in other words, that it 'lead[s] to superior technical product performance'".[117] And while the Commission has recently shown a positive attitude towards the efficiency defence under Article 102,[118] the legal parameters for this second objective justification have nonetheless remained very vague indeed.

---

[114] *Ibid.*, para. 86.

[115] *France Télécom* v. *Commission*, Case T-340/03 (supra n. 66), esp. para. 217.

[116] *Microsoft* v. *Commission*, Case T-201/04 (supra n. 80).   [117] *Ibid*, para. 1159.

[118] For an attempt to provide such guidelines, see now Commission, "Guidance on Article 82" (supra n. 25), para. 30. The Commission here suggests four criteria that parallel the four conditions under Article 101 (3).

Index